LIFE WRITING AND THE SOUTHERN HEMISPHERE

New Directions in Life Narrative

New Directions in Life Narrative explores the concept of life narrative across the mediums of written work, oral narratives, photography, documentary film, visual art, performance and social media. The series nurtures theoretical, methodological and interpretive innovation in life writing research, supporting projects that apply new combinations of philosophy, critical theory and methodology to the study of life narrative, providing new ways of reading diverse and always evolving forms. It advances interdisciplinary approaches to life narrative, combining the insights of life writing scholarship with those of cognate fields such as art history, history, anthropology, comparative literary studies, law, sociolinguistics, media studies, medicine, philosophy, psychology and sociology. The series strives towards an international scope that mirrors its community, offering a forum for the study of works in translations not previously studied as well as publishing studies of non-Anglophone works.

Series Editors:
Kate Douglas, Flinders University, Australia
Anna Poletti, Utrecht University, Netherlands
John Zuern, University of Hawaii, USA

Editorial Advisory Board:
Dr Ebony Coletu (Penn State University, USA); Dr Ana Belen Martinez Garcia (University of Navarra, Spain); Associate Professor Claire Lynch (Brunel University, UK); Professor Pramod K Nayar (The University of Hyderabad, India); Dr Nick Tembo (The University of Malawi); Professor Jianling Liu (Shanghai Jiao Tong University, China); Professor Gerardo Necoechea (Instituto Nacional de Antropologia e Historia, Mexico); Dr Laurie McNeill (University of British Columbia, Canada)

Available Titles:
Human Rights in Graphic Life Narrative: Reading and Witnessing Violations of the 'Other' in Anglophone Works, Olga Michael
Children and Biography: Reading and Writing Life Stories, Kate Douglas
Life Writing and the End of Empire, Emma Parker
Refugee Lives in the Archives: A Pacific Imaginary, Gillian Whitlock
Reading Mediated Life Narratives: Auto/Biographical Agency in the Book, Museum, Social Media, and Archives, Amy Carlson

Forthcoming Titles:
The Death Memoir in Contemporary Culture, Claire Nally
Ecological Life Writings from India: Marginalisation, Environmental Justice and Told-to Autobiography, Shalini M and Moncy Mathew
Cricket and its Life Narratives: From Tour Diaries to Podcasts, edited by Claire Westall and Rakesh Ramamoorthy
Digital and In/Visible Lives in Autobiographical Webcomics, Shannon Sandford

LIFE WRITING AND THE SOUTHERN HEMISPHERE

TEXTS, SPACES, RESONANCES

Edited by
Elleke Boehmer and Katherine Collins

BLOOMSBURY ACADEMIC
LONDON • NEW YORK • OXFORD • NEW DELHI • SYDNEY

BLOOMSBURY ACADEMIC
Bloomsbury Publishing Plc
50 Bedford Square, London, WC1B 3DP, UK
1385 Broadway, New York, NY 10018, USA
29 Earlsfort Terrace, Dublin 2, Ireland

BLOOMSBURY, BLOOMSBURY ACADEMIC and the Diana logo are
trademarks of Bloomsbury Publishing Plc

First published in Great Britain 2024

Copyright © Elleke Boehmer, Katherine Collins, and Contributors, 2024

Elleke Boehmer and Katherine Collins have asserted their right under the
Copyright, Designs and Patents Act, 1988, to be identified as Editors of this work.

For legal purposes the Acknowledgements on p. xvi constitute an
extension of this copyright page.

Series design by Rebecca Heselton
Cover image © Abstract Aerial Art/Getty Images

All rights reserved. No part of this publication may be reproduced or transmitted in any form or by any means, electronic or mechanical, including photocopying, recording, or any information storage or retrieval system, without prior permission in writing from the publishers.

Bloomsbury Publishing Plc does not have any control over, or responsibility for, any third-party websites referred to or in this book. All internet addresses given in this book were correct at the time of going to press. The author and publisher regret any inconvenience caused if addresses have changed or sites have ceased to exist but can accept no responsibility for any such changes.

A catalogue record for this book is available from the British Library.

Library of Congress Cataloging-in-Publication Data
Names: Boehmer, Elleke, 1961- editor. | Collins, Katherine (College teacher), editor.
Title: Life writing and the Southern Hemisphere: texts, spaces, resonances / edited by Elleke Boehmer and Katherine Collins.
Description: London; New York: Bloomsbury Academic, 2024. | Series: New directions in life narrative; vol 6 | Includes bibliographical references and index.
Identifiers: LCCN 2024013526 (print) | LCCN 2024013527 (ebook) | ISBN 9781350360808 (paperback) | ISBN 9781350360754 (hardback) | ISBN 9781350360778 (pdf) | ISBN 9781350360785 (ebook)
Subjects: LCSH: Biography as a literary form. | Developing countries–In literature. | Southern Hemisphere–In literature. | LCGFT: Essays.
Classification: LCC CT21.L5125 2024 (print) | LCC CT21 (ebook) | DDC 808.06/692–dc23/eng/20240404
LC record available at https://lccn.loc.gov/2024013526
LC ebook record available at https://lccn.loc.gov/2024013527

ISBN:	HB:	978-1-3503-6075-4
	PB:	978-1-3503-6080-8
	ePDF:	978-1-3503-6077-8
	eBook:	978-1-3503-6078-5

Series: New Directions in Life Narrative

Typeset by Integra Software Services Pvt. Ltd.

To find out more about our authors and books visit www.bloomsbury.com
and sign up for our newsletters.

To Ben, Sam, Seren, Thomas

CONTENTS

List of Figures	ix
List of Contributors	xi
Acknowledgements	xvi

Introduction *Elleke Boehmer and Katherine Collins*   1

Part I Reading the south

1. Life writing and imagining across southern space *Elleke Boehmer*   13
2. Prosthetics, souvenirs and settlement: South-south connections in Janet Frame's and Doris Lessing's life writing *Emma Parker*   25
3. Antarctic futures: Francisco Coloane and literary nationalism *Elizabeth Chant*   39
4. Cross-cultural life writing: Juxtaposing Adivasi/Tribal Indian and Indigenous Australian texts *Priyanka Shivadas*   53

Part II Imagining spaces and spatiality

5. Unknowing a southern life: Writing around the abyss *Katherine Collins*   67
6. Minority life in Nigeria's south-south: Ken Wiwa's *In the Shadow of a Saint* *Obari Gomba*   81
7. Southwards from the Northeast *Archie Davies*   91
8. The south as a continuous space *Pablo Wainschenker*   103
9. J. M. Coetzee's Hispanic south *Cristóbal Pérez Barra*   115

Part III Reading and writing in southern waters

10. Tsunami, tornado, tide: Life and writing of the oceanic south in selected nonfiction by Amitav Ghosh *Charne Lavery*   131
11. The representation of water spirits in southern African Literature *Confidence Joseph*   145
12. 'All water has a perfect memory': In search of Dambudzo Marechera's stream *Tinashe Mushakavanhu*   157

Contents

Part IV Sounds, images and resonances in the far south

13 The plankton net at the door: Scott's hut and the poetics of 'intimate immensity' *Joanna Price* — 171
14 The musical lives of Mawson's men *Carolyn Philpott* — 187
15 Signals from the south: Decoding the life of an Antarctic wireless operator *Elizabeth Leane* — 201
16 Remote imag(in)ing the Antarctic: Life writing and the resonant page *Elizabeth Lewis Williams* — 215

Part V Embodying the south

17 The fugitive lives of David Stuurman *Sarah Comyn and Porscha Fermanis* — 239
18 Recovering a biography of a southern city, Bulawayo *Isaac Ndlovu* — 257
19 From the far bank: *Two-Body Problem* in the south *Louis Rogers* — 269
20 Mogau Grace *Khutso Mabokela* — 279

Index — 289

FIGURES

0	Southern Lives Workshop (2021) poster. Designed by Joe Shaughnessy. Albatross photograph copyright Elleke Boehmer. Used with permission	xvii
1.1	Basket from Northern Queensland. Copyright Pitt Rivers Museum, University of Oxford (1897.1.2)	16
1.2	Basket from Tasmania. Copyright Pitt Rivers Museum, University of Oxford (1893.38.24)	17
2.1	Maize, Tobacco etc. Southern Rhodesia Pavilion, British Empire Exhibition, Wembley 1925	26
5.1	Sailing chart from the Marshall Islands. Copyright Pitt Rivers Museum, University of Oxford (1897.1.2)	68
5.2	Ostrich egg from southern Africa. Copyright Pitt Rivers Museum, University of Oxford (2004.142.1110)	68
13.1	Jane Ussher. The first peek through the cold porch into the interior of Captain Scott's last expedition base. Copyright Jane Ussher / Antarctic Heritage Trust	174
13.2	Herbert Ponting. Nelson and Day landing the townet. March 15, 1911. Copyright Scott Polar Research Institute, University of Cambridge	178
13.3	Judit Hersko, *Scott's Terra Nova Hut with Herbert Ponting's darkroom*, 2009. Courtesy of the artist	180
13.4	Judit Hersko, Anna's Cabinet (detail). 2011. Courtesy of the artist	181
13.5	Judit Hersko, *Portrait of Anna Schwartz. 2008.* Courtesy of the artist	182
14.1	The AAE's original pump organ, as it sits today in the Mawson's Huts Replica Museum in Hobart, Tasmania. Photo: Carolyn Philpott, with permission from the Mawson's Huts Foundation	188
14.2	Frank Hurley, 'A winter evening at the hut' (1911), National Library of Australia, http://nla.gov.au/nla.obj-136188901. Used with permission	189
14.3	The 'Southern Sledging Song' as printed in *The Adelie Blizzard*, with notes likely made by McLean. Courtesy of the Australian Polar Collections, South Australian Museum, Adelaide	194
14.4	Original programme for *The Washerwoman's Secret.* Courtesy of the Australian Polar Collections, South Australian Museum, Adelaide	195
17.1a	David Stuurman to Governor Darling, 19 December 1828, MHNSW – StAC: NRS 905 [4/2015] 29/853. Used with permission	244

Figures

17.1b David Stuurman to Governor Darling, 19 December 1828,
MHNSW – StAC: NRS 905 [4/2015] 29/853. Used with permission 245

17.2 David Stuurman Statue at the National Heritage Monument in Pretoria,
South Africa [currently touring] 248

CONTRIBUTORS

Elleke Boehmer is Professor of World Literature in English and OCLW Executive Director. She is a Fellow of the Royal Society of Literature and the Royal Historical Society. She is a Fellow at Wolfson College and an Honorary Fellow of St John's College, Oxford. Since 2023, she has been an Extraordinary Professor in English at the University of Pretoria. She is the author of seven monographs including *Postcolonial Poetics, Indian Arrivals* (2015–16 ESSE prize-winner), *Stories of Women* and *Southern Imagining* (2025). Boehmer's fiction includes *To the Volcano* and *The Shouting in the Dark* (Olive Schreiner Prize-winner 2018).

Emma Parker is Lecturer in Literature and Gender at the University of Bristol, UK. Her research focuses primarily on global Anglophone literatures, particularly on autobiographical narratives and settler cultures. She has published on postcolonial literatures, life writing and graphic narratives. Books include *Life Writing and the End of Empire: Homecoming in Autobiographical Narratives*, and she is the co-editor, with Josh Doble and Liam J. Liburd, of *British Culture After Empire*. She is the Anne Ball Bodley visiting fellow (2024–5) at the Bodleian Libraries, University of Oxford, researching exiled South African women writers in Britain during apartheid.

Elizabeth Chant is Assistant Professor in Global Sustainable Development at the University of Warwick, UK. An interdisciplinary scholar, her background is in Latin American cultural studies, with a focus on environmental humanities. Liz is currently developing a monograph on the trope of desolation in literature and visual culture depicting Patagonia while also advancing a project that examines domestic tourism to industrial sites across Argentina, Chile and the western United States in the early twentieth century. She has published on the maritime charting of Patagonia in the eighteenth century and the development of tourism in Juan Fernández (with Natalia Gándara).

Priyanka Shivadas is a lecturer at Trinity College, the University of Melbourne, Australia. She specializes in global Indigenous literary studies, with a focus on Indigenous Australian and Adivasi/tribal literatures. She also holds the title of Adjunct Associate Lecturer at UNSW Canberra. Her work has been published in the *Journal of the Association for the Study of Australian Literature, Performance of the Real* and *The Culture of Dissenting Memory: Truth Commissions in the Global South*.

Katherine Collins is a researcher in the Faculty of English Language and Literature at the University of Oxford and a Fellow of the Oxford Centre for Life-Writing at Wolfson College. Her research interests include creative practice as research, critical pedagogies

Contributors

and research cultures. She has published on the intersections of research and poetry, and fiction and the archive. She is currently a co-investigator on the Wellcome Trust funded project *Leading Across Boundaries*. She is also a poet, with work in *Propel Magazine*, *The Rialto*, *bath magg*, *Shearsman Magazine*, and *Finished Creatures*, among others.

Obari Gomba, an International Writing Program Fellow of the University of Iowa, USA and the Associate Dean of Humanities at the University of Port Harcourt, Nigeria, has been the TORCH Global South Visiting Professor and Visiting Fellow at All Souls College, University of Oxford, UK. He has won the Nigeria Prize for Literature (2023), the PAWA Prize for African Poetry (2022), the Association of Nigerian Authors Drama Prize (2018), and the Association of Nigerian Authors Poetry Prize (twice, 2016 and 2017). His latest book of essays is *Free Troubles: A Writer's Eyes on the World*.

Archie Davies is a lecturer in Geography and Fellow of the Institute of Humanities and Social Sciences at Queen Mary, University of London, UK. His book, *A World Without Hunger: Josué de Castro and the History of Geography*, analyses the life and work of Josué de Castro (1908–73), a Brazilian activist, politician and geographer. He has translated Milton Santos's 1978 classic work, *For a New Geography*, and with Christen Smith and Bethânia Gomes is translator and editor of *The Dialectic Is in the Sea: The Black Radical Thought of Beatriz Nascimento*.

Pablo Wainschenker is a researcher at Gateway Antarctica at the University of Canterbury, New Zealand. He is an active member of the Standing Committee on the Humanities and Social Sciences within the Scientific Committee on Antarctic Research and the Editor of the Secretariat of the Antarctic Treaty. He has published on Antarctica in South American fiction; works also include *Trapped in the End of the World*, a documentary film about the Nordenskjöld Expedition to Antarctica (1901–3) (Hiperkinesis Films; with Eduardo Sánchez and Fernando Moyano), *La Antártida, enigmático mundo sin misterios* (Artefacto, 2015) and other articles published in Argentine media.

Cristóbal Pérez Barra obtained his DPhil from the English Faculty in the University of Oxford, UK. Prior to his involvement in literary studies, he was a lecturer of History of Law at the Pontifical Catholic University of Chile and worked as a lawyer in Santiago. He has published a short-story collection, *El descorazonamiento*; a novel, *Una sombra en la noche*; and translations of J. M. Coetzee, *Two Elizabeth Costello Lessons*, and Julian Barnes, *In the Land of Pain*. His monograph, *Hispanic Coetzee*, will be published in 2025.

Charne Lavery is Senior Lecturer in the Department of English at the University of Pretoria, South Africa. She is also co-director, with Isabel Hofmeyr, of Oceanic Humanities for the Global South (www.oceanichumanities.com). Her publications include *Writing Ocean Worlds: Indian Ocean Fiction in English*, and the co-edited collections *Maritime Mobilities in Anglophone Literature and Culture*, *Reading from the South* and *Reading for Water*. She is leading a project to pilot an African Antarctic Artists and Writers Programme and co-edits a Palgrave book series on Maritime Literature and Culture.

Contributors

Confidence Joseph is a postdoctoral fellow in English at the University of Pretoria. Her work combines decolonial and environmental approaches to explore the representation of water in southern African Literature. In this, she foregrounds water as a critical tool for, and object of, analysis as she explores notions of displacement, identity, home and belonging. Reading for water surfaces the complex entanglements between the human and non-human, the natural and the supernatural, in ways that speak to the multiple ways of being in the world. Her other research interests include African postcolonial literatures, African migration narratives, the environment and gender studies.

Tinashe Mushakavanhu is a Junior Research Fellow in African and Comparative Literature at St Anne's College, Oxford University. The central theme of his research is the role of literary culture in documentation, historical knowledge and political power, particularly the aesthetics and materiality of writing; archives and archival theory; translation; and African print cultures. His work manifests in interdisciplinary modalities, blurring creative and critical methods, and writing genres, to imaginatively reconfigure the strictures that conventionally separate the poetic and the theoretical. His publications include *Reincarnating Marechera: Notes on a Speculative Archive* and *Some Writers Can Give You Two Heartbeats*.

Joanna Price is a Visiting Research Fellow at the Research Institute for Literature and Cultural History, Liverpool John Moores University. She has written about affect and place, particularly in relation to trauma, memory and mourning. Her recent publications include articles about Antarctica and 'the traumatic sublime' as well as affective landscapes in Antarctic travel memoirs. She is writing an 'affective biography' of R. F. Scott's Terra Nova hut, which will form part of a book about how, through literature, art and photography, the material spaces of Antarctica become affective both locally and globally.

Carolyn Philpott is Senior Lecturer in Musicology at the University of Tasmania's Conservatorium of Music and Adjunct Senior Researcher at the Institute for Marine and Antarctic Studies (IMAS). Her research interests include Australian music and intersections between music, sound, place and the environment, especially music and soundscape-based works composed in connection with Antarctica. She has travelled to Antarctica as a researcher multiple times and has published her research in musicology and polar studies journals, books and encyclopaedias. She is author of *Composing Australia: Nostalgia and National Identity in the Music of Malcolm Williamson* and lead editor of *Performing Ice*.

Elizabeth Leane is Professor of Antarctic Studies in the School of Humanities, College of Arts, Law and Education, University of Tasmania, Australia. She has a career-long drive to understand how non-specialists can connect with remote or seemingly inaccessible places and ideas. With degrees in both science and literature, she uses the insights of the humanities to understand how humans relate to the Antarctic, the 'continent for science'. She has visited Antarctica as a writer-in-residence, an educator and a researcher. Her

Contributors

books include *Antarctica in Fiction* and *South Pole: Nature and Culture* and the co-edited collections *Anthropocene Antarctica* and *Performing Ice*.

Elizabeth Lewis Williams is a poet, teacher and Visiting Fellow at the University of East Anglia, UK. Her creative-critical PhD explored the idea of scientific and poetic measure in Antarctic poetry, and her research interests include representations of Antarctica, the intersections between poetry and science, the poetics of place and the value of poetry and the poetry workshop in promoting multi-disciplinary dialogue and public engagement, particularly around narratives of climate change. She has published two books of poetry, *Deception Island* and *Erebus*, and toured an immersive poetry-film-sound installation in a replica Antarctic hut.

Sarah Comyn is an Assistant Professor and Ad Astra Fellow in the School of English, Drama and Film at University College Dublin, Ireland. Her research interests are in the literary institutions of the long nineteenth century, settler colonial literature, the literary cultures of nineteenth-century mineral mining, and the transhistorical relationship between literature and political economy. Recent publications include *Political Economy* and *Worlding the South: Nineteenth-Century Literary Culture and the Southern Settler Colonies* (ed. with Porscha Fermanis).

Porscha Fermanis is Professor of Romantic Literature at University College Dublin. She is the principal investigator of the 'SouthHem' project, funded by the European Research Council from 2016–22. Her most recent books are *Romantic Pasts: History, Fiction and Feeling in Britain, 1790–1850* and *Worlding the South: Nineteenth-Century Literary Culture and the Southern Settler Colonies* (ed. with Sarah Comyn). Her latest book, *Settler Fiction from the Southern Hemisphere, 1820–1890*, is forthcoming from Oxford University Press.

Isaac Ndlovu is a senior lecturer in the Department of English at the University of Pretoria, South Africa. His research interests are in African narratives of crime and imprisonment, contemporary South African and Zimbabwean fiction and life writing. His recent publications are: 'Ghostly National Imaginings and the (Il)logic of Capitalism in Meg Vandermerwe's *Zebra Crossing*' in *African Identities*, 'Writing and Reading Zimbabwe in the Global Literary Market: A Case of Four Novelists' in the *Journal of Postcolonial Writing* and 'Rewriting the Colonial Gaze? Black Middle Class Constructions of Africa in Sihle Khumalo's Travel Writing' in *a/b: Auto/Biography Studies*.

Louis Rogers is a writer and editor based in London, UK. His writing and photography have appeared in *Granta*, *Tank Magazine*, *New Left Review*, the *Financial Times*, *Architectural Review*, *Literary Review*, *The Plant* and others. Crossing media – and often needling their intersections – his work engages with memory, materiality, documentary form, live performance, architecture, colonial history and translation. His play *Two-Body Problem*, a one-woman show set in Antarctica, toured UK venues between 2018 and 2020. He is a commissioning editor at the art publisher MACK.

Khutso Mabokela is a lecturer in the School of Languages and Communication at the University of Limpopo, South Africa. Before her tenure at the University of Limpopo, she garnered significant professional experience as an nGAP lecturer at the University of Venda over a span of five years. Alongside her academic pursuits, she has contributed to the field of journalism, serving as a junior reporter at *Cue Newspaper*, a local publication based in Makhanda, as well as working as a writer for the Department of Cooperative Governance, Human Settlements and Traditional Affairs in Polokwane, Limpopo province.

ACKNOWLEDGEMENTS

We are indebted to a number of people and organizations whose support was invaluable in running the 'Southern Lives' series of workshops and developing this collection of essays. To Hermione Lee and Kate Kennedy of the Oxford Centre for Life-Writing, who were unstinting and enthusiastic in their encouragement of this project. To Freya Marshall Payne, Joe Shaughnessy and Charles Pigeon for their fantastic support with organizing the 'Southern Lives' workshops and their skill as panel chairs, and to Tom McLean for stepping in at the last moment to chair the panel 'Perspectives on Time, Change, and the Environment'. Kind thanks to Joe Shaughnessy for his beautiful poster. We would like to thank Maria Rita Drumond Viana, David Mills, Darshini Nadarajan, Sam Sneddon and Yusra Price, who have been generous with their time and insights.

We are grateful to our funders: the British Academy for the Small Grant 'Tracing southern latitudes: legends, languages, life-writing' (SRG19\190295) awarded to Elleke Boehmer, and the Leverhulme Trust for the Early Career Fellowship (ECF-2018-210) awarded to Katherine Collins. We are also grateful to the curators of the Pitt Rivers Museum for setting up the display for our Southern Lives workshop in 2021; the Events and Catering teams at Wolfson College and TORCH | The Oxford Research Centre in the Humanities; and the English Faculty at the University of Oxford. We thank those individuals and institutions who have given permission for the materials to which they hold copyright to be reproduced in this book.

We are also hugely indebted to all who participated in the three 'Southern Lives' workshops, two on-line, one hybrid, including the lively and stalwart audience who turned up for the hybrid workshop in December 2021. We want to say a special thank you to the contributors to this book who have all helped to make it the rich and varied collection that it has become.

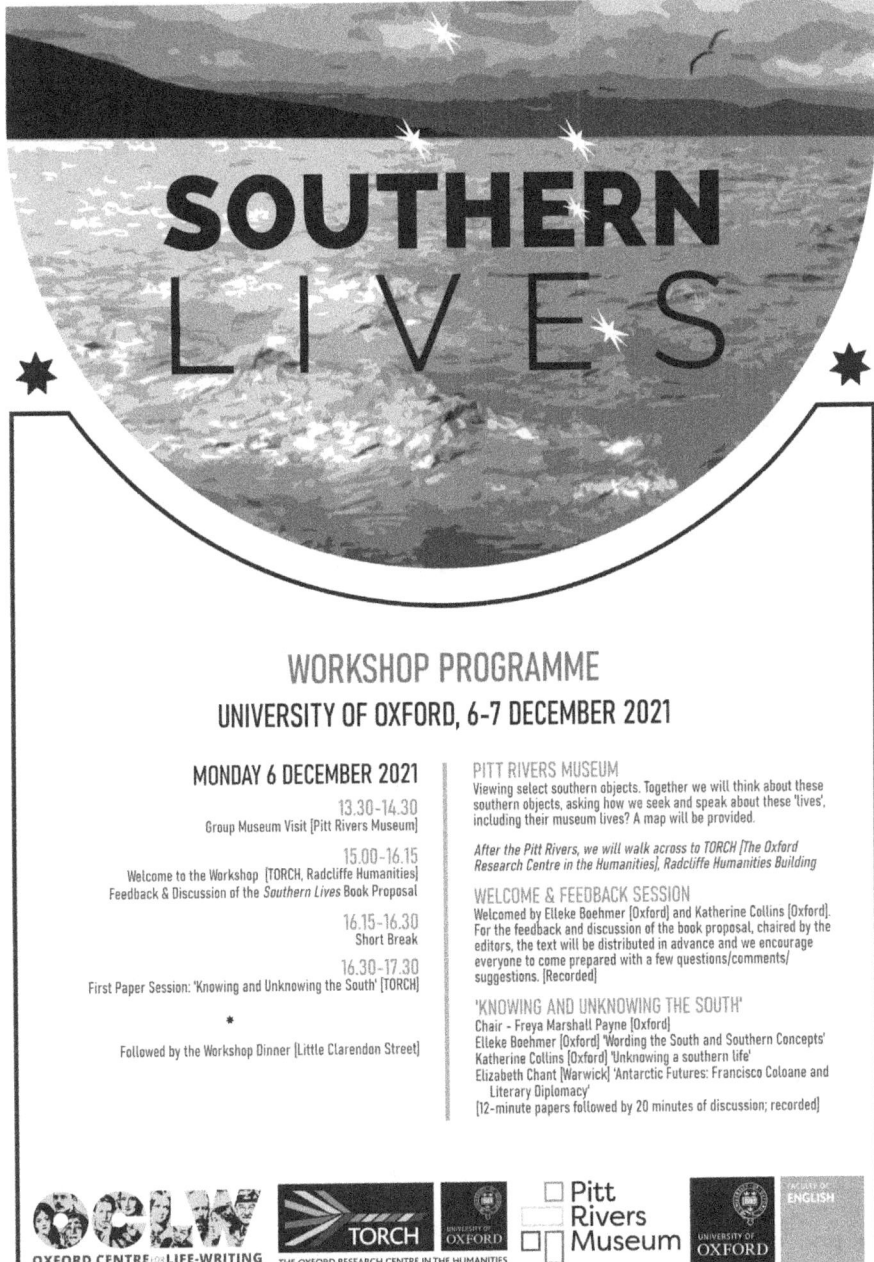

Figure 0 Southern Lives Workshop (2021) poster. Designed by Joe Shaughnessy. Albatross photograph copyright Elleke Boehmer. Used with permission.

INTRODUCTION
Elleke Boehmer and Katherine Collins

The surface of the Southern Hemisphere is almost entirely water and, as such, has been called the blue hemisphere.[1] The South Pacific, South Atlantic and Indian Oceans wash into the Southern Ocean that surrounds Antarctica, which forms the pulse of all the world's currents.[2] Storms here turn clockwise and summer runs from December to February. The Southern Hemisphere is famously home to albatrosses, penguins, marsupials, llamas, capybaras, maned wolves and many other creatures that do not occur on the northern continents. Landscapes range from the dusty sandstone rocks at the Cape of Good Hope to the white sand and turquoise waters of islands in the South Pacific; from the stone-grey Patagonian shore to the dense green of the Amazon; and from rolling humps of pampas with snow-capped mountains in the distance to lonely blue-white icebergs reflected in the sea.

However, though the Southern Hemisphere makes up one-half of the earth's surface, southern geographies, histories and lives tend to be defined from a northern perspective. Consider the expressions 'down under', 'upside down' or 'the far side of the world', and the many phrases we use that take as read that the north is 'the top', the right side up. Think about how maps and globes give prominence to the northern continents. Meg Samuelson, writing on the Anthropocene, rightly points out that not only does the dominance of northern perspectives 'cast more than half of the world into its shadow, but the attempt to view the planet from a singular vantage point must also introduce blind spots which would obscure the very totality that the Anthropocene is expected to represent'.[3]

It is this apparent overlooking, and the associated tension between addressing the exclusion of southern perspectives while resisting the tendency to universalize, that drives this collection of essays on life writing and the Southern Hemisphere. On the premise that life writing presents singular views from the vantage of specific situations, the book brings together life stories, memoirs, biographies, autobiographies and poetics set in the south, or told from the perspective of southern lands, that give views on the hemisphere from within. Contributions are drawn from scholars and writers living and working in, and on, South America, Africa, Australia, Asia and Europe. Our continental representation, therefore, includes three of the major southern continents and makes prominent reference to the fourth, Antarctica.

As Elleke Boehmer points out in the first chapter in this book, the phrase 'the Southern Hemisphere', to anyone writing from the Global North, is also likely to mean, among other possibilities, distance and faraway-ness. For Elleke, born in the south, this farness has a sound, 'the ringing, shirring sound of a device like a high-frequency radio, out of focus, trying and failing to communicate across the miles'.[4] Another aspect of distance, of course, is time. Not simply travel time but time measured by the sun's path across meridian lines. We felt this distance most acutely when organizing the three workshops that crystalized this collection, which, for reasons of distance and the Covid-19 pandemic, all met online or in hybrid form. In this way, we experienced a disconcerting sense of remote togetherness, despite some of us being nearly eighteen thousand kilometres and fourteen hours apart.[5]

Hemispheric demarcations and long distances, however, are far from the only media through which 'the south' has been or can be understood. Various terminologies, which attempt to capture not just the south as a geographic designation but also as the intersection of histories of northern colonialism and economic inequity, have risen and fallen in popularity in the twentieth and twenty-first centuries in a multitude of disciplines. Different essays in this collection speak to and sometimes combine these varying definitions. True, many have been contested, such as the contemporary term 'Global South', the coining of which is often attributed to Carl Oglesby, an American political activist writing on the Vietnam War in 1969.[6] The South African Australian writer J. M. Coetzee regards the term as a wholly negative construction that, as an analytical category, can mean several things.[7] Even so, this term and its opposite, the Global North, have largely taken over from terms like Third World or developing world.[8] As Archie Davies writes in this volume, the Global South is often used as 'a kind of spatial metaphor for underdevelopment and coloniality'.[9] It has also served as a category descriptor for alliances such as the Non-Aligned Movement and the G77 at the United Nations. And, more radically, it has been suggested that the grouping 'reterritorializes global space in the interests of repossession by the dispossessed'.[10] Though the term has been criticized for the ways in which it may elide the many differences between the lands and peoples it includes, for Siba Grovogu, therein lies its importance:

> as a movement, the Global South has no central structure, no central command, and no appointed spokesperson. It has had multiple custodians, all of them self-selected, in reaction to the deepening and multifaceted violence experienced at different moments by its members.[11]

The aspect that these economic, political, postcolonial, conceptual, semantic and even geographical definitions have in common is that they originate in the north. So, too, do cognate terms such as 'Northropocene' that Meg Samuelson and others have discussed. Nirmal Puwar has written about the 'staging' of Global North individuals and institutions in the attempt to centre southern knowledge, asking '[w]ho gets recognised? Whose tracks are in the sand? What do we risk tracing over? Who is illuminated? What is leap frogged over?'[12] Elleke Boehmer, in her previous work, posits, by contrast, an understanding of the south rising from the 'contact zone' of 'cultural and political exchange' between southern peripheries, one that allows us to be in 'intellectual partnership with epistemologies grounded in south-south relations', sharing conceptual ground whilst also reflecting critically upon it.[13] Sarah Comyn and Porscha Fermanis, who have also contributed to this work, further suggest that a combination of Indigenous and Black knowledge can help us to question the predominance of northern ways of thinking, thereby integrating southern worlds with the rest of the planet in a process that they call worlding the south. Citing Isabel Hofmeyr, they explore a more 'southern latitude' in their work by tracing and creating ways of seeing lines of connection and exchange across the hemisphere.[14] Likewise, Marcio D'Olne Campos and Paulo Freire's concept of 'Sulear' seeks to counter the ways in which the north is presented as the universal referent.[15]

The scholarly discipline, if not the genre, of life writing can be aligned to northerly institutions, perhaps most clearly in the case of travel writing, which tends to be written from the powerful vantage-point of the European, with their 'imperial eyes'.[16] And yet life writing can also give a view from below. If the generic idea of a life nearly always features a northern subject, whether in sports, in politics or in literature, southern life stories can offer countervailing and alternative perspectives that open up our understanding of what counts as the subject of life writing, to say nothing of *how* we understand life stories whether in the north or the south.

The *Life Writing and the Southern Hemisphere* essays all explore the idea of lives lived, written, and narrated in and from southern places. The lives include animal and plant life, as well as musical lives, and lives captured in performance, the visual arts and photography. Collectively, the essays ask how southern lives and life writing from antipodean and other southern compass points impact how we understand and read life writing and even, in some cases, how our planet is perceived.

To define life writing can be complicated, comprised as it is of an eclectic array of sources and both shorter and longer literary forms.[17] As well as letters and diaries, journals and emails, the genre also embraces the 'vast literary netherworld of court reports, ledgers, household accounts, marginalia, and graffiti'.[18] 'Netherworld' in Patrick Hayes's formulation is an interesting image construct in the context of the Southern Hemisphere. Literary forms of life writing include memoir, biography, case history, creative-critical writing and testimony, as well as hybrid genres such as autofiction, biographical fiction, the non-fiction novel and auto-theory, not to mention responsiveness to the lives of artists and thinkers when reading their texts. Attention to what might be called the margins, peripheral or subaltern perspectives has come more recently, with scholars such as Gillian Whitlock, Sidonie Smith and Julia Watson's focus on the lives and writings of enslaved people, refugees and women experiencing various forms of oppression world-wide.[19] What might be termed 'southern' forms of life writing include the Latin American form *testimonio*,[20] of which perhaps the most famous example is *I, Rigoberta Menchú*,[21] and the Indigenous Australian *story* or *yarning*.[22]

However, with the legacies of colonialism including language loss and archiving practices that prioritize some lives over others, the 'authoritative life' still tends to be the northern life, as are the dominant historical narratives. And so, in this book, we turn to different forms to give a more complex and attuned picture of southern lives – including the lives of objects, stories of hauntings and ghostly presences, lives lived and written in and through southern waters and airwaves, and ways of reading historical accounts differently – all of which may allow us better to conceptualize the planet from below, from its nether-regions, if you will. As Obari Gomba, one of the scholars who contributed to this volume, said during our meetings, 'Let's not assume that we'll be able to put a definition or cap on what life writing is or what it isn't. It's impossible, because the very idea of creating either life or art means that the borders will constantly be shifted.' Therefore, we have approached this book as involving a multidisciplinary conversation spanning all compass points, which includes many more voices than ours, and which we hope will continue to grow.

We have grouped the essays in this collection broadly into five themes: reading the south; imagining spaces and spatiality; reading and writing in southern waters; sounds, images and resonances in the far south; and embodying the south. In the first section, 'Reading the south', Elleke Boehmer reflects upon what it is to think and write about the state of being far and south, and how life writing might help to bridge the hemisphere's mythic vastness by attending to the lives of objects crafted by peoples of the south, to southern etymologies and to southern thought-worlds. Emma Parker's reading of Doris Lessing's (1919–2013) and Janet Frame's (1924–2004) autobiographical writing extends Siba Grovogu's interpretation of the Global South, emphasizing these two writers' anti-colonial critique. Through both authors' descriptions of their respective fathers' prosthetics and discarded souvenirs from the First World War, Parker shows how they eschew a shared sense of colonial belonging and instead offer interlocking accounts of a collapsing imperial identity. Elizabeth Chant's reading of Chilean writer Francisco Coloane (1910–2002), a member of the first Chilean Antarctic Expedition in 1947, shows how Coloane's literary nationalism furthers Chilean interests while simultaneously critiquing the human occupation of the Antarctic and the environmental damage it causes. In this way, Chant seeks to unravel the personal and the political in what are some of Coloane's most overtly nationalist ruminations, while also underscoring the didactic concern that echoes across his corpus. Priyanka Shivadas offers a comparative reading of two texts produced collaboratively and cross-culturally, one Indigenous Australian, the other Adivasi/tribal Indian literature. Her analysis spans questions of orality and textual and paratextual elements, highlighting ways in which the Indigenous memoirists of these texts assert agency and control over their written narratives.

In various forms, figurative and geographical, Katherine Collins, Obari Gomba, Archie Davies, Pablo Wainschenker and Cristóbal Pérez Barra explore southern spaces and spatiality. Through the lives of two objects, a stick chart and an ostrich-egg water carrier, Collins traces what she terms 'abyssal' metaphors for the imbalance of information and representation of the lives once lived around these objects. She outlines a metaphorical cartography originating in the amity lines of the sixteenth century, extended today into a compound metaphor that represents physical division and epistemic and economic inequality. Gomba considers the life of Ken Wiwa (1968–2016), son of acclaimed writer and environmentalist Ken Saro-Wiwa, who was one of nine Ogoni activists judicially murdered by the Nigerian state in 1995. He demonstrates that the ways in which Nigeria's region of south-south is minoritized and subjugated relates critically to the marginalization of the south in other geographical contexts. The name 'south-south' on its own seems to enforce a double *southness*. Davies' contribution deepens this insight, showing, through his analysis of the lives of three intellectuals of the Brazilian Northeast, how geographical categories – like the south – come into being in relation to individual biographies. His study thus offers different pathways through which we might think about southern-ness. During their lives, his three subjects, Josué de Castro (1908–73), Milton Santos (1926–2001) and Beatriz Nascimento (1942–95), moved southwards, outwards and back to the Northeast in imaginary, intellectual and physical terms.

Staying with South America, and specifically its Southern Cone, Wainschenker and Pérez Barra both consider continuities across southern spaces. Wainschenker's chapter explores the idea of the far south as a continuous space, both in a North to South sense, where Antarctica can be seen as a part of South America, and East to West, in which Antarctica and the Southern Ocean are seen as an entity in themselves. Pérez Barra presents a fascinating case study of the South African Australian J. M. Coetzee's aim to build bridges between the literary communities and cultures of hemispheric cities like Buenos Aires, Cape Town and Sydney without the intervention of the Global North, namely New York or London.

In the section titled 'Reading and writing in southern waters', Charne Lavery, Confidence Joseph and Tinashe Mushakavanhu each consider southern oceans, rivers and lakes through various lenses. Drawing upon the non-fictional prose of novelist Amitav Ghosh, Lavery highlights the ways in which the Indian writer theorizes the differing capacities of life writing and literary novels for conceptualizing environmental futures and the centrality of the oceanic south in that vision. Joseph explores how water spirits have been represented in southern African literature as figures of resistance for social, political and environmental purposes, and thus how mythic and the material are inextricably intertwined with how lives are lived and perceived in the Global South. Mushakavanhu poses several provocative questions about the life of the Zimbabwean writer Dambudzo Marechera and his canonical text *The House of Hunger*. Mushakavanhu wonders what would have happened if editorial intervention hadn't changed the book's title from the original, *At the Head of the Stream*. What if we search again for the stream which so inspired Marechera's work?

From water to ice, the section 'Sounds, images and resonances in the far south' contains chapters by Joanna Price, Carolyn Philpott, Elizabeth Leane and Elizabeth Lewis Williams, all concerned with the Antarctic. Price's subject is the work of Jane Ussher and Judit Hersko, two artists who have engaged with Scott's *Terra Nova* hut on Cape Evans. A plankton net, hanging near the door, captured both artists' attention and embodied in their work, for Price, both the 'intimate immensity' of the hut and the threshold between human and non-human worlds. Philpott and Leane both write about aspects of Douglas Mawson's Australasian Antarctic Expedition in the 1910s. Philpott's chapter draws upon diaries, musical items and the expedition's 'newspaper', the *Adelie Blizzard*, to recognize the role of music in these men's lives in Antarctica. It reveals how they used music to fill space and mark time during the expedition and how they (ironically) adapted northern music and traditions to suit their own experiences as 'Southern' men and to aid their survival in the far south. Leane excavates the life and achievements of little-known radio operator Sidney Jeffryes (1884–1942) who accompanied Mawson. This pioneer of Antarctic telecommunications was admitted to the Hospital for the Insane (as it was then called) a few weeks after the expedition returned from Antarctica. Leane argues that the pressures that surrounded his efforts to send telegraphic messages across the Southern Ocean had a significant effect on when and how his illness unfolded. The section concludes with poet Elizabeth Lewis Williams's reflections on remoteness and the poetic imagination, illustrated with poems that explore how the technologies of remote imaging and sensing, as well as meteorological observations and radio communication, become metaphors for relationship: with the self, with others and with the planet.

In the final section, 'Embodying the south', Sarah Comyn and Porscha Fermanis show how interiority models of life writing fail to give an account of the plural and fragmented lives of the late eighteenth-century Indigenous Khoi resistance leader David Stuurman (1773–1830). They argue that fugitive lives require fugitive modes and methods of reading that cut across or act aslant to colonial dichotomies, so presenting life writing from the south as a means of resisting the naturalization of the subaltern status of individuals like Stuurman. Through his reading of Melina Rorke's autobiographical travelogue, *Melina Rorke: Her Amazing Experiences in the Stormy Nineties of South Africa's Story Told by Herself* (1939), Isaac Ndlovu pursues the partial recovery of a biography of Bulawayo. His chapter shows how, in the gaps, silences and absences of the colonial text, the reader can 'tilt differently' and thus imagine and recover a broader town life than one offered by Rorke's narrative. Louis Rogers and Khutso Mabokela conclude the section, and the book, with powerful creative-critical responses to southern embodiment. Rogers offers a critical reflection on his polarity-reversing play, *Two Body Problem* (2018). In a comparative reading of his script in dialogue with two key influences, Jenny Diski's memoir *Skating to Antarctica* and J. M. Coetzee's novel *Elizabeth Costello*, he shows how life writing and a far-southern setting relate to performance and self-revelation for both character and author. In Mabokela's story, Mogau Grace imaginatively reflects on her painful experiences as a South African woman born in the mid-1980s. Combining autobiographical and biographical material with the motifs of god(s) and dream(s), the piece thinks through multiple forms of southern-ness in its depiction of the typical emotional and physical violence an ordinary South African township woman encounters. Together, the contributions in this section join with the essays in the rest of the collection to show that, adapting Samuelson's words, reflections on lives and life writing in half of the planetary sphere must still always recognize that 'there is only one earth'.[23]

Notes

1. Meg Samuelson, 'An "International Author, but in a Different Sense": J. M. Coetzee and "Literatures of the South"', *Thesis Eleven* 162, no. 1 (2021): 137–54.
2. Joy McCann, *Wild Sea: A History of the Southern Ocean* (Chicago: University of Chicago Press, 2019).

3. Meg Samuelson, 'Thinking the Anthropocene South', *Contemporary Literature* 61, no. 4 (2021): 537–49, 538.
4. Elleke Boehmer, 'Life Writing and Imagining across Southern Space', p. 13.
5. See also Elleke Boehmer, 'Faraway Close', *English Academy Review* 38, no. 1 (2021): 67–8.
6. Carl Oglesby, 'Vietnamism Has Failed … The Revolution Can Only Be Mauled, Not Defeated', *Commonweal* 90 (1969): 11–12. See also Elleke Boehmer and Dominic Davies, 'Postcolonialism and South-South Relations', in *Routledge Handbook of South-South Relations*, ed. Elena Fiddian-Qasmiyeh and Patricia Daley (London: Routledge, 2018), 48–58.
7. See J. M. Coetzee, 'Literatures of the South: Introductory Remarks', unpublished lecture, notes by Cristóbal Perez Barra, San Martín National University, Buenos Aires (11 April 2016).
8. The division of First, Second and Third Worlds was first proposed by demographer Alfred Sauvy in 1952, see Eugénia Palieraki, 'The Origins of the "Third World": Alfred Sauvy and the Birth of a Key Global Post-war Concept', *Global Intellectual History* (2023): 1–30; and Elleke Boehmer and Dominic Davies, 'Postcolonialism and South-South Relations', 48–58.
9. Archie Davies, 'Southwards from the Northeast', p. 99.
10. Matthew Sparke, 'Everywhere but Always Somewhere: Critical Geographies of the Global South', *The Global South* 1, no. 1 (January 2007): 117–26, 117.
11. Siba Grovogu, 'A Revolution Nonetheless: The Global South in International Relations', *The Global South*, 5, no. 1 (2011): 175–90, 176–7. Or, in the words of artist Ellen Gallagher, 'all of no man's land is ours'. Available online: https://www.museum.nl/nl/stedelijk-museum-amsterdam/tentoonstelling/ellen-gallagher-all-of-no-mans-land-is-ours (accessed 12 February 2024).
12. Nirmal Puwar, 'Puzzlement of a Déjà vu: Illuminaries of the Global South', *The Sociological Review* 68, no. 3 (2020): 540–56, 552.
13. Elleke Boehmer, *Empire, the National, and the Postcolonial, 1890–1920: Resistance in Interaction* (Oxford: Oxford University Press, 2002), 2–4.
14. Sarah Comyn and Porscha Fermanis, 'Introduction: Southern Worlds, Globes and Spheres', in *Worlding the South*, ed. Sarah Comyn and Porscha Fermanis (Manchester: Manchester University Press, 2021), 1–33. See also: Isabel Hofmeyr, 'Southern by Degrees: Islands and Empires in the South Atlantic, the Indian Ocean, and the Subantartic World', in *The Global South Atlantic*, ed. Kerry Bystrom and Joseph R. Slaughter (New York: Fordham University Press, 2018), 82; Immanuel Wallerstein, *The Modern World-System* (New York: Academic Press, 1964), 98; Peter Hitchcock, *The Long Space: Transnationalism and Postcolonial Form* (Stanford, CA: Stanford University Press, 2010), 35.
15. See the website SULear, https://sulear.com.br/beta3/english/; Paulo Freire, *Pedagogy of Hope: Reliving Pedagogy of the Oppressed* (London: Bloomsbury Publishing, 2021), 218.
16. See Mary Louise Pratt, *Imperial Eyes: Travel Writing and Transculturation* (Abingdon: Routledge, 2007).
17. Zachary Leader, *On Life-Writing* (Oxford: Oxford University Press, 2015).
18. Patrick Hayes, 'What Is "Life-writing" and Why Does It Matter?' *OUPblog*. Available online: https://blog.oup.com/2022/11/what-is-life-writing-and-why-does-it-matter/.
19. Gillian Whitlock, *Postcolonial Life Narratives: Testimonial Transactions* (Oxford: Oxford University Press, 2015); Sidonie A. Smith and Julia Watson, eds., *Before They Could*

Vote: American Women's Autobiographical Writing, 1819–1919 (Madison: University of Wisconsin Press, 2006).

20. See Guadalup Escobar, 'Testimonio at 50', *Latin American Perspectives* 48, no. 2 (2021): 17–32.
21. Rigoberta Menchú, *I, Rigoberta Menchú: An Indian Woman in Guatemala*, trans. Ann Wright (London: Verso Press, 1983). See also David Damrosch, 'Rigoberta Menchú in Print', in *What Is World Literature?* (Princeton, NJ: Princeton University Press, 2003), 231–59.
22. The authors thank Alexus Davies for introducing them to the concept of yarning. There are many possible citations for 'yarning' and 'storywork' as methodologies, often in health and education contexts. We have chosen to cite Indigenous scholars Carmen Parter and Shawn Wilson 'My Research Is My Story: A Methodological Framework of Inquiry Told Through Storytelling by a Doctor of Philosophy Student', *Qualitative Inquiry* 27, no. 8–9 (2021): 1084–94.
23. Meg Samuelson, 'Thinking the Anthropocene South', 539.

Bibliography

Boehmer, Elleke. *Empire, the National, and the Postcolonial, 1890–1920: Resistance in Interaction*. Oxford: Oxford University Press, 2002.

Boehmer, Elleke. 'Faraway Close'. *English Academy Review* 38, no. 1 (2021): 67–8.

Boehmer, Elleke. 'Life Writing and Imagining across Southern Space'. In *Life Writing and the Southern Hemisphere: Texts, Spaces, Resonances*, edited by Elleke Boehmer and Katherine Collins, 13–24. London: Bloomsbury Academic, 2024.

Boehmer, Elleke, and Dominic Davies. 'Postcolonialism and South-South Relations'. In *Routledge Handbook of South-South Relations*, edited by Elena Fiddian-Qasmiyeh and Patricia Daley, 48–58. London: Routledge, 2018.

Coetzee, J. M. 'Literatures of the South: Introductory Remarks', unpublished lecture, notes by Cristóbal Perez Barra, San Martín National University, Buenos Aires (11 April 2016).

Comyn, Sarah, and Porscha Fermanis. 'Introduction: Southern Worlds, Globes and Spheres'. In *Worlding the South,* edited by Sarah Comyn and Porscha Fermanis, 1–33. Manchester: Manchester University Press, 2021.

Damrosch, David. 'Rigoberta Menchú in Print', in *What Is World Literature?*, 231–59. Princeton, NJ: Princeton University Press, 2003.

Davies, Archie. 'Southwards from the Northeast'. In *Life Writing and the Southern Hemisphere: Texts, Spaces, Resonances*, edited by Elleke Boehmer and Katherine Collins, 91–102. London: Bloomsbury Academic, 2024.

Escobar, Guadalup. 'Testimonio at 50'. *Latin American Perspectives* 48, no. 2 (2021): 17–32.

Freire, Paulo. *Pedagogy of Hope: Reliving Pedagogy of the Oppressed*. London: Bloomsbury Publishing, 2021.

Grovogu, Siba. 'A Revolution Nonetheless: The Global South in International Relations'. *The Global South*, 5, no. 1 (2011).

Hayes, Patrick. 'What Is "Life-writing" and Why Does It Matter?' *OUPblog*. Available online: https://blog.oup.com/2022/11/what-is-life-writing-and-why-does-it-matter/.

Hitchcock, Peter. *The Long Space: Transnationalism and Postcolonial Form*. Stanford, CA: Stanford University Press, 2010.

Hofmeyr, Isabel. 'Southern by Degrees: Islands and Empires in the South Atlantic, the Indian Ocean, and the Subantartic World'. In *The Global South Atlantic*, edited by Kerry Bystrom and Joseph R. Slaughter. New York: Fordham University Press, 2018.

Leader, Zachary. *On Life-Writing*. Oxford: Oxford University Press, 2015.
McCann, Joy. *Wild Sea: A History of the Southern Ocean*. Chicago: University of Chicago Press, 2019.
Menchú, Rigoberta. *I, Rigoberta Menchú: An Indian Woman in Guatemala*, translated by Ann Wright. London: Verso Press, 1983.
Oglesby, Carl. 'Vietnamism Has Failed ... The Revolution Can Only Be Mauled, Not Defeated'. *Commonweal* 90 (1969): 11–12.
Palieraki, Eugénia. 'The Origins of the "Third World": Alfred Sauvy and the Birth of a Key Global Post-war Concept'. *Global Intellectual History* (2023): 1–30.
Parter, Carmen, and Shawn Wilson. 'My Research Is My Story: A Methodological Framework of Inquiry Told Through Storytelling by a Doctor of Philosophy Student'. *Qualitative Inquiry* 27, no. 8–9 (2021): 1084–94.
Pratt, Mary Louise. *Imperial Eyes: Travel Writing and Transculturation*. Abingdon: Routledge, 2007.
Puwar, Nirmal. 'Puzzlement of a Déjà vu: Illuminaries of the Global South'. *The Sociological Review* 68, no. 3 (2020).
Samuelson, Meg. 'An "International Author, but in a Different Sense": J. M. Coetzee and "Literatures of the South"'. *Thesis Eleven* 162, no. 1 (2021): 137–54.
Samuelson, Meg. 'Thinking the Anthropocene South'. *Contemporary Literature* 61, no. 4 (2021): 537–49.
Smith, Sidonie A., and Julia Watson, eds. *Before They Could Vote: American Women's Autobiographical Writing, 1819–1919*. Madison: University of Wisconsin Press, 2006.
Sparke, Matthew. 'Everywhere but Always Somewhere: Critical Geographies of the Global South'. *The Global South* 1, no. 1 (January 2007): 117–26.
Wallerstein, Immanuel. *The Modern World-System*. New York: Academic Press, 1964.
Whitlock, Gillian. *Postcolonial Life Narratives: Testimonial Transactions*. Oxford: Oxford University Press, 2015.

PART I
READING THE SOUTH

CHAPTER 1
LIFE WRITING AND IMAGINING ACROSS SOUTHERN SPACE
Elleke Boehmer

The phrase 'Southern Hemisphere', one of the two key terms in the title of this collection, immediately signifies distance and faraway-ness to anyone writing from the Global North. In the Southern Hemisphere lie remote landmasses that many of the world's peoples will never visit. For the writer Teju Cole, to travel south-west from America across the Pacific to New Zealand evokes feelings of farness so resonant and suggestive that together they constitute an independent matrix of sensation, a complex set of feelings that blends together yet at the same time goes beyond the well-described five senses.[1]

The travelling protagonist in Olga Tocarczuk's *Flights* (2007) relatedly comments that to speak of distance implies speaking 'from somewhere, some centre or axis, some human habitation'.[2] It requires a point of reference against which to relativize the space traversed. On a journey south-east from Poland once again to New Zealand, she writes that she misses in the green islands of Aotearoa the sense of a fixed centre, a 'real' or recognizable place to arrive at. Even after having traced one of the longest arcs of flight in the world, the country denies her the clear point of geohistorical focus to which Europeans like herself, travelling away from or back to their subcontinent, are accustomed. Their subcontinent is an established centre of world history, after all.

For me, Southern Hemisphere–born, the idea of farness calls up not so much images of continents and islands in the far south, as for Tokarczuk, but associations of the Southern Ocean. To many southerners, this ocean, with its charging currents, its steely horizons and 'enormous flashing seas' (in Joseph Conrad's phrase) and its proximity to Antarctica, is the epitome of the farthest south. There is in fact far more ocean in the Southern Hemisphere (about 81 per cent of its surface is water), and far fewer people live there (only about 11 per cent of the world's population).[3] For me, southern farness also has a sound – the ringing, shirring sound of a device like a high-frequency radio, out of focus, trying and failing to communicate across miles and time-zones. Considering the hemisphere's vast watery distances, it is perhaps no accident that several of the essays in this collection discuss radio communications.[4] From the late nineteenth century on, the technology made real and realizable encounters across distance that till then were imaginable only through the more numinous media of telepathy and haunting.

The idea of linking up across great distance through radio and, later, the telephone, then satellite, raises a more general question about imaginative identification across the planet, along the lines of longitude. How do we bridge vast north-south distances in the mind, especially when most of us will never descend below the Equator, yet when cross-border solidarities are as important as at any other time in human history, perhaps even more so? This essay reflects first upon what it is to think and write about the state of being far and south, both geopolitically and temporally. The far south of the world, with latitudes *above* (not below!) 35 degrees south, is not only at a great distance from the global centres of economic power and cultural influence; historically, the region has also always been considered to represent the essence of the unknown.

The essay then goes on to offer thoughts on how life writing, the second key term in the title, might help to bridge the hemisphere's mythic vastness, and how the writing of lives that intersect or conjoin across the miles affords ways of interpreting and managing distance. For the purposes of the discussion, 'lives' here includes the lives of objects crafted by the peoples of the south and also southern etymologies, the history or lives of words from the indigenous languages of the Southern Hemisphere, that may help to give us insight into southern thought-worlds. These different life forms and textures, I suggest, open channels across great planetary distances. They provide entry-points into the remote and sometimes faded cultural spaces of the lesser known and (by the north) more objectified hemisphere.

Central to this approach is the 1930s linguistic theory of Edward Sapir and Benjamin Whorf, who proposed that our understanding of the world is, in part, shaped by the words we have to name it.[5] The theory gains melancholic traction in the context of European colonialism in the Southern Hemisphere. For most parts of the far south, including Tierra del Fuego, the Cape of Good Hope, Tasmania and the islands of Aotearoa/New Zealand, including Te Waipounamu or South Island (though not only these), empire brought the imposition of European knowledge systems and the destruction of peoples and their cultures. Southern things came to be named using northern words. Many Indigenous Southern languages – Khoikhoi, Selk'nam, Yaghan and hundreds of languages in Australia – were lost to the memory of most, and, as they dwindled, vital environmental knowledge and understandings of nature and country faded also. Important aspects of the Southern Hemisphere's reality came to elude people's ability to interpret them even where they lived those realities. The lands, oceans and living creatures of the south were (and are still) imagined not through local words that had grown up in those contexts but by words from elsewhere, that necessarily bore little relation to those spaces and that required adaptation, revision and readjustment to fit.

In what follows, I consider three pathways that we might follow to work against these at once linguistic, epistemological and technological impositions. I look at the identifications afforded by crafted objects, in particular baskets, then at the reawakening of words, and finally at link-ups through life writing. Each pathway explores how we might set about retrieving or reawakening southern knowledges from beyond the divide of power and knowledge separating the Global North from the South. The divide here takes temporal as well as spatial form, especially for those who have been and remain subject to empire and the processes of uneven globalization and extraction that split southern peoples, cultures and lands away from the rich and powerful north.

Life Writing and Imagining Across Southern Space

Objects

This section asks about what happens when we thoughtfully engage with cultural objects from far away – in this case, the remote Southern Hemisphere. The governing idea here is the question of whether the close-up observation of the craft that went into the making of the objects might help bring the life of their makers more proximate to us and imaginatively bridge the power-knowledge divide separating the south from the north. As any museum visitor will know, this divide is often further reinforced by the objectifying information lists and labels that accompany the objects. In the case of the Pitt Rivers Museum in Oxford, the ethnographic museum I know best, which features a range of Southern Hemisphere objects, information sheets about exhibits, without exception, contain more information about the collectors than about the makers of the objects and the cultures from which they came.

Yet, though those original makers' names and identities are now mostly lost, it is immediately clear on looking at the objects that they testify in multiple ways to the skills and life experiences of trained craftswomen and craftsmen. The objects palpably emerge from ways of life long adapted to their environments – from fishing, hunting and gathering practices, from modes of navigation and from life processes of reproduction, loss and death – and could arguably be related back to them.

The important research of the anthropologist Laura Peers, formerly of the Pitt Rivers Museum, has laid down generative pathways through which we might explore how a particular group, the living descendants of such cultural objects' first makers, might handle and engage with them.[6] In her work, Peers describes how the handling process sparks in people strong feelings of connection and a sense of closeness with the ancestral spirits who are still believed to inhabit the objects that they once used when they were living people. My own position in relation to exhibited objects in the Pitt Rivers is of course different than this, more at-arms'-length, and, in any case, handling the objects is generally not permitted. Yet, even so, it is possible to observe at close quarters the objects' contours, volume, proportions and the details of their decoration. We can take in the once-living textures of flax and reed, of eggshell and wood, and follow with our eyes the processes of weaving, plaiting, winding, knotting, engraving, threading and so on that has gone into their making.

The southern objects in the Pitt Rivers Museum that I particularly relate to are two Indigenous Australian baskets or dilly (also, *dhili*) bags, a rounded one from Tasmania in white iris plant fibre and a bigger 'bicornual basket' in twined weave from what is now Northern Queensland, painted with a zigzag design in red. I noticed even before reading more about the uses of the *dhili* bag that the bottom of the larger one was unmistakeably made to take the shape of the fish that must once have lain in it, with the creatures' dorsal curves mirrored in the basket's bellied lower edge.

To me, the close-up contact with the bags' rounded depth and evident utility solicits the viewer's attention in a certain precise way. As with the other indigenous southern objects on display – the boomerang and the Fuegian slingshot – they unlock points of entry into histories that have otherwise now evanesced. The shape of the baskets and the

Figure 1.1 Basket from Northern Queensland. Copyright Pitt Rivers Museum, University of Oxford (1897.1.2).

craft that has gone into their making offer means of understanding and relating to the life ways and practices of the individuals who produced them, even if over 150 or so years ago. (The information sheet suggests that they had both been crafted 'by' the 1860s and 1890s, respectively, when they were collected.) After all, the things people make and use are shaped to their bodies and the needs for which they are made. And the signs of an object's wear and tear bear the imprint of a daily life, the round of work and rest, of going out and coming back in. Even the twist and turn of the fibres, like the curve of the handles, give some sense of the objects' habitual use, how they might be hooked over a shoulder or hunched up on a hip, such as after walking home from foraging in rock pools. More than that, to adapt from Joseph Conrad's comment on hearing the human voice in a Southern Ocean gale, the signs of making and usage communicate 'the mark of human consciousness' upon the character of time.[7]

Life Writing and Imagining Across Southern Space

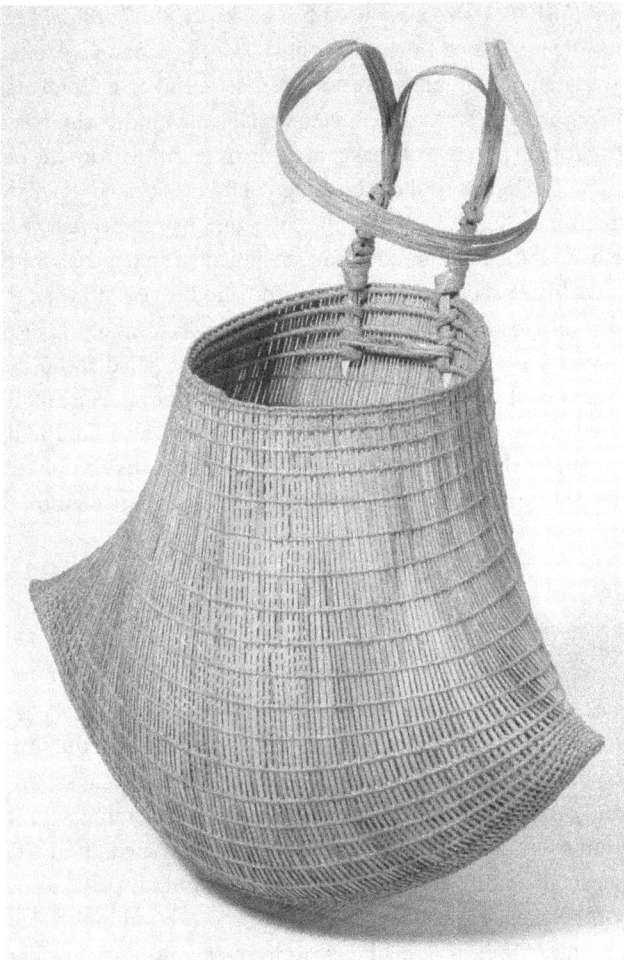

Figure 1.2 Basket from Tasmania. Copyright Pitt Rivers Museum, University of Oxford (1893.38.24).

These speculations were reinforced on a research trip to the University of Tasmania in Hobart in December 2022, which included a visit to the Tasmanian Museum and Art Gallery. In a display in the very first room of the gallery, I was met with *dhili* bags that looked much like the one from Tasmania in the Pitt Rivers Museum. It was a curious moment of recognition and return. I was revisiting objects that I had repeatedly weighed and turned around in my imagination back in Oxford. Now, I was able better to place them in some of the contexts in which they had been used and made.

The object labels accompanying the display cases filled in more of the cultural stories of the bags' making and of the craft that had produced their curves and decoration. I learned that the bags were used as fish baskets and that their strong bendable size afforded compact and efficient transport for sea food. I also read that the important cultural

17

leader Trukanini (1812–76) probably used fish baskets just like these. I learned that the fibre used, the white flag iris or Tasman flax lily (*Dianella tasmanica*), offers flexibility in weaving and strength and durability over time. I also found on an information board the story of a contemporary Tasmanian educator, Colleen Mundy, who has continued her community's traditional practice of basket making by learning from the older, 'respected weavers' in her family. She has studied the design of baskets passed down the generations, from mother to mother, that have eluded the collector's net. In her daily life, Mundy says, she has tried to live 'off the land' and has 'collected plants and lichens for bush dyeing and fibre crafts', always inspired by the 'love of the land and the sea and what they give to us'.[8]

Taking all this in, I experienced at close hand there in front of the display cases how crafted objects offer ways of narrating histories that have faded and of recognizing the important relations of stewardship of land and sea that have been woven into them. I saw how objects such as these not only embed skills but also hold temporality. They reawaken life practices that have continued despite the incursions of colonialism. The marks of making they carry are places where the historical imagination can shift south and take flight.

Words

In this section I consider how Indigenous southern words, for their part, might evoke southern contexts and sensations and unlock southern stories. In the sounds, meanings and etymologies of these words, southern peoples past and present step forward, even if only intermittently, as speakers and thinkers and as agents operating within their history, not outside it – in short, as 'active subjects', not simply as acted upon.[9] The idea here is that elements as small as single words and phrases can hold spatial knowledge or give some account of the experience of feeling in place and centred in the south, not 'upside down' or 'on the edge'.[10] The words challenge us to re-examine how our knowledge of the world has been naturalized, so that northern concepts are always seen as prior. Where the words fall into recognizable patterns, they can also tell us something more about the ways in which indigenous southern peoples inhabited, imagined and interpreted their environments, how they organized their mental worlds, where they paid attention, looked more closely and placed emphasis.[11]

The interconnection of Indigenous words, their contexts and their speakers' thought-worlds, including their sense of space-time, is especially clear in the case of languages where tense is spatially conceived and non-linear, as, for example, in Indigenous Australian languages like Gamilaraay, Warlpiri, Noongar or Kaurna. As Marnie Hughes-Warrington and Anne Martin write, for such languages, 'Country [or place] is the organiser' of the understanding of time. Conversely, ideas of time are also indistinguishably bound up with those of space. Temporal words denote position and direction; spatial words duration, recurrence, and senses of distant and near time.[12]

The Indigenous writer Tara June Winch's novel *The Yield* (2020) offers a remarkable case in point. Winch has made it her mission through the structures of her fiction to reclaim her Wiradjuri people's linguistic landscape and, in this way, story-sized pieces of their history. Her central protagonist, the grandfather, Albert Gondiwindi, takes it as his life's project to compile a word-list of Wiradjiri, something that commits him to telling mini cultural tales about the words. His poetic definitions of, for example, *dharrang-dharrang* (messenger, but also librarian), or *murru* (marks or tracks, also lifeways), or *gibirrban*, the Southern Cross constellation, form part of the texture of the story and revitalize and update the language within the novel itself.[13]

A personal back-story is attached to many of the words, such as about Albert's time in the children's home, or his relationship with his wife and family, a backdrop which then threads the individual story in with the wider group's. For a language, as Winch writes, is a handbook of culture; it explains how kinship works; which feelings count; how to read the stars.[14] She also endeavours to capture the emplacement of time in her language, as it is reflected in the interchangeable prepositions of directionality, position and sequence that characterize many Indigenous Australian languages. Or, as Albert Gondiwindi explains, *yandu* – 'yet, if, then, when, at the time'. Therefore, *yandu* is also 'the glue' of stories.[15]

Indigenous place-names and names for geographic features, too, carry the memory of associations with the land and so can centre southern contexts in the mind. *Hoerikwaggo* or 'Mountain in the sea' for Cape Town's Table Mountain, *Uluru* for the great sacred rock at the heart of Australia, and so on give modern listeners and speakers a plastic, embodied sense of what it was to inhabit those geographies before colonization, even where the languages themselves are no longer spoken outside of small groups. For the South African language activist Denver van Breda, 'when you lose land and language you lose identity'. However, by retrieving the Khoi words that live on in place-names and in Afrikaaps (the Khoisan-inflected version of Afrikaans, itself a creole of Dutch), he is nonetheless able to '[find his] ancestors'.[16] In his view, too, a south-centred understanding can be reawakened through the medium of southern words seen as knowledge-objects, even if they now occur only as borrowings into other languages. As in van Breda's work with Afrikaans, a key way of driving this retrieval can be by reading the 'perverse' colonial archive slant, for example, by backlighting the indigenous words that crop up in the word-lists compiled by missionaries and ethnographers ('Indigenous', 97–104).[17]

Writing

And so, to writing – the writing of others' lives: how life writing helps to build identification and bridge global distances. Writing that calls to mind others distanced in both time and space has the capacity to create or re-create what I call faraway closeness. It allows us to be together in some sense despite being physically far apart, using coordinated thinking or even something as mundane and everyday as a phone call or a text message. Life writing, as well as the identifications offered by storytelling, gossip and anecdote, arguably offer channels for feeling and thinking our way into the lives of others, on related lines to the weave of the *dhili* bags.

The role of writing and conversation about writing in bridging space-time gaps was brought home to everyone during the Covid-19 global lockdowns. Being proximate in spite of distance became a condition shared by millions of people, not least the contributors to this book. The workshops where many of the essays collected here were honed were held either on-line or in hybrid form. We experienced at first-hand a virtual looping across the time-zones and observed that sharing experiences held in common despite the separations of geography encouraged the imagination to cross the gulfs of space that the impossibility of travel had thrown up between countries.

These identifications bore parallels in spatial terms with the exercise of reading southern histories into objects and words. Early navigation offered another useful analogy, harking back to a time when ships' captains, ancient mariners and other people of the sea often saw no one other than the crew they were sailing with for months on end. With their letters and logbooks, these navigators were, however, continually relating to each other, identifying in the imagination with those they would later report to and live with. Travel to the moon forms the twentieth-century equivalent of these journeys. The astronaut Michael Collins circling around the dark side of the moon on the Apollo 11 voyage interestingly described the experience of being the remotest human in the solar system, or anywhere, as 'rounding the Horn'. The first few decades of Antarctic exploration, which several essays in this book discuss, also offers a striking example of how we might hold each other in mind through a kind of willed telepathy, by focussing on an object in common at a certain agreed time of day even when we lack more direct means of communication.

For me during the Covid-19 lockdown, writing about remote identification and distant proximity between the north and the south turned into a double project – first, a novel about an epistolary love affair conducted between England and Antarctica, and second, a literary and cultural history of the Southern Hemisphere. I happily discovered that the creative writing helped to develop new vocabularies for talking about being remote together. It offered an oxymoronic lexicon for feeling each other across distance, or for thinking as one across the miles, faraway but close. I often used as a guide the lines that Paquita, the wife of Australian Antarctic explorer Douglas Mawson, wrote him in a letter he would only read about two years later, in 1913, on his return home from not just one but two winters spent in an ice-bound hut on the edge of the frozen continent: 'O darling … if only nothing is happening to you but I think I should feel it.'[18] She was trying, as I was, to give concrete words to the intangible yet real experience of choreographed telepathy.

Others' experiences of being at distance also helped my writing. As I worked, stories jumped out from the newspaper and social media that spoke directly to my interest in how people might have an affair long distance or keep a new relationship alive. In my novel, the characters, separated by 10,000 miles, work out what the other might be doing at each hour of a normal day and try to bring their mental worlds into synch. On the hour, each one concentratedly thinks of the other, a bit like Paquita and Douglas.

As for the Southern Hemisphere history, analyzing how courageous if overreaching ship's captains like Vasco da Gama or James Cook navigated vast, uncharted distances around the southern continents brought to mind not only the seemingly unending quality of the Southern Ocean horizon but also how to interrelate across it. In the 'storm-blasted' southern seas, Samuel Taylor Coleridge's Ancient Mariner famously encounters threatening ice-fields – and a bird that shows his crew fellowship. Writing their stories, I imagined their tiny ships rounding wild Cape Horn and the stormy Cape of Good Hope, proceeding mostly by happenstance and instinct. I sensed their joy at meeting a passing ship that might be heading back to Lisbon or London, the ports that they had left from. I felt the resistance or push-back of the great quantities of turbulent water that separated them from home. I was struck by how often ships meeting one another on the 'everlasting terra incognita' of the Southern Ocean, in Herman Melville's phrase, take pains to draw close and cross wakes, to exchange letters and greetings.

In my novel, the two characters in love yet 10,000 miles and a hemisphere apart and without reliable email decide to look at the moon at the same time every night as a way of keeping virtually in touch. Though they see different constellations, they are at least joined by longitude and the moon's orbit. The triangulation bridges the vast distance between them – and, in a very particular way, also provides a guiding motif for weathering life-events during lockdown, as happened to me on the last night of 2020.

On the evening of 30 December 2020, my eldest niece started to give birth to her first child, my grand-niece. By midnight, though, little was happening. Pacing up and down, I was trying to think hard of them both, as was her mother, my sister-in-law, who texted to say she, too, was awake and restless. There was a full moon that night, a bright one, and I stepped outside for a while to look at it and take some pictures. I sent my sister-in-law these, and she wrote back to say that she, too, was looking out at the moon. Reading her text, I felt suddenly reassured. Together, we were thinking in a coordinated and hence (it felt) sustaining way about the near mother-to-be and the new baby.

Like people reading in a group, or sharing stories on-line, we were joining up our anxieties and expectations through a common point of reference. The experience of new life and the bright moon connected us across the distance. The baby was born a few hours later, in the very early hours of the morning. Though we have happily met in person since, from the beginning the baby's extended family was able to follow the story of her first half-year through a range of media, WhatsApp photographs, FaceTime, phone calls and SMS, as do many dispersed families from around the world. This has kept us in touch with her life in meaningful ways. At each month's end for the first year of her life, her parents took a picture of the baby alongside a card showing her age – *I am one month old*, etc. These are the moments, the chapters in the story, that I most value. For me, they confirm something potent about storytelling at distance, and something about the powers of imaginative identification, of feeling intimately connected with others, even across huge distances.

Conclusion

Object identifications, word associations, life writing – each one of these processes not only bridges distance but also validates forms of relational understanding. If the naming of the south by the north is at once a correlate for, and an instance of, the latter's geopolitical domination, then these forms of imaginative closeness contribute to deconstructing that planetary imbalance. The techniques of object and word biography join with forms of life writing across space-time to help to unlock learnings and perceptions 'from below'. The channels of hemispheric connection allow us to upturn perceptions of these areas as too out there and faraway to count – such perceptions as underwrote empire, and vice versa. We see that the so-called edges of the world can be linked in the mind even despite their remoteness. We are prompted to view the planet more holistically, as a conglomerate of many different centre-points and axes. Or, finally, as Albert Gondiwindi in *The Yield* defines Wiradjiri *manhang* or 'soil, earth, dirt':

> Over and over that cycle never ended ... I read that inside the soil there are the same number of microbes as there are stars in the universe ... Once you find a piece of something you know about, afterward you end up getting given more and more pieces of the puzzle everywhere you go. One thing comes and then the world tells you to look out for all the other missing information. *Manhang* – that's where the body goes eventually, and everything else from the *manhang* to the stars is eternally alive with our spirits.[19]

Notes

1. Elleke Boehmer, 'Time and Distance', *Agenda* 35, no. 4 (2021): 99–104.
2. Olga Tokarczuk, *Flights*, trans. Jennifer Croft (London: Fitzcarraldo, 2006).
3. Meg Samuelson, 'An "International Author, but in a Different Sense": J. M. Coetzee and "Literatures of the South"', *Thesis Eleven* 162, no. 1 (2021): 137–54.
4. I try to capture the simultaneous allure and blur of long-distance radio communication in my short story 'The Father Antenna'. See Elleke Boehmer, *Sharmilla, and Other Portraits* (Auckland Park: Jacana, 2010), 7–15.
5. Madeleine Mathiot, *Ethnolinguistics: Boas, Sapir and Whorf Revisited* (The Hague: Mouton, 1979), 163.
6. Peers's area of expertise is north-west Canada. See Laura L. Peers and Alison K. Brown, *Visiting with the Ancestors: Blackfoot Shirts in Museum* Spaces (Athabasca: Athabasca University Press, 2016).
7. Joseph Conrad, *The Mirror of the Sea* (London: J. M. Dent and Sons, 1949), ch. 14.
8. Information board, Tasmanian Museum and Art Gallery, author photograph, 10 December 2022.
9. Nicholas Evans, *Dying Words: Endangered Languages and What They Have to Tell Us* (Oxford: Blackwell, 2010), 160–5.
10. Song-lines or dreaming tracks work as a kind of memorized orientation that makes possible at once sensing and singing the land while moving through it. Though he did not use Indigenous knowledge responsibly, Bruce Chatwin's *The Songlines* remains evocative for western audiences in outlining the concept. Against Chatwin's claims, Indigenous Australians believe that they have always lived in Australia; they did not migrate to the continent from Africa.

11. Elleke Boehmer, *Empire, the National, and the Postcolonial 1890–1920* (Oxford: Oxford University Press, 2002), 2–5. See also Néstor García Canclini, *Imagined Globalization*, trans. George Yúdice (Durham and London: Duke University Press, 2014).
12. Marnie Hughes-Warrington and Anne Martin, *Big and Little Histories: Sizing Up Ethics in Historiography* (Abingdon: Taylor and Francis, 2021), 262. From the online Gamilaraay course I took with Tracey Cameron at the University of Sydney, March–May 2021, I gained a comparable sense of how temporality operated in the language, or of how space-time was designated. Gamilaraay notably uses the same suffix (*-ga*, or *-dha*) to denote nearby position: 'in', 'on', 'at', 'near', etc.
13. Tara June Winch, *The Yield: A Novel* (London, HarperVia, 2019), 125–6.
14. Ibid., 341.
15. Ibid., 24.
16. Denver van Breda, Deidre Jantjies, and Menán du Plessis, '!Hub Di Gowab – 'n Taal van ons Land', Woordfees festival discussion, Stellenbosch, 11 March 2020. As part of this same conversation, van Breda noted that language recognition and relearning were ways of healing a community and connecting to the ancestors. While colonial 'Hollander' forces had worked with destructive effect, inflicting '*kakapoesa*' or erasure of identity, Afrikaans and Griqua speakers had ('till 1875') kept indigenous Khoi-San languages alive.
17. Kennedy argues that the 'challenge is to use such records – what I am calling *perverse archives* – to create an Indigenous cultural memory of dehumanization and survival' (p. 90).
18. Emma McEwin, *An Antarctic Affair* (Bowden, South Africa: East Street Publications, 2008), 69.
19. Tara June Winch, *The Yield*, 76–7.

Bibliography

Archibald, Jo-Ann, Jenny Lee-Morgan, and Jason De Santolo, eds. *Decolonizing Research: Indigenous Storywork as Methodology*. London: Zed, 2019.
Boehmer, Elleke. *Empire, the National, and the Postcolonial, 1890–1920*. Oxford: Oxford University Press, 2002.
Boehmer, Elleke. *Sharmilla, and Other Portraits*. Auckland Park: Jacana, 2010.
Boehmer, Elleke. 'Time and Distance'. *Agenda* 35, no. 4 (2021): 99–104.
Canclini, Néstor García. *Imagined Globalization*, translated by George Yúdice. Durham and London: Duke University Press, 2014.
Chatwin, Bruce. *The Songlines*. London: Jonathan Cape, 1987.
Conrad, Joseph. *The Mirror of the Sea*. London: J. M. Dent and Sons, 1949.
Evans, Nicholas. *Dying Words: Endangered Languages and What They Have to Tell Us*. Oxford: Blackwell, 2010.
Hughes-Warrington, Marnie, and Anne Martin. *Big and Little Histories: Sizing Up Ethics in Historiography*. Abingdon: Taylor and Francis, 2021.
Kennedy, Roseanne. 'Indigenous Australian Arts of Return: Mediating Perverse Archives', in *Rites of Return: Diaspora Poetics and the Politics of Memory*, edited by Marianne Hirsch and Nancy K. Miller, 88–104. New York: Columbia University Press, 2011.
Mathiot, Madeleine. *Ethnolinguistics: Boas, Sapir and Whorf Revisited*. The Hague: Mouton, 1979.
McEwin, Emma. *An Antarctic Affair*. Bowden, South Africa: East Street Publications, 2008.
Peers, Laura L., and Alison K. Brown. *Visiting with the Ancestors: Blackfoot Shirts in Museum Spaces*. Athabasca: Athabasca University Press, 2016.

Samuelson, Meg. 'An "International Author, but in a Different Sense": J. M. Coetzee and "Literatures of the South"'. *Thesis Eleven* 162, no. 1 (2021): 137–54.
Tokarczuk, Olga. *Flights*, translated by Jennifer Croft. London: Fitzcarraldo, 2006.
van Breda, Denver, Deidre Jantjies, and Menán du Plessis. '!Hub Di Gowab – 'n Taal van ons Land', Woordfees festival discussion, Stellenbosch, 11 March 2020.
Whorf, Benjamin. *Language, Thought, and Reality: Selected Writings of Benjamin Lee Whorf*, edited by John B. Carroll, Stephen C. Levinson and Penny Lee. Boston: MIT Press, 2012.
Winch, Tara June. *The Yield: A Novel*. London: HarperVia, 2019.

CHAPTER 2
PROSTHETICS, SOUVENIRS AND SETTLEMENT: SOUTH-SOUTH CONNECTIONS IN JANET FRAME'S AND DORIS LESSING'S LIFE WRITING
Emma Parker

In July 1874, Mary Paterson, an eighteen-year old Scot, disembarked from the *Mairi Bhan* in Otago harbour on the South Island of Aotearoa New Zealand. A reporter for *The Otago Witness* entered the ship as it docked, writing approvingly that the several hundred 'single girls [onboard] were well-behaved' and would be a welcome 'accession to the population of the Province'.[1] Mary was illiterate at the time of her arrival, having worked in a Glaswegian cotton mill from the age of eight. Throughout the mid-nineteenth century, many families in her hometown had been 'kept from actual starvation by the means of soup kitchens' after the local weaving industry collapsed.[2] A significant portion of these communities from the Lowlands, including Mary and her future husband Alexander Frame, subsequently accepted government-supported passage to Aotearoa New Zealand, where they were welcomed as means to bolster the colony's white population. The Frame family, like many settlers, nevertheless maintained close ties with Britain over the ensuing decades. Their second-youngest child, George, dutifully 'responded to the call of King and Empire' in 1916, volunteering to serve as a sapper in Gallipoli and later on the Western Front.[3] Although he hoped to stay in Britain after the war, George returned to Otago in 1919, assisted by a rehabilitation loan which outlined an agreement between 'his Majesty the King and George Samuel Frame'.[4] Over several successive generations, this family's lives became embedded within the complex networks of empire, preserving ties which linked the distant archipelagos of Britain and Aotearoa New Zealand.

In 1924, exactly fifty years after Mary departed from Scotland, a young English bank manager named Alfred Tayler visited the Empire Exhibition at Wembley, where he encountered an advertisement for government-subsidized farms in Southern Rhodesia. In front of the poster were piles of glossy cobs stacked high on a display stand, with accompanying pamphlets promising that quick fortunes could be made from this staple crop (see Figure 2.1). The amputation of Alfred's right leg shortly before the battle of Passchendaele meant that he was the sole survivor of his company, left to insist that 'England was a country that had betrayed its promises to its people'.[5] Accompanied at the Exhibition by his wife Emily, a former nurse, Alfred was on the hunt for new opportunities in the mid-1920s and the Southern Rhodesia stand seemed to promise

Figure 2.1 Maize, Tobacco etc. Southern Rhodesia Pavilion, British Empire Exhibition, Wembley 1925.

freedom for a disabled veteran who had 'never had the capital to farm' in England.[6] So rather than returning to their previous home in Persia (now Iran), where he managed a branch of the country's Imperial Bank, Alfred and Emily relocated to southern Africa with their two small children, hoping to forge new, successful lives on the settler frontier. Despite making endless plans to return to Britain over the ensuing decades, the Taylers became trapped by their debts to the country's land bank, and the increasingly infirm Alfred eventually died in Salisbury (now Harare, Zimbabwe) in 1947.

These outward voyages from Britain to the so-called 'colonial peripheries' of the Southern Hemisphere might initially be attributed to the vagaries of fate, the result of chance encounters and individual decisions. But such 'journeys out' were far more than happenstance. Bill Schwarz reminds us that throughout the nineteenth century, numerous official and philanthropic schemes actively promoted '[white] emigration, motivated in part by fears *of the impending "over-population"* of Britain' (emphasis my own).[7] When the Frames left the Clyde Valley in the 1870s, 'the New Zealand government had seventy-three agents in Scotland alone and advertised in 288 Scottish newspapers'.[8] Mass white emigration continued long into the next century when, after the First World War, 'the establishment of the Overseas Settlement Committee [was] designed to promote the emigration of veterans and their dependents to the dominions'.[9] These policies viewed Britain's colonial territories as a solution to domestic problems, accommodating communities that the government neither wanted as citizens nor needed as a labour force. While injured soldiers like George Frame were supported to return home, disabled veterans like Alfred were encouraged to consider new lives out in the empire. Elsewhere Elleke Boehmer has written of the exchanges and south-south connections caused by 'imperial policies which had been developed in relation to one particular dependency or colony' being transferred to others.[10] These ensured that those living in settler colonies, including former soldiers like George and Alfred, were connected by a series of horizontal exchanges, rather than being confined to a vertical core-periphery relationship with the metropole. The lives of these two men suggest how 'lateral, networked, and periphery-periphery lines of connection' developed in southern, late colonial contexts during the final decades of the British Empire.[11]

Excepting recent scholarship by Jean Smith (2022), previous studies of colonial 'emigration [being used] as a solution to social problems' have focussed largely on the Victorian era.[12] Yet resettlement schemes worked to address 'complex problems of demobilisation, veterans' discontent, industrial regeneration and chronic unemployment' far into the twentieth century.[13] This chapter traces how Alfred's and George's disappointed post-war lives in settler societies confront official narratives of imperial prosperity, where white emigration was expected to secure the future of a global Anglosphere. It uncovers lateral connections between white communities in Southern Rhodesia and Aotearoa New Zealand which challenge the foundations of a settler-colonial project premised on white land ownership, health and prosperity.

Alfred and George are also, of course, connected by the extensive life writing projects of their respective daughters. The Nobel Prize–winning writer Doris Lessing recorded her father's life across multiple autobiographical narratives, remembering how Alfred 'valiantly fought the disadvantages of a wooden leg', yet 'infected' his children with talk of 'the scarred pitiful shrunken stump, the war, the war, the *war* – the Trenches'.[14] George is remembered in the autobiographies of the New Zealand writer Janet Frame as a distant parent who was 'so often either sad or angry', plagued by the terrible memories that – unlike Alfred – he largely refused to discuss.[15] Previous comparative studies of these authors (including my own) begin with Frame's and Lessing's 'journeys in', emphasizing their respective arrivals in London after the Second World War (McLeod 2004; Parker 2024). But this chapter suggests that their life writing intersects through an earlier series of south-south connections, forged by disillusioned veteran fathers who felt, to borrow Lessing's phrase, 'surplus to requirements' after active service.[16] These accounts consistently describe white colonial emigration as entrapment, rather than personal liberation. The lateral exchanges between these southern lives build on Siba Grovogu's argument that the Global South is delineated by 'a set of practices, attitudes and relations' which disavow those 'institutional and cultural practices associated with colonialism'.[17] Lessing's and Frame's life writing is rooted in the south not because their childhoods took place geographically below the equator but because their anti-colonial critique challenges white settler society from within. Both women define settlerdom through failure, viewed through the prism of paternal figures who felt forgotten by and jettisoned from the metropole.

In order to tease out these connections between war, white settlers and southern lives, this chapter focuses on autotopographical objects associated with Alfred and George, drawing on Jennifer A. Gonzalez's term for personal possessions where 'memories

[are] made manifest in a material form'.[18] Whether in descriptions of Alfred's wooden leg, or in the assortment of souvenirs that George brought back from his wartime service, Lessing and Frame returned over and over to totemic objects which ultimately became symbols of waste and failure. As we will see, rather than being memories of – or even memorials to – each man's wartime service, these objects reveal an imperilled imperial identity at the end of empire. Ostensibly autotopographies are intended to be 'witnesses of [an individual's] existence'.[19] We look at such objects to discern, 'above all, what they disclose about *us*'.[20] Yet for Lessing and Frame, possessions like medals or a government-sponsored prosthetic – both designed to commemorate wartime sacrifice – instead represent redundancy and colonial malaise. Such useless material objects bring the south-south connections between these life writers sharply into focus, revealing the contradictions of the settler imaginary. By undoing the false promises of a glossy corn cob, or an advertisement for subsidized emigration to the colonies, these autotopographical objects form exhibitions of their own, displays of debris which challenge empire's official narratives of prosperous white settlement.

Prosthetics and wartime memories in Southern Rhodesia

In the first volume of her autobiography, Lessing describes how her father never stopped talking 'through my days and through my sleep, too, [about] the war, the betrayal of the soldiers, the wicked stupidities and corruption of government'.[21] As Alfred obsessively recited his memories of 'tanks, star-shells, shrapnel, howitzers', his daughter was – even in her final memoir *Alfred and Emily* (2008) – always trying to escape: 'crouching in the bush, my hands right over my ears "I won't, I will not. Stop. I won't listen"'.[22] Although their Rhodesian home was both geographically and culturally remote from the battlefields of France, the Taylers' farmhouse was filled with ghostly 'men in uniforms'.[23] In Lessing's life writing, memories of 'the Great War' are secured to objects which act as proxies for missing bodies, like the framed image of her mother's 'great love, a doctor, [who] drowned in the Channel'.[24] Those survivors who returned or retreated to the colony were left to compulsively repeat their stories, and Alfred often exchanged 'war memoirs, war histories' with friends and neighbours in Southern Rhodesia.[25] Yet these official, printed accounts were hardly straightforward expressions of nationalist or imperial belonging; Alfred Tayler championed texts like *All Quiet on the Western Front* (1928) because he identified with German soldiers who had been 'betrayed [just] like the English tommies by their generals'.[26] None of the public and private sites of memory from Lessing's childhood made any mention of Black African companies like the Rhodesia Native Regiment (comprised of over 2,600 men) who also fought and died in the conflict.[27] Solidarity between veterans could, in the settler colony, cross enemy lines but not racial ones.

Many former soldiers who lived nearby were physically disabled, from 'Mr Livingstone [who had] a wooden leg' to 'Mr McAuley [who] had a steel plate over his stomach, to keep his intestines in – so they said'.[28] Along with these visceral reminders of the battlefield, *Under My Skin* contains numerous descriptions of prostheses and bodily fragmentation which emphasize the distance between the colony and metropole. Lessing recalls the self-inflected mutilation of her parents 'both [having] all their teeth out' while visiting England, on the advice that 'there would not be any good dentists in Southern Rhodesia' and natural teeth 'were of no use to anyone'.[29] Frame, too, viewed 'the general opinion [...] that natural teeth were best removed' as 'a kind of colonial squandering, like the needless uprooting of forests'.[30] In Alfred and Emily's case, the unnecessary dentures became a symbol of how unprepared they were for frontier life; the 'ill-fitting teeth' troubled a couple who, after realising that they would never make enough money to return to England, would lie huddled and defeated in bed, next to 'glasses of water with their false teeth in'.[31] As Ryan Sweet notes, cosmetic prostheses were 'synonymous with representations of ageing' in late Victorian literature, with dentures in particular viewed as grotesque and comic.[32] Alfred and Emily's uncomfortable teeth are emblems of loss, of a prosperous colonial future that had failed to arrive *and* of the false promises of empire, which caused them to prematurely age. Yet in Lessing's life writing, these items also emphasize the distance between her family's past lives in the northern hemisphere and their southern present. These artificial body parts are a tragic, rather than comic, reminder of their sacrifices for the myths of British imperialism, emblematic of their shared, remote existence in a landlocked settler colony.

While prosthetics feature in many of Lessing's childhood memories, Alfred's wooden leg is the autotopographical object which most clearly connects her view of a declining empire to the physical and emotional devastation of the war. As her family were marooned in Southern Rhodesia, Lessing used this geographical position to develop a critical, anti-imperial account of the First World War from the south. Here the conflict becomes inseparable from waste and failure, throwing previous models of robust, imperial masculinity into crisis. The leg is at the centre of Lessing's earliest memory where she sits, aged two, propped up against her father and astride a horse: 'I am inside the heat of the horse, the smell of the horse [...] I lean back my head and shoulder into my father's stomach and feel there the hard straps of the wooden-leg harness'.[33] The artificial wooden leg – that 'hard slippery hidden thing' – was attached to Alfred's thigh with heavy leather straps, concealing the 'pitiful shrunken stump [...] with its shrapnel scars' that Lessing always thought of as 'the dead leg'.[34] In this earliest recollection, the wooden leg is a 'thing' distinct from the embodied, sensory realities of the child, man and animal. The saddle and the leather straps of Alfred's leg hold the trio together, locking them into place. While the leg allowed Alfred some practical mobility, it was also a symbol of his imprisonment, a visual reminder of the restrictions placed on his adult life. He viewed the appendage as his only 'real capital' – because the Land Bank would 'think twice before making a cripple from the war a bankrupt' – but it also ensured that he could never 'dominate the bush' as a successful farmer.[35] Lessing's memory of the leather straps emphasizes how the leg tethered both Alfred and his family to their unsuccessful colonial lives. This object reverses the trajectory of the nineteenth and early twentieth-century imperial romance, where a male English protagonist journeys from north to south, conquering uncharted lands in the latter, before returning, enriched and triumphant, to the former.[36] Instead, Alfred became stuck in the colony, living amongst objects that confirmed both his estrangement from his former home and his inability to successfully work the land.

Yet we should remain cautious of reading this wooden leg (or, indeed, any prostheses) purely for its metaphoric functions. Vivian Sobchack has rightly critiqued posthumanist analysis which relegates the 'human beings who use prosthetic technology ... into the background' of cultural analysis, emphasizing instead the literal and material realities from which these technologies are constructed.[37] With this in mind, the wooden leg is a condition of daily life in Lessing's autobiographical writing, whether for Alfred who struggled with the uncomfortable limb as he tended to his ailing crops, or for Lessing, whose awareness of her own body was framed by the 'dead leg'.[38] But this object *also* indicates how Lessing's autobiographical view from the south challenges the mythologies of an imperial nation. The badly fitted prosthetic suggests how colonies like Southern Rhodesia were transformed, through official emigration schemes, into distant spaces where unwanted veterans could be relegated to the empire's southern margins. As Sweet notes, former soldiers with physical injuries 'tended to be jobless' in Britain and amputees, in particular, were categorized as 'similar to that of elderly men, who were also often excluded from the workplace'.[39] Alfred believed that the resettlement scheme, and his perpetual loan extensions from the Land Bank, were a means of jettisoning this unwanted labour force. As a result, his wooden leg is an autotopographical object which undermines the integral structures and even the futurity of colonial rule itself.

In one sense, the prosthetics in *Under My Skin* all suggest personal sacrifices: Alfred's leg underscores his wartime service, and the Taylers' dentures reveal their initial fidelity to an imperial cause, as they saw 'the British Empire [as] a boon and benefit to the whole world'.[40] Yet these objects also highlight why a family who quickly realized that the promises of empire 'had little to do with reality' emigrated in the first place; in the early 1920s, Alfred and Emily were traumatized by their memories of war and unable to imagine adult lives in Britain.[41] If new prosthetic technologies during this period complicated social 'understanding[s] of the healthy body as a whole', then Alfred's wooden leg is an autotopographical object which disputes the future of a united empire.[42] Through it Lessing challenges the body politic of white settlerdom from an insubordinate, anti-colonial perspective directed from the south. By turning next to Janet Frame's fascination with the detritus of war in Aotearoa New Zealand, this chapter traces further, horizontal connections between life writers who make objects integral to their white, southern, anti-settler memoirs. Whether in Lessing's semi-useless prosthetics, or Frame's discarded souvenirs from the war, these artifacts offer south-south connections which eschew a shared sense of colonial belonging, and instead offer interlocking accounts of an unravelling imperial identity.

Souvenirs from the battlefield in Aotearoa New Zealand

Although Frame was also raised by a First World War veteran, her father's experiences were rarely discussed in a home where it seemed 'that war happened in history and in places far away, in other nations'.[43] Instead, official commemorations of Anzac Day (which marked the landing of Australian and New Zealand soldiers at the Gallipoli Peninsula in 1915) were used by her school teachers to proclaim 'the British Empire's glorious deeds in battle'.[44] Throughout the 1920s and 1930s, service to the empire was, in Jock Phillips's words, 'seen as being consistent with, not opposed to, the claim that Gallipoli represented the birth of [New Zealand's] nationhood'.[45] On the few occasions that George Frame's war years were mentioned, these were 'used only by Mum to explain why Dad was so often sad or angry'.[46] Lottie Frame's exclamation that '[y]our father fought in the trenches, kiddies', was usually an end to the subject.[47] Memories of the war belonged to an increasingly public narrative regarding the young nation's position within a wider empire and were seldom discussed in private. Yet like Lessing's family home, the Frames' property was filled with leftover objects from the conflict, many of which seemed to underpin her father's personal sense of frustration. These horizontal parallels between different settler colonies suggest a more uneasy sense of Aotearoa New Zealand's southern position in the Empire than national or official narratives would allow.

While George rarely articulated his memories of the war, he preserved many possessions that reminded the family of his active service. Unlike Alfred's leg (which had some, limited utility value), George's objects could only function as mnemonic devices, punctuating the silence that surrounded his war-years. He had a habit of taking 'the gas mask he had brought home from the war, and putting it over his face' advancing on Frame's frightened younger sister, who cowered when she saw 'the monster and stranger approach'.[48] The family's 'most hallowed keeping place' was the top drawer of a duchesse dresser, where they kept a collection of personal treasures including 'Dad's foreign coins, mostly Egyptian, brought home from the war'.[49] The five-year-old Frame was dismayed to find that she could not exchange these for the soft pillows of chewing gum sold in her local shop. When, decades later, she returned home after the death of her parents, Frame opened 'the sewing machine drawer where the bullets used to be kept, and there they were, two or three, shining with a point at the end like bronzed rockets'.[50] She and her siblings were forbidden from touching these objects, but they often took the bullets out to play 'school with them'.[51] The items that George transported home are marked by uncanny combinations of the familiar and the unfamiliar; the mask that could transform a parent's face into a monstrous threat, the mysterious coins that had no exchange value, and the ostensibly dangerous bullets, which were repurposed as dollies in childhood games. Unlike Lessing, Frame regularly handled her father's autotopographical objects, yet the mask and the bullets (like the prostheses) hold an ambivalent, even dangerous, relationship to their owners' bodies. This potential threat is underscored by all of George's war-mementoes being concealed in boxes and drawers, only to be surreptitiously uncovered by the children. The meaning of these possessions to George, their original owner, is never fully clarified.

Such fragments of unspoken, private experiences run counter to the public memories of the First World War that, throughout Frame's childhood, were being transformed into myths of imperial glory. During the immediate post-war period, a rising nationalism 'celebrated colonialism's continuing success' in Aotearoa New Zealand, despite the country's official status as dominion.[52] This worked to emphasize the linkages between north and south along an imperial centre-periphery axis, suggesting that the settler nation was in, but not of, the south. Yet the leftover objects of George's wartime service question these calcifying narratives, emphasizing how Frame's critical, distinctly southern, perspective connects horizontally with Lessing's anti-imperial life writing. Technically George's wartime possessions were souvenirs – traces of his journeys across both North Africa and Europe – but they were practically useless. There was nothing unusual about his returning with personal mementos; so many soldiers came home from the war with 'found and scavenged objects' from the battlefield that official guidelines were issued 'about which items [made] safe and acceptable war souvenirs'.[53] Yet George's objects did not allow him to narrate his years serving on the Western Front and in the Middle East. Instead, these possessions are the leftovers of his travels to and from an imperial nation that had first driven his Scottish relatives to the colonies during the nineteenth century. These possessions overcome the seemingly rigid dichtonomies between colony and metropole, private and public lives, or south and north. Like the Tayler families' prostheses in southern Africa, once these possessions are transported to Aotearoa New Zealand, they reveal how the south was viewed by colonial authorities as a zone of relegation for unwanted communities. George, after all, was sent home along with his defunct gas mask and a handful of unspent ammunition. Frame's descriptions of such surplus items – the 'homeless bits and pieces' – offer tantalizing, south-south connections with Lessing's Rhodesian childhood through the debris of empire.[54]

Several of Frame's novels and short stories depict veteran characters who serve on the Western Front before returning to Aotearoa New Zealand (such disorientating repetitions are a defining feature of Frame's interconnected oeuvre). Tom Livingstone, the protagonist of *Intensive Care* (1970), returns 'with remnants of gas in his lungs, shrapnel in his back', and bearing a gas mask that he stored 'under my pillow' for comfort.[55] Like the real George, Tom frightens his daughters by donning the mask at home and distorting his own features. But it is in the short story 'Between My Father and the King' (published after Frame's death in 2004) where these memories of war are fully transformed into an anti-colonial critique from the south. The story repeats a familiar narrative of a 'father [who] fought in the First World War' before coming home 'with a piece of shrapnel in his back, remnants of gas in his lungs, a soldier's paybook, an identity disc, a gas mask, and a very important document which gave details of my father's debt to the King'.[56] The resettlement loan demands that he 'allow the King's Representative to inspect' any goods purchased with the crown's financial support, leading the narrator to realize that the familiar coordinates of her childhood were 'the King's property on gracious loan to my father'.[57] At any moment her parents might have been asked by an official representative to conduct 'a tour of the far-flung colonial furniture'.[58] In this fiction the father answers back to the document of loan with his own corresponding litany: '[b]ack, shrapnel in; lungs, remains of gas in; nights, nightmares in; days, memories in'.[59] This list of personal casualties is an alternative to the receipt of payment and debt demanded by the sovereign. In the story's closing sentence, he demands that the original loan be cancelled 'or passing by Buckingham Palace I shall drop in to inspect you and claim settlement for your debt to me'.[60]

The fictive father's retort suggests that all these possessions, including his mind and body, were initially claimed by the imperial crown. When he collapses the geographical distance between his suburban home at Richardson Street, Dunedin and Buckingham Palace, London, this exchange offers a reconfigured relationship between northern metropole and southern colony through a distinctly Antipodean perspective. Once he returns with memorabilia from the trenches (paybook, identity disc, gas mask), the veteran cannot return to the expectations of colonial life, where settler families promised fealty to the crown, and would be drawn to, or expelled from, Britain as and when required. The real legacies of the war are concealed, with traces lingering either beneath the skin (the gas-damaged lungs) or hidden in the recesses of private memory and nightly terrors. This fictionalized list of possessions, payment and debt reorients the established networks of colonial rule, as the father interrupts empire's unidirectional flow. He challenges a northern centre which extracts labour and resources from its southern peripheries, only to deposit surplus materials and citizens back when its needs are served. But when read comparatively, this scene emphasizes the south-south connections between Frame's and Lessing's critical accounts of white, late colonial life. The unsettling comparisons between their disenchanted soldier-fathers, who felt abandoned and left to stagnate among the debris of their imperial service, imagines different locations across the colonial South as interconnected zones of relegation and neglect.

Yet it remains important to insist on the contrasts between the souvenirs that George Frame transported to the settler society in which he was born and Alfred Tayler's reliance on a prosthetic leg in Southern Rhodesia. The comparative readings in this chapter do not work to collapse the material and cultural distinctions between these two southern lives, nor to homogenize the very different histories of colonial settlement in Aotearoa New Zealand and the former Southern Rhodesia. Yet both Lessing and Frame return to paternal objects which question the stability of white colonial rule during their interwar childhoods. Their life writing evacuates tokens of national loyalty (from medals to prosthetic limbs) of their intended meaning. These manoeuvres undo an imperial, nineteenth-century fascination with portable, domestic objects which, as John Plotz notes, historically produced 'a [shared] sense of belonging at an empire's far-flung margin[s]'.[61] Frame and Lessing would use the depletion of material possessions to narrate empire's dismantlement and eventual collapse. In their life writing, objects intended to affirm enduring models of imperial masculinity instead challenge the future of British colonialism. By further suggesting that these useless possessions *always* belonged to dejected men, both memoirists undo the myths of successful white emigration which underpinned Britain's global Empire.

As Bill Brown notes, we might first imagine objects as reassurance of a 'place of origin', a stabilizing centre for personal histories.[62] But in these intersecting accounts of Alfred's and George's southern lives, there is no discernible future for either these objects or their owners. Once they are detritus, these totemic possessions cannot become heirlooms for subsequent generations, like the 'heavy table silver [and] Persian carpets' that the Taylers carefully shipped out to southern Africa.⁶³ Neither George's souvenirs nor Alfred's unwanted prosthetic will secure a stabilizing settler genealogy for the future. When, at the end of her autobiographies, Frame attempts to salvage possessions from her abandoned family home, she discovers that these become 'a heap of apparent rubbish' after being removed from the derelict property.⁶⁴ If autotopographical objects should 'form a visible and tactile map of subjectivity', in Lessing's and Frame's life writing they reveal how an anti-imperial view of and from the settler South might reimagine the rose-shaded cartographies of empire.⁶⁵ In their critical accounts of life at the end of empire, neither the colonial frontier nor the Western Front can sustain lasting narratives of imperial glory, which might themselves offer sources of shared national pride. Instead, these surplus items, much like their owners, point towards a simultaneously hopeful and unsettling future, one where former symbols of imperial power can now track empire's inevitable ruin.

Notes

1. 'The Mairi Bhan', *Otago Witness*, 1 August 1874, 16.
2. Jock Phillips and Terry Hearn, *Settlers: New Zealand Immigrants from England, Ireland and Scotland, 1800–1945* (Auckland: Auckland University Press, 2008), 1.
3. Michael King, *Wrestling with the Angel: A Life of Janet Frame* (London: Picador, 2000), 16.
4. Janet Frame, *Janet Frame: The Complete Autobiography* (London: The Women's Press, 1990), 9.
5. Doris Lessing, *Under My Skin: Volume One of My Autobiography, to 1949* (London: HarperCollins, 1994), 36.
6. Ibid., 46.
7. Bill Schwarz, *The White Man's World* (Oxford: Oxford University Press, 2011), 61.
8. Ibid., 61.
9. Kathleen Paul, *Whitewashing Britain: Race and Citizenship in the Postwar Era* (Ithaca, NY: Cornell University Press, 1997), 28.
10. Elleke Boehmer, *Empire, the National, and the Postcolonial, 1890–1920: Resistance in Interaction* (Oxford: Oxford University Press, 2002), 13.
11. Dominic Davies and Elleke Boehmer, 'Postcolonialism and South-South Relations', in *Routledge Handbook of South-South Relations*, eds. Elena Fiddian-Qasmiyeh and Patricia Daley (Abingdon: Routledge, 2019), 48.
12. Fariha Shaikh, *Nineteenth-Century Settler Emigration in British Literature and Art* (Edinburgh: Edinburgh University Press, 2018), 9.
13. Kent Fedorowich, 'The Assisted Emigration of British Ex-servicemen to the Dominions, 1914–1922', in *Emigrants and Empire: British Settlement in the Dominions Between the Wars*, ed. Stephen Constantine (Manchester: Manchester University Press, 1990), 46.
14. Lessing, *Under My Skin*, 102; 173.
15. Frame, *The Complete Autobiography*, 122.

16. Doris Lessing, *Alfred and Emily* (London: Fourth Estate, 2008), 92. In Josephine A. McQuail, ed., *Janet Frame in Focus* (Jefferson, NC: McFarland, 2018), Cyrena Mazlin notes that Lessing and Frame believed their fathers' memories of war had been transferred to them, raising further questions as to how this conflict informed their settler-colonial childhoods.
17. Siba N. Grovogui, 'A Revolution Nonetheless: The Global South in International Relations', *The Global South* 5, no. 1 (2011): 177.
18. Jennifer A. Gonzalez, 'Autotopographies', in *Prosthetic Territories: Politics and Hypertechnologies*, ed. Gabriel Brahm Jr. and Mark Driscoll (Boulder, CO: Westview Press, 1995), 138.
19. Gonzalez, 'Autotopographies', 133.
20. Bill Brown, 'Thing Theory', *Critical Inquiry* 28, no. 1 (2001): 4.
21. Lessing, *Under My Skin*, 85.
22. Lessing, *Alfred and Emily*, 170.
23. Lessing, *Under My Skin*, 99.
24. Lessing, *Alfred and Emily*, viii.
25. Lessing, *Under My Skin*, 100.
26. Ibid., 110.
27. For details of Black regiments from southern Africa during the First World War, see: Tim Stapleton, 'The Composition of the Rhodesia Native Regiment during the First World War', *History in Africa* 30 (2003): 283–95.
28. Lessing, *Under My Skin*, 99.
29. Ibid., 46.
30. Frame, *The Complete Autobiography*, 202.
31. Lessing, *Under My Skin*, 159.
32. Ryan Sweet, *Prosthetic Body Parts in Nineteenth-Century Literature and Culture* (New York: Palgrave Macmillan, 2022), 229.
33. Lessing, *Under My Skin*, 18.
34. Ibid., 18; 19; 22.
35. Ibid., 129; 59.
36. See Anne McClintock's *Imperial Leather* (1995), particularly Chapter one, for a full discussion of the eroticized nature of the imperial romance.
37. Vivian Sobchack, 'A Leg to Stand on: Prosthetics, Metaphor, and Materiality', in *The Prosthetic Impulse: From A Posthuman Present to a Biocultural Future*, ed. Marquard Smith and Joanne Morra (Cambridge, MA: MIT Press, 2006), 23.
38. Lessing, *Under My Skin*, 22.
39. Sweet, *Prosthetic Body Parts*, 223.
40. Lessing, *Under My Skin*, 50.
41. Ibid.
42. Sweet, *Prosthetic Body Parts*, 10.
43. Frame, *The Complete Autobiography*, 121.
44. Ibid.

45. Jock Phillips, 'The Quiet Western Front: The First World War and New Zealand Memory', in *Race, Empire and First World War Writing*, ed. Santanu Das (Cambridge: Cambridge University Press, 2011), 240.
46. Frame, *The Complete Autobiography*, 122.
47. Ibid.
48. Ibid., 63.
49. Ibid., 10.
50. Ibid., 432.
51. Ibid.
52. Felicity Barnes, 'Settler Colonialism in Twentieth-Century New Zealand', in *The Routledge Handbook of the History of Settler Colonialism*, ed. Edward Cavanagh and Lorenzo Veracini (Abingdon: Routledge, 2016), 441.
53. Rolf Potts, *Souvenir* (London: Bloomsbury, 2018), 76.
54. Frame, *The Complete Autobiography*, 433.
55. Janet Frame, *Intensive Care* (New York: George Braziller, 1994), 4; 23.
56. Janet Frame, 'Between My Father and the King', in *Between My Father and the King: New and Uncollected Stories* (Berkeley, CA: Counterpoint, 2012), 10.
57. Ibid., 11.
58. Ibid.
59. Ibid., 12.
60. Ibid.
61. John Plotz, *Portable Property: Victorian Culture on the Move* (Princeton, NJ: Princeton University Press, 2008), 18.
62. Brown, 'Thing Theory', 1.
63. Lessing, *Under My Skin*, 51.
64. Frame, *The Complete Autobiography*, 433.
65. Gonzalez, 'Autotopographies', 134.

Bibliography

Barnes, Felicity. 'Settler Colonialism in Twentieth-Century New Zealand'. In *The Routledge Handbook of the History of Settler Colonialism*, edited by Edward Cavanagh and Lorenzo Veracini, 439–55. Abingdon: Routledge, 2016.

Boehmer, Elleke. *Empire, the National, and the Postcolonial, 1890–1920: Resistance in Interaction*. Oxford: Oxford University Press, 2002.

Brown, Bill. 'Thing Theory'. *Critical Inquiry* 28, no. 1 (2001): 1–22.

Davies, Dominic, and Elleke Boehmer. 'Postcolonialism and South-South Relations'. In *Routledge Handbook of South-South Relations*, edited by Elena Fiddian-Qasmiyeh and Patricia Daley, 48–58. Abingdon: Routledge, 2019.

Fedorowich, Kent. 'The Assisted Emigration of British Ex-servicemen to the Dominions, 1914–1922'. In *Emigrants and Empire: British Settlement in the Dominions Between the Wars*, edited by Stephen Constantine, 45–71. Manchester: Manchester University Press, 1990.

Frame, Janet. 'Between My Father and the King'. In *Between My Father and the King: New and Collected Stories*. Berkeley, CA: Counterpoint, 2012.

Frame, Janet. *Intensive Care*. New York: George Braziller, 1994.

Frame, Janet. *Janet Frame: The Complete Autobiography*. London: The Women's Press, 1990.

Gonzalez, Jennifer A. 'Autotopographies'. In *Prosthetic Territories: Politics and Hypertechnologies*, edited by Gabriel Brahm Jr. and Mark Driscoll, 133–50. Boulder, CO: Westview Press, 1995.

Grovogui, Siba N. 'A Revolution Nonetheless: The Global South in International Relations'. *The Global South* 5, no. 1 (2011): 175–90.

King, Michael. *Wrestling with the Angel: A Life of Janet Frame*. London: Picador, 2000.

Lessing, Doris. *Alfred and Emily*. London: Fourth Estate, 2008.

Lessing, Doris. *Under My Skin: Volume One of My Autobiography, to 1949*. London: HarperCollins, 1994.

'The Mairi Bhan'. *Otago Witness*, 1 August 1874.

Mazlin, Cyrena. 'A Soldier's Daughter: The Autobiographies and Autobiographical Fiction of Janet Frame and Doris Lessing'. In *Janet Frame in Focus: Women Analyze the Works of the New Zealand Writer*, edited by Josephine A. McQuail, 39–61. Jefferson, NC: McFarland and Company, 2018.

McClintock, Anne. *Imperial Leather: Race, Gender and Sexuality in the Colonial Contest*. New York: Routledge, 1995.

McLeod, John. *Postcolonial London: Rewriting the Metropolis*. Abingdon: Routledge, 2004.

Parker, Emma. *Life Writing and the End of Empire: Homecoming in Autobiographical Narratives*. London: Bloomsbury, 2024.

Paul, Kathleen. *Whitewashing Britain: Race and Citizenship in the Postwar Era*. Ithaca, NY: Cornell University Press, 1997.

Phillips, Jock. 'The Quiet Western Front: The First World War and New Zealand Memory'. In *Race, Empire and First World War Writing*, edited by Santanu Das, 231–48. Cambridge: Cambridge University Press, 2011.

Phillips, Jock, and Terry Hearn. *Settlers: New Zealand Immigrants from England, Ireland and Scotland, 1800–1945*. Auckland: Auckland University Press, 2008.

Plotz, John. *Portable Property: Victorian Culture on the Move*. Princeton, NJ: Princeton University Press, 2008.

Potts, Rolf. *Souvenir*. London: Bloomsbury, 2018.

Schwarz, Bill. *The White Man's World*. Oxford: Oxford University Press, 2011.

Shaikh, Fariha. *Nineteenth-Century Settler Emigration in British Literature and Art*. Edinburgh: Edinburgh University Press, 2018.

Smith, Jean. *Settlers at the End of Empire: Race and the Politics of Migration in South Africa, Rhodesia, and the United Kingdom*. Manchester: Manchester University Press, 2022.

Sobchack, Vivian. 'A Leg to Stand on: Prosthetics, Metaphor, and Materiality'. In *The Prosthetic Impulse: From a Posthuman Present to a Biocultural Future*, 17–41. Cambridge, MA: MIT Press, 2006.

Stapleton, Tim. 'The Composition of the Rhodesia Native Regiment during the First World War'. *History in Africa* 30 (2003): 283–95.

Sweet, Ryan. *Prosthetic Body Parts in Nineteenth-Century Literature and Culture*. New York: Palgrave Macmillan, 2022.

CHAPTER 3
ANTARCTIC FUTURES: FRANCISCO COLOANE AND LITERARY NATIONALISM
Elizabeth Chant

Despierto de pronto en la noche pensando en el extremo sur
(Pablo Neruda, *Canto General*)

Reflecting as an octogenarian on his definitive relocation to Santiago in 1936, Chilean author Francisco Coloane (1910–2002) calls to mind the musings of his friend, the great poet Pablo Neruda (1904–73): 'I awaken suddenly in the night thinking about the far south'.[1] Coloane repeats this line from Neruda's Latin American epic, the *Canto General* (General Song), in his 2000 autobiography as he remembers his own struggle to put down roots in the Chilean capital. Like his southern compatriot, Coloane remains often disturbed by thoughts of the far south, and this line still 'comes to mind' after many decades in Santiago.[2]

One of austral Chile's great storytellers, Coloane spent the majority of his literary career examining the southern reaches of his homeland. Born in Quemchi, Chiloé, just south of continental Chile, Coloane moved to the southern Patagonian city of Punta Arenas as a teenager. It was here that the seeds of Coloane's literary career were sown; he won a community literature competition in 1927 and later that year had a column published in the local newspaper, *El Magallanes*.[3] Coloane undertook a series of arduous jobs in the area, which included ranching and butchering sheep on an *estancia* in Tierra del Fuego, as well as a spell in the Chilean Navy, where he built upon the navigational skills he had learnt from his father, a whaler.

Coloane is mostly known in Chilean literature for his short stories detailing life in the far south of the country, which focus on interactions between humans and nonhuman life forms, and on the sea. Although well known in Chile, his work was not disseminated in translation until late in his career, most notably by French publisher Phébus beginning in the 1990s.[4] This led to further publication of his works in more than fourteen languages, many of which have appeared posthumously. An English translation of his 1956 short story collection *Tierra del Fuego* was published in 2009. Italian publisher Guanda, which first published his collection *Cape Horn* (1941) in 1997, has reissued eight of Coloane's works since 2016 alongside a new digital edition of the compilation volume, *Il meglio di Francisco Coloane* (*The Best of Francisco Coloane*), in 2022. Academic interest in his work has grown concurrently.[5] Recent Coloane scholarship has sought to tease out the didactic elements of his corpus in relation to sociopolitical issues and ecological concerns. This has included highlighting Coloane's recuperation of the role played by marginalized Chilotes in the Patagonian workers strikes of the early 1920s[6] and the ability of nonhuman life to seek justice in his stories.[7]

Further research has underlined Coloane's preoccupation with the far south beyond the confines of the American continent.[8] Coloane coveted the idea of visiting Antarctica long before he set foot there, exploring an imagined version of the landmass in his second young adult novel *Los conquistadores de la Antártida* (*The Conquerors of Antarctica*), which won the 1945 annual Novel Prize awarded by Chile's most important publishing house, Zig-Zag. The following year, Coloane was working as a civil servant in the Ministry of Health in Santiago when he met Vice-admiral Immanuel Holger, who was preparing for the first Chilean Antarctic Expedition, due to depart in January 1947. Coloane recalls in his autobiography, *Los pasos del hombre: Memorias* (*The Footsteps of Man: Memories*), how he believes Holger perceived his 'intimate desire' to see Antarctica, not least due to the recent success of *Los conquistadores*.[9] 'I think the admiral was aware of my intentions',[10] Coloane muses, as several days later he received an invitation to participate in the voyage aboard the transport *Angamos*, complete with permission to report for newspapers and magazines.

The 1947 voyage marked the consolidation of Chile's Antarctic claim, which had been staked by President Pedro Aguirre Cerda in November 1940 against a backdrop of growing tensions with the UK, US, Norway and Argentina.[11] While having an express geopolitical aim, the cultural impact of the expedition was carefully considered by the Chilean authorities. Coloane was one of several civilian crew members chosen to disseminate news of the voyage in their respective fields, which also included author Raúl Silva Maturana, who published the travelogue *Antártida blanca* (*White Antarctica*) (1947), and zoologist Guillermo Mann, after whom one of Chile's Antarctic research bases is named. Indeed, when he went to accept the invitation, Holger told Coloane, 'I hope it helps you to write a story'.[12] His role on board was clear: to document, describe and make people aware of this new Chilean territory. Coloane dutifully fulfilled this task. Retellings of the expedition, including the labours of establishing Chile's first Antarctic base, and tense encounters with British soldiers, are present across his corpus in both fiction and non-fiction, appearing for the final time in the story 'El inglés de Lockroy' (The Englishman in Port Lockroy), published in the posthumous collection *Antártico* (*Antarctic*) (2008).

This chapter analyzes Coloane's Antarctic literature, exploring how his literary nationalism furthers Chilean interests while simultaneously critiquing the human occupation of the Antarctic and the environmental damage it causes. I show how these purposes are often at odds, since in Coloane's later work, he denounces human presence in Antarctica while maintaining that it is an inherently Chilean territory. Examining narrations of the 1947 visit both in fiction and non-fiction, as well as Coloane's pre-visit imaginings of the continent in *Los conquistadores*, I flesh out the Antarctic element in his work, reflecting upon the impact of this event across his corpus and defining it as one of the most important case studies for understanding the complex role of autobiography and memory in Coloane's realist writing. In so doing, I seek to unravel the intertwining of the personal and the political in what are some of Coloane's most overtly nationalist ruminations, while also underscoring the ultimate didactic nature of his tales that echo across his long career.

Coloane and the Chilean Antarctic

Coloane's depictions of Antarctica have drawn interest from scholars working across Antarctic literary and historical studies. His work has been analyzed both in relation to Chilean sovereignty in the Antarctic region by polar historian Adrian Howkins[13] and as an example of how Antarctica manifests in Latin American literature as the 'alien next door' by Pablo Wainschenker and Elizabeth Leane,[14] also contributors to this volume. Chilean literary scholar Tatiana Calderón Le Joliff has further sought to examine Coloane's stories as a form of what she terms 'escritura "tempanesca" (iceberg writing)',[15] which builds on Grínor Rojo's metaphorical reading of Coloane's first young adult novel and the prequel to *Los conquistadores*, *El último grumete de la Baquedano* (*The Last Cabin Boy of the Baquedano*) (1941), as a mirror of 'the reconnaissance voyage of Chile's territory and history undertaken by the fatherland in the first half of the twentieth century'.[16]

Against a backdrop of geopolitical change and uncertainty, Neruda (and Coloane's) nightmares about the far south reveal the geographical anxiety that plagued Chilean intellectuals in the period identified by Rojo. Chilean sovereignty had only been definitively staked in Patagonia with the founding of Fuerte Bulnes on the Strait of Magellan in September 1843, an undertaking that produced ongoing diplomatic crises with Argentina. This annexation brought cultural challenges as Chile sought to familiarize its citizens with the frigid expanses of the south and to rid them of their association with Indigenous conflict. Articles such as '¡No hay INDIOS en MAGALLANES! (There Are No INDIANS in MAGALLANES!)', published in the travel magazine *En Viaje* (1933–73), produced by the Empresa de Ferrocarriles del Estado (EFE, or Chilean State Railways), attest to the need to remind would-be travellers that this region was firmly part of a euro-descendant nation.[17]

Coloane was a regular contributor to *En Viaje*, which also published accounts of touristic visits to Chilean Patagonia and Tierra del Fuego. This was part of an effort to usher in a new touristic vision of southern Chile to support territorial nationalism.[18] The attention paid to Chile's southern reaches was further part of a broader attempt to evoke an image of Chile as a cold country on the international stage, seeking to assert influence by distancing itself from the 'stigma of the banana republic' that plagued other American nations, which were seen as unstable and underdeveloped by the west.[19] This focus brought Chile's Antarctic whaling and fishing activities into view, many of which were operated out of Magallanes, Chile's southernmost province prior to the 1940 Decree.[20] EFE proclaimed that Magallanes was the 'land of the future',[21] and so it was only natural that the annexation of the Chilean Antarctic would continue to build on this projected success. In this vein, literary critic David Perry Barnes describes Magallanes in a 1945 *En Viaje* article as 'the prow of the continent that advances southward', alluding to the destiny of Chile's austral expansion.[22]

Against this backdrop, Magellanic authors such as Coloane were particularly important for building literary and cultural connections with the Antarctic. Coloane's preoccupation with depicting the far south has meant that his work is often situated in the extensive Hispanic American genre of *criollismo,* which emerged in the late nineteenth century and espouses a focus on rural regional settings explored in a realist style. Unlike the 'rural idealism' that characterizes the works of renowned early Chilean *criollistas* such as Mariano Latorre (1886–1955) and Federico Gana (1867–1926),[23] Coloane examines the brutality of regional life, often drawing on examples from his own experiences.[24] In the short story 'Cabo de Hornos (Cape Horn)', for example, one of Coloane's most well-known tales, two brothers who hunt South American sea lion pups for their pelts team up with a fugitive from Ushuaïa prison to raid an island rookery where they club the newborns to death, 'piling up their small bodies'.[25] One of the brothers, Jackie, is directly inspired by a man Coloane knew from his ranching days who enjoyed torturing and killing small animals, whom he remembers stacking foal and guanaco corpses 'in a strange spectacle'.[26]

Coloane's forays beyond the remit of conventional *criollista* writing place him firmly alongside other socially-charged writers of the Chilean literary Generation of '38. His focus on rural space offered Chileans a 'familiar way of understanding an unfamiliar landscape' by means of an established genre.[27] In *Los conquistadores,* for example, radio operator Alejandro and Chilean Sergeant Ulloa connect the strange electric storms of the Drake Passage and the frequent earthquakes experienced across Chile to the presence of the Andes by hypothesizing that 'that enormous spine that runs throughout the Americas, and that finishes exactly in this location, must produce some kind of atmospheric malaise'.[28] In so doing, Coloane takes a cherished national symbol and links it to climatic activity beyond the Chilean mainland, enabling the reader to see how Chilean sovereignty logically extends southwards via the geomorphological connection between America and Antarctica. In Coloane's revisits to his Antarctic odyssey throughout his career, we see this locale become a space for the negotiation of his own relationship with national identity, particularly as a former serviceman, and of his personal values, especially as an ecological writer.

Reading Coloane's White Continent

Coloane's association with Antarctica has yielded a misremembering of his journey to the far south in Chilean Letters. In the 'Dictionary of Chilean Authors' published serially in *En Viaje*[29], Coloane's participation in the expedition is said to have inspired the fictional narrative of *Los conquistadores,* which was not the case, as Coloane himself has emphasized:

> I did not know the Antarctic when I wrote this book. I knew Cape Horn, and I based the Antarctic part on an old book by Nordenskjöld: *Voyage to the South Pole,* which I pirated, shall we say, so much so that some of the elements I adapted are scientifically accurate.[30]

During the voyage's return leg, Coloane penned the preface to fellow writer Óscar Vila Labra's account of the expedition, *Chilenos en la Antártica* (*Chileans in the Antarctic*) (1947). Moored in Punta Arenas, Coloane laments what he terms the 'dryness' and 'sobriety' of Antarctic exploration travelogues, which, he argues, makes them 'tiring to read'.[31] His early reflections foreground the challenge of trying to capture Antarctic space in writing: 'The grandeur of Antarctic nature is so overwhelming that it mutes the word of the prose writer.'[32] Coloane contends that travel writing is not the best medium for understanding such scenery: 'Faced with that crowding of ice floes that we encountered in Marguerite Bay ... we thought how only a piece of abysmal or desolate music, or a poem, would be able to express the sensation that such a view produces in the human spirit.'[33] Although Coloane did not himself turn to music or verse to resolve the inadequacies of language, his later writing following the visit both in fiction and nonfiction combines national concerns with more profound reflections on the democratizing power of Antarctic space, including the right of humans to be there at all.

Coloane advances a vision of Antarctica that melds both imagined and real experiences of the region that employ 'certain kinds of language which we might think of as being inherently diplomatic'.[34] This is particularly evident in Coloane's initial foray into his imagined Antarctic in *Los conquistadores*, written prior to the 1947 visit. The text details the adventures of the Chilean Navy's Walaia Radio Station on Navarino Island, just south of the main Island of Tierra del Fuego, and primarily follows Alejandro Silva, a radio operator, his brother Manuel, also known as 'Jefe Blanco (White Chief)', who is the leader of a group of Yahgan in the area; Félix, a Yahgan man under Manuel; and Sergeant Ulloa, who is based at the station. The first half of the novel mainly follows their exploits assisting ships that have met with danger around Cape Horn, and putting a criminal named Gaban to rights. In Chapter VI, they return to the station to hear that President Aguirre Cerda has passed away. Sergeant Ulloa, obsessed with knowing his country from top to bottom, decides that he will travel to Antarctica to plant a flag in his name.[35] Coloane's nationalism is particularly overt in this text: Aguirre Cerda is remembered fondly as the man who 'enlarged Chile's soul and body'.[36] Félix succumbs to the inclement conditions shortly after they reach the continent, and Ulloa dies falling from a precipice after planting the flag for his beloved president. The two brothers are rescued by the Navy after reaching a whaling outpost and eventually return to Walaia, where the novel concludes.

The journey to Antarctica has been read by Rojo as a foil to the conquest of the Americas by Spain, only on this occasion, the two men's sacrifice is not for the Empire but rather for the 'unfaltering glory of the republican fatherland'.[37] This parallel is further echoed by the fact that Félix is seemingly collateral damage in Ulloa's quest for glory. Félix's presence on the voyage is a key part of the geopolitical argument being advanced: as Howkins has noted, Chilean writers including Coloane 'sought to create a literary case for Chilean sovereignty by transplanting the myths and legends of southern Chile to the shores of the Antarctic Peninsula'.[38] Coloane had a keen interest in the oral tradition of the Indigenous populations of Southern Patagonia and Tierra del Fuego, namely the Selk'nam, Haush, Kawésqar and Yahgan. He collected and retold static versions of origin myths in the pages of *En Viaje*[39] and has cited the ethnographer Martin Gusinde's (1886–1969) studies of the Fuegian populations, which included recorded stories from the Selk'nam, Haush and Yahgan, as one of the key 'footprints' on his writing.[40]

In the context of the Antarctic, though, the appearance of these narratives extends Chilean sovereignty southwards by contending that the waterways south of Cape Horn have been transited by the Yahgan since time immemorial. In Chapter V, for example, Miguel relays the Yaghan myth of the 'phantom penguin' to Alejandro detailing how the Yahgan came to respect the penguin species that inhabit the Beagle Channel.[41] Later, in Chapter IX, as they venture into the Antarctic, the group come across a beached Yahgan *anan* (canoe) with three skeletons aboard. They wonder, 'How did a boat, so small to have crossed these seas, and so big to have been picked up by the rocky river, end up in the interior of this calm valley?'[42] Although they have no answers, the presumed transport between the South American continent and Antarctica decisively links the region to austral Chile, the visible presence of Indigenous Americans tapping into the 'visuality of our indigenous populations' that Luis Horta has identified as being integral to the presentation of the Antarctic as an inherently Chilean space.[43]

Coloane further advances the geomorphological element of the Chilean claim by highlighting the connections between Chilean and Antarctic fauna. In *Los conquistadores*, the group come across unidentifiable mammal prints that display 'claws similar to those of the *huemul*, the beautiful deer that adorns the Chilean coat of arms'.[44] His qualification of the *huemul*'s role in national heraldry ensures that even a foreign reader will understand the geopolitical implications of finding similar footprints in Antarctica. He further uses descriptions of colour to connect the white continent to the Chilean flag. This begins in *Los conquistadores* with the mention of 'meadows of pale red lichen on the snow' on the banks of the river the group believes carried the *anan* upstream.[45] Though Coloane does not refer to it explicitly, he is here invoking the red, white and blue of the Chilean flag.

Coloane develops this image further in his autobiography, describing the actual flag placed atop the first Chilean Antarctic base, which he helped to erect in 1947: 'Atop the trusses of the first base being constructed fluttered our Chilean flag, displaying its Andean white complete with polar star, and the red of the Chilotean *copihues* (Chilean bell-flowers) that were carried by the [naval schooner] *Ancud* when it took possession of the Strait of Magellan.'[46] Here Coloane suggests that Chilean presence in Antarctica was foretold in the national flag, further linking this conquest to the *copihue*-dotted region of Araucanía. The mid-nineteenth-century invasion of this territory saw republican Chile quash the Mapuche resistance that had long resisted Spanish colonial endeavours in order to annex the region. In this allusion, Coloane thus positions the Antarctic as the final piece in the puzzle of Chile's southward expansion and Indigenous repression, one that is paradoxically staked upon connections to indigenous flora. Like many earlier *criollista* authors, we thus see Coloane turning to images of a safe, memorialized Indigenous past in order to further a cohesive idea of national identity that is founded upon successful acts of dispossession. If, indeed, the Yahgan did reach Antarctica, Chile's claim represents an ongoing displacement that echoes the violent annexation of their ancestral lands and waters in southern Patagonia. Yet Coloane does not acknowledge this, positioning the Fuegian populations as arbiters of Chilean identity via whom geopolitical claims can be reinforced.

This interest in Chilean Antarctic sovereignty also combines with Coloane's nonhuman agenda, whereby he advocates for all forms of life to coexist sustainably. In the nonfiction bilingual photography book *Antártica: una visión gráfica del continente helado* (*Antarctica: A Graphic View of the Frozen Continent*) (1985), Coloane's recollection of the 1947 expedition is rendered in prose alongside images captured by Chilean Lithuanian photographer Jack Ceitelis in January 1982.[47] This text and its accompanying images were reprinted in an expanded 2005 bilingual edition simply titled *Antártica* as part of Editorial Puelche's series *Chile: Colección Destinos Turísticos y Culturales* (*Chile: The Touristic and Cultural Destinations Collection*). The collection was intended to provide a 'useful tool' to help the reader get to know Chile,[48] yet interestingly, both Ceitelis's prologue and Coloane's text are less overtly nationalistic than the escapades on the ice imagined in *Los conquistadores* and recounted in his later autobiography. While there are still geopolitical concerns, these are coupled with a growing awareness of environmental threats to Antarctica, which Ceitelis highlights in the prologue, and Coloane mentions again several years later in his 1989 conversations with Chilean journalist and author Virginia Vidal.[49]

Ceitelis and Coloane's work focuses primarily on what they perceive to be the democratizing power of the space. Ceitelis writes, 'I have to mention in human terms that the Antarctic is the last place on the globe where money does not prevail and where all nationality differences are erased and only solidarity and camaraderie count.'[50] Coloane's account is mainly concerned with describing flora and fauna, including crabeater seals, skuas and the aforementioned red lichen, this time without recourse to their role as Chilean symbols. He echoes Ceitelis's reflections upon the human condition: in one instance, he imagines a diatom telling him, 'I am barely a particle in the universe.'[51] Faced with millennial life forms, Coloane thus encourages the reader to examine human exceptionalism. While the competing annexations of foreign nations are not mentioned, he closes by recalling the sight of 'faded rainbows' in the Drake Passage during the 1947 expedition 'as in the myth of the Yamana tribes who dwelt for a span of two thousand years in che [*sic*] Capes of Horn'.[52] It is noteworthy that Coloane includes this reference to Yahgan tradition despite the broader claim of the texts that the Antarctic prompts reflections on the universal human experience and supersedes the description attempts of individual cultures. Although Coloane's fiction is noteworthy for its creation of a counternarrative to the official history of southern Chile that calls out settler violence against the Indigenous populations,[53] his advocacy for the coexistence of all forms of life sustainably harbors a contradiction. It holds a fatalistic attitude towards the Yahgan that does not recognize their presence in the Drake Passage as analogous with the Chilean annexation, despite their continued habitation in the region.[54]

The accompanying texts in *Antártica* from the Chilean Antarctic Institute articulate this Chilean vision more explicitly, reminding the reader of the book's diplomatic aim by highlighting that the Antarctic coastline is six times the distance from Arica to Punta Arenas.[55] Coloane's contribution is much shorter than that of the Institute, in spite of the fact that he is listed as the sole author on the front cover in large print, directly under the title. This prominence speaks to his enduring power in Chile as the nation's southern writer, one who 'expanded the geographical limits of the nation's literature' in line with Aguirre Cerda's Antarctic decree.[56]

In Coloane's final posthumous publication, the short story collection *Antártico*, we find a melding of both geopolitical and environmental aims. Although no date is given to the story, in 'El inglés de Lockroy' Coloane rewrites an event detailed in his autobiography which constitutes a key example of intertextuality in his life writing. In *Los pasos*, Coloane recalls Jorge González, a Chilean official and expedition crewmember, ascending the high point of Port Lockroy in the Gerlache Canal to plant a flag, after they come across a British soldier and his assistant who have been stationed there alongside a painted plaque that declares the area 'British Crown Land'.[57] This echoes Sergeant Ulloa's fatal flag planting in *Los conquistadores*, a fictitious event previously imagined by Coloane. The men decide to show the soldier some 'Chilean hospitality' and invite him to dine onboard their vessel, where they talk until midnight, 'sidestepping' discussion of nations and politics which 'among the polar ice have no more of an echo than the nocturnal crowing of penguins'.[58] In 'El inglés de Lockroy', Coloane takes this disavowal even further:

> What are conventions, treaties, nationalisms and prejudices, other than symbols that are incapable of understanding the majesty of this solitude? ... Be they Chilean, Argentinean, or English, in Antarctica, one is only man, and that is how we felt before the Englishman in Port Lockroy.[59]

Although Coloane does not shy away from the staking of Chilean claims in the fictional tale, describing a flag-planting exercise that echoes that of González, there is an evident criticism of all human attempts to quantify, divide and colonize the Antarctic.

The story's close emphasizes this sentiment as the Chilean crew come across the blade of a broken propellor from a boat that has run aground and presumably been repaired, leaving this memento behind. The narrator ponders whose boat it might have been, concluding that whoever it was, they were flying 'an anonymous flag that arrived there fluttering not in the air but in the depths of the sea'.[60] Coloane's reminder of the tragedy and death that so often mar Antarctic exploits encourages the reader to question the rationalization of these voyages. This echoes the words spoken by an iceberg about death as it converses with a man in a story, 'La Voz del Témpano' (*The Iceberg's Voice*), published by Coloane in the *Angamos* onboard magazine *Aurora Antártica* in 1947:

> I dissolve on the surface of the sea, sinking to its submarine currents until I arrive in the tropics, where I become a cloud and overlook your fields, fertilising them so that you can be born and survive. Don't you recognise me in yourself? In the fruit that you eat? In your blood?[61]

Like Sergeant Ulloa, the naming of Coloane's posthumous collection 'Antártico' plants his final literary flag at the apex of the white continent. Yet across his corpus we can identify numerous moments like this where the glory of sovereignty is brushed aside to advocate for the nonhuman by rejecting settler incursions, especially in his later work. While it is important to note the expansionist element in Coloane's writing, which operates on the basis that these territories are fundamentally Chilean, a claim levied in part via potential Indigenous connections, we might expand this understanding to suggest that he advocates for an Antarctic democracy beyond the human. Following his first-hand experience of the frozen continent, Coloane becomes critical of men that position sovereignty above all else. His daring to publish a tale such as 'La Voz del Témpano' to an audience largely comprised of Chilean servicemen demonstrates his deep running commitment to environmental justice and the need to remind people of it as Chile advanced southwards. As life writing, then, we can read Coloane's retellings of his Antarctic exploits as in the service of national interests in his country's far south but also as a documentation of his enduring personal convictions about safeguarding its environment, ones that prompted him to continue looking south, even in the middle of the night.

Notes

1. Pablo Neruda, *Canto General*, 50th anniversary edition, trans. Jack Schmitt (Berkeley and Los Angeles: University of California Press, 2000), 65.
2. Francisco Coloane, *Los pasos del hombre: memorias* (Barcelona: Mondadori, 2000), 107.
3. Coloane, *Los pasos del hombre*, 75–6.
4. Tatiana Calderón Le Joliff, 'Coloane, Hemingway y Le Clézio: los "témpanos" de la imaginación', *Anales de literatura chilena* 11, no. 14 (2010): 304.
5. Key examples include Jorge Ricardo Ferrada, *Los cuentos de Francisco Coloane: espacios de realidad y deseo* (Santiago de Chile: Editorial Universidad de Santiago, 2004); Rachel VanWieren, 'Exploring the Margins of Patagonia in Chilean Fiction' (PhD thesis, UCLA, 2010); and Jenny Haase, 'Abismos bajo el hielo. Experiencias desintegradoras en los cuentos de Francisco Coloane', in *Trans*Chile: cultura-historia-itinerarios-literatura-educación. Un acercamiento transareal*, ed. Ottmar Ette and Horst Nitschack (Madrid and Frankfurt am main: Iberoamericana and Vervuert, 2010), 125–36.
6. Rachel VanWieren, 'Reconsidering the Patagonian Worker Movements of the 1920s: Francisco Coloane's and Luis Sepúlveda's Rebellious Chilotes', *A Contracorriente: una revista de estudios latinoamericanos* 14, no. 3 (2017): 127–42.
7. Juan Gabriel Araya Grandón, 'Un territorio más allá: convergencias ecológicas en la cuentística de Francisco Coloane', *Literatura y Lingüística* 20 (2009): 41–55; Eliana Rojas and Pablo Vargas, eds., *Coloane: literatura y ecología al sur del mundo* (Santiago de Chile: Ocho Libros, 2010); Elizabeth Chant, 'Reading Fuegian Narratives and Nonhuman Sensibility in Francisco Coloane's Patagonian Tales', *Journal of Latin American Cultural Studies* 33, no. 1 (2024): 1–20.
8. Tatiana Calderón Le Joliff, 'La teoría del iceberg y la práctica de la alusión en los cuentos de Ernest Hemingway y de Francisco Coloane', *Acta Literaria* 32 (2006): 97–105, https://revistas.udec.cl/index.php/acta_literaria/issue/view/353; Calderón Le Joliff, 'Coloane, Hemingway y Le Clézio'; Grínor Rojo, 'Sobre "El último grumete de la Baquedano" y algo más', *Anales de literatura chilena* 10, no. 12 (2010): 85–98; Eddie Morales Piña, 'En torno al

9. escritor chileno Francisco Coloane … y un cuento gélido', *Estudios Hemisféricos y Polares* 2, no. 2 (2011): 26–34; Alejandra Mora, 'De cómo la imaginación crea una tierra. Divagaciones sobre los viajes imaginarios y reales de Francisco Coloane a la Antártica', *Aura Austral*, July 2018. Available online: https://auraaustral.cl/cronicas-territorio/de-como-la-imaginacion-crea-una-tierra-divagaciones-sobre-los-viajes-imaginarios-y-reales-de-francisco-coloane-a-la-antartica/.
9. Coloane, *Los pasos del hombre*, 147.
10. 'Parece que el almirante percibió mi intención'. Coloane, *Los pasos del hombre*, 147. This and all future translations are the author's own.
11. Pablo Fontana, 'The Antarctic Extension of Latin America', in *The Cambridge History of the Polar Regions*, ed. Adrian Howkins and Peder Roberts (Cambridge: Cambridge University Press, 2023), 680.
12. 'Ojalá le sirva para escribir un cuento'. Coloane, *Los pasos del hombre*, 148.
13. Adrian Howkins, 'Appropriating Space: Antarctic Imperialism and the Mentality of Settler Colonialism', in *Making Settler Colonial Space: Perspectives on Race, Place and Identity*, ed. Tracey Banivanua Mar and Penelope Edmonds (London: Palgrave Macmillan, 2010), 45; Adrian Howkins, *Frozen Empires: An Environmental History of the Antarctic Peninsula* (Oxford and New York: Oxford University Press, 2016), 81.
14. Pablo Wainschenker and Elizabeth Leane, 'The "Alien" Next Door: Antarctica in South American Fiction', *The Polar Journal* 9, no. 2 (3 July 2019): 324–39.
15. Calderón Le Joliff, 'La teoría del iceberg', 97.
16. Rojo, 'Sobre "El último grumete de la Baquedano" y algo más', 87.
17. José Kramarenko, '¡No hay INDIOS en MAGALLANES!', *En Viaje*, February 1944, 32.
18. Rodrigo Booth, '"El paisaje aquí tiene un encanto fresco y poético": las bellezas del sur de Chile y la construcción de la nación turística', *HIB: Revista de Historia Iberoamericana* 3, no. 1 (2010): 10–32.
19. Sylvia Dümmer Scheel, *Sin tropicalismos ni exageraciones: la construcción de la imagen de Chile para la Exposición Iberoamericana de Sevilla en 1929* (Santiago de Chile: RIL Editores, 2014), 169.
20. Nancy Nicholls Lopeandía, 'La Sociedad Ballenera de Magallanes: de cazadores de ballenas a "héroes" que marcaron la soberanía nacional, 1906–1916', *Historia (Santiago)* 43, no. 1 (June 2010): 68.
21. Empresa de los Ferrocarriles del Estado, *Guía del Veraneante 1948* (Santiago de Chile: Talleres Gráficos de los Ferrocarriles del Estado, 1948), 297.
22. David Perry Barnes, 'Magallanes, crisol de razas, es himno al trabajo y la solidaridad', *En Viaje*, July 1945: 158.
23. Patrick Barr Melej, 'Cowboys and Constructions: Nationalist Representations of Pastoral Life in Post-Portalian Chile', *Journal of Latin American Studies* 30, no. 1 (February 1998): 44.
24. Morales Piña, 'En torno al escritor chileno Francisco Coloane … y un cuento gélido', 30.
25. Francisco Coloane, *Cabo de Hornos*, 12th ed. (Santiago de Chile: Editorial Orbe, 1973), 21.
26. Coloane, *Los pasos del hombre*, 86.
27. Howkins, 'Appropriating Space', 45.
28. ' … ese enorme lomo que corre a través de las Américas, y que termina precisamente en este lugar, debe producir algún malestar atmosférico'. Francisco Coloane, *Los conquistadores de la Antártida*, 17th ed. (Santiago de Chile: Zig-Zag, 1985), 12.

29. Claudio del Solar, 'Diccionario de autores de la literatura chilena. 14º parte', En Viaje, June 1969, 428: 31–32.
30. 'Yo no conocía la Antártida cuando escribí este libro. Yo conocía el Cabo de Hornos y la parte de la Antártida la hice basándome en un viejo libro de Nordenskjöld: Viaje al Polo Sur, a quien piratée, digamos, de manera que tienen una veracidad científica algunas cosas que adapté'. Francisco Coloane and Virginia Vidal, *Testimonios de Francisco Coloane* (Santiago de Chile: Editorial Universitaria, 1991), 46.
31. Francisco Coloane, 'Prólogo', in *Chilenos en la Antártica*, by Óscar Vila Labra (Santiago de Chile: Editorial Nascimiento, 1947), 5–6.
32. 'La grandiosidad de la naturaleza antártica es tan sobrecogedora que enmudece la palabra del prosista'. Coloane, 'Prólogo', 6.
33. 'Frente a esa trabazón de témpanos que presenciamos en la Bahía Margarita … hemos pensado que sólo una música abismante o desolada, o un poema, podrían expresar la sensación que aquello produce en el espíritu humano'. Coloane, 'Prólogo', 6.
34. William T. Rossiter, 'Literature and Diplomacy', in *The Encyclopedia of Diplomacy*, ed. Gordon Martel (Chichester: John Wiley & Sons, Ltd, 2018), 6.
35. Coloane, *Los conquistadores de la Antártida*, 68.
36. 'El agrandó el alma y el cuerpo de Chile'. Coloane, *Los conquistadores de la Antártida*, 68.
37. Rojo, 'Sobre "El último grumete de la Baquedano" y algo más', 97.
38. Howkins, *Frozen Empires*, 11.
39. See, for example, Francisco Coloane, 'La leyenda de la laguna de Agamaca', *En Viaje*, December 1969.
40. Coloane, *Los pasos del hombre*, 89.
41. Coloane, *Los conquistadores de la Antártida*, 55.
42. '¿Cómo esa embarcación tan pequeña para atravesar esos mares y tan grande como para ser arrastrada por ese pedregoso río había llegado hasta el interior de ese apacible valle?' Coloane, *Los conquistadores de la Antártida*, 103.
43. Luis Horta, *El sexto continente: filmaciónes en la Antártica Chilena 1919–1973* (Santiago de Chile: Cineteca Universidad de Chile, 2018), 7.
44. Coloane, *Los conquistadores de la Antártida*, 102.
45. ' … pastizales de rojo claro sobre la nieve, una especie de liquen florecido'. Coloane, *Los conquistadores de la Antártida*, 98.
46. 'Sobre los tijerales de la primera base en construcción, ondeaba nuestra bandera chilena identificando su blanco andino con estrella polar, y el rojo de los copihues chilotes llevados por la goleta Ancud cuando tomó posesión del estrecho de Magallanes' Coloane', *Los pasos del hombre*, 156.
47. Francisco Coloane and Jack Ceitelis, *Antártica: una visión gráfica del continente helado* (Santiago de Chile: Editorial Andrés Bello/ Editorial Ceitelis-Rast, 1985).
48. Francisco Coloane and Jack Ceitelis, *Antártica* (Santiago de Chile: Editorial Puelche, 2005), inside cover.
49. Coloane and Vidal, *Testimonios de Francisco Coloane*, 59.
50. Jack Ceitelis, 'Dos Palabras/Two Words', in *Antártica*, by Francisco Coloane and Jack Ceitelis (Santiago de Chile: Editorial Puelche, 2005), 3.
51. Francisco Coloane, 'Antártica', in *Antártica*, by Francisco Coloane and Jack Ceitelis (Santiago de Chile: Editorial Puelche, 2005), 29.

52. Coloane, 'Antártica', 30.
53. Rachel VanWieren, 'La amenaza del femicidio: mujeres selk'nam e inmigrantes fueguinos en El guanaco blanco (1980) de Francisco Coloane y El corazón a contraluz (1996) de Patricio Manns', in *América Latina en el nuevo milenio: procesos, crisis y perspectivas*, ed. Elena Oliva et al. (Santiago de Chile: Centro de Estudios Culturales Latinoamericanos, Universidad de Chile, 2009), 107.
54. Jude Isabella, 'Declared Extinct, the Yaghan Rise in the Land of Fire', *Hakai Magazine*, 31 March 2022. Available online: https://hakaimagazine.com/features/declared-dead-the-yaghan-rise-in-the-land-of-fire/.
55. Instituto Antártico Chileno, 'El Continente Antártico/The Antarctic Continent', in *Antártica*, by Francisco Coloane and Jack Ceitelis (Santiago de Chile: Editorial Puelche, 2005), 6.
56. Carlos Droguett, 'Francisco Coloane, o la séptima parte visible', *Mensaje* 23, no. 235 (December 1974): 624.
57. Coloane, *Los pasos del hombre*, 155.
58. Coloane, *Los pasos del hombre*, 155.
59. '¿Qué significan las convenciones, los tratados, los nacionalismos, los prejuicios, sino símbolos incapaces de entender la majestuosidad de esa soledad? ... Pero sea chileno, argentino o inglés, en la Antartica sólo se es hombre, y eso fue lo que nos sucedió con el inglés de puerto Lockroy'. Francisco Coloane, *Antártico* (Santiago de Chile: Alfaguara, 2008), 152.
60. 'Era una bandera anónima que llegó hasta allí flameando no en los aires, sino en las profundidades del mar', Coloane, *Antártico*, 154.
61. 'Me diluyo en la superficie del mar para bajar a sus corrientes submarinas y en ellas llegar hasta los trópicos, transformarme en una nube y recorrer tus campos fertilizándolos para que nazcas y puedas vivir. ¿No me reconoces en tí mismo, entonces? ¿En tu sangre? ¿En el fruto que comes?' This tale is related by Óscar Pinochet de la Barra, who later founded the Chilean Antarctic Institute in 1963. 'Con Pancho Coloane en la Antártica', *La Segunda*, 13 August 2002, 6.

Bibliography

Araya Grandón, Juan Gabriel. 'Un territorio más allá: convergencias ecológicas en la cuentística de Francisco Coloane'. *Literatura y Lingüística* 20 (2009): 41–55.
Barr Melej, Patrick. 'Cowboys and Constructions: Nationalist Representations of Pastoral Life in Post-Portalian Chile'. *Journal of Latin American Studies* 30, no. 1 (February 1998): 44.
Booth, Rodrigo. '"El paisaje aquí tiene un encanto fresco y poético": las bellezas del sur de Chile y la construcción de la nación turística'. *HIB: Revista de Historia Iberoamericana* 3, no. 1 (2010): 10–32.
Calderón Le Joliff, Tatiana. 'Coloane, Hemingway y Le Clézio: los "témpanos" de la imaginación'. *Anales de literatura chilena* 11, no. 14 (2010): 301–14.
Calderón Le Joliff, Tatiana. 'La teoría del iceberg y la práctica de la alusión en los cuentos de Ernest Hemingway y de Francisco Coloane'. *Acta Literaria* 32 (2006): 97–105.
Chant, Elizabeth. 'Reading Fuegian Narratives and Nonhuman Sensibility in Francisco Coloane's Patagonian Tales'. *Journal of Latin American Cultural Studies* 33, no. 1 (2024): 1–20.
Coloane, Francisco. *Antártico*. Santiago de Chile: Alfaguara, 2008.
Coloane, Francisco. *Cabo de Hornos*, 12th ed. Santiago de Chile: Editorial Orbe, 1973.

Coloane, Francisco. *Los conquistadores de la Antártida*, 17th ed. Santiago de Chile: Zig-Zag, 1985.
Coloane, Francisco. *Los pasos del hombre: Memorias*. Barcelona: Mondadori, 2000.
Coloane, Francisco. 'Prólogo', in *Chilenos en la Antártica*, by Óscar Vila Labra, 5–6. Santiago de Chile: Editorial Nascimiento, 1947.
Coloane, Francisco, and Jack Ceitelis. *Antártica: Una visión gráfica del continente helado*. Santiago de Chile: Editorial Andrés Bello/ Editorial Ceitelis-Rast, 1985.
Coloane, Francisco, and Jack Ceitelis. *Antártica*. Santiago de Chile: Editorial Puelche, 2005.
Coloane, Francisco, and Virginia Vidal. *Testimonios de Francisco Coloane*. Santiago de Chile: Editorial Universitaria, 1991.
del Solar, Claudio. 'Diccionario de autores de la literatura chilena. 14º parte', *En Viaje*, June 1969: 428: 31–32.
Dümmer Scheel, Sylvia. *Sin tropicalismos ni exageraciones: la construcción de la imagen de Chile para la Exposición Iberoamericana de Sevilla en 1929*. Santiago de Chile: RIL Editores, 2012.
Ferrada, Jorge Ricardo. *Los cuentos de Francisco Coloane: espacios de realidad y deseo*. Santiago de Chile: Editorial Universidad de Santiago, 2004.
Fontana, Pablo. 'The Antarctic Extension of Latin America'. In *The Cambridge History of the Polar Regions*, edited by Adrian Howkins and Peder Roberts, 672–701. Cambridge: Cambridge University Press, 2023.
Guia del Veraneante 1948. Santiago de Chile: Talleres Gráficos de los Ferrocarriles del Estado, 1948.
Haase, Jenny. 'Abismos bajo el hielo: experiencias desintegradoras en los cuentos de Francisco Coloane'. In *Trans*Chile: Cultura-Historia-Itinerarios-Literatura-Educación. Un acercamiento transareal*, edited by Ottmar Ette and Horst Nitschack, 125–36. Madrid and Frankfurt am main: Iberoamericana and Vervuert, 2010.
Horta, Luis. *El Sexto Continente: Filmaciónes en la Antártica Chilena 1919–1973*. Santiago de Chile: Cineteca Universidad de Chile, 2018.
Howkins, Adrian. 'Appropriating Space: Antarctic Imperialism and the Mentality of Settler Colonialism'. In *Making Settler Colonial Space: Perspectives on Race, Place and Identity*, edited by Tracey Banivanua Mar and Penelope Edmonds, 29–52. London: Palgrave Macmillan, 2010.
Howkins, Adrian. *Frozen Empires: An Environmental History of the Antarctic Peninsula*. Oxford and New York: Oxford University Press, 2016.
Kramarenko, José., '¡No hay INDIOS en MAGALLANES!', in *En Viaje*, February 1944, 32.
Mora, Alejandra. 'De cómo la imaginación crea una tierra. Divagaciones sobre los viajes imaginarios y reales de Francisco Coloane a la Antártica'. *Aura Austral*, July 2018. Available online: https://auraaustral.cl/cronicas-territorio/de-como-la-imaginacion-crea-una-tierra-divagaciones-sobre-los-viajes-imaginarios-y-reales-de-francisco-coloane-a-la-antartica/.
Morales Piña, Eddie. 'En torno al escritor chileno Francisco Coloane ... y un cuento gélido'. *Estudios Hemisféricos y Polares* 2, no. 2 (2011): 26–34.
Neruda, Pablo. *Canto General*, 50th anniversary edition, translated by Jack Schmitt. Berkeley and Los Angeles: University of California Press, 2000.
Nicholls Lopeandía, Nancy. 'La Sociedad Ballenera de Magallanes: de cazadores de ballenas a "héroes" que marcaron la soberanía nacional, 1906–1916'. *Historia* (Santiago) 43, no. 1 (June 2010): 41–78.
Rojas, Eliana, and Pablo Vargas, eds. *Coloane: Literatura y ecología al sur del mundo*. Santiago de Chile: Ocho Libros, 2011.
Rossiter, William T. 'Literature and Diplomacy'. In *The Encyclopedia of Diplomacy*, edited by Gordon Martel, 6. Chichester: John Wiley & Sons, Ltd, 2018: 1–13.
VanWieren, Rachel. 'Exploring the Margins of Patagonia in Chilean Fiction' (PhD thesis, UCLA, 2010).

VanWieren, Rachel. 'La amenaza del femicidio: mujeres selk'nam e inmigrantes fueguinos en El guanaco blanco (1980) de Francisco Coloane y El corazón a contraluz (1996) de Patricio Manns'. In *América Latina en el nuevo milenio: procesos, crisis y perspectivas*, edited by Elena Oliva, Alondra Peirano, Elisabet Prudant and Javiera Ruiz, 107. Santiago de Chile: Centro de Estudios Culturales Latinoamericanos, Universidad de Chile, 2009: 93–108.

VanWieren, Rachel. 'Reconsidering the Patagonian Worker Movements of the 1920s: Francisco Coloane's and Luis Sepúlveda's Rebellious Chilotes'. *A Contracorriente: Una revista de estudios latinoamericanos* 14, no. 3 (2017): 127–42.

Wainschenker, Pablo, and Elizabeth Leane. 'The "Alien" Next Door: Antarctica in South American Fiction'. *The Polar Journal* 9, no. 2 (3 July 2019): 324–39.

CHAPTER 4
CROSS-CULTURAL LIFE WRITING: JUXTAPOSING ADIVASI/TRIBAL INDIAN AND INDIGENOUS AUSTRALIAN TEXTS
Priyanka Shivadas

This chapter considers selected cross-cultural, collaboratively produced Adivasi/tribal Indian and Indigenous Australian life writing texts alongside each other. It explores the thematic concerns and structural features these texts share and asks how they reflect on commonalities and divergences between life writing narratives from Indigenous southern communities. The selected texts are *The Town Grew Up Dancing: The Life and Art of Wenten Rubuntja* (2002) and *Mayilamma: The Life of a Tribal Eco-warrior* (2018). Both texts are as-told-to life narratives, a form of life writing which 'involves one person telling their life story to another, who, with varying degrees of creative intervention writes it up on their behalf'.[1]

Firstly, tracing trans-south solidarities and alliances, this chapter demonstrates how the Indigenous memoirists of these texts, asserting agency and control over the written narratives, speak to Indigenous Australian writer Alexis Wright's (Waanyi) vision of a 'self-governing' Indigenous literature. It is to be noted that one text is situated in Australia, an Anglophone white settler-nation which has the economic status of the Global North. The other is in India, a non-Anglophone postcolonial nation-state, which, although in the hemispheric North, is considered part of the Global South. Divisions, as Wright says, can render some people 'invisible' to others in the world.[2] She adds, 'Aboriginal people [of Australia], with more in common with people deemed to be of the Global South geographically and economically, find [them]selves divided from the south, and included in the distant Global North'.[3] By the same token, Adivasi/tribal peoples of India continue to be subjected to violent processes of colonization of their lands and cultures even though they are situated in a postcolonial nation-state. One of the aims of this chapter is to render the connections between the metaphorical and literal south visible by juxtaposing life writing texts from Australia and India alongside each other.

Reading across the south can be revealing not just in terms of tracing commonalities. The position and status of the selected texts, as well as the current material and political realities that surround them in a 'globalized' literary world, are different. The juxtaposition of *Mayilamma,* from the Adivasi/tribal context, with a similarly focused but differently produced text from the Indigenous Australian context, *The Town Grew Up Dancing*, reveals a lack of protocols in India to protect the rights of Adivasi/tribal peoples to determine how their stories are represented and disseminated. Moreover, close attention to the paratextual devices which frame *Mayilamma* demonstrates how assigning the text to the genre of environmental justice life writing from the Global South diminishes the distinctiveness of its substance and aesthetics as an Indigenous life writing text. On the other hand, *The Town Grew Up Dancing* is shown as enacting a collective memoir, thus speaking to the importance assigned to kinship and country in Indigenous lives.

In the following section of this chapter, I begin by briefly outlining what is shared between these Indigenous life writing texts. In greater detail, I provide an analysis of the editorial apparatus surrounding *Mayilamma* and *The Town Grew Up Dancing*, to emphasize how it is important not only to draw links and trace connections across the south and the Global South but also that the contrasts can be equally revealing, too.

Mayilamma and *The Town Grew Up Dancing*

Transcribed by Jothibai Pariyadath, *Mayilamma* is the life narrative of Mayilamma from Eravallar Adivasi community. Originally published in Malayalam in 2006, the English translation of the text is by Swarnalatha Rangarajan and Sreejith Varma. *The Town Grew Up Dancing* is Wenten Rubuntja's (Arrernte) story told predominantly in his first language Arrernte, transcribed and translated into English by linguist and artist Jenny Green. Both texts retell the lives of prominent Indigenous activists who spoke from positions of leadership, providing insight into their respective communities. They hint at the non-text-based cultures of the Indigenous/Adivasi communities of Eravallar and Arrernte peoples, where the voice is a major means of communication. Moreover, a distinctive feature of the narratives told by Mayilamma and Rubuntja is their focus on a selfhood, which defines itself in terms of place-based affiliations. It is recorded in the text that Mayilamma's earliest memories are of her grandfather 'leading men into the forest to collect honey from the bees'.[4] She says, 'I have heard that back in my grandfather's father's time, our community was "number one" in the forest'.[5] Mayilamma is thus establishing her position as part of a lineage of Adivasi people – her grandfather's father's – who are traditional custodians of the forests.

Likewise, Rubuntja narrates by way of introducing himself, 'They call me Wenten Lterrkapante, Lterrkapante from Mpweringke – Burt Crossing…. My grandfather, old Short Bob, gave me that name. That old man was from Mpweringke and when I was born he said, "That's my little grandson, that one, little Lterrkapante." This was my first name, before I was baptized'.[6] In this identification of self as Wenten Lterrkapante, relations to country (Mpweringke) and kin (grandfather, old Short Bob) are simultaneously established, and the cardinal importance of these relations are stressed by Rubuntja by saying this was his first name.

As Alexis Wright formulates in a 2019 essay published in the *Sydney Review of Books*, it is an important aspect of textual sovereignty for Indigenous writers to define themselves in relation to land. In Wright's vision of a self-governing Indigenous literature, a sovereign literary space made through the agency of Indigenous writers, land is the ancient library from where knowledge originates. Moreover, in this vision, Indigenous peoples establish

Cross-Cultural Life Writing

'a long vision' of themselves through their relationship to land, community, and culture.[7] Relationship to land, which is fundamental to physical and spiritual sustenance for Indigenous peoples, is further established by both Rubuntja and Mayilamma by relating personal experiences that are specific to certain locations and landscapes. Rubuntja recalls, 'Our grandmothers used to dampen the bush onions with milk and make them like [native] seed porridge and feed it to us kids. That was Artepe Ulpaye [Todd River]'.[8] Similarly, Mayilamma says, 'I remember going to a school as a child in Attayampady. The school near Kuttentan's field remains the same even today.'[9]

Rubuntja and Mayilamma's narratives also emphasize the intimate knowledge they possess of the land, as demonstrated by their use of plants and herbs for traditional medicines. 'The eremophilia plant – called arrethe – was like Vicks. [...] If you had a cold you'd boil up the eremophilia leaves, pour the mixture into a bottle, and then rub yourself with it – just like Vicks', remarks Rubuntja.[10] In her narrative, Mayilamma regards highly the knowledge of Pappal, one of the oldest and one of the 'most important' members of the community, who is well-versed in traditional medicine. 'Whenever we caught a fever or cold, she would light a fire using stones and drop *thumba* leaves and castor leaves in water and make us inhale the steam. The fever would flee in no time', notes Mayilamma.[11] These narrative practices, which establish 'land as a storied site of human interaction', are indispensable to Indigenous peoples and vitally important to Indigenous sovereignty and belonging, according to Native American scholar Mishuana Goeman (Tonawanda Band of Seneca).[12] As Goeman explains, these 'narrative practices' are the obverse of the 'discourses of property and territory' by which ownership to land has been claimed in colonial-imperial formations, and as such 'uniquely pivotal' to Indigenous sovereignty and serve as a point of difference from 'other minority cultures and statuses'.[13] In this chapter, these narrative practices also outline vivid thematic congruences between texts from Indigenous southern communities.

As mentioned earlier, *The Town Grew Up Dancing* and *Mayilamma* share structural similarities, too. They are both flanked and framed by paratextual devices. The lives of Rubuntja and Mayilamma have been documented and translated by non-Indigenous biographers and translators while drawing on living traditions of Indigenous orality. The paratextual elements brought into play by the biographers and translators have an instrumental effect on these texts, as is often the case in as-told-to life writing. *Mayilamma* begins with a full 39 pages of front-matter, numbered in lower-case Roman numerals. Of the 111 pages that proceed, only 64 pages constitute the body of the text or, in this case, the autobiographical account. The remaining end-matter is 47 pages. Printed on the top-left of the dust jacket of the 2018 hard copy edition from the publisher Orient Blackswan is the title *Mayilamma: The Life of a Tribal Eco-Warrior*. The original book in Malayalam by Mathrubhumi Books bears the title *Mayilamma: Oru Jeevitham*, literally meaning 'Mayilamma: A Life'. Through this renaming, the translated English version positions the book in the field of environmental literature alongside life writing.

The foreword is written by American scholar Scott Slovic, who served as the founding president of the Association for the Study of Literature and Environment (ASLE) from 1992 to 1995. As Slovic notes, 'It does not matter that Mayilamma herself was unable to read or write or that she was a tribal woman – rather, these aspects of her life contribute to the profound authenticity and make it all the more admirable that she became such a strong activist in the face of multinational power and misdeeds.'[14] The assertion is that her tribal identity and lack of a formal education made Mayilamma an unlikely candidate to spearhead protests against Coca-Cola, a multinational corporation founded in America more than a century ago and whose yearly revenue runs into millions of dollars. As documented in the book, the company had set up a bottling plant in Plachimada, Mayilamma's village. Within six months of the beginning of its operation in 2000, wells in the village ran dry because of unlimited extraction of groundwater by the plant. The remaining sources of water were contaminated by the wastes released by the industrial operations, making it unfit for human consumption or agricultural use. To Mayilamma and other residents of the village, the activities of the company in Plachimada sounded a death knell. A protest was launched in 2002 on Earth Day, 22 April, with the intention to shut the plant down.

In the introduction to *Mayilamma*, the English translators and editors of the book, Swarnalatha Rangarajan and Sreejith Varma, speak of the protest in the following manner: 'The course of the Plachimada struggle that began as a silent vigil by adivasi [sic] villagers and soon cascaded into full-blown war fought by actors, both local and international, for the cause of environmental justice jeopardized Coca-Cola's symbolic cultural capital.'[15] They point out that unlike scientific and legal accounts of the events that took place in Plachimada, *Mayilamma* helps the reader visualize the 'slow violence' wrought by long-term damage done to the environment.[16] *Slow violence* is a term borrowed from Rob Nixon's *Slow Violence and the Environmentalism of the Poor*, which lays stress on environmental deterioration that because of its slow nature is rendered invisible by the powerful forces of industrialization and capitalism. Slow violence affects especially those from historically disadvantaged communities such as Indigenous peoples. Elsewhere, Rangarajan has asserted that such 'narratives of slow violence […] are rescued from invisibility and representational bias by women writing nature in the Global South.'[17]

Mayilamma emerges from the Global South according to the introduction of the book. As a geopolitical space often associated with erstwhile colonized nations, the Global South performs an important denotative function in Rangarajan and Varma's introduction to *Mayilamma*, which locates the narrative in that sphere. Having taken the place of the term *the Third World*, the Global South, it has been rightly noted, continues to imply substandard, poor conditions of living which characterize the Third World in public imagination.[18] At the same time, says Rangarajan, 'the Global South is an emerging new expression of political and socio-cultural entities from multiple locations and cultures in which questions of identity, culture, sustainable development and environment governance become vital in the articulation of a new world order.'[19]

Mayilamma has been aligned with other similar autobiographies published in the Global South and areas of the Global North that have seen severe environmental disregard and human rights violation. In the foreword, Slovic connects Ken Saro-Wiwa's Nigerian memoir and Rigoberta Menchu's Guatemalan autobiography to *Mayilamma*.[20] Similarly, Rangarajan and Varma draw parallels between *Mayilamma* and Wangari Maathai's *Unbowed: A Memoir* from Kenya and Terry Tempest Williams' *An Unnatural History of Family and Place* from North America. They argue that all these texts have a common feature. They belong to environmental justice life writing, which as a discursive paradigm bridges the domains of jurisprudence and ecological care.[21] Additionally, the issues of pollution, corporate control of common resources and environmental justice are repeatedly used in the paratext to present *Mayilamma* to its readers. These readers are characterized on the jacket of the book as 'students of environmental studies, ecological activists, and everyone who feels responsible for their only home – the earth'.[22]

By contrast, Pooja Parmar, in *Indigeneity and Legal Pluralism in India: Claims, Histories, Meanings*, shifts the analytical emphasis from questions of environmental degradation and justice to issues concerning Indigenous rights and claims in her work on the Plachimada dispute. She notes:

> Pollution and global capital are familiar concepts and urban readers are able to relate to a story that contains these words. An Adivasi's refusal to leave, on the other hand is unfamiliar. For many it is in fact an unreasonable assertion since it does not fit into the popular belief that everyone must want to leave what is seen as the most backward part of the state.[23]

Parmar, who is trained as a legal scholar, looks outside legal frameworks and into 'articulations of everyday experiences of injustice, stories about humans and nonhumans, personal life histories and oral histories of a community' to better understand the Plachimada dispute.[24] She posits two vital facts that are rarely mentioned in general accounts of the conflict, which can make a significant difference to our reading of *Mayilamma*. Firstly, in the early days of the protest, it was thought necessary to rename the Adivasi Samara Samithi (Adivasi Struggle Committee), led by Mayilamma, as the Coca-Cola Virudha Samara Samithi (Anti-Coca-Cola Struggle Committee). Parmar advises, 'This change was necessary because many do not wish to support an Adivasi struggle. [...] the words "Adivasi struggle" are generally associated with the long-standing demands by Adivasis in Kerala for restoration of their lands that are currently occupied by non-Adivasi settlers.'[25]

Secondly, in August 2006, a few months before her death in early 2007 and two years after the bottling plant was forced to stop its operation, Mayilamma left the *samara pandal*[26] in anger, never to return. While the reasons behind Mayilamma's decision are not entirely clear, the primary cause has been attributed to a difference of opinion between Mayilamma and a non-Adivasi supporter of the anti-Coca-Cola struggle named Subramaniam. Without offering further details, Parmar implies that they did not see eye-to-eye regarding the end-goal of the protest.[27] Consequently, Parmar asserts that the popular understanding of the Plachimada dispute shared among environmental and human rights activists, journalists, politicians and other actors who wanted the bottling plant shut down differs in significant ways from the understanding shared among the Adivasis in the region.

In *Mayilamma*, the conceptual categories that populate and structure the paratext – environmental justice life writing from the Global South – are tenable, powerful ideas that can resonate across ideological and demographical divides. However, I would like to argue that these categories are not intrinsic to Mayilamma's own narration. In the book, Mayilamma says that if she ever met Sonia Gandhi (the president of the Indian National Congress, in power at the Center at the time of the protests), she would say: 'There is a small well in front of my house. All these days we were drinking water from that well. Now the water is not good. We are not against you giving any company a permit or an award. But can you bring the good water back to our well?'[28] This excerpt from *Mayilamma* directly relates to Parmar's point: 'When the Adivasis say they need and want water, they do not want just any water. [...] The well-water is significant because it is connected to, and connects them to, the land.'[29]

In an interview included in the paratext of *Mayilamma*, Jothibai Pariyadath is asked whether the Plachimada struggle should be viewed within this broader picture of 'indigenous struggles' for land alienated from them.[30] Pariyadath replies, 'Though the struggle was begun mostly by the adivasis [sic], later on the whole local population of Plachimada rallied around them. It shaped up as a local people's movement against a global corporate.'[31] This response not only minimizes the strength of Adivasi struggles for right to land but repeats the popular understanding of the Plachimada dispute as an anti-Coca-Cola struggle. The translators of the English book, Rangarajan and Varma, who were awarded the ASLE Translation Grant which helped them take the 'translation project forward in so many ways',[32] have chosen to situate the book firmly in the genre of environmental justice life writing. In doing so, I argue that the paratext assigns a lesser role to the complex history of Indigenous struggles for alienated lands, which is inseparably connected to events in Plachimada and Mayilamma's lived experience. By the same token it is crucial to note that in the paratext, *Mayilamma* is not addressed as Indigenous life writing, a genre which emphasizes the distinctiveness of Indigenous experiences. This has a direct implication for how the lived experiences of Mayilamma narrated in the text are comprehended and accorded significance by readers. By rendering the value of Mayilamma's narrative in purely environmental terms, the paratext directs readers' attention away from Indigenous concerns and aesthetics. And, furthermore, by appealing specifically to eco-conscious readers as mentioned earlier, the distribution of the book in the market has also been managed.

On the other hand, Wenten Rubuntja's *The Town Grew Up Dancing* is a remarkable example of a text that marshals its paratextual elements to broaden the range of contextual information available to the reader. Crucial among the paratext are several full-color reproductions of Rubuntja's paintings and drawings, photographs, posters and maps of places in Central Australia mentioned in his account. Reflecting the primal importance of country to Rubuntja, a historical timeline of Mparntwe/Alice Springs and 'notes on skin names' have also been appended to the body of the text. A 'skin name is part of a complex system of social labelling that locates an [Aboriginal] individual within interconnected systems of kin and country'.[33] Published by Jukurrpa books, an imprint of the Indigenous Australian publishing house IAD Press, *The Town Grew Up Dancing* flags the voice of the non-Indigenous transcriber/translator/editor visibly throughout the text. The following is an excerpt from its preface:

> *PIPE INGKERRE MWERRE ANTHURRE PIPE nhenge itne read-em-iletyeke,* 'Oh arratye anthurre good story nhenhe kwenhe'. *Antirrkwetyeke akwete. Akwete mapele aneme ingkernenye mapele aneme read-em-ilerltanerle,* 'Ah that's story from the Creation of the world'. *Iwetyakenhe. Antirrkwetyeke akwete, akweke ingkernenye mapele areme,* grandchildren get-em properly true story.
>
> This book is really good – people have got to read it and say, 'This is a really good story'. These stories must be kept forever. Then all the little ones can read about it in the future and say, 'Ah, that's the story from the Creation of the world.' This story mustn't be thrown away – it must be kept forever so that all the young ones in the future can read it and the grand children can get the proper true story. (Wenten Rubuntja 2000)

In 1998 Wenten Rubuntja approached the Aboriginal Areas Protection Authority (AAPA) and asked them to assist him with the recording of his life story. Work commenced on the project in 1999, with a grant from the Australian Institute for Aboriginal and Torres Strait Islander Studies (AIATSIS) to help finance the research. A second grant was subsequently awarded to complete the research.[34]

The above excerpt is representative of the design and style of narration the text adopts. According to the preface, *The Town Grew Up Dancing* is based on taped interviews with Rubuntja held between 1975 and 2001. It showcases an approach of 'long-term immersion'[35] of the non-Indigenous collaborator within the Indigenous family and community of the autobiographical subject. A vast majority of the interviews were recorded by non-Indigenous linguist Jenny Green, who shares the authorial credit for the book alongside Rubuntja. During the interviews, Rubuntja spoke in Arrernte, Aboriginal English and a mix of Arrernte and English, and these different forms are transcribed in the text in a visual format which seeks to delineate the work of translation and transcription that produced the final text.

As in the excerpt above, the original transcript is in grey and italics if spoken in Arrernte, with the English translation printed in grey, without italics, appearing immediately afterwards. Since the interviews were conducted over many years, linking text printed in black is provided by Jenny Green and the non-Indigenous historian Tim Rowse to construct a narrative from the material shared during separate interviews. In most cases, the linking text provides historical detail or explanatory notes. 'The resulting drafts of the text have been read to Wenten and in this process he has corrected the text and provided further detail', notes the preface.[36] It continues, 'As translators we are aware of the many complex issues involved, and of the power the style of translation has to affect the overall impact of the narrative. We also recognise that in some instances alternative interpretations of the text are possible.'[37] Most of the translation work is attributed to

Green, who was helped by senior Arrernte woman Veronica Dobson Perrurle. The preface also acknowledges that Green 'inevitably represents the "white listener" in this context, irrespective of her two and a half decades of experience working in the area, and her considerable knowledge of the Arrernte language'.[38]

The introduction of the book describes Rubuntja as 'a remarkable person, well known both as an artist and as a major spokesperson, negotiator, and ambassador for Aboriginal Australia'.[39] He played a key role in the passing of the Aboriginal Land Rights (Northern Territory) Act 1976, the first legislation in Australia that enabled Aboriginal peoples to claim land title based on traditional occupation. *The Town Grew Up Dancing* chronicles other significant achievements of Rubuntja. The final narrative weaves in the words of many people who were closely associated with him – family members, most notably his sister Ruby Rubuntja, his wife Cynthia, and others who worked with him at Aboriginal organizations in Central Australia. This collective memoir is a fitting way to tell the story of a man who was actively involved in community welfare and wore many hats (literally and metaphorically) in his life. He was a member of different Aboriginal organizations, an activist, a cook, a brickmaker, a drover, a butcher and a family man committed to 'the support of a large extended family'.[40]

In her review, Mary Eagle, calling the book a 'biography-cum-autobiography', praises it for its multilayered narrative approach: 'It is at one level the biography of Alice Springs (Mparntwe), a town that "grew up dancing". At another, it is a story of some decades of policy making on questions of land rights.'[41] European scholar Oliver Haag puts Rubuntja's book under the category of published Indigenous autobiographies.[42] Apart from Eagle's positive review and Haag's mention of the book in his survey of Indigenous Australian autobiographies and biographies, critical responses to the text are lacking. This is despite its attention to the ethics of cross-cultural collaboration, self-reflexivity in editorial apparatus and its attempt to translate the words of Rubuntja as close to the original recording as possible.

The Town Grew Up Dancing provides a useful contrast to *Mayilamma*. As shown, the categorization of *Mayilamma: The Life of a Tribal Eco-Warrior* as 'environmental justice writing' closes off readings crucial to the centering of Indigenous land rights. Despite the urgency and critical status of the environmental championing of Adivasi voices, in the context of *Mayilamma*, non-Indigenous mediation weakens Indigenous claims for land redress and right to land. On the other hand, recognizing its own ambivalence, *The Town Grew Up Dancing* refers to itself as autobiography and biography. It enacts a collective memoir, emphasizing the importance assigned to kinship and country in Indigenous lives.

Crucially, the transcriber, Jothibai Pariyadath, is assigned sole authorship of *Mayilamma*, appropriating Mayilamma's moral right to claim her own story, and the copyright of *Mayilamma* rests with the publisher. One of the key principles for ethical and responsible use of Indigenous cultural knowledge and expression in collaborative works is that benefits will be shared among the contributors, including copyright and the monetary benefits that arise from it. This is reflected in *The Town Grew Up Dancing*, which shares the copyright among Rubuntja, Green and Rowse. In this way, the juxtaposition of *Mayilamma* with *The Town Grew Up Dancing* magnifies a lack of centrally governed frameworks or protocols in India to affirm Adivasi/tribal rights to 'own and control representation and dissemination of their stories, knowledge and other cultural expression', which currently guide the Australian publishing industry and are dictated in *Protocols for Using First Nations Cultural and Intellectual Property in the Arts* produced by the Australia Council for the Arts.[43]

Writing: Protocols for Producing Indigenous Australian Writing, a more specific document directed at authors and publishers, also produced by the Australia Council for the Arts, states clearly that in the case of recording oral stories, '[w]here the work closely follows the words of the Indigenous storyteller, copyright ownership should be recognised as belonging to that person'.[44] For life stories of Indigenous peoples, 'if it is primarily their story (for example, if transcribed from tapes), then the life story subject should own copyright' and 'if it is a collaboration (for example, where the writer has brought his or her skill to the work), then there may be some scope for sharing copyright'.[45] These protocols are followed in *The Town Grew Up Dancing*, but not in *Mayilamma*. This is a highly problematic issue highlighted by the trans-south Indigenous-to-Indigenous lens of this chapter.

In focusing largely on the paratexts embedded within the texts by non-Indigenous collaborators, I do not wish to take attention away from the important narrative relationships to land established by Rubuntja and Mayilamma highlighted at the start. This chapter foregrounds Indigenous life stories which are often absent from dominant narratives and discourses. It emphasizes the strengths and agency of Indigenous texts and voices, especially in their connectedness. Finally, it reflects on the role of non-Indigenous collaborators working with Indigenous writers to address critical issues impinging on sustainable, ethical futures for cross-cultural Indigenous life writing emerging from the south/Global South.

Notes

1. Sandra Lindemann, 'As-Told-to Life Writing: Narratives of Self and Other', *a/b: Auto/Biography Studies* 32, no. 2 (2017): 385–6.
2. Alexis Wright, 'A Self-Governing Literature: Who Owns the Map of the World?', *Meanjin* 79, no. 2 (2020): 92–101.
3. Wright, 'A Self-Governing Literature'.
4. Jothibai Pariyadath, *Mayilamma: The Life of a Tribal Eco-Warrior* (Hyderabad: Orient Blackswan, 2018), 17.
5. Pariyadath, *Mayilamma*, 17.
6. Wenten Rubuntja, Tim Rowse and Jenny Green, *The Town Grew Up Dancing: The Life and Art of Wenten Rubuntja* (Alice Springs, NT: Jukurrpa Books, 2002), 17–18.
7. Alexis Wright, 'The Ancient Library and A Self-Governing Literature', *Sydney Review of Books*, 2019.
8. Rubuntja, *The Town Grew Up Dancing*, 37.

9. Pariyadath, *Mayilamma*, 25.
10. Rubuntja, *The Town Grew Up Dancing*, 43.
11. Pariyadath, *Mayilamma*, 16.
12. Mishuana Goeman, 'From Place to Territories and Back Again', *International Journal of Critical Indigenous Studies* 1, no. 1 (2008): 23.
13. Ibid., 23.
14. Pariyadath, *Mayilamma*, xv.
15. Ibid., xxix–xxx.
16. Ibid., xxii.
17. Swarnalatha Rangarajan, 'Women Writing Nature in the Global South: New Forest Texts from Fractured Indian Forests', in *Handbook of Ecocriticism and Cultural Ecology*, ed. Hubert Zapf (Berlin: De Gruyter, 2016), 439.
18. Russell West-Pavlov, *The Global South and Literature* (Cambridge: Cambridge University Press, 2018), 4.
19. Rangarajan, 'Women Writing Nature in the Global South', 439.
20. Pariyadath, *Mayilamma*, xv.
21. Ibid., xxv.
22. Ibid.
23. Pooja Parmar, *Indigeneity and Legal Pluralism in India: Claims, Histories, Meanings* (Cambridge: Cambridge University Press, 2015), 85–6.
24. Parmar, *Indigeneity and Legal Pluralism in India*, 10.
25. Ibid., 58.
26. *Samara pandal* can be translated as a hut or shelter built for protestors to gather.
27. Parmar, *Indigeneity and Legal Pluralism in India*, 136.
28. Pariyadath, *Mayilamma*, 63.
29. Parmar, *Indigeneity and Legal Pluralism in India*, 54.
30. Pariyadath, *Mayilamma*, 83, 103.
31. Ibid., 83.
32. Ibid., xi.
33. Rubuntja, *The Town Grew Up Dancing*, 191.
34. Ibid., vii.
35. Jennifer A. Jones, *Black Writers, White Editors: Episodes of Collaboration and Compromise in Australian Publishing History* (Sydney: Australian Scholarly Publishing, 2009), 226.
36. Rubuntja, *The Town Grew Up Dancing*, ix.
37. Ibid., viii.
38. Ibid.
39. Ibid., 1.
40. Ibid., 1, 5.
41. Mary Eagle, 'The Town Grew Up Dancing: The Life and Art of Wenten Rubuntja', *Aboriginal History* 27 (2003): 261
42. Oliver Haag, 'From the Margins to the Mainstream: Towards a History of Published Indigenous Australian Autobiographies and Biographies', in *Indigenous Biography and*

Autobiography, ed. Peter Read, Frances Peters-Little and Anna Haebich (Canberra: ANU E Press, 2008), 21.
43. *Protocols for Using First Nations Cultural and Intellectual Property in the Arts* (Sydney: Australia Council for the Arts, 2019).
44. *Writing: Protocols for Producing Indigenous Australian Writing* (Sydney: Australia Council for the Arts, 2007), 35.
45. Ibid., 35.

Bibliography

Eagle, Mary. 'The Town Grew Up Dancing: The Life and Art of Wenten Rubuntja'. *Aboriginal History* 27 (2003): 261–4.

Goeman, Mishuana. 'From Place to Territories and Back Again'. *International Journal of Critical Indigenous Studies* 1, no. 1 (2008): 23–34.

Haag, Oliver. 'From the Margins to the Mainstream: Towards a History of Published Indigenous Australian Autobiographies and Biographies'. In *Indigenous Biography and Autobiography*, edited by Peter Read, Frances Peters-Little and Anna Haebich, 5–28. Canberra: ANU E Press, 2008.

Jones, Jennifer A. *Black Writers, White Editors: Episodes of Collaboration and Compromise in Australian Publishing History*. Sydney: Australian Scholarly Publishing, 2009.

Lindemann, Sandra. 'As-Told-To Life Writing: Narratives of Self and Other'. *a/b: Auto/Biography Studies* 32, no. 2 (2017): 385–6.

Nixon, Rob. *Slow Violence and the Environmentalism of the Poor*. Cambridge, MA: Harvard University Press, 2011.

Pariyadath, Jothibai. *Mayilamma: The Life of a Tribal Eco-Warrior*. Hyderabad: Orient Blackswan, 2018.

Parmar, Pooja. *Indigeneity and Legal Pluralism in India: Claims, Histories, Meanings*. Cambridge: Cambridge University Press, 2015.

Protocols for Using First Nations Cultural and Intellectual Property in the Arts. Sydney: Australia Council for the Arts, 2019. Available online: https://australiacouncil.gov.au/wp-content/uploads/2021/07/protocols-for-using-first-nati-5f72716d09f01.pdf (accessed 26 March 2023).

Rangarajan, Swarnalatha. 'Women Writing Nature in the Global South: New Forest Texts from Fractured Indian Forests'. In *Handbook of Ecocriticism and Cultural Ecology*, edited by Hubert Zapf, 438–58. Berlin: De Gruyter, 2016.

Rubuntja, Wenten, Tim Rowse, and Jenny Green. *The Town Grew Up Dancing: The Life and Art of Wenten Rubuntja*. Alice Springs, NT: Jukurrpa Books, 2002.

West-Pavlov, Russell. *The Global South and Literature*. Cambridge: Cambridge University Press, 2018.

Wright, Alexis. 'The Ancient Library and A Self-Governing Literature'. *Sydney Review of Books*, 2019. Available online: https://sydneyreviewofbooks.com/essay/the-ancient-library-and-a-self-governing-literature/.

Wright, Alexis. 'A Self-Governing Literature: Who Owns the Map of the World?' *Meanjin* 79, no. 2 (2020): 92–101. Available online: https://meanjin.com.au/essays/a-self-governing-literature/ (accessed 26 March 2023).

Writing: Protocols for Producing Indigenous Australian Writing. Sydney: Australia Council for the Arts, 2007. Available online: https://www.austlit.edu.au/images/documents/Writing.pdf (accessed 26 March 2023).

PART II
IMAGINING SPACES AND SPATIALITY

CHAPTER 5
UNKNOWING A SOUTHERN LIFE: WRITING AROUND THE ABYSS

Katherine Collins

In the Pitt Rivers Museum in Oxford are two objects that were made and used in different parts of the Southern Hemisphere. One is a stick chart, a navigational aid from Jaluit Atoll in the Marshall Islands, made from thin strips of wood and seashells (see Figure 5.1).[1] The other is a water carrier from the Northern Cape Province in South Africa, an ostrich egg engraved with shapes and schematic figures such as antelopes and ostriches, into which has been cut a lateral hole (see Figure 5.2). The stick chart was obtained by Georg Irmer in 1896, brought to the UK and donated to the museum the following year; the egg was collected by Edward John Dunn in 1872 and donated in 1936. A more recent companion to these objects is the museum catalogue, which contains information about where they originated, their local names (in these two cases, unknown), the materials from which they were made and processes through which they were created. The catalogue also includes information about their collectors, donors, and a history detailing their listing and illustration in various academic publications.[2]

Viewing these two objects and their catalogue entries side-by-side, I was struck by the imbalance of the two sections; the information about the objects themselves was typically less than half a page, the other running to two, even three pages. I do not wish to suggest that curators at the Pitt Rivers are indifferent to these imbalances – for instance, Laura Peers has worked to reconnect community members with their material heritage, and Alice Stevenson, Dan Hicks and colleagues have worked to understand the Museum's collection as 'a kind of archaeological site'.[3] Nonetheless, these catalogue entries are a stark reminder that here, in this northern institution, we seem to know more about how these two southern objects came to be in the museum, and who has documented them in which academic publication since they arrived, than we do about the objects themselves.[4] When I mentioned my observation to another contributor to this volume, Obari Gomba, we spoke about the kinds of questions we would probably never be able to answer, a century after the objects came to be part of the Museum's collections: Who made this? What did this object mean to them? Who taught them this craft and what stories were exchanged as they learned? Who did they teach in turn? How did they spend their time once their work of carving and measuring was done? My experience with two of these objects and their catalogue entries in the Pitt Rivers Museum underpins my thinking in this chapter on life writing and the Southern Hemisphere.

One way of conceptualizing the imbalance in the information we have about the objects is to consider it a product of abyssal thinking, a term introduced by Portuguese academic Boaventura de Sousa Santos during a lecture in New York in

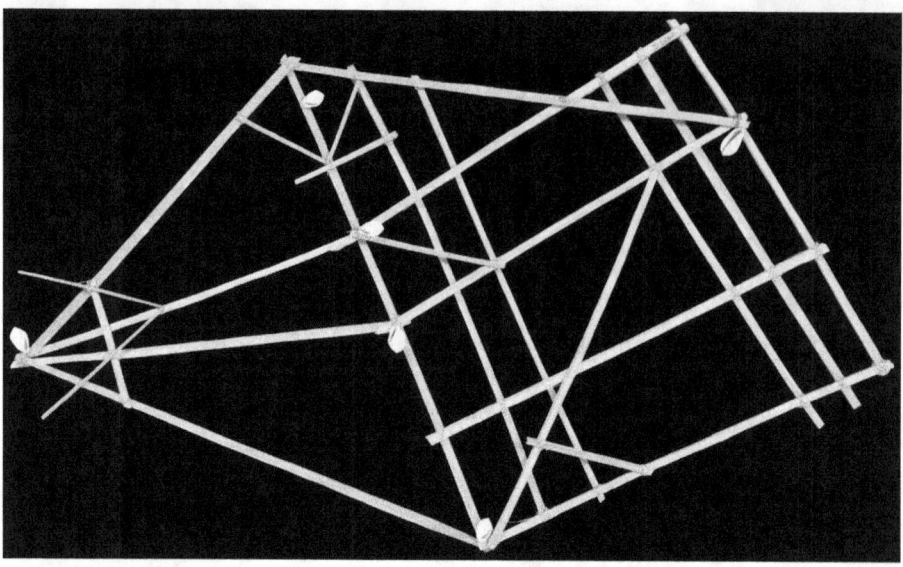

Figure 5.1 Sailing chart from the Marshall Islands. Copyright Pitt Rivers Museum, University of Oxford (1897.1.2).

Figure 5.2 Ostrich egg from southern Africa. Copyright Pitt Rivers Museum, University of Oxford (2004.142.1110).

2006. Abyssal thinking is 'a system of visible and invisible distinctions, the invisible ones being the foundation of the visible ones. The invisible distinctions are established through radical lines that divide social reality into two realms, the realm of "this side of the line" and the realm of "the other side of the line".'[5] Thus, the phrase 'the abyssal line' entered the Anglophone lexicon and has since become a popular way to write and speak about Epistemicide[6] in multiple languages – English, Portuguese and Spanish primarily, but also Japanese, Afrikaans and Catalan – in fields such as linguistics, education, cultural studies and Indigenous studies.[7] In this chapter I trace the history of the abyssal line concept in its evolution from a metaphorical cartography originating in the amity lines of the sixteenth century, to a compound metaphor that is both a territory to be mapped and a means of inscription. I analyze the 'abyss' as a poetic and as a conceptual metaphor, identifying source domains from ancient Mediterranean cosmologies to the Black Atlantic and the relational poetics of Édouard Glissant.

Abyssal lines

For de Sousa Santos, abyssal lines are the inheritors of the amity lines that emerged in the middle of the sixteenth century. Amity lines were actual lines, albeit contested and shifting, drawn on the world map to delineate places where conflict, piracy and violence between European actors would not, ostensibly, affect international treaties or influence diplomatic relations between European states. Described by Mark Netzloff as '[o]ne of the abiding fictions underwriting the history of international law', amity lines 'held an imaginative currency because they served as a moving horizon that could maintain a conceptual boundary separating Europe from its messy entanglements across the globe'.[8] Comparing the amity lines and modern abyssal lines, de Sousa Santos writes:

> The abyssal character of the lines manifests itself in the elaborate cartographic work invested in their definition, in the extreme precision demanded from cartographers, globe makers, and pilots, and in vigilant policing and the harsh punishment of violations. In its modern constitution, the colonial represents not the legal or illegal but rather the lawless. [...] 'Beyond the equator there are no sins'.[9]

In his early work, de Sousa Santos argued that while there are no longer literal lines that delineate places in the world where it is agreed openly that lawlessness may prevail, the 'metaphorical cartography'[10] of such lines remains. As a result, 'modern western thinking' divides 'the human' from 'the sub-human in such a way that human principles are not compromised by inhuman practice'. Examples of these inhuman practices include Guantánamo and 'the savage zones of the mega-cities, in *ghettos*, in sweatshops, in prisons, in the new forms of slavery, in the black market of human organs, in child labour and prostitution'.[11]

These early iterations of abyssal lines represent a pluralistic approach within a socio-legal framework. Later, the concept is expanded theoretically and epistemically to emphasize that realities on the other side of the lines are not just 'made invisible'[12] but actively 'produced as non-existent'.[13] Concomitantly, the definition simplifies into a line that 'marks the radical division between forms of metropolitan sociability and forms of colonial sociability'.[14]

As the scope and definition evolve, de Sousa Santos moves away from the plural, *abyssal lines*, in favour of the singular *abyssal line*,[15] and explicit comparisons between abyssal and amity lines and their cartographies cease to be drawn.[16] My reading of this evolution is that as abyssal lines become less overtly associated with the form of metaphorical cartography associated with literal lines 'that define borders as fences and killing fields, that divide the cities',[17] so *the abyssal line* itself becomes the symbol of a variety of ways that exclusion and oppression manifest. In *Epistemologies of the South*, for example, abyssal *lines* are part of the map, interrelated lines that can be conceptual, epistemic, or temporal. These include 'civil society and the state of nature'; science and 'incomprehensible magical or idolatrous practices';[18] the visible and invisible; the existent and non-existent; and present and past. Together, these cartographic lines combine to produce the predominant division between human and sub-human. Four years later, in *The End of the Cognitive Empire, the abyssal line* itself has come to symbolize the territory that requires mapping: 'The sociology of absences is the cartography of the abyssal line' and its 'official cartographer' is 'the modern archive'.[19] Such is the case for the stick chart and ostrich egg, represented in the modern archive of the Pitt Rivers catalogue primarily as museum objects, while knowledge of the southern relationality of these object's biographies is absent.

As a compound metaphor, the abyssal line is a 'meandering',[20] 'elusive'[21] and 'ghostly presence',[22] frequently described as 'invisible' throughout de Sousa Santos's work.[23] Yet the sense of an ethereal, barely present line coexists with the line's other, fiercer, qualities, such as being 'radical', resilient and persistent. The line is sometimes personified, for example, as the 'collective unconscious of capitalism, colonialism, and patriarchy'. It produces an 'inaudible voice',[24] hides 'behind the mask of liberal ideology and its abstract political ethics',[25] and moves 'insidiously'.[26] It is at the same time a territory to be mapped and is itself 'drawn'[27] on a map or 'inscribed in the lived experience of racialized and sexualized bodies'.[28] Conversely, when she is conducting research, the 'researcher herself is, as it were, a map crossed over by the abyssal line'.[29] Thus, the abyssal line occupies a duality whereby it can both cross and itself be crossed in ways that are 'fatal'.[30] An example, often repeated, is that of a woman 'in a sexist society' who experiences abyssal and non-abyssal exclusions – the latter if she is paid less than her male colleague for the same job, the former if she is a victim of sexual violence,[31] at which point she has crossed the abyssal line 'from the world of metropolitan sociability to the world of colonial sociability, the realm of subhumanity [sic]'.[32] The abyssal line can also be 'witnessed', 'identified', 'made visible', 'confronted' and 'denounced'; 'ignored', 'reproduced' and 'legitimized'; and 'overcome' and 'superseded'.[33]

The abyss metaphor

Metaphors can shape how we think and interact conceptually, materially and relationally. Conceptual metaphor theorists propose that this structuring occurs via our attempts to understand complex, abstract ideas by relating them, through metaphor, to those which are familiar.[34] As a compound metaphor, the abyssal line is based on two simpler metaphors: the line and the abyss.[35] While much has been written in the service of articulating the literal and metaphorical aspects of the line, I suggest that de Sousa Santos introduced the 'abyssal' not as a conceptual metaphor but a poetic one, a linguistic flourish to reinforce his thesis that northern epistemologies render other ways of knowing invisible. I have two reasons to propose this. The first is that the seeds of the abyss metaphor may have been sown at least ten years earlier than the 2006 lecture, in the article 'Depois do dilúvio neoliberal' (After the neoliberal deluge/biblical flood), published in a São Paulo daily newspaper.[36] In this article, de Sousa Santos writes that neoliberalism is reaching exhaustion due to the 'abyssal/abysmal increase in social inequality and exclusion and their effects in democratic governability'. In Portuguese, the words *abissal* and *abysmal* are close synonyms,[37] whereas in English the meanings have diverged, *abysmal* being 'an exceptionally poor standard or quality; extremely bad, appalling' and *abyssal* for the hellish depths, the unfathomable, the oceanographic and the geological.[38] Therefore, when de Sousa Santos uses the term 'abyssal', it is plausible he intended to convey a meaning such as 'especially destructive' akin to the biblical flood, rather than to invoke the abyss with all its associated symbolism in English. Secondly, in previous work, when de Sousa Santos has intended a term to be understood as deliberately, conceptually metaphorical, he identifies it as such; examples include the 'metaphorical cartography' discussed previously, intercultural translation[39] and the metaphorical 'South',[40] which has of course been greatly expanded since 1995 (see the introduction to this volume). It is possible, therefore, that the 'abyssal' is not metaphorical but rather results from its translation from Portuguese to English and might equally be named something like 'destructive' thinking or the 'eradication' line. There is certainly a point to be made here about the dominance of English as an academic language and the importance of thinking carefully about translation when working with concepts originating with speakers of other languages. However, it must also be acknowledged that 'abyssal' thinking and the 'abyssal' line/s have been used conceptually and widely in English for over fifteen years, and bobbing in their wake is all their symbolic baggage packed with chasms, underwater depths, darkness and primordial chaos. Perhaps the translation of 'abyssal' has not yet been scrutinised closely by Anglophone academia precisely because the metaphor does seem to resonate so well, poetically?

The source domain[41] for the abyss that comes most readily to mind for those educated in Northern institutions originated in theology – the Hebrew, Babylonian or Egyptian primordial deep waters that existed before creation;[42] the chaos of early Greek cosmology; or the underworld of Tartarus – and continued as a strong theme throughout western philosophy. In the case of the stick chart and ostrich egg, the symbolism is consistent with de Sousa Santos's arguments on the abyssal line, in that it reinforces the idea that what was known about the objects in their original context, for the object's nineteenth-century collectors at least, was 'incomprehensible', or perhaps their 'utter strangeness' led Dunn and Irmer to deny, consciously or not, the 'very human nature'[43] of the southern people who made and used them. Consequently, these collectors may have had little curiosity about those southern people's lives and their relationships to these objects, which is why this information is now lost to the Pitt Rivers, a northern institution on 'this side' of the line. However, despite its ability to explain the absence of southern knowledge in this way, it must be acknowledged that these source domains are themselves (per de Sousa Santos) abyssal. As Martin Bernal has argued, the discipline 'Classics' has

> incorporated social and cultural patterns in society as a whole and has reflected them back, to provide powerful support for the notion of Europe possessing a categorical superiority over all other continents, which in turn justifies imperialism or neo-colonialism as *missions civilisatrices*.[44]

In addition to the entangled nature of the classical and western philosophical abyss as a source domain, metaphor itself can be 'a technique ultimately of avoidance. Even as it illuminates, it makes the actual disappear'.[45] This is a perspective taken also by Eve Tuck and Wayne Yang in their influential essay 'Decolonization Is Not a Metaphor'.[46] Tuck and Yang's contention is that the realm of the symbolic should not supersede or complicate what is really at stake, which is Indigenous peoples' rights to, and return of, their land, on their own terms[47] and not defined in a settler colonial sense as 'property'. 'Until stolen land is relinquished', they write, 'critical consciousness does not translate into action that disrupts settler colonialism.'[48] It is powerfully symbolic to imagine knowledge of the stick chart and ostrich egg – their makers, caretakers, those who knew how to use them, those who benefited from their use, those who knew their cultural and symbolic meanings, their names, their stories – as simply swallowed by the unfathomable darkness and depth of the abyss. The potential loss of knowledge of these objects and their relations to the lives of southern peoples is not anyone's fault, the metaphor could suggest; rather the loss has happened because of a force beyond human control, the 'abyss' possessing as it does the physical and temporal scale of a geological event. This aspect of the abyss symbolism, therefore, might enable a 'move to innocence', which 'represent[s] [...] fantasies of easier paths to reconciliation' for those within the northern metropole.[49] Conversely, Tapji Garba and Sara-Maria Sorentino have argued that we cannot discount the 'relationship between history and contingency, materiality and the symbolic' in theorizing.[50] Their analysis is of a different colonial practice, slavery, a context in which the abyss metaphor has been used powerfully by writers such as Édouard Glissant, upon which I will now expand.

Lines in the sea

As I have shown in this chapter, abyssal lines are often explained and illustrated using cartographic metaphors to refer to legal and epistemic divisions. As with the 'abyss' in abyssal lines, the mapping metaphor isn't much elaborated, but I want to suggest that the 'representation of spaces'[51] that emerges from de Sousa Santos's cartography is primarily of dry land. In part, this is because land is where the social movements and radical organizations that form the core of his analysis tend to be located. There is some textual evidence as well; for instance, when discussing problems of scale, de Sousa Santos offers representations of 'land use'[52] as an example, and he writes of 'the savage zones of the megacities'.[53] When water is discussed, it is primarily in a context of its significance to the environment, as a subject of political struggle and, occasionally, as a metaphor for, for example, globalization as an 'unstoppable flood'.[54] And yet, the Southern Hemisphere is the watery hemisphere, connecting to the north, too, through water.

Tracing de Sousa Santos's references on the origins of his cartographic thinking in the lines of amity as previously mentioned, as well as the Treaty of Tordesillas between Portugal and Spain, which proposed a line in the Atlantic between the Cape Verde islands and the Caribbean, another reading of abyssal cartography is possible, one with its source in the ocean and the fragmentation of the archipelago, rather than the unity of the continent. For Édouard Glissant, as John Drabinski explains, the Caribbean is at the centre of his thinking, not just because that was his home, but because the Caribbean

> is simultaneously local – hemispheric, specifically historical, particular in its memories – and global – the crossroads of the world, from the beginning. That is, Caribbeanness is *tout-monde*, not as an aesthetic or ethical idea or ideal, but as a direct description of the material histories and memories of the archipelago.[55]

Glissant takes the trauma of the Middle Passage as the source of history, and for him, the abyss represents at the same time a profound sense of loss and, at the shoreline, of beginning.[56] Glissant's conception of the abyss also includes a line: the tracings of slave ships from African countries in the East to the Americas in the West. This line he calls a 'creature' and identifies it as a 'fibril'.[57] Typically, a fibril is part of a biological system, such as a plant root, muscle fibre or protein. Thus, here the 'abyssal line' (a phrase Glissant does not use) does not divide but rather is part of a system of relation.

Connections across oceans with traces of sadness and loss, though incomparable in scale and impact, can also be read into the journeys of the stick chart and ostrich egg. And therefore, I want to suggest that Glissant's concepts of opacity and transparency offer alternative ways of recognizing such 'abyssal' absences. For Glissant, opacity is neither a lack of transparency or translucency nor the obscurity of a difficult text,[58] which is often accompanied by exclusion. Rather, opacity 'is that which cannot be reduced, which is the most perennial guarantee of participation and confluence'.[59] Opacity is, as Drabinski explains, therefore an ontological and epistemological concept, which sustains the 'constant reinvention of not just meaning, but the meaning of meaning'.[60]

Transparency, typically the opposite of opacity, in this case is associated with the verb *grasp* figuratively to attain intellectual mastery over a subject and literally 'the movement of hands that grab their surroundings and bring them back to themselves. A gesture of enclosure if not appropriation'.⁶¹ The desire for transparency then, in Glissant's terms, becomes a demand for formulation, a series of clarifications, in pursuit of a particular kind of Western universality.⁶² And I can't help but notice the parallel in the way the stick chart and ostrich egg were grasped, brought back across the ocean to Oxford and in the process, most of what was known about the people who made and used them was washed away. Seeking to recover lost knowledge about the stick chart and ostrich egg, to answer the questions I have posed throughout this chapter about the lives that once surrounded them, might well, in Glissant's terms, represent yet another gesture of enclosure and appropriation.

So, what can we do with the concept of opacity, when it comes to the lives of, and those surrounding, the stick chart and ostrich egg? Taken literally, the formulation of a *right to* opacity could result in another move to innocence, in this case absolving the northern institution of any obligation towards understanding or restitution on the basis that the waters ought to remain murky. Instead, I suggest that Glissant's work suggests that the loss can be mourned, and that mourning – reading with the frame of melancholy, trauma, memory and traces – like the ocean itself, has its own shape and texture. It is not an absence to be grasped, claimed or filled in.

Conclusion

The stick chart and the ostrich egg are not split, broken or fragmented. Yet both are fragments of the lives that once gave them their different watery purposes: allowing people in southern Africa to carry water and people in the Marshall Islands to navigate between islands in the South Pacific. The stick chart was obtained from Chief Nelu by Dr Georg Irmer, in 1896 then governor of the Marshall Islands, who gave it to the educationalist Sir Graham Balfour, at that time travelling in the Pacific.⁶³ The ostrich egg came into the possession of Edward John Dunn in 1872.⁶⁴ Both objects travelled from the Southern Hemisphere to the Northern, likely by water, washing up on the shore of the Pitt Rivers Museum in Oxford. Balfour gave the stick chart to the Museum in 1897; Dunn donated the Ostrich egg in 1936, where it was left unentered until 2004.

The catalogue entries are also full of fragments, of crossing places. The language, if it can be read as a form of life writing, is dense, coded, staccato. It is shattered by slashes, intruded upon by capital letters and punctuation marks:

'Vessel/Animal Figure/Bird Figure/Food Accessory/CLASS: Vessel/Figure/Food and Drink/?'. and 'Illustrated as Fig. 35 "Marshall Islands stick chart, c. 1896. Pitt Rivers Museum 1897.1.2", p. 79, in Talking Maps, Jerry Brotton & Nick Millea (Oxford: Bodleian Library University of Oxford, 2019).'

It does not have the kind of transparency of clear waters, where there seems to be nothing but air between a boat and its shadow on the riverbed below. Neither does it have the opacity of the iron-grey ocean that keeps its secrets close and its wreckage hidden. If these catalogue entries can be read as a kind of chaotic, melancholic life writing of loss, perhaps they can also be read, as John Drabinski puts it, as a move

> toward the unexpected, but always in terms of contact, entanglement, and engagement. And so, opacity does not imply or enact a fundamental passivity – a term that, as Glissant says of 'seize' and 'grasp', has terrifying resonance in the Americas – but rather, with the consciousness of consciousness secured at the end of the world, a kind of vulnerable activity. Vulnerable, that is, because opacity is open to transformative contact.[65]

Acknowledgements

Thank you to Lucy Allen-Goss and David Mills for thoughtful comments on drafts of this chapter.

Notes

1. For reflections on Pacific navigation, see Epeli Hau'ofa, *We Are the Ocean: Selected Works* (Honolulu: University of Hawaii Press, 2008) and Teresia K. Teaiwa, 'Charting Pacific (Studies) Waters: Evidence of Teaching and Learning', *The Contemporary Pacific* 29, no. 2 (2017): 265–82.
2. For example, the first reference for the stick chart is: Listed on page 491 in 'Appendix 13.1: Documented Stick Charts in Museum Collections, Made before 1940' to 'Nautical Cartography and Traditional Navigation in Oceania' by Ben Finney, in *Cartography in the Traditional African, American, Arctic, Australian, and Pacific Societies* (Volume Two, Book Three of The History of Cartography), ed. David Woodward and G. Malcolm Lewis (Chicago: The University of Chicago Press, 1998), 443–92. The provenance is given as follows: 'Dr. Irmer, governor of the Mrshall [*sic*] Islands, obtained it from Chief Nelu, Jaluit, 1896. Graham Balfour, who traveled [*sic*] in the Pacific in the 1880s and 1890s, presented it to the museum. (Graham Balfour may have been a cousin of Henry Balfour, the museum's first curator.)' A note (note 5, page 492) reads: 'H. Lyons, "The Stick charts of the Marshall Islanders: A Paper Read at the Afternoon Meeting of the Society, 14 May 1928", *Geographical Journal* 72 (1928): 325-8; this item is referenced as 18" x 11".' [JC 26 2 1999].
3. See Laura Peers and Alison K. Brown, *Visiting with the Ancestors: Blackfoot Shirts in Museum Spaces* (Edmonton, AB: Athabasca University Press, 2016); and Alice Stevenson and Dan Hicks, *World Archaeology at the Pitt Rivers Museum: A Characterization* (Oxford: Archaeopress Archaeology, 2013), 2.
4. This is not a new observation. See, for example, Isabelle Parsons, 'Artefacts That Travel: The Changing Contexts and Meanings of Archaeological Objects Collected by Edward J. Dunn', *Southern African Humanities* 25 (2013): 53–63.
5. The lecture was published in 2007 as 'Beyond Abyssal Thinking: From Global Lines to Ecologies of Knowledges', *Review (Fernand Braudel Center)* 30, no. 1 (2007): 45–89, 45.

6. Jairo I. Fúnez-Flores has been researching the genealogy of this term and has attributed its introduction to Raul Pertierra in 1988 in 'The Rationality Problematique: An Anthropological Review of Habermas's "The Theory of Communicative Action" Volume I'. *Social Analysis: The International Journal of Social and Cultural Practice* 23 (1988): 72–88.
7. Field and language information was obtained via a search for 'abyssal line' in the Bodleian library catalogue on 14 April 2023.
8. Mark Netzloff, 'Lines of Amity: The Law of Nations in the Americas', in *Cultures of Diplomacy and Literary Writing in the Early Modern World*, ed. Tracey A. Sowerby and Joanna Craigwood (Oxford: Oxford University Press, 2019), 55, 56.
9. Boaventura de Sousa Santos, 'Beyond Abyssal Thinking', 49; and Boaventura de Sousa Santos, *Epistemologies of the South: Justice against Epistemicide* (London, New York: Routledge, 2016), 121.
10. Santos, 'Beyond Abyssal Thinking', 53; and Santos, *Epistemologies of the South*; Santos, *Decolonising the University: The Challenge of Deep Cognitive Justice* (Newcastle: Cambridge Scholars Publishing, 2018), 124.
11. Santos, 'Beyond Abyssal Thinking', 53 (emphasis in original).
12. See Santos, 'Beyond Abyssal Thinking'; *Epistemologies of the South*; Santos, *The End of the Cognitive Empire: The Coming of Age of Epistemologies of the South* (Durham, NC: Duke University Press, 2018); Santos, 'The Alternative to Utopia Is Myopia', *Politics & Society* 48, no. 4 (2020): 572.
13. Boaventura de Sousa Santos, 'Epistemologies of the South and the Future', *From the European South* 1 (2016): 21. See also Santos, *Decolonising the University*.
14. Santos, 'The Alternative to Utopia Is Myopia', 572.
15. This shift is most apparent between two of the most highly cited books published in English, *Epistemologies of the South* in 2016, in which he uses the singular and plural forms with similar frequency, and *The End of the Cognitive Empire* in 2018, in which he uses the plural once, while the singular appears in the text over a hundred times. This comparison was made on Santos's scholarly books and essays in English between 2007 and 2020 using the text search function in the qualitative analysis software NVivo.
16. He does make reference to the sixteenth century in *The End of the Cognitive Empire*, in a context of tracing capitalism's relationship with colonial domination.
17. Santos, 'Beyond Abyssal Thinking', 57.
18. Santos, *Epistemologies of the South*, 122.
19. Santos, *The End of the Cognitive Empire*, 25, 30 and 198.
20. Santos, *Epistemologies of the South*, 126.
21. Santos, 'Myopia', 754.
22. Santos, *The End of the Cognitive Empire*, 23 and 191.
23. See, for example, Santos, *Epistemologies of the South*, 119 and 120; Santos, *Decolonising the University*, 161 and 372; and Santos, *The End of the Cognitive Empire*, 6, 24, 108 and 128.
24. Santos, *The End of the Cognitive Empire*, 8, 24, 173 and 177.
25. Santos, 'Myopia', 573.
26. Santos, *The End of the Cognitive Empire*, 42; see also Santos, 'Myopia', 583.
27. Santos, *Decolonising the University*, 158 and 372.
28. Santos, 'Myopia', 573.

29. Santos, *The End of the Cognitive Empire*, 173.
30. Santos, 'Myopia', 574; Boaventura de Sousa Santos, 'The Resilience of Abyssal Exclusions in Our Societies: Toward a Post-Abyssal Law', *Tilburg Law Review* 22, no. 1–2 (2017): 251 and 253.
31. There has been very limited engagement in Santos's work thus far about sexual harassment and abuse within 'non-abyssal' settings, such as Northern institutions of higher education. For a discussion of the wider phenomenon, see Erin Pritchard and Delyth Edwards, Sexual Misconduct in Academia: Informing and Ethics of Care in the University (London: Routledge, 2023).
32. See Santos, *The End of the Cognitive Empire*, 23; 'Resilience', 253; Santos, 'Myopia', 574.
33. Santos, *The End of the Cognitive Empire*, 135, 137, 220, 250, 251, 265, 276 and 297; Santos, *Decolonising the University*, 166, 166 and 342; Santos, 'Myopia', 578 and 584.
34. Originating in cognitive linguistics, notably George Lakoff and Mark Johnson, *Metaphors We Live By* (Chicago: Chicago University Press, 1980). More recently, see Raymond W. Gibbs, *Metaphor Wars* (Cambridge: Cambridge University Press, 2017); and Zoltán Kövecses, *Extended Conceptual Metaphor Theory* (Cambridge: Cambridge University Press, 2020). An example supported by ample linguistic evidence is using the metaphor of war to conceptualize arguments.
35. Zoltán Kövecses, *Metaphor in Culture: Universality and Variation* (Cambridge: Cambridge University Press, 2005).
36. Boaventura de Sousa Santos, 'Depois do dilúvio neoliberal', *O Estado de S. Paulo*, 29 September 1996.
37. Thanks are due to Maria Rita Drumond Viana, who located the article in *O Estado de S. Paulo*, brought it to my attention and explained the closer relationship between *abissal* and *abysmal* in Portuguese. All translations to English from Portuguese in this paragraph were by Maria Rita Drumond Viana (2023).
38. Abyss, Noun. *Oxford English Dictionary*, Oxford University Press, July 2023. Available online: https://doi.org/10.1093/OED/1111046421.
39. Santos, *Epistemologies of the South*, 215.
40. Boaventura de Sousa Santos, 'Three Metaphors for a New Conception of Law: The Frontier, the Baroque, and the South', *Law and Society Review* 29, no. 4 (1995): 569–84.
41. Kövecses, *Extended Conceptual Metaphor Theory*.
42. Kathryn Madden, 'Abyss', in *Encyclopedia of Psychology and Religion*, ed. D. A. Leeming, K. Madden and S. Marlan (Boston: Springer, 2010).
43. Santos, *Epistemologies of the South*, 122.
44. Martin Bernal, 'The Image of Ancient Greece as a Tool for Colonialism and European Hegemony', in *Social Construction of the Past*, ed. George C. Bond and Angela Gilliam (London: Routledge, 2020), 119.
45. Deborah Tall, *A Family of Strangers* (Louisville, KY: Sarabande Books, 2006), 85.
46. Eve Tuck and K. Wayne Yang, 'Decolonization Is Not a Metaphor', *Decolonization: Indigeneity, Education & Society* 1, no. 1 (2012): 1–40.
47. A similar debate rages, of course, about the return of museum objects; see, for example, Dan Hicks, *The Brutish Museums: The Benin Bronzes, Colonial Violence and Cultural Restitution* (London: Pluto Press, 2020).

48. Santos, 'Decolonization Is Not a Metaphor', 19.
49. Tuck and Yang discuss a variety of moves to innocence in the settler colonial North American context; different factors may be at play in the Southern African and Micronesian contexts as to how these moves to innocence might be grounded.
50. Tapji Garba and Sara-Maria Sorentino, 'Slavery Is a Metaphor: A Critical Commentary on Eve Tuck and K. Wayne Yang's "Decolonization Is Not a Metaphor"', *Antipode* 52, no. 3 (2020): 11.
51. Santos, *Epistemologies of the South*, 140.
52. Ibid., 142.
53. Ibid., 124.
54. Santos, *Decolonising the University*, 210.
55. John E. Drabinski, *Glissant and the Middle Passage: Philosophy, Beginning, Abyss* (Minneapolis: University of Minnesota Press, 2019), preface.
56. Drabinski, *Glissant and the Middle Passage*, 54.
57. Édouard Glissant, *Poetics of Relation*, trans. Betsy Wing (Ann Arbor: University of Michigan Press, 1997), 5.
58. Glissant's examples of 'difficult texts' are myth or tragedy, which I find supportive of the point made earlier about the relationship of the Western canon to 'abyssal' exclusion.
59. Glissant, *Poetics of Relation*, 191.
60. Drabinski, *Glissant and the Middle Passage*, 13.
61. Glissant, *Poetics of Relation*, 191–2.
62. Édouard Glissant, *Caribbean Discourse: Selected Essays*, trans. J. Michael Dash and Kandioura Dramé (Charlottesville: University Press of Virginia, 1999), 2. Glissant explains in his own footnote on this page, that, much like Santos's metaphoric definition of the South, '[t]he West is not in the West. It is a project, not a place'.
63. Pitt Rivers Museum Catalogue. Oxford: University of Oxford. Item 1897.1.2.
64. Pitt Rivers Museum Catalogue. Oxford: University of Oxford. Item 2004.142.1110.
65. Drabinski, *Glissant and the Middle Passage*, 20.

Bibliography

Bernal, Martin. 'The Image of Ancient Greece as a Tool for Colonialism and European Hegemony'. In *Social Construction of the Past*, edited by George C. Bond and Angela Gilliam, 119–28. London: Routledge, 2020.

Drabinski, John E. *Glissant and the Middle Passage: Philosophy, Beginning, Abyss*. Minneapolis: University of Minnesota Press, 2019.

Garba, Tapji, and Sara-Maria Sorentino. 'Slavery Is a Metaphor: A Critical Commentary on Eve Tuck and K. Wayne Yang's "Decolonization Is Not a Metaphor"'. *Antipode* 52, no. 3 (2020): 764–82.

Gibbs, Raymond W. *Metaphor Wars*. Cambridge: Cambridge University Press, 2017.

Glissant, Édouard. *Caribbean Discourse: Selected Essays*, translated by J. Michael Dash and Kandioura Dramé. Charlottesville: University Press of Virginia, 1999.

Glissant, Édouard. *Poetics of Relation*, translated by Betsy Wing. Ann Arbor: University of Michigan Press, 1997.

Hau'Ofa, Epeli. *We Are the Ocean: Selected Works*. Honolulu: University of Hawaii Press, 2008.
Hicks, Dan. *The Brutish Museums: The Benin Bronzes, Colonial Violence and Cultural Restitution*. London: Pluto Press, 2020.
Kövecses, Zoltán. *Extended Conceptual Metaphor Theory*. Cambridge: Cambridge University Press, 2020.
Kövecses, Zoltán. *Metaphor in Culture: Universality and Variation*. Cambridge: Cambridge University Press, 2005.
Madden, Kathryn. 'Abyss'. In *Encyclopedia of Psychology and Religion*, edited by D. A. Leeming, K. Madden and S. Marlan. Boston: Springer, 2010.
Netzloff, Mark. 'Lines of Amity: The Law of Nations in the Americas'. In *Cultures of Diplomacy and Literary Writing in the Early Modern World*, edited by Tracey A. Sowerby and Joanna Craigwood, 54–68. Oxford: Oxford University Press, 2019.
Peers, Laura, and Alison K. Brown. *Visiting with the Ancestors: Blackfoot Shirts in Museum Spaces*. Edmonton, AB: Athabasca University Press, 2016.
Santos, Boaventura de Sousa, 'The Alternative to Utopia Is Myopia', *Politics & Society* 48, no. 4 (2020): 567–84, 572.
Santos, Boaventura de Sousa. 'Beyond Abyssal Thinking: From Global Lines to Ecologies of Knowledges'. *Review (Fernand Braudel Center)* 30, no. 1 (2007): 45–89.
Santos, Boaventura de Sousa. *Decolonising the University: The Challenge of Deep Cognitive Justice*. Newcastle: Cambridge Scholars Publishing, 2018.
Santos, Boaventura de Sousa. *The End of the Cognitive Empire: The Coming of Age of Epistemologies of the South*. Durham, NC: Duke University Press, 2018.
Santos, Boaventura de Sousa. *Epistemologies of the South: Justice against Epistemicide*. London, New York: Routledge, 2016.
Santos, Boaventura de Sousa. 'Epistemologies of the South and the Future'. *From the European South* 1 (2016): 17–29.
Santos, Boaventura de Sousa. 'The Resilience of Abyssal Exclusions in Our Societies: Toward a Post-Abyssal Law'. *Tilburg Law Review* 22, no. 1–2 (2017): 237–58.
Santos, Boaventura de Sousa. 'Three Metaphors for a New Conception of Law: The Frontier, the Baroque, and the South'. *Law and Society Review* 29, no. 4 (1995): 569–84.
Stevenson, Alice, and Dan Hicks. *World Archaeology at the Pitt Rivers Museum: A Characterization*. Oxford: Archaeopress Archaeology, 2013.
Tall, Deborah. *A Family of Strangers*. Louisville, KY: Sarabande Books, 2006.
Teaiwa, Teresia K. 'Charting Pacific (Studies) Waters: Evidence of Teaching and Learning'. *The Contemporary Pacific* 29, no. 2 (2017): 265–82.
Tuck, Eve, and K. Wayne Yang. 'Decolonization Is Not a Metaphor'. *Decolonization: Indigeneity, Education & Society* 1, no. 1 (2012): 1–40.

CHAPTER 6
MINORITY LIFE IN NIGERIA'S SOUTH-SOUTH: KEN WIWA'S *IN THE SHADOW OF A SAINT*
Obari Gomba

Five years after the Nigerian state executed nine Ogoni activists, including the globally acclaimed writer and environmentalist Ken Saro-Wiwa, his son, Ken Wiwa, published a memoir entitled *In the Shadow of a Saint* (which won the Hurston-Wright Nonfiction Award in 2002). Wiwa was born in Lagos in 1968, raised for a few formative years in Port Harcourt (between 1970 and 1978) and lived for the greater part of his life in London from 1978 to his death in 2016. In January 1978, his father, Saro-Wiwa, had relocated his wife and young children to London, then stayed back in Nigeria and visited his family occasionally.[1] Alienated, the young Wiwa sought to mute the echoes of a distant homeland that had become a turf of discontent. His education deepened his immersion in London, but the politics of his country was too unsettling to allow him to ignore his native land.

After Wiwa's tertiary education at University College London, he served for a while as the Internet editor of the *Guardian*, and his journalism featured in other media outlets. Then, after civilian rule was restored in Nigeria, he returned to the country in 2005 and served as a special assistant or advisor, in one stretch, to three presidents (Olusegun Obasanjo, Umaru Yar'Adua and Goodluck Jonathan). The events that are chronicled in his memoir in focus here occurred before his service in the presidency.

Wiwa's memoir evokes both trauma and posttraumatic growth in response to personal and communal tragedies. The author's family, ethnicity and country are at the centre of his narrative. The immediate provocation for the story is the execution of his father on 10 November 1995, in the oil-city of Port Harcourt, Nigeria, and the aftermath of that event was a long-drawn-out turmoil of both resistance and state-inflicted terror that spread beyond Ogoni to the rest of the Niger Delta region. It played a role in the decision of the state to make certain provisions in its laws.

Citing Ogoni as an example, this chapter examines how Wiwa's life writing has presented the significance and insignificance of tragic minority life in the Niger Delta, a region which is also designated in Nigeria's 1999 Constitution as the south-south, as if to enforce a double *southness*. Although Nigeria is, strictly speaking, not located south of the equator, the ways in which its south-south region is minoritized and/or subjugated, and turned into a site of extraction, relates in critical ways to the marginalization of the south in other geographical contexts that are detailed in this book.

Of Nigeria's thirty-six states, divided into six geo-political zones, the six states between the Old Calabar River and the Benin River cover the same area that was known since colonial times as the Niger Delta. It has been the homeland(s) of diverse ethnic minorities, subject to the operation of both external and internal systems of power since the fifteenth century. It has been a region of ruthless resource extraction (ivory, palm oil, crude oil, etc.); it has suffered mass displacement (via the Slave Trade) and disruption through wars of conquest. Ogoni is one of the ethnic nationalities in this region, and crude oil has been extracted from its land since the 1950s, before Nigeria's self-rule.[2]

As the oil industry grew in the area from the 1950s to the 1990s, and the international oil company, Shell, extracted resources worth billions of dollars, the industrial process destroyed the environment and traditional modes of livelihood. Karl Maier[3] writes that it was against this backdrop that the Movement for the Survival of the Ogoni People (MOSOP) was founded by Ken Saro-Wiwa and his compatriots in 1990 to seek redress and secure development,[4] and to present an Ogoni Bill of Rights, a text of its demands, to the Nigerian state.[5] The movement had expected the state to feel uneasy, but members could not have imagined to what extent it would, in the coming years, exploit internal schism in Ogoni, enforce military occupation, sanction so-called wasting operations, hound thousands into exile, and effect mass incarceration, rape and looting, executing activists on the verdict of a kangaroo tribunal. The Ogoni were truly forced to bear the brunt of the state's anxieties.

To come to terms with the individual and collective trauma that the Nigerian state had inflicted on his family's life, Wiwa found that he had to unearth his father's words. He wrote: 'When I decided to confront my feelings about my father, he had been dead for two years, but in many respects, not least in my mind, he was very much alive.'[6] There was no difference between the essence of his father and his perception of home. He had to latch on to his father's words to be able to understand both patrimony and homeland:

> In one of his letters, he urged me to write, and I took that as my cue. I felt it was my duty to set the record straight about Ken Saro-Wiwa, to expose his critics and accuse his killers. I imagined that this book would be my contribution to the struggle – my opportunity to right the wrongs done to my father and my people.[7]

Home and alienation

On one of Wiwa's few visits to Ogoni in his adult life, he noted the 'oil wells, pipelines and gas flares that have helped to enrich Nigeria but have jeopardized the viability of village communities that once made a simple living from farming and fishing'.[8] This situation was the basis of his people's discontent. It was important for him and his people to understand the contrast between their poverty and the resource that was extracted from their south-south land. His life and his father's life were tied to that knowledge.

To be able to write about himself and his family, he realized that he had to locate his home. At the core of the memoir lie the themes of selfhood, family and community that translated to the local and global circumstances that impacted his and his father's lived experience. So, he wrote: 'My father. Where does he end and where do I begin?'[9] He knew that his nativity represented a continuum even though the restrictions of time and space had jeopardized the filial relationship, and it was ironic that a tragic loss was what had necessitated reevaluation and repair.

In 1978 when Saro-Wiwa moved his wife and young children to London and stayed back in Nigeria,[10] he took a complicated decision to raise a family in a foreign country without living in that country to watch and help with the pressures on the family. It was also paradoxical that he chose to work hard in the Global South to raise the resources that maintained his family in one of the most expensive cosmopolitan cities of the Global North, a classic case of capital flight from the south. His experience of western education in Nigeria had established his faith in education, built his sense of nationalism and appeared to have driven him to conceive Britain as a place for his children's education and upbringing (despite the racism of the time). On the one hand, then, it was a 'prestige project' to place his children in a cosmopolitan city and give them the best education that money could buy, as he liked to put it.[11] But, on the other hand, Saro-Wiwa's decision was an effort to insulate his family from a postcolony that had lost its hope of greatness too soon. In the 1970s, Nigeria's postwar toxicity was obvious, ethnic squabbles and maneuvers were rife, and there were daily provocations for a person like him who had become a target of post-Biafra war animus and was wont to be daring. He understood the difficulties of positioning himself as a leader of the Ogoni. His native land was an exploitable southern minority of minorities, prone to its own divisions and acrimonies.

If the migration of his nuclear family was intended as an escape from the challenges or difficulties of minority life in Nigeria, London presented a different kind of minoritization in that his family became part of a migrant black population. Wiwa remarked that his brother, Gian, was the only other African with him 'out of 150 boys at our boarding school in Derbyshire' and they 'were mercilessly teased at first' just as their 'father had predicted'.[12] It was a dislocation, a challenging experience that Wiwa defined as the loss of the simple joys of his childhood.[13] London was a far from perfect place even though it kept the young children distant from the abrasions of their father's life in Nigeria. The cost was enormous, the goal was clear and the outcome was ironic. The children grew up and got quality education, but they were alienated from their father and their homeland.[14]

The tension of that alienation was most manifest in the relationship between Saro-Wiwa and his first-born son, whom he had been careful to christen after himself. The son's revolt was exemplified by his decision to change his name (from Ken Saro-Wiwa Jr. to Ken Wiwa) to forge an identity of his own. He was a son who had grown up to idolize his father's accomplishment and to resent his father for being more absent than present. He knew his father's success as a writer, cultural icon, astute businessman and community leader, but he wanted him to be *more* of a father to the family than a father to the community. His father's remarkable sacrifices to meet the family's needs paled due to his absence.

But if Wiwa judged his father harshly, his father judged harshly in return, setting high expectations of him.[15] In many ways, he became entangled in his own sort of 'oedipality'. He saw his father through the lens of his mother's matrimonial struggle,[16] a difficult, absent and unfaithful husband who indulged in various affairs. As the oldest child, he became a sharer of his mother's heartbreaks yet carried her pain so deeply that it stood in the way of his relationship with his father. At the same time, his mother activated Wiwa's ethnic commitment in a manner that her husband's paternal authority and entreaties could not do. She was a migrant mother who knew that the heritage of children was in the south of Nigeria regardless of their transplantation to the West. In due course, Wiwa scaled up his activism in support of his father and his people. As he stated, 'I put the active in "activist"', believing that his father 'would have been proud'.[17] He switched from his earlier detachment and resentment to embracing his father's struggle: 'the simplest and most profound truth I have learned is that you can never truly know who you are until you know your father'.[18] The crisis of his father's incarceration and execution brought him to a point of self-evaluation and self-discovery.

The intensity of Wiwa's awakening and involvement was noticed by the obdurate military leaders of Nigeria. Lt. Col. Dauda Komo, the military administrator who oversaw state-sanctioned terror in Ogoni, had dismissed him (Wiwa) as follows: 'Just because he … speaks Queen's English, everyone applauds, but he's just a spoilt child who wouldn't know the way to his own village.'[19] Rattled by his efforts to protect his father's image, the state struck back with bullying tactics, harping on what it interpreted as Wiwa's alienation. Yet it was impossible to dismiss a person who had so fully embraced the cause of his people, who felt it was his 'duty to set the record straight about Ken Saro-Wiwa, to expose his critics and accuse his killers'.[20]

Minority politics, state integration and colonial hangovers

Nigeria's central government is powerful because the country has a federal system that ensures that resource control is vested in the centre. A quasi-unitary state privileges hegemony and accumulation over a fair and just integration of its component units. The ethnic majorities (Hausa-Fulani, Yoruba and Igbo) are all given support by the windfalls of Big Oil. For example, over 80 per cent of the oil wells in the Niger Delta are concessioned to entities from Northern Nigeria. Oilfields and facilities are operated with little regard for the economic wellbeing of host communities, extraction processes constitute sheer industrial nihilism to the detriment of the environment and the state apparatus is a twin to transnational interest.

These postcolonial ethnic hegemonies have their roots in colonialism.[21] The origin of Nigeria, particularly as it pertained to its deltaic south, typified the power of the Global North over the Global South. This was only confirmed during the Nigerian Civil War (1967–70) when Britain supported the Federal side in the interest of controlling 'the vast and largely untapped oilfields'.[22] Or, as Wiwa writes, resource extraction and 'the stew of economically unequal multi-ethnic identities sowed the seeds of the troubles that have plagued Nigeria since its independence in October 1960'.[23] Nigeria, as he also wrote, 'should be God's own country in Africa. Spread over a million square kilometres in West Africa, it is richly endowed with mineral and human resources. It is the sixth-largest producer of crude oil in the world, and it has one of the largest deposits of natural gas.'[24] But there was a stark gap between the availability of resources and the application of resources with poor quality of life, deplorable basic amenities and widespread discontent.[25] Nowhere was this situation more manifest than in oil-producing Ogoni, one more sad example of the petro-cultures of the Global South where extractive industries and governments turn resources to curses. Like his father, he was troubled by 'the oil wells, pipelines, and gas flares that have helped to enrich Nigeria but have jeopardized the viability of village communities'.[26] In truth, Nigeria was not enriched; rather business oligarchies and ethnic behemoths were ruthless in their accumulation of wealth at the expense of the oil-bearing ethnic minorities of the south.

Both Wiwa and his father knew that the actual devolution of power, if the term could be applied in this context, was between ethnic and economic hegemons. They knew that the condition of the southern minorities of the Niger Delta indicated that a combination of state power and foreign businesses from the Global North had created a system of neocolonialism that was both internal and external. It was against that system that the Ogoni people rose to defend their homeland. As Wiwa outlines, his father championed the formation of MOSOP in 1990 as a platform 'to "mobilize the Ogoni people and empower them to protest against the devastation of their environment by Shell, and denigration and dehumanization by Nigeria's military dictators". He had very modest expectations of what he conceived as a non-violent grass-roots organization'.[27] But his huge investment (of courage, intellect, creativity, money, public relations, etc.) in one sense paid off. Ogoni mobilization not only shaped and reshaped Wiwa's family but also impacted on and inspired the narrative of resistance in the deltaic south of Nigeria.

The significance of the Ogoni movement was clear to see: a southern minority dared to confront the abuses of a multinational business and the misgovernance of a postcolonial nation-state. But to do so was to challenge entities that were tied to the patronage and/or profiteering systems of powerful states of the Global North. The movement caught the people's imagination: on 4 January 1993, for example, about three hundred thousand people came out to support one of its protest marches. 'That day', Wiwa comments, 'it was a peaceful demonstration' and 'the Ogoni declared Shell *persona non grata* until it paid rents and cleaned up the environment'.[28] The environment was a key subject because MOSOP realized that 'the incidence of oil spills in Ogoni was one of the highest recorded in the world'.[29] The Ogoni argued that the double standard of the extractive industries of the West, such as Shell, allowed them to operate in the Global South in a manner that they would never do in the Global North. It was the success of that large awakening that sent jitters through the establishment.

For a postcolonial nation-state that was sure of its overarching power, it was usual for the government to dismiss southern minorities as supine and incapable of stirring up a movement. The energy of the Ogoni caused the state and the multinationals to fear that the model of the resistance would inspire other minority nationalities in the south to resist the status quo of exploitation. J. Timothy Hunt[30] noted that the three major oil companies in Port Harcourt urged the military administrator of Rivers State, Lt. Col. Dauda Musa Komo, 'to take urgent measures in Ogoniland'.[31] The result was the formation of a brutal taskforce called the Rivers State Internal Security (RSIS). It was a classic case of how multinational entities, deriving their leverage from the power and clout of their home countries in the Global North, are able to set agendas for governments in the Global South and compel action to secure profit. Ogoni was viewed as a disruptor. It was marked and Saro-Wiwa was marked. The Nigerian regime began to crack down on the people in what resembled a colonial-style military pacification.[32] A postcolonial nation-state visited atrocities on one of its southern minorities because it was sure it would get away with this. The government was methodical and clear about its objective, and resolute in its programme to inflict tragedies and to break the Ogoni resistance totally. Every action was fair as long it was targeted at the people, stretching their resilience and punishing their doggedness.

One of the arrowheads of the onslaught was the head of the RSIS taskforce, Lt. Col. Paul Okuntimo, whose villainy was only matched by his flippancy.[33] The Civil Liberties Organization described Lt. Col. Okuntimo as a psychopath.[34] This point was well-known and was corroborated by Ike Okonta and Oronto Douglas, who had accused Shell of funding criminal military operations in Ogoni.[35] For its part, Shell's spin was constantly shifty, full of outright denials or attempts at obfuscation,[36] a situation that Michael Peel (2009) also observed.[37] Shell is repeatedly depicted in Wiwa's writing as a multinational overlord in cahoots with a military regime, a travesty that placed profit over southern lives, a naked show of might that exploited the military's disregard for the lives of southern minorities. To serve Shell and the Nigerian state, Lt. Col. Okuntimo's RSIS taskforce, as Okonta and Douglas stated, allegedly wrote a secret memo recommending a series of destructive and murderous operations to the military administrator of Rivers State, Lt. Col. Dauda Musa Komo.[38] As Wiwa observes, Lt. Col. Okuntimo 'boasted that he had perfected 221 ways to kill' and had no restraint when he made his chilling recommendations in the memo: 'wasting operations during MOSOP and other gatherings, making constant military presence justifiable' and 'wasting targets to cutting across communities and leadership cadres'.[39] Like Okonta and Douglas, Wiwa implied that the incident in Giokoo on 21 May 1994, which led to the death of four Ogoni chieftains, for which Saro-Wiwa and his compatriots were tried and executed, was the act of the government's taskforce.

As the atrocities in Ogoni escalated, the operation drew condemnation from activists, writers and journalists around the world, but the global system of power did not intervene to bring succour to a suffering people. Until Saro-Wiwa and his compatriots were executed, global power players fell for the convenience of realpolitik. Neither the United States (which had immense leverage as the leading purchaser of Nigeria's oil), nor the United Kingdom (which enjoyed its major stake in Anglo-Dutch Shell), saw the necessity for a more pointed repudiation of the atrocities. Many other countries chose to pussyfoot around the matter until the hangman went to work on 10 November 1995. The decisions to impose a few sanctions on the officers of the Nigerian state and to suspend Nigeria from the Commonwealth (which was meeting in New Zealand at that time) were token actions to massage their international conscience. Shell and the Nigerian state got away with their actions in part because the abuses happened in the south of the country where such things might be said always to have happened. They were also hidden or at least less discoverable. Wiwa's memoir of his father dutifully puts the abuses on record and calls attention to a global system that was wired to fail the south.

In its small corner of the Global South, Ogoni was a minority matter – little or nothing in the eyes of those who wanted Big Oil and Big Government to succeed at their profiteering. The contrived uproar of western states was soon quietened by the wheel of profit. Wiwa comments, 'I realized that the politicians didn't care that my father was dead. All the moral indignation in the world wasn't going to change the fact that Ken Saro-Wiwa was, to them, a minor detail in a bigger picture.'[40] Whether in Nigeria or in the larger world, Saro-Wiwa and his people were treated as expendables 'as long as the oil continued to flow in the right direction and at the right price, as long as the system worked to the advantage of the multinational oil companies and their hired thugs in vicious military regimes'.[41] Wiwa had painfully realized that his father's tragedy had barely troubled the status quo and certainly did not transform it for good. However, even though his posttraumatic growth did not allow him to dwell on personal grief, his coming face to face with his father's legacy in the book led him to see that one seemingly ignorable movement of resistance could ignite the possibilities of future resistance and the hope of eventual victory.

The Ogoni story, as presented by Wiwa, exposes one of the most severe and disturbing narratives of loss from the Global South since the 1990s. The narrative proved that the powerful would stop at nothing to protect their interests, particularly where natural resources were involved. 'Natural resources', to cite Michael Klare, 'are the building blocks of civilization and an essential requirement of daily existence'.[42] We still live in a world that, as Paul Middleton argued, is 'increasingly' dependent 'on cheap energy' and global powers are resolute in their 'desire to control' any 'source of that energy' because energy is 'power'.[43] According to Human Rights Watch (1999), 'politics has become an exercise in organized corruption – a corruption perhaps most spectacularly demonstrated around the oil industry'.[44]

Conclusion

It is significant that Wiwa adopted writing as a strategy against his family trauma and as a means of coming to terms. By telling his story as his father's son, he laid bare the challenges that faced his family and his community in a world where abusive power had upset everything that was secure and yet could get away with it. Seeking catharsis by exposing his family's truth, Wiwa also forged the ability to empathize with other victims of power. For example, through his visit to the children of Steve Biko and Nelson Mandela, he looked for ways of sharing feelings of defeat and triumph. He cites Joe Slovo's letter to his daughter, Gillian Slovo, in which he observed that the 'world would be a poorer place if it was peopled by children whose parents risked nothing in the cause of social justice for fear of personal loss'.[45] Thus, to Wiwa, his life writing became a form of redress, at least at a personal level, as well as a journey into the past to find children whose parents had made sacrifices. It was significant that the journey from South Africa to Myanmar, where he met Aung San Suu Kyi, turned into a mission to bear witness to a pattern of abusive power in the Global South.[46]

Through recounting his experiences of pain, Wiwa found strength and the possibility of healing and growth. Even as he continued to negotiate living with the legacy of a divided and contested Ogoni, he wrote about recovery as much as loss and about life as much as death.[47] His memoir is a son's exploration of his place in his family's turmoil, at the same time as it is also a portrayal of the local and global dimensions of his slain father's life and legacy – a portrait of a key personage who dared to mobilize an ethnic minority against a rentier post-colony, and a host of neocolonial powers masquerading as multinational corporations. Intersecting persons and places north and south across the globe, the memoir depicts the tension and division in a political family and a community pitched against Big Oil and Big Government. But it is also a call to action. While exposing immediate theatres of pain and grief, it celebrates the triumph of the human spirit over the worst impulses of power and in that sense encourages Ogoni and other southern minorities to keep on fighting.

Notes

1. Ken Wiwa, *In the Shadow of a Saint* (Ibadan: Spectrum Books, 2002), 19.
2. Ibid., 62.
3. Karl Maier, *This House Has Fallen: Nigeria in Crisis* (Boulder, CO: Westview Press, 2000).
4. Ibid., 90–1.
5. Wiwa, *Shadow*, 98–9; Ken Saro-Wiwa, *A Month and a Day: A Detention Diary* (Ibadan: Spectrum Books, 1995), 66.
6. Wiwa, *Shadow*, 9.
7. Ibid.
8. Ibid., 28.
9. Ibid., 1.
10. Ibid., 19.
11. Ibid., 16.
12. Ibid., 74.
13. Ibid., 55–8.
14. Ibid., 77.
15. Ibid., 9, 16–22.
16. Ibid., 89, 136.
17. Ibid., 144.
18. Ibid., 13.
19. Ibid., 15.
20. Ibid., 9.

21. Ibid., 35.
22. Ibid., 38.
23. Ibid., 37.
24. Ibid., 4.
25. Ibid.
26. Ibid., 28.
27. Ibid., 6.
28. Ibid.
29. Ibid., 64–5.
30. J. Timothy Hunt, *The Politics of Bones: Dr. Owens Wiwa and the Struggle for Nigeria's Oil* (Toronto: McClelland & Stewart, 2005).
31. Ibid., 168.
32. Wiwa, *Shadow*, 112.
33. Ibid.
34. Civil Liberties Organization, *Annual Report: A CLO Report on the State of Human Rights in Nigeria* (Lagos: Civil Liberties Organization, 1999), 200.
35. Ike Okonta, and Oronto Douglas, *Where Vultures Feast: Shell, Human Rights, and Oil in the Niger Delta* (San Francisco: Sierra Club Books, 2001), 129–37.
36. Wiwa, *Shadow*, 104.
37. Michael Peel, *A Swamp Full of Dollars: Pipelines and Paramilitaries at Nigeria's Oil Frontier* (London: I. B. Tauris & Co., 2009), 161.
38. Okonta and Douglas, *Vultures*, 35–6, 129.
39. Wiwa, *Shadow*, 112.
40. Ibid., 159.
41. Ibid.
42. Michael T. Klare, *Resource Wars: The New Landscape of Global Conflict* (New York: Henry Holt, 2001), 226.
43. Paul Middleton, *The End of Oil: The Gulf, Nigeria and Beyond* (London: Magpie Books, 2007), 5–6.
44. Human Rights Watch, *The Price of Oil*, 6.
45. Wiwa, *Shadow*, 177.
46. Ibid., 209–29.
47. Ibid., 241–52.

Bibliography

Civil Liberties Organization. *Annual Report: A CLO Report on the State of Human Rights in Nigeria*. Lagos: Civil Liberties Organization, 1999.

Human Rights Watch. *The Price of Oil: Corporate Responsibility and Human Rights Violations in Nigeria's Oil Producing Communities*. New York: Human Rights Watch, 1999.

Hunt, J. Timothy. *The Politics of Bones: Dr. Owens Wiwa and the Struggle for Nigeria's Oil*. Toronto: McClelland & Stewart, 2005.

Klare, Michael T. *Resource Wars: The New Landscape of Global Conflict.* New York: Henry Holt, 2001.
Maier, Karl. *This House Has Fallen: Nigeria in Crisis.* Boulder, CO: Westview Press, 2000.
Middleton, Paul. *The End of Oil: The Gulf, Nigeria and Beyond.* London: Magpie Books, 2007.
Okonta, Ike, and Oronto Douglas. *Where Vultures Feast: Shell, Human Rights, and Oil in the Niger Delta.* San Francisco: Sierra Club Books, 2001.
Peel, Michael. *A Swamp Full of Dollars: Pipelines and Paramilitaries at Nigeria's Oil Frontier.* London: I. B. Tauris & Co., 2009.
Saro-Wiwa, Ken. *A Month and a Day: A Detention Diary.* Ibadan: Spectrum Books, 1995.
Wiwa, Ken. *In the Shadow of a Saint.* Ibadan: Spectrum Books, 2002.

CHAPTER 7
SOUTHWARDS FROM THE NORTHEAST
Archie Davies

This chapter thinks with southern lives from the Northeast – the Brazilian Northeast. I want to argue that following the lifepaths of intellectuals can help us see how geographical categories – like the south – come into being in relation to individual biographies. I therefore explore the relationship between the Brazilian Northeast, three intellectuals' lives and their changing spatial conceptualizations of that unique southern region. Thinking biographically, we can track the emergence of geographical and spatial categories, and by untangling the imbrications between the geographies of lives and the geographies of ideas we can enrich our understanding of spatial thinking itself. During their lives, Josué de Castro (1908–73), Milton Santos (1926–2001) and Beatriz Nascimento (1942–95) moved southwards, outwards and back to the Northeast in imaginary, intellectual and physical terms. Their movements suggest different ways of thinking southern-ness, placing an emphasis on the south as multiple and political, and as an orientation, not as a place. Remembering Doreen Massey's notion of space as a 'simultaneity of stories-so-far',[1] we can see how life stories, and individual spatial imaginaries, inform and shape geographical writing. In this way, by following the idea of the Brazilian Northeast through these three intellectual lives, we can see 'the south' in nuanced and relational terms.

The Northeast: a particular kind of south

The south, in Argentine Mexican philosopher Enrique Dussel's terms, is an 'epistemological location'. It is the location 'of the victims, the south of the planet, the oppressed, the excluded, new popular movements, ancestral people colonized by Modernity, by globalized capitalism'.[2] In this context, the Brazilian Northeast is an overdetermined southern space. The Northeast is south of its former European colonial metropole: for centuries, as the Captaincy of Pernambuco under the Portuguese empire, it was the most important space of imperial extraction in Brazil, with its slavocratic cotton, coffee and sugar economy. After independence, the Northeast was freshly inserted into ongoing neocolonial dimensions of dependency in the capitalist world system, but it also became an internal colony, metaphorically south of the Brazilian metropolitan centre of the Centro-Sul and São Paulo. These economic-spatial relations have profound political-spatial correlates. As discussed below, before the military coup of 1964, the Northeast was the hotbed of alternative, anti-imperialist visions of national development, and it remains a vital progressive region in Brazil. It was the leftist regional redoubt which made possible the national defeat of Jair Bolsonaro in 2022's Brazilian election.[3] Anyone who sat into the evening watching the votes file in during the tense second round will have a visceral sense of how, without the Northeast, Brazil would have continued to be dominated by autocratic forces.

The Northeast exists as a paradox within Brazilian national identity: it is described both as the archetypal, most Brazilian of regions,[4] and as the nation's most deprived, unequal region.[5] On the one hand it is a space of recurrent material crisis – of drought and persistent inequality[6] – and on the other hand it is an elusive symbol of an imagined Brazil.[7] As a real and imaginary geography, the Northeast is overdetermined by ideas of environmental crisis, uneven development and the ongoing legacies of extractive plantation economies, primitive accumulation and slavery.[8] The Northeast is both in the Southern Hemisphere and in the tropics. It is both oceanic and continental. It is not a stable or legible spatial category but rather one that crumbles and reformulates as it is used to different ends. It is what the Brazilian geographer Rogério Haesbaert calls an 'arte-fact', 'always with the hyphen in place', always in the entanglement between fact, artifice and political instrument.[9] Haesbaert's concept, like many spatial analyses of the region, can be read as a theorization of space itself, as well as of that particular, political, historical and geographical parcelization of space that is 'the region'. It is not incidental that Haesbaert's postdoctoral mentor was another key thinker of space, Doreen Massey, for whom analyzing the scale of the region (in her case, principally the Southeast of the UK) was a crucial precursor to theorizing space. Thinking about the south from the Northeast does away with any fixed geometric logic in south-ness and reemphasizes the relational qualities of space. Places are only south *of* something that is north of them. The meaning of south is necessarily directional: it only accrues spatial meaning through its relationship with other places. The Northeast, therefore, is a particular kind of south, and Northeastern lives are particular kinds of Southern Hemisphere lives.

Three Northeastern Lives

All born and raised in the Northeast, Josué de Castro, Milton Santos and Beatriz Nascimento were intellectuals with distinctively spatial concerns. Today, we can read them as radical, anticolonial geographers, who offer us new conceptual tools for understanding not only their own region but also space itself.[10] Each came to be intimately associated with the Northeast for political and intellectual reasons. Each proposed very different relational understandings of the Northeast, through distinct kinds of spatial analysis. Their lives wove through the Northeast, and the Northeast was woven through their intellectual praxis. We can trace a relationship between the spatial formulations in their writing and the trajectories, orientations and movements of their lives. Specifically, I want to emphasize their moves southwards, to argue that there is a connection between this orientation and the scalar shifts in their spatial thinking.

At different moments in their lives, Milton Santos, Josué de Castro and Beatriz Nascimento all moved south to the metropoles of Rio de Janeiro and São Paulo.

This movement was a vital precursor to their becoming increasingly global in their practice and analysis. More specifically, they each carried the Northeast into wider scales of practice and theory, into the international (Josué de Castro), the global geography of underdevelopment (Milton Santos) and transatlantic Black space (Beatriz Nascimento). In the links between their physical movements, and their spatial thinking, we can connect *bio*graphy and *geo*graphy; southern lives and life writing.

By seeing their movements as shifting orientations, we can understand the south not as a situation but as a lived set of relations. This means configuring our understanding of southern lives not as located in a fixed geographical space (*the* south) but as involving differential kinds of southern movements, beginning from the coastal Northeast of Brazil, positions southwardness as a movement towards centrality. The south in Brazil is a hegemonic, even colonial, metropole, and it is a condition of possibility for the global and for transnational solidarity. In this section I want to trace the movements of these three intellectuals.

Josué de Castro

Castro was born in 1908 in Recife. He qualified as a doctor, and began to practice in Recife, where he opened the first nutritional clinic in Brazil. In 1932, he wrote his first book, *Conditions of Life of the Working Classes of Recife*, exposing endemic hunger in the city. In the 1940s, he moved to Rio de Janeiro, and after working as a nutritionist, he turned towards geography as a methodology to understand hunger. In 1946 he wrote his masterpiece, *Geografia da Fome* (Geography of Hunger). That book focussed on Brazil, with an emphasis on the national spatial distribution of hunger, beginning from endemic hunger in the Northeast. After assiduously building his international networks, in 1952 he became president of the Council UN's Food and Agriculture Organization, working in Rome and Geneva and becoming an international diplomat. Around the same time, he wrote a book analyzing hunger at a global scale, *Geopolítica da Fome* (Geopolitics of Hunger; but translated into English, confusingly, as *The Geography of Hunger*). As a leading leftist intellectual and political figure, he was exiled in 1964 after the military coup in Brazil. He moved to Paris, where he was a professor of geography at the experimental University of Vincennes until his death in 1973.[11]

Castro's first movement from the capital of the Northeast to the capital of the nation shifted his geographical concerns into new terms, but the Northeast remained a central spatial category in his writing throughout his life. The movement southwards enabled his turn to the international, but he wrote, in 1964, that:

> Travelling all over the world, and seeking always to refresh my spirit with currents of thought that flow in all directions [...] I never stopped feeling like a provincial, with spirit and sentiment impregnated with the substance of the earth of the province[....] It is always possible, scraping back the superficial crust of appearances, to see appearing this same substance, that is made up of the human landscape of the Northeast.[12]

Life Writing and the Southern Hemisphere

I want to draw attention to the affective qualities of Castro's writing. The landscape of the Northeast constitutes an emotional, personal aesthetic world, as well as an analytical category and a sphere of action. Working inside the UN institutions, Castro carried the scale of the Northeast with him, to enact a scalar politics which unsettled the nation state as the key referential category to the international and posited instead that alternate relationships between the global and the regional should be at the centre of international concerns. Working at Vincennes in Paris, in the heart of the European New Left, he insisted on the primacy of thinking geographically beginning from the landscapes, favelas and marginal communities of Brazil and the Third World. When living in both Rio and outside Brazil, he continued to create and maintain regional anti-hunger NGOs and engaged in regional political struggles not because they were subordinate to a national political project but because the Northeast was itself a sphere of action, with direct international meanings and consequences.

Milton Santos

Milton Santos was born in Bahia, in 1926. He came from a middle-class Afro-Brazilian family and studied law at the University of Bahia in Salvador before becoming a geography teacher, a journalist and newspaper editor. In the late 1950s, Santos wrote his doctorate on geography at the University of Strasbourg before returning to Bahia and becoming heavily involved in radical regional politics. During the early 1960s, the Northeast of Brazil was a hotbed of political thinking and activity marked by emergent visions of national and regional economic planning, critical development studies and an alignment with Third Worldist liberation movements.[13] Santos – like Josué de Castro – was right in the middle of this, working as president of the Economic Planning Commission of Bahia and as an important operative for the progressive Brazilian president, Jânio Quadros in Salvador.[14]

After the coup of 1964, Santos was arrested, imprisoned and then forced to leave Brazil. He took up an itinerant, exilic academic life, working in Bordeaux, Caracas, Paris, Toronto, and elsewhere. In the 1970s, he went to work at the University of Dar es Salaam, during a period of intense intellectual activity in the country under the socialist government of Julius Nyerere. The city was a hubbub of intellectual radicalism and a centre for anti-colonial movements across East Africa, from FRELIMO to ZANU-PF and the anti-apartheid movement in South Africa. The university hosted many radical scholars at this time, including Walter Rodney. Santos returned to Brazil in 1977 to finally embed himself in the country's intellectual life. Based in São Paulo until his death in 2001, he became the most influential geographer in Brazil and a nationally prominent black public intellectual. In São Paulo he consolidated his major intellectual achievement, a Marxist-oriented theory of the ontology of space, and methodology for critical geography. But he consistently returned to the Northeast as a category of thought, whether explicitly, writing about the city of Salvador, or implicitly, writing about underdevelopment, poverty and Third World geographies.[15]

Santos defined space iteratively and dialectically, moving between empirical research, methodological reflexivity and spatial conceptualization in a constant process of re-articulation. One of the pivots for his understanding was a conceptualization of space as a system of objects and a system of actions. He expanded on this framework in various ways, cumulatively incorporating new elements into his theory of space. In particular, this involved an iterative development of the concept of socio-spatial formation.[16] This concept, as Ina Elias de Castro has argued, is deeply linked to the idea of the region.[17] As one element of this – a topic too broad for this chapter – we can point to the centrality of a critique of the idea of the mode of production for Santos's work. If there is one mode of production that Santos analyzed more than any other, it was precisely that of the Northeast. Santos's early books all focussed on the Northeast. His first book was *The Settlement of Bahia: Its Economic Causes* (1948), a study of the population of Bahia, followed by *Regional Studies and the Future of Geography* (1953), *Cocoa Zone* (1957), *Studies on the Geography of Bahia* (1958), *The City as Centre of the Region* (1959) and *The Centre of the City of Salvador* (1959). Underpinning his trajectory towards a theory of the nature of space, therefore, was the groundwork of a long body of work on the regional geography of the Northeast, as well as a formative experience in the practical terrain of radical regional economic planning.

After Santos's exile in 1964, his scalar analysis shifted. His first book published after the military coup was *The City in Underdeveloped Countries* (1965), which was followed by a series of works on the Third World and underdevelopment, the beginning of an engagement with international networks of scholars and his imbrication with the history of anglophone geographical ideas.[18] To some extent, of course, this is completely unsurprising: the movement outwards coinciding with a shift towards a more global sphere of concern. What I want to emphasize, though, is how the space of the Northeast – in material, emotional, political and historical terms – continued to underpin Santos's works and reappears in new forms through his spatial theory not only as a socio-economic category and as a spatial imaginary but also as a lived, affective point of reference.

In a 1995 essay to celebrate the work of the economist Celso Furtado – himself a significant political and economic interpreter of the Northeast and its place in the nation – Milton Santos reflected on the legacy of the notion of the region that circulated in the early 1960s in Brazil:

> In that time, when it was still possible to create a viable non-market discourse, the idea of [Northeastern] territoriality as identity strengthened. It lasts until today as a seed for our thought and our action; a seed for our anguish, but also for our hope.[19]

Santos's reminiscence takes us back to his own practice in the Northeast but also to the wider context of a radical moment in the history of the Northeast. Furtado, like Josué de Castro, was involved in the same circles of left governments and radical technocrats as Milton Santos, all attempting in various ways to intervene in the Northeast to challenge inequality and break cycles of underdevelopment. The US-endorsed military coup of 1964 was, not least, a response to these regional efforts. What are most relevant, here, though, are the affective qualities of Santos's imaginary of the Northeast. His relationship with the arte-fact of the Northeast is as *angústia*, anguish and *esperança*, hope. Much more than a cold spatial extension, the Northeast is an emotional space of the intellect and a freighted and expressive category. As for Josué de Castro, this freight was amplified, doubtlessly, by Santos's own experience of exile.

Beatriz Nascimento

Beatriz Nascimento was born in 1942 in Sergipe, in the Northeast. Her family settled in Rio when she was seven. The presence of Sergipe was strong not only in her domestic world but also in the suburban worlds of Rio de Janeiro, which housed thousands of Northeastern migrants, largely Black and *mestiço*. After studying at the Federal University of Fluminense, Nascimento became a key organizer in the black student movement, conducted research on the history of Black people in Brazil, and wrote poetry, essays and cultural criticism. She was murdered in 1995 while defending a friend from an abusive partner.

Across her work, she developed a spatio-political conception of *quilombo* – communities of escaped enslaved people – as a figure for Black liberation, culture and politics. For Nascimento, a transatlantic Black identity was a question of orientations: towards Africa, developed during her research in Angola, towards *quilombos* in Brazil, and historically towards Palmares, the most important *quilombo* in Brazilian history, deep in the Northeastern *sertão*. While her theorization of *quilombo* went far beyond the Northeast, the regional form and regional history were vital to her thinking. Situated in the contemporary Northeastern state of Alagoas, Palmares was a *quilombo* established in 1605. A quasi-state as well as a site of liberation and resistance, Palmares survived for nearly a hundred years and remains a critical point of reference for Black Brazilian political thought. Nascimento visited the site of the *quilombo* during her lifetime and was involved in making the history of Palmares, and its leader Zumbi, central to the politics of Black Brazilian political organization in the second half of the twentieth century. She also analyzed the *quilombo's* historical formation and made an innovative critique of Brazilian historiography and its understanding of the history of Black people in Brazil.[20] This intervention was intimately tied to the Northeast: a large portion of her master's thesis, for instance, took the form of an analysis of the history of the Antonio Conselheiro movement in the Northeast and its intersection with the spatial economies and ethnic make-up of past and present *quilombos*.[21] The Northeast, for Nascimento, served at least two kinds of interconnected spatial imaginary. On the one hand, as described by her daughter Bethânia Gomes, it referred to an atmosphere of Black urban life, revolving around music, spiritual territories, family and joyful modes and memories of collective life.[22] On the other hand, it referred to the complex and multi-faceted forms that historical *quilombos* had taken up in Brazil. Both of these spatial imaginaries had direct connections with African spatial forms, in terms of both the movement of the African *kilombo* into the Brazilian *quilombo*[23] and the contemporary Black Brazilian forms of African spirituality and sociality.

As with Josué de Castro and Milton Santos, the Northeast remained a crucial intellectual, spiritual and personal territory for Beatriz Nascimento. In an unpublished fragment, reflecting on the death of her grandmother, she wrote:

> The truth is that I am a Black girl from Sergipe, moved by so many transmigrations, so many uprootings. I am always seeking an ungrounded territory. A *quilombo* where I know some ancestor of mine lived.

This movement of exile and uprooting is, of course, an essential dynamic in any historical geography of Blackness in the Americas. Nascimento's spatial imaginary takes her away from idealizing sites of escape or authenticity, to turn instead towards the possibilities of a newly 'ungrounded territory'. Such a territory is both material and imaginary. It is a historical continuity drawn out of the histories of *quilombos*:

> To be a descendant of the quilombos of Sergipe is to feel the tragic dimension of the loss of land while at the same time living surrounded by that land, in search of the point where this story was broken.[24]

The spatial process here is distinctively Northeastern as much as it is distinctively Afro-Brazilian. The 'tragic dimension' at work is not, at first remove, the forced transmigration and trauma of enslavement but rather the 'loss of land' of the *quilombo*: settlements which were relentlessly targeted and oppressed by the colonial state before and after the establishment of the Brazilian republic. Nascimento therefore operates through a speculative resettlement of territory: she stages a re-origination for an Afro-Brazilian historical sense of place *inside* the continental space of Brazil. This *quilombo* space is always in dialogue with another, anterior dis-location across the Atlantic, but it is a new kind of continuation, and it has a practical, quotidian history. The history of *quilombo* that Nascimento identifies was not limited to the Northeast, but the place of that region in the history of *quilombo* is originary and essential. Beatriz Nascimento writes of being the 'descendant of the *quilombos of Sergipe*' [emphasis added], not just of *quilombolas*. The Nascimento family's movement southwards to Rio de Janeiro was a dislocation that hundreds of thousands of other Northeasterners undertook throughout the twentieth century. The Northeast was a vital pool of both labour and surplus populations in the development of modern Brazilian capitalism. Its people were forced by drought, loss of land, economic dependency and state policy to seek work in the major cities of the centre south. Nascimento's interpretation of this latest migration – an internal form of exile – is to place it in a continuous line of movement, which generates a continuous search, as she put it elsewhere, for a new existential and physical territory.[25]

Life Writing and the Southern Hemisphere

Life stories

Following Castro, Nascimento and Santos moving in and out of the region, and reconceptualizing the Northeast as they did so, offers some suggestions for articulating the links between thinking about the Northeast as a region and thinking about the south as a spatial category. Remembering Doreen Massey's notion of space as a 'simultaneity of stories so far',[26] we can see how space in the Northeast and the south are both temporal and narrative conditions. Here I want to connect southern lives with southern landscapes, not in terms of particular or stereotypical landscapes of the Southern Hemisphere but in terms of landscape as memory, identity, experience and subjective historicity of place. In this sense, we can read Massey's 'stories so far' as also, and importantly, life stories. When Josué de Castro was a child, he sat and watched the Capibaribe, the river that flows through Recife:

> the river whispered to me in its sweet language as it timorously passed through the green-gray backlands [...] For hours I would sit motionless at the quay, listening to the story of the river [...] It was the river that first taught me the history of the northeast, the history of this land that almost lacks a history.[27]

Here we can see Castro's own spatial imaginary of the Northeast in the story told by its landscape. This recalls how, for Beatriz Nascimento, the loss of land is understood as the breaking of a story. For both Northeasterners, the spatiality of the Northeast is both telluric and aquatic, both historical and experiential. Nascimento speaks of the colour of the earth and continuously returns to the Atlantic and the litoral, while Castro's sense of an interconnected urban and regional identity is intimately associated with the mud of Recife's mangroves.[28] As much as landscape is made up of memory, it is also salty to the taste and gritty to the touch. Story and materiality come together: the region, like the south, is an arte-fact that is imagined, produced and put to work for distinctive political and cultural ends.

From these three lives we can draw out distinct kinds of Northeast spatiality. For Beatriz Nascimento, the Northeast is part of a transatlantic black space, configured through *quilombo*, spirituality and embodiment, captured most intensely in moments of trance, and through spiritual dislocations within *candomblé*.[29] For Josué de Castro, the Northeast is both a continental space tied to geographies of hunger and underdevelopment as well as a personal territory of action, memory and identity. For Milton Santos, the Northeast is a crucial spatial underpinning of a systematic interpretation of economic geography and the production of space.

We can read and interpret distinctive Northeastern geographical imaginaries in different ways in these three writers. They are configured in relation to particular geographical elsewheres: internally towards a continental Brazilian geography of the *sertão*; south towards hegemonic, colonial elites in Rio and São Paulo; north towards Europe, imperialism and dependency; coastally towards the Caribbean; and transcontinentally towards a black spatiality articulated with West Africa. These are all geographical ideas which Santos, de Castro and Nascimento explore and interrogate not just *as* Northeastern ideas but also as the coordinates for rethinking geographical epistemologies of space, nature and race. These, then, are the coordinates of Northeastern southern lives.

Conclusion

A biographical approach to the history of geographical ideas means following the mobile and undetermined relationships between space, social relations and knowledge production which are embodied in the unpredictable routes of a person's life. Whether in terms of the associations between Castro's work on the Northeast and his conceptualization of underdevelopment, between Santos's work on Salvador and his conceptualization of urban informality and economic geography, or between Nascimento's relationship with Sergipe and her conception of a transatlantic Black spatiality, the development of geographical categories is intimately connected to the lifepaths of these scholars.

This mobile approach draws on Edward Said's idea of travelling theory and Donna Haraway's concept of situated knowledges.[30] Bringing these two together suggests that while objectivity is situated, it is also mobile. If spatial ideas come from places, they also come from people's movement between and across places. Knowledge does not only come from somewhere, but it moves, and movement is part of the essence of ideas, not merely something that follows from them. Attending to the lifepaths of southern intellectuals helps emphasize the necessarily mobile and translated qualities of geographical categories such as the Northeast, or the south. Sometimes, the stories and histories of geographical ideas need to be told through the intimate, quotidian details of lived lives.

For these intellectuals, the movement southwards was a process of crossing scales. Going south from Sergipe, Bahia and Pernambuco to Rio and São Paulo meant opening towards the nation, the Atlantic or the global. Their individual trajectories allowed them to conceptualize the Northeast as a space of inequality, underdevelopment and racism but also as a space of potential for new forms of political action, geographical knowledge and liberation. They came to see the Northeast as a relational spatial category with global meanings. In these three scholars, we find less a Global *South* as a kind of spatial metaphor for underdevelopment and coloniality than a Global *Northeast*, a relational geographical category, rich with multi-scalar, personal and political meaning, and open to change and contestation. For each of these three thinkers, their own life trajectories, which took them through around and out of southern spaces, informed how they understood space itself. Our interpretations of their writings on underdevelopment, race and the production of space are enriched by understanding the mobile lives which lay beneath their intellectual production and the enduring significance of their spatial imaginaries of the Brazilian Northeast.

Notes

1. Doreen Massey, *For Space* (London: SAGE, 2005), 9.
2. Enrique Dussel, *Politics of Liberation: A Critical World History*, trans. Thia Cooper (London: SCM Press, 2011), 549–50.
3. Federico Acosta Rainis, 'Brazil Election: How Lula Won the Runoff, from São Paulo to the North-east', *Guardian*, 1 November 2022. Available online: https://www.theguardian.com/world/2022/nov/01/brazil-election-how-lula-won-the-runoff-from-sao-paulo-to-the-north-east.
4. Francisco Julião, *Cambão – The Yoke: The Hidden Face of Brazil* (Harmondsworth: Penguin Books, 1972).
5. Celso Furtado, *Diagnosis of the Brazilian Crisis* (Berkeley and Los Angeles: University of California Press, 1965).
6. Josué de Castro, *Death in the Northeast: Poverty and Revolution in the Northeast of Brazil*, 1st ed. (New York: Random House, 1966).
7. Durval Muniz de Albuquerque Jr, *The Invention of the Brazilian Northeast* (Durham, NC and London: Duke University Press, 1999).
8. Archie Davies, *A World Without Hunger: Josué de Castro and the History of Geography*, Chapter 5 (Liverpool: Liverpool University Press, 2022).
9. Rogério Haesbaert, 'Região, regionalização e regionalidade: questões contemporâneas (Region, Regionalization and Regionality: Contemporary Questions)', *ANTARES: Letras e Humanidades* no. 3 (2010): 2–24.
10. Methodologically, my relationship with these three lives is different. I have written a kind of intellectual biography of Josué de Castro, translated one of Milton Santos's books, and translated and edited Beatriz's work, in collaboration with Christen Smith and Nascimento's daughter Bethânia Gomes.
11. Archie Davies, *A World Without Hunger: Josué de Castro and the History of Geography* (Liverpool: Liverpool University Press, 2022).
12. Josué de Castro, *Documentário do nordeste* (Documentary of the Northeast), 2nd ed. (São Paulo: Editôra Brasiliense, 1959), 7–8.
13. Federico Ferretti and Breno Viotto Pedrosa, 'Inventing Critical Development: A Brazilian Geographer and His Northern Networks', *Transactions of the Institute of British Geographers*, 2 May 2018. Available online: https://doi.org/10.1111/tran.12241.
14. Breno Viotto Pedrosa, 'O périplo do exílio de Milton Santos e a formação de sua rede de cooperação (The Long Journey of Milton Santos's Exile and the Formation of His Network of Cooperation)', *História, Ciências, Saúde-Manguinhos* 25, no. 2 (June 2018): 429–48. Available online: https://doi.org/10.1590/s0104-59702018000200008.
15. Milton Santos, *Pobreza urbana* (São Paulo: Universidade de São Paulo, 2013).
16. Milton Santos, 'Society and Space: Social Formation as Theory and Method', trans. Stephen Slaner, *Antipode* 9, no. 1 (1977): 3–13.
17. Ines E. de Castro, 'A região como problema para Milton Santos (The Region as a Problem for Milton Santos)', *Scripta Nova. Revista Electrónica de Geografía y Ciencias Sociales* vi, no. 124 (September 2002). Available online: http://www.ub.edu/geocrit/sn/sn-124e.htm.
18. Milton Santos, *For a New Geography* (Minneapolis: University of Minnesota Press, 2021).
19. Milton Santos, 'O Futuro do nordeste: da racionalidade à contrafinalidade (The Future of the Northeast: From Rationality to Counter-Finality)', in *Era da Esperança: Teoria e Política*

No Pensamento de Celso Furtado, ed. Francisco de Sales Gaudencio and Marcos Formiga (Rio de Janeiro: Paz e Terra, 1995), 100.
20. See Beatriz Nascimento, 'For a History of Black People', in *The Dialectic Is in the Sea: The Black Radical Thought of Beatriz Nascimento* (Princeton; Oxford: Princeton University Press, 2023).
21. See 'The Antônio Conselheiro Movement and Abolitionism: A Vision of Regional History', in Nascimento, *The Dialectic Is in the Sea*.
22. See 'On Beatriz Nascimento: A Conversation between Bethânia Gomes, Christen Smith, and Archie Davies', in Nascimento, *The Dialectic Is in the Sea*.
23. See the concept of quilombo and Black cultural resistance in Christen Smith, Archie Davies and Bethânia Gomes, '"In Front of the World": Translating Beatriz Nascimento', *Antipode* 53, no. 1 (January 2021): 279–316. Available online: https://doi.org/10.1111/anti.12690.
24. 'The First Great Loss: Grandma's Death', in Nascimento, *The Dialectic Is in the Sea: The Black Radical Thought of Beatriz Nascimento*.
25. Smith, Davies and Gomes, '"In Front of the World"'.
26. Massey, *For Space*, 9.
27. Josué de Castro, *Of Men and Crabs*, trans. Susan Henterlendy, 1st ed. (New York: Vanguard Press, 1970), xviii.
28. Archie Davies, 'Landscape Semaphore: Seeing Mud and Mangroves in the Brazilian Northeast', *Transactions of the Institute of British Geographers* 46, no. 3 (September 2021): 626–41. Available online: https://doi.org/10.1111/tran.12449.
29. Christen Anne Smith, 'Towards a Black Feminist Model of Black Atlantic Liberation: Remembering Beatriz Nascimento', *Meridians* 14, no. 2 (2016): 71–87. Available online: https://doi.org/10.2979/meridians.14.2.06.
30. Edward Said, 'Traveling Theory Reconsidered', in *Reflections on Exile and Other Essays* (London: Granta, 2001), 436–52; Donna Haraway, 'Situated Knowledge: The Science Question in Feminism as a Site of Discourse on the Privilege of Partial Perspective', *Feminist Studies* 14 (1998): 575–99.

Bibliography

Albuquerque, Durval Muniz de, Jr. *The Invention of the Brazilian Northeast*. Durham, NC and London: Duke University Press, 1999.

de Castro, Ines E. 'A região como problema para Milton Santos (The Region as a Problem for Milton Santos)'. *Scripta Nova. Revista Electrónica de Geografía y Ciencias Sociales* vi, no. 124 (September 2002). Available online: http://www.ub.edu/geocrit/sn/sn-124e.htm.

de Castro, Josué. *Death in the Northeast: Poverty and Revolution in the Northeast of Brazil*, 1st ed. New York: Random House, 1966.

de Castro, Josué. *Documentário do nordeste* (Documentary of the Northeast), 2nd ed. São Paulo: Editôra Brasiliense, 1959.

De Castro, Josué. *Of Men and Crabs*, trans. Susan Henterlendy, 1st ed. New York: Vanguard Press, 1970.

Davies, Archie. 'Landscape Semaphore: Seeing Mud and Mangroves in the Brazilian Northeast'. *Transactions of the Institute of British Geographers* 46, no. 3 (September 2021): 626–41. Available online: https://doi.org/10.1111/tran.12449.

Davies, Archie. *A World Without Hunger: Josué de Castro and the History of Geography*. Liverpool: Liverpool University Press, 2022.

Dussel, Enrique. *Politics of Liberation: A Critical World History*, translated by Thia Cooper. London: SCM Press, 2011.

Ferretti, Federico, and Breno Viotto Pedrosa. 'Inventing Critical Development: A Brazilian Geographer and His Northern Networks'. *Transactions of the Institute of British Geographers*, 2 May 2018. Available online: https://doi.org/10.1111/tran.12241.

Furtado, Celso. *Diagnosis of the Brazilian Crisis*. Berkeley and Los Angeles: University of California Press, 1965.

Haesbaert, Rogério. 'Região, regionalização e regionalidade: questões contemporâneas (Region, Regionalization and Regionality: Contemporary Questions)'. ANTARES: *Letras e Humanidades* no. 3 (2010): 2–24.

Haraway, Donna. 'Situated Knowledge: The Science Question in Feminism as a Site of Discourse on the Privilege of Partial Perspective', *Feminist Studies* 14 (1998): 575–99.

Julião, Francisco. *Cambão – The Yoke: The Hidden Face of Brazil*. Harmondsworth: Penguin Books, 1972.

Massey, Doreen. *For Space*. London: SAGE, 2005.

Nascimento, Beatriz. *The Dialectic Is in the Sea: The Black Radical Thought of Beatriz Nascimento*. Princeton; Oxford: Princeton University Press, 2023.

Pedrosa, Breno Viotto. 'O périplo do exílio de Milton Santos e a formação de sua rede de cooperação (The Long Journey of Milton Santos's Exile and the Formation of His Network of Cooperation)'. *História, Ciências, Saúde-Manguinhos* 25, no. 2 (June 2018): 429–48. Available online: https://doi.org/10.1590/s0104-59702018000200008.

Rainis, Federico Acosta. 'Brazil Election: How Lula Won the Runoff, from São Paulo to the Northeast'. *Guardian*, 1 November 2022. Available online: https://www.theguardian.com/world/2022/nov/01/brazil-election-how-lula-won-the-runoff-from-sao-paulo-to-the-north-east.

Said, Edward, 'Traveling Theory Reconsidered'. In *Reflections on Exile and Other Essays*. London: Granta, 2001.

Santos, Milton. *For a New Geography*. Minneapolis: University of Minnesota Press, 2021.

Santos, Milton. 'O futuro do nordeste: da racionalidade à contrafinalidade (The Future of the Northeast: From Rationality to Counter-Finality)', in *Era Da Esperança: Teoria e Política No Pensamento de Celso Furtado*, edited by Francisco de Sales Gaudencio and Marcos Formiga, 99–107. Rio de Janeiro: Paz e Terra, 1995.

Santos, Milton. *Pobreza Urbana*. São Paulo: Universidade de São Paulo, 2013.

Santos, Milton. 'Society and Space: Social Formation as Theory and Method', translated by Stephen Slaner. *Antipode* 9, no. 1 (1977): 3–13.

Smith, Christen Anne. 'Towards a Black Feminist Model of Black Atlantic Liberation: Remembering Beatriz Nascimento'. *Meridians* 14, no. 2 (2016): 71–87. Available online: https://doi.org/10.2979/meridians.14.2.06.

Smith, Christen Anne, Archie Davies, and Bethânia Gomes. '"In Front of the World": Translating Beatriz Nascimento'. *Antipode* 53, no. 1 (January 2021): 279–316. Available online: https://doi.org/10.1111/anti.12690.

CHAPTER 8
THE SOUTH AS A CONTINUOUS SPACE
Pablo Wainschenker

For many years, the South Polar Regions have been perceived in the popular imagination as bizarre, distant locales. They are disjointed from the known world as if there were a gap, an almost insurmountable wall of water between Antarctica and the rest of the planet. This assumption is rooted in ancient traditions and has influenced classic works of fiction including Edgar Allan Poe's *The Narrative of Arthur Gordon Pym of Nantucket*, a dystopic novel about a journey to the South Pole and the encounter with its imagined inhabitants, first published in 1838.

Against the classic perspective that puts Antarctica as an isolated area of the world, my recent work with Elizabeth Leane has focused on representations of the South Polar regions in writings from South America's Southern Cone. This has pointed to an alternative narrative in fiction that to date has been little researched, which presents the Drake Passage as a connector between South America and Antarctica.[1] Through the analysis of three fiction works by Liborio Justo,[2] Francisco Coloane[3] and Roberto Fontanarrosa,[4] this study has shown that South America's Antarctic fiction challenges the Anglocentric view of the Antarctic space. Even though the stories analyzed there are widely disparate – ranging from a heroic tale of Chilean nationalism (Coloane), to a satirical and, at times, absurd re-creation of Argentina's early history (Fontanarrosa) – they share a sense of geographic proximity between southern Patagonia and the Antarctic Peninsula. However, the representations of a continuous multinational southern environment encompassing Tierra del Fuego, the Islas Malvinas/Falkland Islands, South Georgia and beyond can be contentious politically. First, the idea goes against the image of a motherland with neatly demarcated borders, where the national government acts as the custodian of the territory and oversees human movements, as Argentine authorities in the first decades of the nineteenth century wished to achieve.[5] Second, it is incompatible with the establishment of Antarctic sovereignty claims.[6]

In this chapter, I extend previous work on the spatial relationship between Argentina and the South Polar regions, focussing here on Argentine non-fiction. The discussion will explore the features of the spatial imagination about Antarctica that originates in that South American country, concentrating on a representative group of authors. In doing this, I do not mean to exhaust spatial perspectives on Antarctica, the Southern Ocean and South America, but I do want to probe whether Argentine life writing presents the icy continent as a disjointed region, separated from the rest of the world, or whether it offers alternative views. After describing the European perspective on the South Polar regions as an isolated environment, I look by contrast at the relationship between the south of South America and the Southern Ocean as it emerges in Argentine non-fiction.

Life Writing and the Southern Hemisphere

The South Polar regions in the European tradition

The physical features of the South Polar regions lend themselves to their construction as an isolated realm. Unlike their northern counterpart – composed of the relatively small and shallow Arctic Ocean, which is surrounded by the inhabited continental masses of North America and Eurasia – Antarctica is a vast uninhabited continent encircled by the Southern Ocean, a mass of water that reaches depths of over 7,000 metres. The sea around the icy continent undergoes regular low-pressure systems that can create waves as high as twenty metres and a continuous east-to-west circumpolar current encompasses the continent. The Antarctic Polar Front creates a natural barrier between the cold and dense waters around the continent and the warmer northern waters, which are not only more temperate and less dense but also saltier and less oxygenated (and hence, harbour life forms different from those found further south).[7]

Fiction written in English in the nineteenth century draws on the idea of the southernmost regions of planet Earth as distant, otherworldly areas cut off from the rest of the globe by the sea. In the well-studied Antarctic novel of Edgar Allan Poe, *Narrative of Arthur Gordon Pym of Nantucket*, the Southern Ocean lies between the known world and mystery. While the beginning of the journey features classic elements of oceanic environments such as winds and waves, as the ship moves closer to the South Pole, the sea takes on more sinister overtones. At one point, Pym and his colleagues pick up from the water the carcass of a strange short-legged beast armed with scarlet claws and teeth, silky hair and a head resembling that of a cat with canine ears.[8] The finding marks the passage from the familiar north to the alien south. When Pym and his colleagues land on an Antarctic island the following day, this transition is apparent: 'At every step we took inland the conviction forced itself upon us that we were in a country differing essentially from any hitherto visited by civilized men.'[9] The Southern Ocean separates two unmatchable worlds.

Roughly until the mid-twentieth century, such representations of the South Polar Regions in fiction written in the English language often constructed Antarctica as a sealed-off environment plagued by danger. This is neatly encapsulated in Howard Phillips Lovecraft's *At the Mountains of Madness* (first published in 1936 and inspired by Poe):

> That seething, half-luminous cloud-background held ineffable suggestions of a vague, ethereal beyondness far more than terrestrially spatial; and gave appalling reminders of the utter remoteness, separateness, desolation, and aeon-long death of this untrodden and unfathomed austral world.[10]

Spatial representations of the icy continent are not exempt from geopolitical implications. Ignacio Cardone notes that depicting Antarctica as a remote, separated continent (what he calls *Continental Antarctica*) harmonized with British aspiration to integrate the Antarctic Peninsula region into the UK's overseas territories in the 1920s. As no man's land, the continent was 'the last frontier for exploration and colonization'.[11]

Yet, on the other hand, as he argues, emphasizing the connectedness between the frozen continent and its surroundings (the *Hemispheric Antarctica*), in both Argentina and Chile, contributed to the establishment of a sense of belonging, favouring these countries' sovereignty claims over roughly the same area claimed by the UK.[12] In narrative, though, the spatial imagination was not necessarily tied to territorial ambitions. Sergio Piñero's *El puñal de Orión* (Orion's Dagger), published in 1925, presents the Southern Ocean as a spatial continuation of the Argentine pampas and simultaneously naturalizes British hegemony over the same space.[13] Although the coexistence of spatial connections decoupled from nationalism could be seen as incongruous (see Pedro Luis Barcia's study *La literatura antártica argentina*), it constitutes a fundamental feature of Piñero's and other authors' work.[14] And this is what we might come to expect. Rather than being exceptional, contradictions are engrained in Antarctic narratives.[15]

Antarctica's geopolitical connections with regions and events further north became apparent during the Cold War. At the time, the overlapping sovereignty claims of Argentina, Chile and the United Kingdom over the Antarctic Peninsula were a source of grave concern for the US government since those three countries were US allies (and hence a confrontation among them would benefit the Soviet Union).[16] After testing different ideas in search of a peaceful solution, in 1959 the US hosted a diplomatic conference that led to the signing of the Antarctic Treaty in Washington.

Later on, environmental anxieties added another layer of connectedness between Antarctica and its surrounding area. Elizabeth Leane notes that in fiction, during the last decades of the twentieth-century, action-thrillers and eco-thrillers about the region became dominant, fuelled by environmental concerns. These works transmit and magnify some of the tensions around Antarctica and its place in the world order.[17]

The Southern Cone tradition: A controversial image

The nineteenth-century emergence of literature of and about Argentina was shaped by the development of travel writing in English, German and other European languages. In his work on the influence of English travellers on early Argentine literature, Adolfo Prieto notes that, between 1820 and 1835 alone, at least fourteen English authors published accounts of their journeys across this South American country.[18] The role of these narratives in Argentine literature is evident in the works of local writers, who often used the style, descriptions and perspectives of European texts in their own texts.[19] Sometimes, English authors influenced their Argentine counterparts even beyond literary production. Analyzing the life and works of Esteban Echeverría – a key Argentine author who penned the seminal epic poem *La cautiva* (The Captive) in 1837 – José Luis Lanuza contends that Echeverría not only was inspired by Byron's writing but even aspired to become a 'Byronian' character himself.[20]

More relevant here than the general spell of English literature on Argentine writers is the more specific influence of British and European narratives on the spatial representations of Argentina by local authors. A repeated image in those European texts is that of the pampas as an extension of the sea. Enrique Williams Álzaga traces this analogy back to the mid-1700s when, in a letter to his brother Angelino, Italian Jesuit Carlo Gervasoni described the journey from Buenos Aires across the pampas as a maritime undertaking:

> I will inform you about our navigation across the land. You would use the same expression if you saw the immense fields that extend boundlessly from Buenos Aires to Córdoba and Tucumán, where I am currently, thank God, safe and sound. [...] I said 'navigation' mainly for two reasons: first, because during our one-month journey, we have not seen a single mound or a hill [...]. They are all low fields, resembling an ocean. [...] The second reason why I said 'navigation' is that before setting out it is necessary to make the same provisions as if you were going to travel by sea. Thus, before leaving Buenos Aires we provided ourselves with what was necessary for the entire journey, that is, bread, biscuits, eggs, salted fish, a good quantity of cattle [...].[21]

In the same vein, in a narrative of his journey to South America, first published between 1814 and 1825, Alexander von Humboldt resorts to the ocean to describe his travels through Venezuela:

> The monotony of these steppes is imposing, sad and oppressive. Everything appears motionless; only now and then from a distance does the shadow of a small cloud promising rain move across the sky. The first glimpse of the plains is no less surprising than that of the Andean chain. It is hard to get accustomed to the views on the Venezuelan and Casanare plains, or to the pampas of Buenos Aires and the Chaco when, for twenty to thirty days without stopping, you feel you are on the surface of an ocean.[22]

In Argentina, the analogy between the pampas and the sea also shows in the work of local writers. In a narrative of his expedition to *Sierra de la Ventana* published in 1837, Captain Pedro Andrés García notes:

> Such is the admirable effect of these works of nature, in the middle of a seemingly endless pampa, and such is the surprise that they provoke in the observer when he sees them for the first time at a distance in a desert country; similar to an ocean, in which he wanders like a ship, with no more help than that provided by chance![23]

García's likening of the pampas to the ocean resonates with other contemporary Argentine narratives. In *Memoria descriptiva sobre Tucumán*, an account of his journey to Argentina's north-west, first published in 1834, Juan Bautista Alberdi acknowledges the influence of British captain Joseph Andrews's report of a voyage to the same region entitled *Journey from Buenos Aires* and published a few years before.[24] Adolfo Prieto notes that, despite being born in the region he was visiting, Alberdi imitates Andrews's perspective as a foreigner traveller.[25] More important here, however, is that Alberdi also borrows from the British author his descriptions of the pampas as an ocean. Although he had never seen the sea, the Argentine writer presents the area where Tucumán was found as follows: 'Standing on the edge of the elevation on which the village is situated, one sees beneath one's feet a vast, bluish ocean of woods and meadows stretching eastwards as far as the eye can see.'[26]

In his analysis of the travel narratives of Colonel Pedro García – written during the advances of Argentina's army across the pampas as part of the political and economic expansion of capitalism at the beginning of the 1800s – Néstor Cremonte argues that the appealing image of a boundless landscape where people could move and settle to their hearts' content was, in practice, a nightmarish burden for new landowners and rural authorities. At the time, the nascent government in Buenos Aires was engaged in a war with Patagonia's native population with the goal of appropriating their land, plotting it for future exploitation and extending governance. The rise of agriculture and livestock farming – mainly cows and sheep – as export commodities, demanded control over and monitoring of land, cattle and people across a vast area where the government's reach was weak or non-existent. Free movement hampered the consolidation of landowners as a hegemonic group while it threatened the power of the developing Argentine state as a competent authority in rural areas.[27] Hence, although extending a sense of familiarity to contested areas lends itself to nationalist discourse, at the same time it thwarts ambitions of territorial control.

Life writing at the end of the world: An unexpected friendship

With the increase of expeditions from Buenos Aires to South Georgia and Antarctica during the first decades of the twentieth century, a new spatial perspective arises in Argentine narratives. The idea of a continuous space comprising Tierra del Fuego, the Malvinas/Falklands archipelago, South Georgia, the Southern Ocean and Antarctica lies in the background of works written then but little known today. For example, Sergio Piñero's *El puñal de Orión* (Orion's Dagger) (1925) narrates a journey from Buenos Aires to the Argentine *Base Orcadas* (South Orkney Station) on Laurie Island, Antarctica, including a stop in the whaling factory *Compañía Argentina de Pesca* in Grytviken, South Georgia, where he takes part in the activities of Norwegian whalers and meets with the British governor.[28]

Unlike the unspecific oceanic references employed by authors in the 1820s to describe the expanse of inland South America as if it were a sea ('It was Byron's Sea, muse of the Romantic', says Lanuza),[29] in the 1920s Piñero flips the relationship, presenting the Southern Ocean as a mass of water that resembles the Argentine pampas. In some cases, the sea is constructed as a horse 'that jumps over the ship with the agility of an equestrian contest',[30] leaving the vessel powerless as a piece of flotsam. At other times, the likeness does not come from the ocean itself but from those who wander about its waters:

I scan the horizon and it is impossible for me to distinguish the announced whale. Meanwhile, Larsen has seen that there are five, altogether sailing towards us. And, what is more, he has singled out the one that will yield the most profits. He is a gaucho in between his aquatic roundup.[31]

These types of references constructing the Southern Ocean as a familiar place of the pampas, abound in *El puñal de Orión*. At the same time, Piñero does not conceal the fact that South Georgia, considered by Argentina part of its domains, is under British rule. Not himself speaking any English, he describes a hilarious encounter with the British governor in Gryviken, for whom Spanish was not a familiar language. The experience starts when the governor takes Piñero to shore from the ship *Guardia Nacional*:

His boat is nervous like those ponies from our childhood. Adding insult to injury, it hiccups or maybe it stutters, for its exhaust isn't regular. Be that as it may, we resolve in unison to steer with the oars. And at that time, I notice the surprising affinity that binds me to the governor.[32]

Continuing to the end of the day, the narrative encounter condenses the harmonious coexistence of spatial familiarity and lack of nationalism that pervades the whole book.

Ice, water lilies and teasels

Between the 1950s and the 1990s, there is an upsurge of narratives that focus on the presence of Argentina's military in Antarctica and the value of the icy continent not so much as one more element in a bigger spatial continuum but as a far corner of the motherland that needs to be occupied. Emilio Díaz's *Relatos antárticos* (Antarctic Narratives) published in 1958, *Antártida, mi hogar* (Antarctica, my Home) by José María T. Vaca (1962) and *Un viaje a las montañas blancas* (A Journey to the White Mountains) by Ángel Mafezzini (1986), are three of these types of Antarctic non-fiction narratives that carry strong nationalist and heroic undertones. Unlike the stories penned by Liborio Justo, Francisco Coloane and Roberto Fontanarrosa mentioned at the beginning of this chapter,[33] most of these other works follow a pattern in which personal sacrifice, dedication to service and commitment to national goals are the main priority.

A dissentient contemporary approach is that of Alberto Soria in *La vida en la Antártida* (Life in Antarctica), a narrative about his stay in Argentina's *Base Melchior* (Melchior Station) in 1952.[34] Against the backdrop of a national expedition, *La vida en la Antártida* focuses on Soria's personal encounter with Antarctic space and on his efforts to watch over the emotional well-being of the overwintering crew. Relevant here is Soria's likening of the Antarctic icescape to features of Argentina's environment. Describing the round pieces of sea ice known in English as pancake ice, he notes: 'The small pieces of ice that remain adrift, due to mutual and constant friction, become rounded and raise their edges, like the leaves of the irupé.'[35] He also finds familiar elements on land around the station: 'On calm, very cold nights, the flakes form needles that stick to wires and icicles like metal particles attracted by magnets. They cover them from top to bottom, reminding us of the teasels of our plains with their straight sticks full of thorns.'[36]

More recently, other non-fiction works have also focused on Antarctic space. Federico Bianchini's *Antártida: 25 días encerrado en el hielo* (Antarctica: 25 Days Locked Up in the Ice) compares Antarctica with life further north, but for very different reasons than Soria's:

> Before coming to Antarctica, I was asked several times if I was not afraid of isolation. However, what I long for now is loneliness. Here, one is in contact with more people than in Buenos Aires. Every morning after waking up, I greet sixty people. Every night, before I fall asleep, again. At home, I kiss my girlfriend during breakfast, exchange a few words with the bus driver who takes me to work, spend hours reading a computer screen, and have lunch with four or five colleagues. If I have any meetings, at the end of the day, hopefully, I may have interacted with fifteen people. In the heart of the city, within a radius of eight kilometres.[37]

Bianchini's sense of confinement in Argentina's Marambio station resonates with the diaries of the photographer Adriana Lestido. In *Antártida negra: los diarios* (Black Antarctica: The Diaries), she describes her days in Antarctica as 'the closest situation to being in jail I have gone through'.[38] She records repeatedly the anguish she feels due to the lack of privacy 'sharing a room with six more people in a military base'.[39]

Contrasting with Northern Hemisphere traditions in which the South Polar regions are isolated from civilization, in our work with Elizabeth Leane we have shown that fiction narratives from Argentina and Chile present a sense of continuity between southern South America and Antarctica. These narratives are not necessarily tied to patriotism, nor are they completely detached from English writing.

In this chapter, I have focused on a selection of southern life writing works from an Argentine perspective, published from the beginning of the 1900s to the present, to probe whether the assumptions of Antarctica as an inverted space held true to them. Drawing on previous scholarship on the influence of British writers in nineteenth-century Argentine literature, I have demonstrated here that the engagement of Argentine authors with the south reveals a sense of closeness between the regions north and south of the Drake Passage. Instead of equating the South with ideas of inversion and disconnection, the southern life writing texts discussed here show, to varying degrees, a pattern of connectedness between southern Patagonia, Tierra del Fuego, the Southern Ocean and Antarctica. While in the texts published in the twentieth century, this sense of continuity draws on metaphors likening the southern landscape to the Argentine pampas on a positive note (as in the aforementioned descriptions by Soria), later works equate Antarctica with rather unpleasant elements of life in Argentina (see, for example, Lestido's parallel between the cramped conditions in an overcrowded Antarctic station with the situation in Argentine prisons).[40] Either as a southern version of a bucolic scene from the Pampas, a gelid stronghold of national consciousness or an unwelcoming and uninhabited backyard, in southern life writing from Argentina, the south is anything but an isolated and inverted space.

Notes

1. Pablo Wainschenker and E. Leane. 'The "Alien" Next Door: Antarctica in South American Fiction', *The Polar Journal* 9, no. 2 (2019): 324–39.
2. Lobodón Garra, 'La borrasca', in *La tierra maldita. Relatos bravíos de la Patagonia salvaje y de los mares australes*, 1st ed. (Buenos Aires: Editorial Cabaut y Cía., 1932): 145–54.
3. Francisco Coloane, *Los conquistadores de la Antártida*, 1st ed. (Santiago de Chile: Zig-Zag, 1945).
4. Roberto Fontanarrosa, 'La Carga de Membrillares', in *El mundo ha vivido equivocado y otros cuentos*, 11th ed. (Buenos Aires: Ediciones de la Flor, 1988), 38–40.
5. Néstor Cremonte. 'Un coronel ilustrado hacia las tierras yermas del sur', in *Viaje y relato en Latinoamérica*, ed. Mónica Marinone and Gabriela Tineo (Buenos Aires: Ediciones Katatay, 2010), 220–1.
6. Argentina and Chile made formalized claims over the Antarctic Peninsula in the 1940s – which, in turn, overlap with British ambitions over the same territories.
7. Joy McCann, *Wild Sea: A History of the Southern Ocean* (Chicago: University of Chicago Press, 2020).
8. 'We also picked up a bush, full of red berries, like those of the hawthorn, and the carcass of a singular-looking land animal. It was three feet in length, and but six inches in height, with four very short legs, the feet armed with long claws of a brilliant scarlet, and resembling coral in substance. The body was covered with a straight silky hair, perfectly white. The tail was peaked like that of a rat, and about a foot and a half long. The head resembled a cat's with the exception of the ears – these were flapped like the ears of a dog. The teeth were of the same brilliant scarlet as the claws.' In Edgar Allan Poe, *The Narrative of Arthur Gordon Pym of Nantucket* (Bungay, Suffolk: Penguin Books, 1975), 188–9.
9. Ibid., 195.
10. Howard Phillips Lovecraft, *At the Mountains of Madness and Other Tales of Terror* (New York: Del Rey, 2007), 30.
11. Ignacio Cardone, 'The Continental, the Hemispheric and the Global Antarctica: Southern Perspectives of Climate Change and the Governance of Antarctica', *The Polar Journal* 12, no. 1 (2022): 70.
12. Ibid., 67 and 71.
13. Sergio Piñero, *El puñal de Orión* (Buenos Aires: Proa, 1925), 171–5.
14. Pedro L. Barcia, *La literatura antártica argentina. Estudio y antología* (Buenos Aires: Academia Argentina de Letras, 2013).
15. Discussing Antarctic fiction, Elizabeth Leane contends that 'Ultimately, perhaps, the fascination of Antarctica lies in its contradictions: it is a place of compressed time and extended time; haunted by monsters from the past and threatened by its own prophesies of the future; ancient and primeval, but forever young, pristine and wrinkle-free.' Leane's list of Antarctic contradictions could probably be expanded. The narratives of Piñero and others show that Antarctica can also be proximate and alien. Elizabeth Leane, *Antarctica in Fiction: Imaginative Narratives of the Far South* (Cambridge: Cambridge University Press, 2012), 179.

16. Adrian J. Howkins, *Frozen Empires: An Environmental History of the Antarctic Peninsula* (Oxford: Oxford University Press, 2017), 15.

17. Elizabeth Leane, 'Yesterday's Tomorrows and Tomorrow's Yesterdays: Utopian Literary Visions of Antarctic Futures', *The Polar Journal* 3, no. 2 (2013): 339–40.

18. These include Francis Head's *Rough Notes Taken during Some Rapid Journeys across the Pampas and among the Andes* (London: John Murray, 1826); J. A. B. Beaumont's *Travels in Buenos Ayres, and the Adjacent Provinces of the Rio de la Plata, with Observations Intended for the Use of Persons Who Contemplate Emigrating to That City; or Embarking Capital in Its Affairs* (London: James Ridgway, 1828); Alexander Caldcleugh's *Travels in South America during the Years 1819-20-21. Containing an Account of the Present State of Brazil, Buenos Ayres, and Chile*. 2 vols. (London: John Murray, 1825); H. M. Brackenridge's *Voyage to Buenos Ayres Performed in the Years 1817 and 1818 by Order of American Government* (London: Sir Richard Phillips, 1820); John Miller's *Memoirs of General Miller in the Service of the Republic of Peru* (London: Longman, Rees, Orne, Brown & Green, 1828) and more. For a comprehensive list, see Kristine Jone's study 'Nineteenth-century British Travel Accounts of Argentina', *Ethnohistory* 33, no. 2 (1986): 195–211.

19. There is an extensive body of scholarly literature on the contribution of British narratives to the representations of Argentina, including the studies by Leila Gómez (*Iluminados y tránsfugas*), Jean Franco ('Un viaje poco romántico') and Santo Samuel Trifilo (*La Argentina vista por viajeros ingleses*).

20. José Luis Lanuza, *Esteban Echeverría y sus amigos* (Buenos Aires: Raigal, 1951): 15, 33, 37.

21. Here, and elsewhere throughout this chapter unless otherwise stated, the translation from Spanish is mine. The original letter by Gervasoni quoted here was translated from Italian to Spanish by Mario J. Buschiazzo and included in Enrique Álzaga's *La pampa en la novela argentina*, 1st ed. (Buenos Aires: Ángel Estrada, 1955): 35–6.

22. Alexander von Humboldt, *Personal Narrative* [of a journey to the equinoctial regions of the new continent] (London: Penguin Books, 1995), 162.

23. This excerpt from García's account is taken from Adolfo Prieto, *Los viajeros ingleses y la emergencia de la literatura argentina, 1820-1850* (Buenos Aires: Sudamericana, 1996), 25 (footnote 14).

24. Juan Bautista Alberdi, *Memoria descriptiva sobre Tucumán* (Buenos Aires: Libertad, 1834). The excerpts mentioned here are taken from Prieto, *Los viajeros ingleses*. The British account mentioned by Alberdi is Joseph Andrews, *Journey from Buenos Ayres, through the Provinces of Cordova, Tucuman, and Salta, to Potosi, thence by the Deserts of Caranja to Arica, and Subsequently, to Santiago de Chili and Coquimbo, Undertaken on Behalf of the Chilian and Peruvian Mining Association in the Years 1825-26* (London: John Murray, 1827).

25. Prieto, *Los viajeros ingleses*, 101.

26. Ibid. Alberdi was not the only local writer in Argentina who replicated the spatial perspectives of European travellers and acknowledged this influence explicitly. Having descriptions penned by foreign explorers was very useful for local authors since most Argentine writers in the nineteenth century had never been to the places they depicted. In addition, the readership was very small at the time. According to the national census of 1869, out of a total population of 1,736,923, illiteracy reached at least 1,000,000 people throughout the country. Among the merchants, illiteracy reached 50 per cent. In Buenos Aires, 77 per cent of the workers could not read (data from Alejandro Eujanian and Alejandro Cattaruzza. 'Del éxito popular a la canonización estatal del Martín Fierro: tradiciones en pugna (1870-1940)'. In *Prismas-Revista de historia intelectual* 6, no.1 (2002): 102).

27. Cremonte, 'Un coronel ilustrado', 220.
28. The book was based on articles previously published in *La Razón* – a leading newspaper of the era – but was never reprinted. In the early 1930s, the chapter about the journey from South Georgia to Argentina's meteorological observatory on the South Orkney Islands in Antarctica was included in *Hojas Sueltas*, a schoolbook for the fifth and sixth grades by Elvira Rawson de de la Serna, y Laura S. Solari (52–58).
29. Lanuza, *Esteban Echeverría*, 37.
30. Piñero, *El puñal*, 40. The pampas, those wide and grassy plains stretching as far as the eye can see, have a special place in Argentina's national imagination. In literature, the image of a *gaucho* (a mostly illiterate man living in rural areas) riding a horse across the pampas is typical of the *gauchesca*, a literary genre that thrived from the 1870s to the 1920s. Horses, gauchos and pampas were also present in the fine arts, including the drawings and paintings of Florencio Molina Campos and other *Costumbrismo* artists.
31. Ibid., 143.
32. Ibid., 172.
33. Wainschenker and Leane, 'The "Alien" Next Door'.
34. Alberto A. Soria, *La vida en la Antártida* (Buenos Aires: Editorial Guillermo Kraft, 1954).
35. Ibid., 229. The irupé, or water platter (*Nymphaeaceae* spp.), is a species of water lilies native to South America and common in north-east Argentina.
36. Ibid., 184.
37. Federico Bianchini, *Antártida: 25 días encerrado en el hielo* (Buenos Aires: Tusquets Editores, 2016), 89.
38. Adriana Lestido, *Antártida negra: los diarios* (Buenos Aires: Tusquets Editores, 2017), 117.
39. Ibid., 70.
40. Ibid., 51 and 117. Lestido's likening of Argentina's Deception Station to a prison is significant since she has a deep understanding of life in prisons. Her own father served time in jail when she was a child, and in the early 1990s she regularly attended a female prison in La Plata to produce a photographic essay later published as *Mujeres Presas* (Women in prison).

Bibliography

Alberdi, Juan Bautista. *Memoria descriptiva sobre Tucumán*. Imprenta de la libertad 1834. Available online: http://www.jstor.org/stable/60234296.

Barcia, Pedro L. *La literatura antártica argentina. Estudio y antología*. Buenos Aires: Academia Argentina de Letras, 2013.

Bianchini, Federico. *Antártida: 25 días encerrado en el hielo*. Buenos Aires: Tusquets Editores, 2016.

Cardone, Ignacio. 'The Continental, the Hemispheric and the Global Antarctica: Southern Perspectives of Climate Change and the Governance of Antarctica'. *The Polar Journal* 12, no. 1 (2022): 62–87.

Coloane, Francisco. *Los conquistadores de la Antártida*. Santiago de Chile: Zig-Zag, 1945.

Cremonte, Néstor. 'Un coronel ilustrado hacia las tierras yermas del sur'. In *Viaje y relato en Latinoamérica*, edited by Mónica Marinone and Gabriela Tineo, 215–35. Buenos Aires: Ediciones Katatay, 2010.

De la Serna, Elvira Rawson de y Laura S. Solari. *Hojas Sueltas. Lecturas para 5° y 6° grados*. Buenos Aires: Isely & Cía, 1933. Facsimile retrieved from Biblioteca Nacional de Maestros. Available online: http://www.bnm.me.gov.ar/giga1/libros/00022231/00022231.pdf.

Díaz, Emilio Luis. *Relatos antárticos*. Buenos Aires: Editorial Losada, 1958.

Fontanarrosa, Roberto. 'La Carga de Membrillares'. In *El mundo ha vivido equivocado y otros cuentos*, 11th ed., 38–40. Buenos Aires: Ediciones de la Flor, 1988.

Franco, Jean. 'Un viaje poco romántico: viajeros británicos hacia Sudamérica, 1818-28'. *Escritura* 4, no. 7 (1979): 129–42.

Garra, Lobodón. 'La borrasca'. In *La tierra maldita. Relatos bravíos de la Patagonia salvaje y de los mares australes*, 1st ed., 145–54. Buenos Aires: Editorial Cabaut y Cía., 1932.

Gómez, Leila. *Iluminados y tránsfugas: relatos de viajeros y ficciones nacionales en Argentina, Paraguay y Perú*. Madrid, Frankfurt am Main: Iberoamericana; Vervuert, 2009.

Howkins, Adrian J. *Frozen Empires: An Environmental History of the Antarctic Peninsula*. Oxford: Oxford University Press, 2017.

Humboldt, Alexander von. *Personal Narrative* [of a Journey to the Equinoctial Regions of the New Continent]. Introduction and translation from *Relation historique du voyage aux régions équinoxiales du nouveau continent* (first published in 1814–25) by Jason Wilson. Historical introduction by Malcolm Nicolson. London: Penguin Books, 1995.

Justo, Liborio (Lobodon Garra). *La tierra maldita. Relatos bravíos de la Patagonia salvaje y de los mares australes*. Editorial Cabaut y Cía., 1932.

Justo, Liborio. *Prontuario*. 1st ed. Buenos Aires: Ediciones B, 2006.

Lanuza, José Luis. *Esteban Echeverría y sus amigos*. Buenos Aires: Raigal, 1951.

Leane, Elizabeth. *Antarctica in Fiction: Imaginative Narratives of the Far South*. Cambridge: Cambridge University Press, 2012.

Leane, Elizabeth. 'Yesterday's Tomorrows and Tomorrow's Yesterdays: Utopian Literary Visions of Antarctic Futures'. *The Polar Journal* 3, no. 2 (2013): 333–47.

Lestido, Adriana. *Antártida negra: Los diarios*. Buenos Aires: Tusquets Editores, 2017.

Lovecraft H. P. *At the Mountains of Madness and Other Tales of Terror*. New York: Del Rey, 2007.

Mafezzini, Ángel. *Un viaje a las montañas blancas*. 1986.

McCann, Joy. *Wild Sea: A History of the Southern Ocean*. Chicago: University of Chicago Press, 2020.

Piñero, Sergio. *El Puñal de Orión: Apuntes de viaje*. Buenos Aires: Editorial Proa, 1925.

Poe, Edgar Allan. *The Narrative of Arthur Gordon Pym of Nantucket*. Bungay, Suffolk: Penguin Books, 1975.

Prieto, Adolfo. *Los viajeros ingleses y la emergencia de la literatura argentina, 1820–1850*. Buenos Aires: Sudamericana, 1996.

Soria, Alberto A. *La vida en la Antártida*. Buenos Aires: Editorial Guillermo Kraft, 1954.

Trifilo, Santo Samuel. *La Argentina vista por viajeros ingleses: 1810–1860*. Vol. 3. Buenos Aires: Ediciones Gure, 1959.

Vaca, José María Toribio. *Antártida mi hogar*. Buenos Aires: Heraldo, 1962.

Wainschenker, Pablo, and E. Leane. 'The "Alien" Next Door: Antarctica in South American Fiction'. *The Polar Journal* 9, no. 2 (2019): 324–39.

Williams Álzaga, Enrique. *La pampa en la novela argentina*, 1st ed. Buenos Aires: Ángel Estrada, 1955.

CHAPTER 9
J. M. COETZEE'S HISPANIC SOUTH
Cristóbal Pérez Barra

In 2011 the South African–born Australian writer J. M. Coetzee visited Chile for the first time. He had been invited to participate in a seminar organized by the Architecture Faculty of the Pontifical Catholic University in Santiago. At the time I was a junior lecturer at the Law Faculty, beginning to publish fiction and looking for something to translate, and eventually got to know Coetzee during his subsequent yearly visits. In early 2015, Coetzee gave me permission to translate two short stories into Spanish, which would be eventually collected in *Dos lecciones de Elizabeth Costello*, a limited edition signed by him. As I corresponded with Coetzee, he told me that in April of that year he would be taking part in a new series of seminars about the literatures of the south at the San Martín National University (UNSAM) in Argentina.[1] As I was also studying for a master's degree in literature in Santiago, I decided to attend the seminar, but when I arrived in Buenos Aires Coetzee introduced me to his colleagues as his publisher and translator in Chile. Because of that, I had a double perspective: I sat in their private meetings and accompanied them in their visits to the many local cultural landmarks but also sat in the classroom as every other student. This *modus operandi* persisted over the next three and a half years, and I acquired a unique insight into this southern project as a consequence.

The work of the writers who took part in the Buenos Aires seminars was translated from English into Spanish and published by UNSAM press, and the continued interaction with them was a unique opportunity for students, who came from Argentina and other Latin American countries. Therefore, Coetzee's Hispanic south has an important outreach component, and this is one of its key points: the south is something Coetzee tried to bring into being, even if briefly, using his personal cultural capital. In other words, only a writer with his literary prestige could have found the resources to lead this initiative over several years and to invite other important writers and academics to collaborate in it. It is a vision that is very much at odds with Pascale Casanova's idea of a literary system with a centre in Paris or London, for Coetzee's appeal is for the literary practitioners of the south to operate with little regard to the mandates of the northern metropoles. But perhaps even more importantly, it left an indelible mark on students who will eventually become academics with an enduring conscience of what Coetzee meant the south to signify.

Indeed, among the many distinctive features of Coetzee's career, an important element is his elective territory of the south, which comprises the lower portions of three different continents: South Africa, Australia and the Southern Cone of Chile, Argentina and Uruguay. Crucially, this literary land is not exclusively Anglophone, but also Spanish speaking, and one with indigenous languages as well. The combination of these geographical and linguistic factors, the south and the Spanish language, decisively mark the late period of Coetzee's writing but also have ramifications which extend back to the very beginning of his career, both as a writer and as a public intellectual, as I will show in what follows.

However, Coetzee was not the first to try to conceptualize the south as a literary region. In 1998 there was a significant initiative with a similar goal, one that has not been critically assessed until now and one also useful to understanding Coetzee's southern endeavours. The project was marked by the regained democracies of Chile and South Africa and the cultural dialogue established between them and with Australia. In 1997 Jorge Heine, Chilean ambassador to Pretoria and a global studies scholar, co-organized a seminar at the South African Institute of International Affairs (SAIIA) on the Mercosur countries, South Africa, Australia and New Zealand, about 'the things in common they might have and how that might be translated into closer relations between them'.[2] The seminar's organization coincided with Ariel Dorfman's participation in the Grahamstown Festival; his *Death and the Maiden* 'was considered *the* play of South African transition'.[3] Dorfman's visit to South Africa also enabled literary connections: he and Heine met with Nadine Gordimer in Johannesburg and with André Brink and Coetzee in Cape Town.

From the conjunction of these two events arose the idea of an encounter in Chile, to be called Escribiendo el Sur Profundo (Writing the Deep South), to explore the literary side of the SAIIA seminar. As Heine explains,

> The aim was to explore the degree to which the kind of society that is formed in the south moulds in a certain way literary imagination as well, and if there were common elements between these three countries and their respective literatures.[4]

Significantly, in the prologue to the encounter's anthology, Heine offers a critically argued conception that closely anticipates the idea of the south Coetzee was to elaborate in Argentina during the 2010s. Indeed, Heine identifies a new territory as encompassing different areas:

> Una parte significativa de este Nuevo Sur es el Sur Profundo, integrado por los países ubicados al Sur del Trópico de Capricornio; esto es, Australia, Nueva Zelandia, Chile, Argentina, Uruguay y Sudáfrica.[5]

> (A significant part of this New South is the Deep South, formed by the countries located to the south of the Tropic of Capricorn; that is, Australia, New Zealand, Chile, Argentina, Uruguay, and South Africa [own translation]).

Heine also identifies commonalities that extend beyond the geographical, such as a colonial past and a present marked by open economies with a strong emphasis on agricultural exports and mining. However, he is also aware of the need to explore the nation building process in these countries by dint of a literary creation that also addresses ethnic diversity and multiculturalism, and this gave form to the Escribiendo el Sur Profundo project. The encounter, in which Dorfman, Gordimer, Brink, Peter Carey, Helen Garner, Roberta Sykes, Zakes Mda, Mongane Wally Serote and Antonio Skármeta participated, took place in November 1998 at the Santiago Book Fair, followed by further panels in Valdivia and Valparaíso.[6]

Seventeen years later, Coetzee began his own public reflection on what he would come to call 'the south'. Although it is not explicitly formulated, Coetzee's idea of the south has a Borgesian element. The 'on the edge' position from which Borges wrote, as defined by Beatriz Sarlo,[7] was shared by Coetzee, as Peter D. McDonald notes: 'It could be argued that Coetzee emerges as a hero of the margins, as, say, a Kafkaesque hunger artist working in the tradition of a minor literature, always against the odds.'[8] Specifically, Coetzee's operation consisted of stitching fragments of the edge together: realizing that the literary landscapes of the Southern Cone, the Australian continent and South Africa were all on the edge and in the Southern Hemisphere, he strived to build imaginary transoceanic bridges between these territories, both as a world writer and public intellectual.

Coetzee's southern interests in the context of his move to Australia have been well documented by Elleke Boehmer, who notes the change in the fiction's referential aspect. Instead of working at a remove from local references, the relocation to Australia sparked in Coetzee an interest in understanding the make-up of the country:

> The difference is that in Australia, a country that he has acquired by conscious adoption rather than through the accidents of birth, he has been more noticeably concerned not only to establish the country fictionally as a space, but also to *realize* or embody it as an actual, recognizable location.[9]

Therefore, Coetzee's Australian-ness evolved through a conscious and complex embrace, reflected in *Elizabeth Costello*, *Slow Man* and *Diary of a Bad Year* and his acquisition of Australian citizenship in 2006. However, the 'make up' of Australia which Boehmer pinpoints was followed shortly thereafter by a more public display of his sustained interest in the Spanish language and Hispanic cultures, which far precedes the Australian one, for it had begun in London during the early 1960s, as Coetzee explained in his essay 'Homage'.[10] Eventually, this interest directed Coetzee's navigation chart east from Australia, yet still within the Southern Hemisphere.

In fact, Australia and South America featured prominently in the expansion of the literary landscape of Coetzee's late period. Indeed, Coetzee's relocation from South Africa to Australia occurred at the time in which he was progressing in terms of prestige from the periphery to the literary centre of the world, and his gaze was redirected as a consequence. This phenomenon also had a later effect in the form of his Southern Cone travels, which implied changing the backdrop of his southern, regional vision from a static to a moving, panoptic one in the 2010s, connecting the margins and establishing inter-peripheral relations between these three literary lands.

Coetzee's South African identity coupled with his acquired Australian-ness and subsequent immersion in Hispanic literary culture from Chile and Argentina sparked his idea of the south. But to what kind of 'south' was he referring? The categories 'south' and 'Global South' are relatively new in the critical debate and are only briefly considered in Pascale Casanova's *The World Republic of Letters*.[11] Casanova refers to the south when she discusses Faulkner, defining it as 'a rural and archaic world prey to magical styles of thought and trapped in the closed life of families and villages'.[12] The category is an example of what she calls 'lands of literature', one of the components of 'literary space':

> In this broader perspective, then, literary frontiers come into view that are independent of political boundaries, dividing up a world that is secret and yet perceptible by all (especially its most dispossessed members); territories whose sole value and sole resource is literature, ordered by power relations that nonetheless govern the form of the texts that are written in and that circulate throughout these lands; a world that has its own capital, its own provinces and borders, in which languages become instruments of power.[13]

However, even though one way in which these lands of literature take shape is through the kind of dialogue built by the way peripheral writers read one another, the 'south' and the 'Global South' do not gain much traction in Casanova's vision.

These concepts have been more substantially developed during this century in two important studies. One is *Southern Theory*, by Raewyn Connell, which from an Australian perspective aims to 'emphasize relations – authority, exclusion and inclusion, hegemony, partnership, sponsorship, appropriation – between intellectuals and institutions in the metropole and those in the world periphery'.[14] Therefore, Connell's study encompasses different areas of the latter category that do not necessarily belong to the geographical south but that nonetheless share a common history of political or economic dependence distinct from the northern powers. The other is *Theory from the South*, by Jean and John L. Comaroff, which from a South African perspective analyzes the south under two basic premises. Firstly, modernity in the south has long been considered a derivation of its northern version, whereas the authors stress the necessity for it 'to be apprehended and addressed in its own right'.[15] Secondly, the south plays a far more important role in the historical shaping of modernity than has been traditionally acknowledged:

> given the unpredictable, under-determined dialectic of capitalism-and-modernity in the here and now, it is the south that often is the first to feel the effects of world-historical forces, the south in which radically new assemblages of capital and labor are taking shape, thus to prefigure the future of the global north.[16]

Therefore, the Comaroffs grant the south a role in the grand sweep of history that has seldom been considered. However, they also acknowledge that the south 'cannot be defined, *a priori*, in substantive terms', for it 'bespeaks a relation, not a thing in or for itself', one they describe as 'a window on the world at large'.[17] In fact, this lack of substantial definition is also a component of Coetzee's vision of the south but not of Heine's elaboration of the Deep South. Finally, whilst Casanova provides an exclusively literary idea, the conceptions of Heine, Connell, the Comaroffs and Coetzee are firmly rooted in political and social realities.

The *Cátedra Coetzee: Literatura del Sur* Programme materialized after Coetzee was invited by Carlos Ruta, rector of the UNSAM, 'to help with the birth of a new programme in comparative literature' in 2014.[18] When Coetzee started convening writers, some were surprised at the invitation, as Zoë Wicomb recalled in a private email: 'I knew nothing of Coetzee's Argentinian project so, yes, it came as a surprise. I was very keen to go to Buenos Aires and started reading about theories of the South.'[19]

The actual teaching fell on writers, academics or both: Wicomb, Nicholas Jose, Gail Jones, Delia Falconer, Ivor Indyk, Ivan Vladislavić, Antjie Krog and Mia Couto. Coetzee's participation consisted of attending sessions that did not deal with his work and giving his inaugural lectures. Significantly, while Coetzee delved into the idea of the south in his lectures, the other writers analyzed South African and Australian literatures, as Wicomb confirms:

> I was expecting to teach a course on South African writing and in that respect the visit met my expectations, although that was probably about our hosts' admiration for Coetzee. Part of my agreement with John was working closely with Ivan Vladislavić which was a happy and fruitful experience. But I do not recall much theoretical discussion of South-South exchanges.[20]

Therefore, Coetzee's professorship provided a field for the academic unveiling and projection of these two different visions, but his own interest lay in the south. He summarized his aim in an interview with the UNSAM magazine:

> El curso está destinado a facilitar los intercambios directos entre los países del sur. Sin embargo, tales intercambios no son fáciles de lograr, dado que nadan contra la corriente, que fluye desde el norte hacia el sur. Esto es lo que descubrirán aquellos estudiantes que quieran ampliar sus conocimientos sobre otras culturas del sur.[21]

(The course's aim is facilitating direct exchanges between the countries of the south. However, these exchanges are not easy to arrive at, for they swim against the current, which flows from the north to the south. This is what students who would like to expand their knowledge about other southern cultures will discover [own translation]).

Interestingly, Coetzee's idea of the south evolved in tandem with the seminars. In the 2015 inaugural lectures, he spoke of the 'Literature of the South' and offered mostly literary references, like 'The Narrative of Arthur Gordon Pym' and 'The Buladelah-Taree Holiday Song Cycle'. By contrast, in the 2016 lectures Coetzee referred to the '*Literatures* of the South' and an elaborated theoretical reference frame.

I will now turn back to Casanova and consider the south within her system to gloss Coetzee's highly personal conception. Casanova refers to a literary *Weltanschauung* which, although independent in its formulation, is also modelled after a political and geographical map of the world: as such, it contains not only capitals and frontiers but also cardinal points. Nonetheless, Casanova's south has an ephemeral quality demonstrated in the fact that she mentions it only once, parenthetically, when discussing Benet's reading of Faulkner, which provides a perfect example of the myopic northern vision Coetzee strongly criticizes:

> The Spanish writer Juan Benet was indisputably one of the first to have understood this; but after him all writers from the South, in the broad sense of the term, from the West Indies to Portugal and from South America to Africa, recognized that Faulkner had revealed to them a way of attaining the Greenwich meridian without in the least denying their cultural heritage.[22]

According to Casanova, Faulkner attained the Greenwich meridian by being 'consecrated in Paris'.[23] While she asserts that 'it was the great translations of Faulkner's novels by Maurice-Edgar Coindreau that made his consecration and universal recognition possible', she fails to recognize that he had a natural wide avenue into the literary centre as an American writer who wrote in English during the twentieth century.[24]

Peculiarly, Casanova's idea of the south comprises countries from the geographic and economic north with continents from the south in both senses. *Mutatis mutandis*, the north would be Anglo-America and Europe without the Iberian Peninsula, which seems reductive. Casanova is not referring to languages but to national literatures: the Hispanic ones come 'from rural countries with archaic cultural structures', which is a completely different perspective to Coetzee's.[25] Crucially, for Casanova the south's relevance in the global panorama is merely as a point of departure: in fact, according to her, writers become relevant *because* they leave it behind when navigating towards the centre. Therefore, for Casanova the south is a frontier, not a territory. But her vision also contains a misconception about Hispanic literature as a north-driven affair, which affects its understanding on a global scale and is also precisely the mentality Coetzee resists through his southern endeavours, for his crusade is not only for the south but also equally very much against the north. For example, in one of the Buenos Aires seminars, Coetzee declared that 'The North-South paradigm – and I cannot emphasize this strongly enough – is a Northern conception created in the academies and think-tanks of the North. It should be invoked by intellectuals of the south with caution, and only after being seriously rethought.'[26]

By mapping the south as a frontier beyond which she cannot see, Casanova misses the importance of Buenos Aires as a literary centre and of Neruda and Borges as substantial innovators from the Southern Cone. Moreover, Casanova's assertion about Benet is in fact a serious mistake originating in her Eurocentric vision, one which distorts the reality of Hispanophone literature *and* Coetzee's involvement with it. As the only translated author of Minuit, Benet carried a great deal of symbolic capital in Paris, and his literary *distinction* was further enhanced when Bourdieu, Casanova's intellectual mentor, suggested that she interview him.[27] However, by uncritically assuming that Benet's position in world letters was an extension of his Parisian prestige, Casanova overlooked Faulknerian reception in the Hispanic world, which is completely different. In fact, Nora Catelli notes that Borges had reviewed *Absalom, Absalom!*, *The Unvanquished* and *The Wild Palms* during the 1930s, whilst his translation of the latter appeared in 1940. In a similar line, Juan Carlos Onetti had published *A Brief Life* in 1950, while Juan Rulfo's *Pedro Páramo* appeared in 1955.[28]

The bibliographic evidence that Catelli draws on shows that the reception of the American vanguard in Spanish took place first in the Americas, not in Spain; and crucially, Coetzee's essays on Borges and García Márquez also show he is aware of that. Catelli's critique calls into question the duality of peripherality and centre in Casanova, for while the last peninsular Spanish text that resonated globally was *Don Quixote*, during the twentieth century the Hispanic American 'periphery' upstaged Spain in two waves, first through *Modernismo-Creacionismo* in the 1900s–10s and then with the Latin American boom in the 1950s–60s, and thus became the real literary 'centre' of the language.

Consequently, in his elective affinities for Southern Cone writers, Coetzee performed a crucial operation. In fact, he was not really delving into the *literary* peripheries of the Hispanosphere, for while these countries were geographically peripheral, in terms of symbolic capital they became the 'centres', for Neruda from Chile and Borges from Argentina innovated poetry and prose not only in Spanish but also on a global scale – as Coetzee's own reflections in *Summertime* and *Stranger Shores* clearly demonstrates. More generally, Coetzee is also aware that a significant amount of world literature criticism originates in the north and is subject to northern categories and perspectives, resulting in a distorted and partial understanding of the south, which dovetails with his own vision of the problem: namely, that 'the South acts as the Other of the North'.[29] Indeed, his elective territory of the south is partly a reaction for this misconception in the field of world literature. For, if there is a need for a 'southern literature of the South', meaning one 'which is not history-less, not something invented *ab ovo*, but which nevertheless owes almost nothing to the cultural North', as Coetzee declared in Buenos Aires in 2015, this literature also demands its own *southern* criticism.[30]

In contrast to Casanova, Coetzee's gaze from the literary centre was directed southwards in a different way, to the shared experience of the south as one of many possible lands refracted through the force fields of the literary world, but conceived as a *real* territory one inhabits, not as a frontier. Nonetheless, Coetzee's idea is more complicated than it might seem at first glance. Emerging through his collaborations in South America in the 2010s, it also became increasingly clear that this literary territory might only exist by virtue of Coetzee's own personal force field granted by his significant symbolic power. While Casanova referred to the south once in her book, which made it invisible in a book that was hugely influential, Coetzee only conveyed his idea in lectures to small audiences in Buenos Aires, thus gaining less traction and rendering it somewhat ephemeral.

Coetzee's slowly developing vision was enriched by his Southern Cone travels, as he explained during an interview in Buenos Aires in 2015:

> My relations with South America, principally with Argentina, date from late in my life and came as a considerable surprise to me. I encountered from my first visit here to Argentina a reading public that really took books seriously and read books intelligently, that didn't, in my case, put me on the box called 'author of *Disgrace*' [*pause*]. I'm trying to answer your question, why Argentina [*pause*]; it's a country that's been extremely welcoming to me and that I very much enjoy visiting …'[31]

Because of his Borgesian readings, Coetzee was aware of the Buenos Aires location of the southern library before he first visited in 2011. When I asked him how it felt to discover this exceedingly literary capital, Coetzee responded: '[*reflection*] I was prepared'.[32] The somewhat vestigial significance of the literary event in Buenos Aires may have made Coetzee feel particularly attracted to it. As a matter of fact, when I asked him if he would have relocated to Argentina had he visited before emigrating to Australia, he answered: '[*reflection*] Very possibly'.[33]

Buenos Aires was to be crucial in Coetzee's conception of the south because the layers of literary sediment the city contains by dint of Borges's tall and far-reaching construction are comparable to that of a European metropolis. This certainly exerts pressure on Casanova's theory, which presents a world literary system converging into a European centre. Nonetheless, her insistence on the central role of Paris or London shows the limitations of her 'logic of the literary world'.[34] By contrast, for Coetzee the purported centre was only a steppingstone, not a destination: his personal notion of the south tries to create a specific literary territory that circumvents the European centre that anchors Casanova's account. However, Coetzee's notion is also complicated, for while it conveys a certain invitation to cultural emancipation for southern countries, it is also highly idiosyncratic, as it largely stems from his personal experience as a writer who has lived in these territories for more than fifty years and has little critical density, because it has never been published in any written form, but only read to a small audience in Buenos Aires. In other words, Coetzee's south is an exploration based on his personal history and travel across the Southern Hemisphere, a close reading of Borges and the recognition of intersecting points with him, and – crucially – a reflection on his own position, marking a late development in his career as a world writer and public intellectual. Conveniently, in Argentina he found an academic platform on which to develop this conception.

Coetzee initially engaged with economic and sociological texts to approach the globalization phenomenon. However, this proved problematic, for theorists tend to analyze nationally, regionally or globally, but not a discontiguous territory like the south as conceived by Coetzee. He first noted that 'During the 1980s, the term "globalization" began to creep into the discourse of business journalists and management theorists'.[35] He quoted economist Mauro Guillén, who in *The Limits of Convergence* argued that instead of bringing countries and organizations towards increased homogenization, 'the mutual awareness that globalization entails invites them to be different, namely, to use their unique economic, political, and social advantages as leverage in the global economy'.[36]

Nonetheless, according to Coetzee, most sociologists 'replaced the idea of globalization as business or economic strategy with the idea of globalization as *a new form of society*, globalized society'.[37] He cited Martin Albrow, who in *The Global Age* argues that 'The real break, rupture with the modern, shift to a new epoch, comes not with the victory of the irrational over the rational, but when the social takes on a meaning outside the frame of reference set by the nation-state.'[38] He then quoted Zygmunt Bauman, who in *Globalization* argues that 'being local in a globalized world is a sign of social deprivation and degradation', which dovetails with Coetzee's view of a north-driven globalization.[39] Coetzee may have associated this perceived lack of control of local communities noted by Bauman with the 'new global imperialism' he denounced in 'Critic and Citizen: A Response'.[40] He then quoted Michael Hardt's and Antonio Negri's *Empire*, remarking that 'it is no longer possible to demarcate large geographical zones as center and periphery, North and South', which relates to his recognition that Australia lies in the geographical south but is also part of the economic north.[41]

These quotes suggest Coetzee was trying to grapple with the idea of the south himself in these lectures and developing it rather than offering a consistent personal view. After delineating the globalization phenomenon, Coetzee delved into its theoretical consequences, namely the various binary nomenclative options proposed by academics, which have in common the fact that all of them 'describe a pattern of inequality in power, wealth and cultural influence that grew historically out of first European and then later North American imperialism'.[42] All these distinctions are subsumable into the north/south paradigm, and one of the unifying features of the south is the lingering effects of various empires, but this is complicated by the fact that Coetzee's gaze is not historical, as his concern with the term 'Global South' shows. Crucially, he stressed the fact that '*the global South* can all too easily be identified with *the post-colonial* – since most of the global South has a colonial past – and therefore that North-South studies can all too easily simply recapitulate post-colonial studies under a new name.'[43]

This shows Coetzee was reluctant to engage in the nomenclative debate he had described, for he will not define the south according to theory or history. Significantly, Coetzee identifies a problem with the retrospective focus of a post-colonial approach: 'Its critical gaze has been trained not on the present but on the past – on histories of imperialism and colonialism, and the aftermath of those histories.'[44]

But when Coetzee speaks of the south, which of these modes conveys his idea? I will suggest an answer – none of the above – by noting that his reference points are not the nation-state, but geography, not an historical aftermath, but the present. Consequently, the south is *real*, as Coetzee concluded:

> What is left is the real South, the South of this real world, where most of those present in this room were born and most of us will die. It is a unique world – there is only one South – with its unique skies and its unique heavenly constellations. In this South the wind blows in a certain way and the leaves fall in a certain

way and the sun beats down in a certain way that is instantly recognizable from one part of the South to another. In the South, as in the North, there are cities, but the cities of the South all have a somewhat phantasmatic quality. The peoples of the South are all, in one way or another, rough and a bit lazy. We have troubled histories behind us, which sometimes haunt us. It is nothing like this in the North.

I can go on endlessly with my list. And the literatures of the South do indeed go on endlessly as they try to pin down in words their intuitions of what a life in the South consists in.[45]

As can be seen in this passage, Coetzee changed the technical register of the text he used when referring to globalization for a slightly poetic one when describing the south. Although there is no recording of this lecture, I was in the audience when he read it in Buenos Aires, and the inflection with which he read it, which was slightly vatic, emphasized this transition.

It is possible now to venture a definition of the south according to Coetzee, working through Borges: the south is a world formed by people inhabiting a transoceanic regional concatenation, south of the Tropic of Capricorn. It has distinctive characteristics: it is *interregional*, for the strongest common factor is their physical location. It is *anti-global*, although if globalization is perceived by Coetzee as a northern construct and thus to be resisted, it also enables a pan-southern awareness. It is *socially hybrid*: for in these territories there is an uneasy coexistence of Europeanness and nativity. It is *plurilingual*: there is no pre-eminence of English, Spanish, Portuguese, Afrikaans or any other language.

However, the crucial, defining feature of Coetzee's south is that it is a highly personal vision composed of territories in which he has lived or travelled, and he knows their languages and literatures. As he explained:

It is the view not of a social scientist nor of an historian nor of a literary theorist. It is the view of a practising writer who is also a human being who has lived most of his life in two regions of the South – the real South – and is today visiting a third region of the South.[46]

Consequently, Coetzee's vision is similar to the one of Heine, but he was not influenced by the latter. In fact, the *Escribiendo el sur profundo* anthology, which contains Heine's prologue, was only published in Spanish in preparation for the 1998 event in Chile, and Coetzee confirmed in a private email that he 'was unaware of the project'.[47] Therefore, the similarities shown in my comparative analysis are entirely coincidental. The main differences with Heine's vision are Coetzee's use of 'the south' terminology and his emphasis on regions, rather than on countries. Moreover, Coetzee had both deeper existential experience of what he calls the south (by his South African birth, Australian nationality and Southern Cone travelling) and time to reflect on it through an institutional base. In other words – even though he was unaware of Heine's initiative – enabled by the symbolic power acquired as a world writer, it was possible for Coetzee to mentally navigate across the southern seas, doubling its two great capes and exploring along the margins of three continents.

Protesting the Argentine government's measures at UNSAM, which included transferring part of the campus land for a real estate business, Coetzee resigned his professorship in 2018 and has not travelled back to the continent since that year. Although the project has not been picked up by him since then, this chapter reveals that an academic reflection on his vision of the south can take place. Indeed, there seem to be promising signs that his idea, among other meridional conceptualizations, might be gaining currency in academia – as this chapter and the wider collection shows.

Notes

1. J. M. Coetzee, email message to author, 23 March 2015.
2. Jorge Heine, email message to author, 9 April 2021.
3. Ibid.
4. Ibid.
5. André Brink et al., *Escribiendo el sur profundo* (Santiago: El Mercurio/Revista de Libros, 1998), 10.
6. Ibid.
7. Beatriz Sarlo, *Jorge Luis Borges: A Writer on the Edge* (London: Verso, 1993), 4.
8. Peter McDonald, 'The Writer, the Critic, and the Censor: J. M. Coetzee and the Question of Literature', in *J. M. Coetzee and the Idea of the Public Intellectual*, ed. Jane Poyner (Athens: Ohio University Press, 2006), 56.
9. Elleke Boehmer, 'J. M. Coetzee's Australian Realism', in *Strong Opinions*, ed. Chris Danta, Sue Kossew and Julian Murphet (New York: Continuum, 2011), 3.
10. J. M. Coetzee, 'Homage', *The Threepenny Review*, no. 53, Spring 1993.
11. Pascale Casanova, *The World Republic of Letters*, translated by M. B. de Bevoise (Cambridge, MA: Harvard University Press, 2004).
12. Ibid., 337.
13. Ibid., 4.
14. Raewyn Connell, *Southern Theory* (Cambridge: Polity Press, 2007), viii–ix.
15. Jean Comaroff and John L. Comaroff, *Theory from the South* (Boulder, CO: Paradigm, 2012), 7.
16. Ibid., 12.
17. Ibid., 47.
18. J. M. Coetzee, 'The Literature of the South: Introductory Remarks (1)', unpublished lecture (San Martín National University, Buenos Aires, 7 April 2015), 1.
19. Zoë Wicomb, email message to author, 11 April 2021.
20. Ibid.

21. J. M. Coetzee, 'Trascender las fronteras del sur', interview with Jéssica Sessarego, translated by Jimena Reides, *Transas*, dossier 'Miradas de África Meridional desde América Latina', 6 October 2016. Available online: https://www.revistatransas.com/2016/10/06/trascender-las-fronteras-del-sur-entrevista-con-j-m-coetzee/ (accessed 21 April 2021).
22. Pascale Casanova, *The World Republic of Letters*, 338.
23. Ibid., 125.
24. Ibid., 142.
25. Ibid., 338.
26. J. M. Coetzee, 'The Literature of the South: Introductory Remarks (2)', unpublished lecture (San Martín National University, Buenos Aires, 14 September 2015), 4.
27. Pascale Casanova, 'Une critique de solitude', interview with Yves Lacascade, *Journal des anthropologues*, nos. 148–9, 2017. Available online: https://www.acrimed.org/Une-critique-de-solitude-un-entretien-avec#nb1 (accessed 18 January 2021).
28. Nora Catelli, *Juan Benet: Guerra y literatura* (Madrid: Libros de la Resistencia, 2015), 22.
29. J. M Coetzee, 'The Literature of the South: Introductory Remarks (1)', 3.
30. J. M Coetzee, 'The Literature of the South: Introductory Remarks (2)', 6.
31. Interview with Anna Kazumi-Stahl, 'John M. Coetzee, *Cartas de navegación* (English version)', 15 April 2015. Available online: https://www.youtube.com/watch?v=wnfjHQ48EMc (accessed 24 April 2021).
32. J. M. Coetzee, interview with author, 16 April 2015.
33. Ibid.
34. Casanova, *The World Republic of Letters*, 101.
35. J. M. Coetzee, 'Literatures of the South: Introductory Remarks (3)', unpublished lecture (San Martín National University, Buenos Aires, 11 April 2016), 2.
36. Mauro F. Guillén, *The Limits of Convergence* (Princeton, NJ: Princeton University Press, 2001), 3.
37. J. M Coetzee, 'Literatures of the South: Introductory Remarks (3)', 2.
38. Martin Albrow, *The Global Age* (Stanford, CA: Stanford University Press, 1996), 58.
39. Zygmunt Bauman, *Globalization* (New York: Columbia University Press, 1998), 2–3.
40. J. M. Coetzee, 'Critic and Citizen: A Response', *Pretexts: Literary and Cultural Studies* 9, no. 1 (2000): 109–11.
41. Michael Hardt and Antonio Negri, *Empire* (Cambridge, MA: Harvard University Press, 2000), 335.
42. J. M Coetzee, 'Literatures of the South: Introductory Remarks (3)', 3.
43. Ibid., 4.
44. Ibid.
45. Ibid., 5.
46. Ibid.
47. J. M Coetzee, email message to author, 14 September 2023.

Bibliography

Albrow, Martin. *The Global Age*. Stanford, CA: Stanford University Press, 1996.
Bauman, Zygmunt. *Globalization*. New York: Columbia University Press, 1998.
Benet, Juan. *Cartografía personal*. Valladolid: Cuatro ediciones, 1997.
Boehmer, Elleke. 'J. M. Coetzee's Australian Realism'. In *Strong Opinions*, edited by Chris Danta, Sue Kossew and Julian Murphet. New York: Continuum, 2011.
Brink, André et al. *Escribiendo el sur profundo*. Santiago: El Mercurio/Revista de Libros, 1998.
Casanova, Pascale. *The World Republic of Letters*, translated by M. B. de Bevoise. Cambridge, MA: Harvard University Press, 2004.
Catelli, Nora. *Juan Benet: Guerra y literatura*. Madrid: Libros de la Resistencia, 2015.
Cervantes, Miguel de. *Don Quijote de la Mancha*. Madrid: Real Academia Española/Alfaguara, 2004.
Coetzee, J. M. 'Critic and Citizen: A Response'. *Pretexts: Literary and Cultural Studies* 9, no. 1 (2000): 109–11.
Coetzee, J. M. *Diary of a Bad Year*. London: Harvill Secker, 2007.
Coetzee, J. M. *Dos lecciones de Elizabeth Costello*, translated by Cristóbal Pérez Barra. Santiago: El Faro, 2015.
Coetzee, J. M. *Elizabeth Costello*. London: Secker & Warburg, 2003.
Coetzee, J. M. 'Homage'. *The Threepenny Review*, no. 53 (Spring 1993): 5–7.
Coetzee, J. M. *Slow Man*. London: Secker & Warburg, 2005.
Coetzee, J. M. *Stranger Shores: Essays 1986–1999*. London: Secker & Warburg, 2001.
Coetzee, J. M. *Summertime*. London: Harvill Secker, 2009.
Comaroff, Jean, and John L. Comaroff. *Theory from the South*. Boulder, CO: Paradigm, 2012.
Connell, Raewyn. *Southern Theory*. Cambridge: Polity Press, 2007.
Dorfman, Ariel. *Death and the Maiden*. London: Nick Hern Books, 1990.
Faulkner, William. *Novels 1936–1940: Absalom, Absalom!; The Unvanquished; If I Forget thee, Jerusalem [The Wild Palms]; The Hamlet*. New York: Library of America, 1990.
Guillén, Mauro F. *The Limits of Convergence*. Princeton, NJ: Princeton University Press, 2001.
Hardt, Michael, and Antonio Negri. *Empire*. Cambridge, MA: Harvard University Press, 2000.
McDonald, Peter. 'The Writer, the Critic, and the Censor: J. M. Coetzee and the Question of Literature'. In *J. M. Coetzee and the Idea of the Public Intellectual*, edited by Jane Poyner. Athens: Ohio University Press, 2006.
Onetti, Juan Carlos. *A Brief Life*, translated by Hortense Carpentier. New York: Grossman/Viking, 1976.
Rulfo, Juan. *Pedro Páramo*, translated by Lysander Kemp. New York: Grove Press, 1959.
Sarlo, Beatriz. *Jorge Luis Borges: A Writer on the Edge*. London: Verso, 1993.

PART III
READING AND WRITING IN SOUTHERN WATERS

CHAPTER 10
TSUNAMI, TORNADO, TIDE: LIFE AND WRITING OF THE OCEANIC SOUTH IN SELECTED NONFICTION BY AMITAV GHOSH
Charne Lavery

In *The Great Derangement*, Amitav Ghosh proposes that the literary novel as a form struggles to deal with the reality of climate change, partly because that reality includes what seem like a myriad improbable events: 'flash floods, hundred-year storms, persistent droughts, spells of unprecedented heat, sudden landslides, raging torrents pouring down from breached glacial lakes, and, yes, freakish tornadoes'.[1] But novels have shaped our habitual patterns of thought, as perhaps best indicated by the phrase 'If this were in a novel, no one would believe it'.[2] Combine this with what literary critic Margaret Cohen calls 'hydrophasia' – an erasure or forgetting of everything to do with the sea in the twentieth century. In contrast, for instance, nineteenth-century novels were filled with sea travel and imagery, including improbable events that were first recorded as 'remarkable occurrences' in ships' logbooks and sailors memoirs.[3] If the novel form struggles to take into account the wild unknowns of climate change, then life writing and sea writing, particularly from the oceanic south, may be capable of registering its dangerous strangeness.

This chapter explores that intersection, between southern lives, writing and the sea, in the context of the Indian Ocean world as a constitutive part of what Meg Samuelson and I call the 'oceanic south'.[4] The Southern Hemisphere, Samuelson notes, is far more oceanic than the Northern Hemisphere, with 20 per cent higher proportion of ocean to land. The land that does appear in the Southern Hemisphere also houses a relatively impoverished section of the global population, a result of histories of colonization and capitalist expansion that have produced the economic configuration known as the Global South. In a time of both rising inequality and rising seas, we argue that it is useful to bring these two together through the conceptual category of the oceanic south. The Indian Ocean is exemplary of the oceanic south: it has been called the 'ocean of the south', sits largely in the Southern Hemisphere, and is surrounded by the poorer countries of the world (with the significant exception of Australia). While India, in particular, is in the Northern Hemisphere, it is not only generally considered part of the Global South but has even begun to position itself as the 'voice of the Global South'.[5] India, its vast coastline jutting out into the Indian Ocean and its islands like the Andaman and Nicobar archipelagoes, is also both geographically and economically vulnerable to sea-level rise and to the increase in the frequency and intensity of storms which are the products of anthropogenic climate change.[6]

Life Writing and the Southern Hemisphere

Ghosh presents the deranging tendencies of literary fiction, in *The Great Derangement*, through describing an event from his own life, the unlikely yet real event of a tornado occurring in Delhi. This section of non-fictional life writing constitutes the counterexample, a form of non-deranging writing capable of registering both the temporality and geography of climate change. In the chapter he also returns to an earlier work of nonfiction, a work of journalistic life writing published during his time reporting on the effects of the 2004 Indian Ocean tsunami in the Andaman Islands, published later as 'The Town by the Sea' (among other titles, detailed below).[7] While several critics have explored Ghosh's oeuvre as part of the extensive fiction in English of the Indian Ocean world,[8] this chapter focuses on Ghosh's work in nonfiction and life writing as it pertains to the oceanic south and the writing of climate change. In these works Ghosh explores the difficulties involved in the narration of extreme weather events – a tsunami and a tornado, in the context of rising tides – and the potential offered by life writing of the sea and south.

Tsunami

'The Town by the Sea' describes the devastating tsunami of 26 December 2004. Its earlier version appeared just days after the event, on the front page of *The Hindu*, India's national newspaper, on 11–13 January 2005,[9] written after a fact-finding mission Ghosh conducted in the immediate aftermath on the Andaman Islands. It was later called 'The Tsunami of 2004', and earlier 'Chronicling the Devastation', but I have preferred here the title 'The Town by the Sea', which was used in Ghosh's edited collection of essays, *Incendiary Circumstances*.[10] Just as in the title of novelist Abdulrazak Gurnah's Indian Ocean novel, *By the Sea*,[11] the preposition 'by' suggests both proximity and causality, what happens both beside, and by way of, the sea.

The essay begins like this:

> The Andaman and Nicobar islands are one of those quadrants of the globe where political and geological fault lines run on parallel courses. Politically the islands are Union Territories, ruled directly from New Delhi, but geologically they stand just beyond the edge of the Indian tectonic plate. Stretching through seven hundred kilometres of the Bay of Bengal, they are held aloft by a range of undersea mountains that stands guard over the abyssal deep of the Sunda trench.[12]

The Andaman and Nicobar islands are the tips of submarine mountains that overlook a submarine trench that marks the fractious, volcanic meeting of tectonic plates whose slippage against one another caused an undersea earthquake that precipitated the tsunami.[13] This submerged fracture zone is the geologic fault line to which Ghosh refers; almost equally invisible is the political fault line on which the Andamans fall, between colony and postcolony. The postcolonial nation of India inherited the islands from the British empire, such that they retain 'subimperial' status. As Isabel Hofmeyr describes in a different context, some imperial relationships do not operate 'straightforwardly on a North/South axis', creating instead 'subimperial networks of the South'.[14] The Andamans can be seen in this view as a colony of the postcolony, or south of the south, an awkward and potentially explosive paradox. As Ghosh goes on to describe, when the tsunami struck, 'both the fault lines that underlie the islands seem suddenly to have been set in motion: it is as if the hurried history of an emergent nation had collided here with the deep time of geology'.[15] The interlinkage between imperialism and environmental disaster is not only retrospective but prospective. In the days after the tsunami, aid was provided in abundance but did not reach survivors, caught in bureaucratic bottlenecks by unelected officials.[16] The officials responsible had no direct responsibility to their electorate, because the islands are a sub-empire of the Indian mainland, with the in-between status of a Union Territory.[17]

The tsunami has also been used as a symbol of much wider Indian Ocean connectedness by historian Sugata Bose, in the opening lines of his influential *A Hundred Horizons*.[18] He begins his book as follows:

On 26 December 2004, giant tsunami waves triggered by a magnitude 9.0 earthquake off the northwest coast of Sumatra devastated communities around the Indian Ocean rim. [...] The tsunami took about half an hour to reach the Indonesian island of Sumatra and crashed into Thailand in less than two hours. It traveled the approximately two thousand kilometres to Sri Lanka and the southeast coast of India in less than three hours and was pounding the coast of East Africa, some five thousand kilometres away, within seven hours. The unity of the Indian Ocean world had been demonstrated in the most tragic fashion by a great wall of water moving at the speed of a jet aircraft.[19]

Amid debates about the validity of the Indian Ocean world as a historical reality or object of study, particularly into the twentieth and twenty-first centuries, the tsunami of 2004 cut through to establish clear connectedness. Unlike the Southern Hemisphere's association with distance and remoteness, the tsunami connected its shores with dangerous speed. The metaphor is telling too – the tsunami moved at the speed of a jet aircraft, the mode of travel which connects even farflung southern locations with remarkable ease from the second half of the twentieth century. The Indian Ocean rim – including its furthest reaches like southern Africa and Indonesia – was revealed as what Bose calls an 'interregional arena', with the tsunami in this case acting as a kind of biochemical stain, bringing an overlooked or debated unity clearly to light. Moreover, rather than some celebratory constructions of the Indian Ocean world as a space dominated by fluidity, connection and freedom, the tsunami highlights imperial and subimperial relationships, including destruction and tragedy.

The tsunami, importantly, is a tragedy of the sea, caused by the sea, but also by imperial relationships to the sea. For instance, as Ghosh describes, inland infrastructure was much less badly damaged than that which had been situated near the shore. Ghosh asks, bewildered, whether planners were not aware of these risks, but finds that, 'of course, it is all too easy to be wise after the event: given the choice between a view of the beach and a plot in the mosquito-infested interior what would anyone have chosen before 26 December 2004'?[20] The assumption that a sea view is a matter of privilege rather than danger is relatively new, and built, literally, into the structure and position of imperial cities from the seventeenth century onwards, largely by the spread of European empire.[21] Ancient harbor cities of Asia as well as Europe were often situated upriver and inland, far from the reach of storm surges and similar dangers. Later, however, even very different cities like Mumbai and New York were established close to the sea for their strategic location from the point of view of maritime empire: easier to defend from the coast and to supply from the metropolis.[22] These imperial dynamics were exaggerated as British empire in particular expanded in the nineteenth century, creating settlements across what is now the Global South.

As a result of both nature and planning, then, those who had built their homes by the sea, in terms of proximity, had them taken by the sea, in terms of causation. Survivors, Ghosh finds, plan to leave the string of islands and return to the mainland of India, preferring inland areas. 'If nothing else', one of them says to Ghosh, 'we will live in slums besides the railtracks. But never again by the sea.'[23] Their concerns are, post-traumatically, about the possibility of another tsunami or storm surge, but they also pertain to the slower violence of sea level rise, as discussed in the next section.

In addition to Indian Ocean connectedness, the tsunami brought to light the fragile but constitutive links between life and writing in this southern oceanic context. The conjoined geological and the political frames surround what was, in its immediate aftermath, an overwhelmingly human tragedy. The essay is a relentless record of loss. Ghosh describes the experience of the tsunami as recounted by one of the Nicobar islanders that he interviewed, named Obed Tara:

> Looking seawards he saw a wall of water advancing towards his house. Gathering his relatives, he began to run. By the time he looked back, his house, and the neighbourhood in which it stood, had vanished under the waves. Two elderly members of the family were lost and everything they possessed was gone, the car, the phone booth, the house.[24]

The images of water are powerful descriptions of the tsunami – an outsized wall of water under which everything solid vanishes, leaving only waves. Lives are lost, but, as Ghosh goes on to describe, even those who survived suffered the loss of life in a different sense: 'It was the particular nature of this disaster that it targeted not just the physical being of the victims but also the proof of the survivors' identities.'[25] As Ghosh concludes, life is partly a matter of writing – 'identity cards, licences, ration cards, school certificates, cheque books, certificates of life insurance and receipts for fixed deposits'[26] – whose destruction meant for the survivors the loss of 'all the evidentiary traces of their place in the world'.[27] As an example, Ghosh gives us more of Tara's story. Ghosh interviews him in a refugee camp in Port Blair. Tara had been at home visiting his family in Malacca, on the island of Car Nicobar, when the tsunami struck, having travelled there for Christmas from Calcutta where he worked as a soldier in the Indian army. After the tsunami, Tara is unable to claim help from the army because, without identification papers, he cannot prove who he is: 'The sea took my uniform, my ration card, my service card, my tribal papers … Why should they believe me?'[28] Another man had lost the papers which would allow him to claim his pension from the bank; the bank itself had also been swept undersea along with all its records.[29] Each of these interviewees asks Ghosh, the journalist, to write down their names and stories, to begin the kind of paper trail which may eventually allow them to reclaim their identities and thereby their livelihoods.[30] It is a plea for a rewriting into being, which deeply troubles the writer.

At this point in the essay, the features of Ghosh's own life and feelings come more directly into view. He tells a final, longer story of a man whom he calls the Director, who is returning to his hometown of Malacca on the first available flight to search for his missing wife and child.[31] The Director had been away from home on the night of the tsunami, had ignored the final call from his wife, found his son but not his wife and daughter, and lost thirteen years of epidemiological evidence accrued in his position as director of the successful Malaria Research Centre. Ghosh's characterization is factual but also imaginative and empathic. The Director is a man who had rarely expressed his feeling for his family; rather he,

> hoarded it inside himself, in the way a squirrel gathers food for the winter: loathe to spend it in his hectic middle years, he had put it away to be savoured when there was a greater sense of ease in his life, at a time when his battles were past and he could give his hoarded love his full attention. He had never dreamt – and who could? – that one bright December day, soon after dawn, it would be stolen, unsavoured, by the sea.[32]

It is a tragic account of missed opportunities and irreparable loss, which reflect a closeness, and ability to relate, among author, subject and reader. However, when Ghosh accompanies the Director on his search, gaps emerge between them that speak to inevitable empathic limits. When Ghosh drops to the ground in fear at a gas canister exploding, the Director is merely puzzled; when Ghosh wanders casually towards the sea, the Director is distraught. In response to the Director's baffling choice to rescue his malarial slides from the rubble but not his daughter's paintbox, Ghosh asks himself: 'As a husband, a father, a human being, it was impossible not to wonder: what would I have done? what would I have felt? what would I have chosen to keep of the past?'[33] The conclusion is a form of narrative erasure that mirrors the total erasure of the town which had stood by that sea: 'There are times when words seem futile, and to no one more so than a writer.'[34] It is a question of writing and loss, writing in the face of loss and as a net loss – a gesture of impossibility which appears at the end of an act of writerly witness. Yet this writing of and from southern life, in Ghosh's later work, gains in importance as the uneven impacts of climate change begin to be felt.

Life Writing and the Southern Hemisphere

Tornado

The fraught ethical relationship between writing and life is expressed as a disjuncture of scale: against the hugeness of the loss, writing seems trivial. A similar disjuncture opens the essay, as discussed above: the colliding scales of natural and human history. Dipesh Chakrabarty, too, has written of the colliding scales of natural and human history, although rather than in the context of a natural disaster like a tsunami, he is writing in the context of anthropogenic climate change. We have reached a moment in history, he states, when 'the geologic now of the Anthropocene has become entangled with the now of human history'.[35] This is because humanity in species terms has shifted from being acted upon by natural events, to becoming a geological actor itself. And, as Chakrabarty continues, 'to call human beings geological agents is to scale up our imagination of the human'.[36] He also differentiates that imagination, noting that the causes and effects of climate change are not equally distributed across the global North and South. The question of just how to do that scaling and differentiating brings us to Ghosh's return to the tsunami fifteen years later, in *The Great Derangement*. In 2005, what Ghosh does is look out from India across the ocean toward the half-forgotten Andaman Islands and reciprocally back towards India from the sea. What happens, he asks, when the scale of the human life encounters the scale of the ocean's abyssal depths? Does this backwater string of islands have something to tell us of the perils of ignoring the global ocean, both its viciousness and its vulnerability, and the ways in which the vulnerabilities of certain populations are a matter of politics as much as environment? He returns to these questions of the oceanic south in the later work by returning obliquely to the tsunami via another extreme weather event, a tornado. *The Great Derangement* is in fact dedicated, as its epigraph indicates, to Indian historian and essayist Mukul Kesavan, 'in memory of the 1978 tornado'. The tornado he means is described in the book in the form of life writing based on southern experience, a generic choice which Ghosh insists is necessary to its expression at all.

In *The Great Derangement,* Ghosh provides the life-historical context for his initial motivation to report on the tsunami in the first place. The author's fourth novel, *The Hungry Tide*, was published in 2004, just a few months before the tsunami. At the novel's climax, one of the protagonists dies when a storm surge is sent by a cyclone through the Sundarbans. Writing those pages required extensive research on the nature of storm surges, tsunamis and other 'catastrophic waves', Ghosh recounts. This background gave the news of the tsunami, only a few months later, a devastating vividness.[37] As he writes:

> The news had a deeply unsettling effect on me: the images that had been implanted in my mind by the writing of *The Hungry Tide* merged with live television footage of the tsunami in a way that was almost overwhelming. I became frantic; I could not focus on anything.[38]

It was for this reason, the intersection of the historical event with the writerly events of his own life, that he obtained a commission from the newspaper to write about the tsunami.

Tsunami, Tornado, Tide

At the time of writing *The Great Derangement*, a relatively minor point from the original essay, described in the previous section, stands out: the tragic irony that 'the most upwardly mobile people on the island were living at its edges'.[39] This is not a matter of haphazard third-world planning but military precision with imperial origins: the most high-ranking offices had their cottages located closest to the sea. Similarly, in New York, Singapore and Mumbai, the wealthiest select sea-views that leave them vulnerable to the open ocean's rare but vicious assault. Sea-facing planning has its high point in the nineteenth century, a periodization that corresponds also to the precipitous rise in atmospheric concentrations of greenhouse gases. That is causing an increase in cyclones, tornadoes and storm surges, which is in turn leading to steadily climbing risks of violent inundation. Ghosh deploys life writing in his attempt to make sense of the complexity of these causes, risks and effects, returning to the scale of the individual life to regain traction – 'my wife and I were actually in Goa at the time, but since New York is also home to us we watched the storm [Hurricane Sandy] closely'.[40] This is a way of dealing in writerly terms with the challenge Chakrabarty also outlines, of disconnected yet concatenating scales:

> The task of placing, historically, the crisis of climate change thus requires us to bring together intellectual formations that are somewhat in tension with each other: the planetary and the global; deep and recorded histories; species thinking and critiques of capital.[41]

Just as Chakrabarty notes the tensions which climate change brings to the fore in the writing of history, Ghosh meditates on the writing of fiction, and life, in a time of climate change. The overlapping faultlines of politics and environment, such as those centred in the oceanic south, are comprehended by bringing southern lives and oceanic contexts to the fore.

The pattern of seafront settlement, from the later viewpoint of climate change, suggests a widely shared, imperially entrenched belief that 'highly improbable events belong not in the real world but in fantasy' and therefore not in the confines of a realist novel.[42] But these events are hardly as improbable as planning, and literary fiction, makes them seem. The Indian Ocean, Ghosh points out, has always been 'fecund in the breeding of cyclones'. In this and other regions of the Indian Ocean, cyclones are a rare but regular occurrence. In Lindsey Collen's *Mutiny*, a cyclone threatens to make landfall on the island of Mauritius, setting the plot – a prison escape – in motion.[43] Cyclone warnings are a part of life on the island, and their repeated invocations pace the novel, building tension until the climax of the simultaneous storm and breakout. A cyclone in Mauritius, while uncommon, is nevertheless a plausible plot device.

A cyclone in Mumbai, however, is far less plausible. That city, reclaimed from the sea and therefore vulnerable to any kind of oceanic disruption, has historically been largely protected from cyclones and storm surges. But Ghosh discovers that cyclones are becoming more likely in the previously much calmer western half of the Indian Ocean, including the Arabian Sea which washes Bombay's coastline. Moreover, while

Ghosh focuses on the northern part of the Indian Ocean, the same changes are evident in the southern. A few years after the publication of *The Great Derangement*, Cyclone Idai struck the coast of Mozambique, extending the cyclone region by several degrees of latitude and raising widespread calls for climate action. In these cases, the weather events are not only rare but in fact unprecedented, not so much as a result of short-sighted colonial planning but of a deeper climatic change. Climate change is fundamentally a discontinuity with past events, and, as Ghosh writes, 'the discontinuities I have pointed to here have a bearing also on the ways in which worlds are created within novels'.[44]

The tornado to which *The Great Derangement* is dedicated is described early on in the book to make this point about historical discontinuity and fictional plausibility. While walking home from the library at Delhi University, where Ghosh was studying for an MA, the weather turned unseasonably stormy. Suddenly he saw 'a gray tube-like extrusion forming on the underside of a dark cloud [which] came whiplashing down to earth, heading in my direction'.[45] It is a terrifying, barely believable experience, introduced with all the details that make life writing believable: the full date (17 March 1978), the location (the intersection called Maurice Nagar), a description of the weather. Afterwards, what is left is a 'scene of devastation:' 'Buses lay overturned, scooters sat perched on treetops, walls had been ripped out of buildings, exposing interiors in which ceiling fans had been twisted into tulip-like spirals'.[46] Newspapers reported the bizarre event initially as 'Cyclone Hits North Delhi' and the next day corrected it to 'tornado' – the meteorological term for a violent windstorm that forms over land rather than sea and is smaller in size than a cyclone. The terminological confusion, as Ghosh points out, speaks to the rarity of the event: in this case, entirely unprecedented, never before having been recorded in history. The tornado was improbable, and in so extreme a way as to be unsuited for use in a novel. As Ghosh writes, despite the fact that the event loomed large in his memory and imagination, 'oddly enough, no tornado has ever figured in my novels'.[47]

The trouble of course is that serious fiction is realist fiction, and realist fiction depends for its effectiveness on being realist*ic*. Prior to the modern novel, stories like *The Arabian Nights* proceeded from one unlikely event to the next, but in the modern realist novel, dramatic events are rationed and concealed by a filling-in of everyday details, providing a sense of overall plausibility.[48] There is, however, an informative exception in the case of sea fiction. Sea fiction, as Margaret Cohen shows, is formative in the history of the novel: the chronotope of the sea is as productive for the genre as Bakhtin's chronotope of the road.[49] Chronotopes of the sea can in turn be divided into different types, Cohen argues: blue water, brown water, white water, the shore, the island and so on. Blue water is the 'realm of the open ocean containing immense and violent powers of weather, terrain (currents, tide, water depth), monstrous animals, and aggressive warriors, as well as pirates and adventurers seeking gain in unpoliced zones beyond the control of sovereign and law'.[50] While the events of the road need to be plausible in line with reader expectation and familiarity, 'the unthinkable is the limit of the open sea';[51] or, in other words, 'blue-water events are strange *and therefore* true'.[52] Blue water is the home of 'terrifying weather' – like tornadoes in Delhi, cyclones in Mozambique, or tsunamis in the wide Indian Ocean. Significantly, the violations of expectation that are normal on the open sea are themselves dependent on prior forms of life writing, nonfictional narratives of shipping life, ship logbooks and sailor memoirs. In other words, the blue water events that tax standards of plausibility are precisely premised on the writing from, and of, life. While rare, then, the events are not supernatural, magical or inexplicable.

What climate change insists upon is the 'centrality of the improbable', the paradoxical predictability and conscious expectation, of 'terrifying weather'.[53] What this suggests, too, is that rather than the domestic novel of realist fiction, models might be found among the novels of blue water and, I argue, among works of life writing from the oceanic south. Cohen suggests *Moby Dick* as well as Joseph Conrad as exemplars of the earlier tradition of sea writing, novels which invoke yet undermine the convention of plausibility: 'the extravagance of blue water happenings is not a mark of their fanciful status, as in some literary contexts. Rather it is testimony to their existence'.[54] The key example is Conrad's *Typhoon*, a precursor novel about a cyclone at sea. In *Typhoon*, the capable and experienced captain of the steamer SS *Nan-Shan* sails straight into a typhoon in the western Pacific Ocean. Here, the tropical cyclone has a different name, but it is the same phenomenon that occurs in the Indian Ocean. In the case of the novel, it is not the reader who finds the cyclone improbable but, as a kind of proxy, the captain himself. When the mercury falls lower than he has experienced before, he fails to imagine the severity of the weather and therefore the severe consequences of not changing course: 'he had seen some bad weather, and had never doubted his ability to imagine the worst; but this was so much beyond his powers of fancy that it appeared incompatible with the existence of any ship whatever'.[55]

It is the high degree of implausibility of blue water novels that distinguishes them from the 'novelistic depictions of life in land-based domestic and high society'[56] – precisely the kind of novel which Ghosh implicates in deranging culture, in making the impending crisis of climate change so difficult to anticipate. Significantly, both land-centred and high-society settings and experiences are at issue here. The Southern Hemisphere, as noted at the start of this chapter, is far more oceanic than the Northern Hemisphere and is also less developed, less 'high society' on a population level. These overlapping fault lines of the oceanic south are the source of their vulnerability, yet also their relevance to the current crisis. Life writing from the oceanic south provides a better understanding of risks, rarity and plausibility, and is therefore a genre to which, as Ghosh's work shows, we might increasingly turn in uncertain times.

Conclusion: Tides

If the tsunami reveals the connectedness of the Indian Ocean world, it also brings into central focus the ocean itself, not only a connecting southern sea but an environmental ocean that is heating through global warming and producing, as a result, more and more cyclones and other tropical storms. The need to combine these extraordinary events with the ordinariness required for novels is what makes fictional narration so difficult. This is despite the fact that those who live in the Southern Hemisphere and

Global South – especially but certainly not exclusively – can recount extraordinary events as part of ordinary life experience. However, the south is oceanic, and the ocean that is centralized by climate change has also long been the setting of improbability's narration in fictional form. Historically, blue water novels, themselves reliant on the life experience of remarkable occurrences, provide a model for the narration of events that are 'strange and therefore true'. Today, life writing from the oceanic south provides the basis for similar narrative experimentation. In Ghosh's work, as an example, nonfictional life writing registers the remarkable, in ways that may form a bridge to the cultural apprehension of a changing planet in fiction, too.

Notes

1. Amitav Ghosh, *The Great Derangement: Climate Change and the Unthinkable* (London: Penguin, 2018), 23.
2. Ghosh, *The Great Derangement*, 23.
3. Margaret Cohen, *The Novel and the Sea* (Princeton, NJ and Oxford: Princeton University Press, 2010), 14.
4. Meg Samuelson and Charne Lavery, 'The Oceanic South', *English Language Notes* 57, no. 1 (2019): 37–50.
5. Prime Minister Narendra Modi quoted in David Rising, 'Everyone Is Talking about the Global South. But What Is It?', AP World News, 7 September 2023. Available online: https://apnews.com/article/what-is-global-south-19fa68cf8c60061e88d69f6f2270d98b/.
6. Tiffany A. Shaw, Osamu Miyawaki and Aaron Donohoe, 'Stormier Southern Hemisphere Induced by Topography and Ocean Circulation', *Proceedings of the National Academy of Sciences* 119, no. 50 (13 December 2022): e2123512119. Available online: https://doi.org/10.1073/pnas.2123512119.
7. Amitav Ghosh, 'The Town by the Sea', in *Incendiary Circumstances: A Chronicle of the Turmoil of Our Times* (Boston and New York: Houghton Mifflin Co., 2005), 1–25.
8. Gaurav Desai, *Commerce with the Universe: Africa, India, and the Afrasian Imagination* (New York: Columbia University Press, 2013); Charne Lavery, *Writing Ocean Worlds: Indian Ocean Fiction in English* (London: Palgrave, 2021).
9. Amitav Ghosh, 'Overlapping Faults', *The Hindu*, 11 January 2005, sec. National. Available online: https://www.thehindu.com/todays-paper/tp-national/overlapping-faults/article27293242.ece; Amitav Ghosh, 'No Aid Needed', *The Hindu*, 12 January 2005, sec. National. Available online: https://www.thehindu.com/todays-paper/tp-national/no-aid-needed/article27293731.ece; Amitav Ghosh, 'The Town by the Sea', *The Hindu*, 13 January 2005, sec. National. Available online: https://www.thehindu.com/todays-paper/tp-national/the-town-by-the-sea/article27294408.ece.
10. Amitav Ghosh, *Incendiary Circumstances: A Chronicle of the Turmoil of Our Times* (Boston: Houghton Mifflin, 2005). Available online: http://www.loc.gov/catdir/toc/ecip0512/2005012175.html; Alessandro Vescovi, 'Amitav Ghosh as a Secular Essayist', *Postcolonial Text* 18, no. 1–2 (2023): 1–19.
11. Abdulrazak Gurnah, *By the Sea* (London: Bloomsbury, 2001).
12. Ghosh, 'The Town by the Sea', 1.

13. Thorne Lay et al., 'The Great Sumatra-Andaman Earthquake of 26 December 2004', *Science* 308, no. 5725 (20 May 2005): 1127–33. Available online: https://doi.org/10.1126/science.1112250.
14. Isabel Hofmeyr, 'Southern by Degrees: Islands and Empires in the South Atlantic, the Indian Ocean and the Sub-Antarctic World', in *The Global South Atlantic*, ed. Kerry Bystrom and Joseph R. Slaughter (New York: Fordham University Press, 2017), 93.
15. Ghosh, 'The Town by the Sea', 2.
16. Ibid., 9.
17. See Isabel Hofmeyr, 'Styling Multilateralism: Indian Ocean Cultural Futures', *Journal of the Indian Ocean Region* 11, no. 1 (2015): 98–109.
18. Sugata Bose, *A Hundred Horizons: The Indian Ocean in the Age of Global Empire* (Cambridge, MA: Harvard University Press, 2006).
19. Bose, *A Hundred Horizons*, 3.
20. Ghosh, 'The Town by the Sea', 7.
21. Ibid., 6.
22. Ghosh, *The Great Derangement*, 62.
23. Ghosh, 'The Town by the Sea', 8.
24. Ibid., 4–5.
25. Ibid., 2.
26. Ibid.
27. Ibid., 3.
28. Ibid., 5.
29. Ibid.
30. Ibid., 6.
31. Ibid., 14.
32. Ibid., 23.
33. Ibid., 24.
34. Ibid., 25.
35. Dipesh Chakrabarty, 'The Climate of History: Four Theses', *Critical Inquiry* 35, no. 2 (2009): 212.
36. Chakrabarty, 'The Climate of History', 206.
37. Ghosh, *The Great Derangement*, 33.
38. Ibid.
39. Ibid.
40. Ibid., 39.
41. Chakrabarty, 'The Climate of History', 213.
42. Ghosh, *The Great Derangement*, 33.
43. Lindsey Collen, *Mutiny* (London: Bloomsbury, 2002).
44. Ghosh, *The Great Derangement*, 57.
45. Ibid., 11.
46. Ibid., 12.
47. Ibid., 28.

48. Ibid., 17.
49. Margaret Cohen, 'The Chronotopes of the Sea', *The Novel* 2 (2007): 647.
50. Ibid., 650.
51. Ibid., 651.
52. Ibid., 650.
53. Ghosh, *The Great Derangement*, 23; Cohen, 'The Chronotopes of the Sea', 651.
54. Cohen, 'The Chronotopes of the Sea', 651.
55. Joseph Conrad, *Typhoon and Other Tales*, rev. ed., ed. Cedric Watts (Oxford, New York: Oxford University Press, 1903).
56. Cohen, 'The Chronotopes of the Sea', 652.

Bibliography

Bose, Sugata. *A Hundred Horizons: The Indian Ocean in the Age of Global Empire*. Cambridge, MA: Harvard University Press, 2006.
Chakrabarty, Dipesh. 'The Climate of History: Four Theses'. *Critical Inquiry* 35, no. 2 (2009): 197–222.
Cohen, Margaret. 'The Chronotopes of the Sea'. *The Novel* 2 (2007): 647–66.
Cohen, Margaret. *The Novel and the Sea*. Princeton, NJ and Oxford: Princeton University Press, 2010.
Collen, Lindsey. *Mutiny*. London: Bloomsbury, 2002.
Conrad, Joseph. *Typhoon and Other Tales*. Rev. ed. Edited by Cedric Watts. Oxford, New York: Oxford University Press, 1903.
Desai, Gaurav. *Commerce with the Universe: Africa, India, and the Afrasian Imagination*. New York: Columbia University Press, 2013.
Ghosh, Amitav. *The Great Derangement: Climate Change and the Unthinkable*. London: Penguin, 2018.
Ghosh, Amitav. *Incendiary Circumstances: A Chronicle of the Turmoil of Our Times*. Boston: Houghton Mifflin, 2005. Available online: http://www.loc.gov/catdir/toc/ecip0512/2005012175.html.
Ghosh, Amitav. 'No Aid Needed'. *The Hindu*, 12 January 2005, sec. National. Available online: https://www.thehindu.com/todays-paper/tp-national/no-aid-needed/article27293731.ece.
Ghosh, Amitav. 'Overlapping Faults'. *The Hindu*, 11 January 2005, sec. National. Available online: https://www.thehindu.com/todays-paper/tp-national/overlapping-faults/article27293242.ece.
Ghosh, Amitav. 'The Town by the Sea'. *The Hindu*, 13 January 2005, sec. National. Available online: https://www.thehindu.com/todays-paper/tp-national/the-town-by-the-sea/article27294408.ece.
Ghosh, Amitav. 'The Town by the Sea'. In *Incendiary Circumstances: A Chronicle of the Turmoil of Our Times*, 1–25. Boston and New York: Houghton Mifflin, 2005.
Gurnah, Abdulrazak. *By the Sea*. London: Bloomsbury, 2001.
Hofmeyr, Isabel. 'Southern by Degrees: Islands and Empires in the South Atlantic, the Indian Ocean and the Sub-Antarctic World'. In *The Global South Atlantic*, edited by Kerry Bystrom and Joseph R. Slaughter, 81–96. New York: Fordham University Press, 2017.
Hofmeyr, Isabel. 'Styling Multilateralism: Indian Ocean Cultural Futures'. *Journal of the Indian Ocean Region* 11, no. 1 (2015): 98–109.
Lavery, Charne. *Writing Ocean Worlds: Indian Ocean Fiction in English*. London: Palgrave, 2021.

Lay, Thorne, Hiroo Kanamori, Charles J. Ammon, Meredith Nettles, Steven N. Ward, Richard C. Aster, Susan L. Beck et al. 'The Great Sumatra-Andaman Earthquake of 26 December 2004'. *Science* 308, no. 5725 (20 May 2005): 1127–33. Available online: https://doi.org/10.1126/science.1112250.

Rising, David. 'Everyone Is Talking about the Global South. But What Is It'? AP World News, 7 September 2023. Available online: https://apnews.com/article/what-is-global-south-19fa68cf8c60061e88d69f6f2270d98b.

Samuelson, Meg, and Charne Lavery. 'The Oceanic South'. *English Language Notes* 57, no. 1 (2019): 37–50.

Shaw, Tiffany A., Osamu Miyawaki, and Aaron Donohoe. 'Stormier Southern Hemisphere Induced by Topography and Ocean Circulation'. *Proceedings of the National Academy of Sciences* 119, no. 50 (13 December 2022): e2123512119. Available online: https://doi.org/10.1073/pnas.2123512119.

Vescovi, Alessandro. 'Amitav Ghosh as a Secular Essayist'. *Postcolonial Text* 18, no. 1–2 (2023): 1–19.

CHAPTER 11
THE REPRESENTATION OF WATER SPIRITS IN SOUTHERN AFRICAN LITERATURE
Confidence Joseph

The relationship between nature and humans has been a preoccupation of many writers and critics, albeit with a bias towards land. It is only recently, in the Global South at least, that water is being foregrounded in its material and spiritual dimensions.[1] By centring water, the texts privilege other ways of knowing, reading and writing southern lives – ways that are based on intuition and cultural attitudes.[2] Southern waters resist reductive readings, especially reading African lives as those of victims and the African story as destitute. In my reading for water in the selected texts, when characters are aligned with water or when embodying water spirits, they cease to be victims and instead experience agency. This turn towards watery spaces in African literature highlights what Isabel Hofmeyr and Charne Larvey view as 'the new styles of humanities research that speak to environmental and decolonial themes' that have been necessitated by 'rising sea levels'.[3] This turn, among other possibilities, calls for a re-reading of old texts in new ways, foregrounding the improbable and broadening our understanding of the universe as also populated and shaped by the other-than-human. Through a decolonial reading, this chapter explores how water spirits have been represented in southern African literature as figurations of resistance for social, political and environmental purposes. The texts under consideration are Meg Vandermerwe's *The Woman of the Stone Sea* (2019), Lynton Burger's *She Down There* (2020) and *The Return of the Water Spirit* (2002) by Pepetela, which was originally published in 1995 as *O Desejo de Kianda*. In these texts, water and water spirits become protagonists, rather than backdrops for human desires. Acknowledging the 'other than human' that we coexist with, such as spiritual beings, aquatic creatures and nature, might mitigate the effects of the current water pollution crisis, global warming and environmental catastrophes. As the chapter will show, the mythic and the material here become inextricable with how lives are lived and perceived in writing.

Water spirits who manifest in different forms (mermaids, snakes, humans, rainbows, songs and even as water) have different names and personalities depending on socio-historical, cultural contexts and authorial intention. Sometimes we even encounter formless water spirits that emphasize their ethereal attributes. In some cultural products, water spirits are represented as protective spirits that assist people in negotiating the challenges of life. These benevolent spirits seek to bring balance to an unjust world. Elsewhere, they come out as chaotic and vindictive spirits mirroring society's inequalities. Sometimes, they muddy the line between us and the 'other'. Our ambivalent relationship with the element of water seems to inform our characterization of water creatures. In the right circumstances and proportions, water can sustain life but, in excess, it can also kill. Similarly, the water-spirit figure has come to represent both the desires of mankind and the dangers of the ocean. As a result, water and water spirits emerge as significant narrative tools and metaphors in literary texts. The rest of the chapter will unfold as follows. Firstly, I provide a brief overview of southern African water spirits. I then consider how water spirits are used in different forms of writing to protest postcolonial betrayal, environmental degradation and female subjugation.

Southern African water spirits

In some parts of southern Africa, water spirits like *Mamlambo, Njuzu, Nzuzu* and *Kianda*[4] are perceived as protectors of the waters (oceans, rivers, dams, swamps and deep lakes). Some people associate these spirits with their ancestors while some view them as providers and caretakers of different communities. Illustrative is the case of the Tonga people of the Zambezi Valley region in north-west Zimbabwe whose river god *Nyamimyami* sustained them during periods of drought. *Nyaminyami* would expose his back so that people would cut out meat for nourishment.[5] Similarly, the villagers of Matimati in Mia Couto's *Sleepwalking Land* summon and entreat their ancestors who are believed to be in the deep waters of the Indian Ocean.[6] The ancestors offer assistance, which manifests in the form of food and other basic commodities recovered from sinking or sunken ships. In turn, water spirits are expected to be revered and propitiated. For instance, in Angola, those who believe in *Kianda* often express their devotion by offering food and clothing to the sea. Just like other water spirits, if disrespected or neglected, *Kianda* withholds fish and makes the sea ominous.[7] The water spirits are also known as protectors of the environment and will fight back when their abodes are threatened. This is seen when *Nyaminyami* protests the construction of the Kariba Dam on the Zambezi River, a project of assemblage which began in 1956 and concluded in 1959. In 1957, the development of the dam was paused because of excessive damage caused by flooding. Whilst the engineers in charge of the project assured that there were scientific reasons for the dam's crumbling walls, locals maintained that it was *Nyaminyami* expressing his wrath.[8]

While it is tempting to think of indigenous southern African water spirits as homogeneous, figures such as the *Watermeisie* from South Africa complicate this notion. Mapule Mohulatsi argues that the coming together of different cultures such as the European, enslaved and the Khoi in the Cape region over time gave birth to the creolized figure of the *Watermeisie*.[9] This figure also suggests a diffusion of different knowledge-systems across southern Africa. The migration of workers to South Africa from different parts of southern, eastern and central Africa saw a concomitant migration of water-spirit stories and beliefs. In analyzing the representation of water spirits in southern African literature, it becomes apparent that water-spirit beliefs have cross-pollinated. The resultant creolized waters mirror creolized communities, which draws our attention to the possibility of reading and writing human histories and trajectories in water. If anything, the notion of creolized waters illustrates the entangled nature of knowledge systems that we encounter in most southern African writings and the problematic nature of 'authentic' identities that most nationalist narratives insist on. I now turn to the representation of *Kianda* in Pepetela's *The Return of the Water Spirit*.

Kianda: The vindictive water spirit

In *The Return of the Water Spirit*, *Kianda* exemplifies water spirits who are destructive and vengeful in protesting hostile socio-political circumstances. The newly independent nation of Angola is embroiled in a bitter civil war 'as different political ideologies – anti-colonialism, socialism and capitalism – refuse to compromise with each other'.[10] This discord ignites a costly civil war that cripples the nation and prompts the return of *Kianda*. Other instances where we encounter hostile water spirits are in Sara Blecher's film *Otelo Burning* where *Mamlambo* causes havoc, mirroring the anxieties of transitioning from apartheid to democracy in South Africa.[11] In the film, the water snake is a vengeful water spirit that lurks underwater before striking its unsuspecting victims. It is also a figurative embodiment of human greed, jealousy, anger and violence. Another example is in Zimbabwean author Dambudzo Marechera's short story 'Protista' in *House of Hunger* where the malignant figure of the manfish, which I read as the *Njuzu*,[12] symbolizes the bitter hostilities of colonial Rhodesia. The bloodthirsty manfish in the story is reminiscent of the diabolical snake in fellow Zimbabwean writer Charles Mungoshi's *Waiting for the Rain*, which immiserates the Mandengu family.[13]

The Return of the Water Spirit is set in the late 1990s, nearly two decades after Angola's independence from Portugal's colonial rule. While at one level, the novel portrays the political reality of the newly independent state, it also addresses issues of class, gender and the environment. The novel narrates the story of Joao and Carmina Evangelista, whose good fortunes contrast with the impoverishment of most Angolans. Hunger and strife oppose the promise of independence. The postcolonial Luanda that informs the text is filled with the 'non-stop begging of the street kids, the war amputees and the old people thrown out on to the street by poverty'.[14] Suffering in the city transforms the couple's virtuous friend Honorio into a fraudster, and he ends up losing his home, job and family. With nothing left to lose, he and other demonstrators occupy Kinaxixi Square in the central part of Luanda. But the novel is also about *Kianda*, the water spirit whose lagoon was drained to make way for the modern skyscrapers that now dominate Kinaxixi Square. We later discover that *Kianda* is responsible for the mysterious collapse of these buildings as he fights to reclaim his territory. The narrator reveals that '*Kianda* felt asphyxiated with all that weight on top of him. He was unable to swim, and so finally he revolted.'[15] Curiously, the collapse of the buildings does not harm people and animals. One can then argue that through his revolt, *Kianda* is fighting for the oppressed and against the glaring inadequacies of the postcolonial government.

The novel introduces *Kianda* as an angry water spirit in a small lagoon. He assumes the form of a soft song only discernible to a young girl, Cassandra. With time, the song increases in volume and impact as the level of water in the lagoon rises. The strength of the song and the water seem to correlate with the number of buildings that keep crumbling. The song quickly becomes a battle song as *Kianda*'s fight intensifies. Despite Pepetela denying Kianda a tangible form, his wrath is felt all over Luanda. When it reaches its peak, the water in the lagoon bursts and floods the entire city as *Kianda* makes his way back to the ocean. These different but connected threads in the novel (*Kianda* and Carmina's stories) present a non-linear concept of time and space as *Kianda*'s return relaxes rigid boundaries between past and present and between natural and supernatural. His return invokes multiple realities which are juxtaposed in the novel, a multiplicity mirrored and extended by its mythical form.

Before independence, Luanda was known as a cement city built especially for Portuguese settlers.[16] These buildings represented Portugal's colonial control in Angola, and after independence, these structures continued to symbolize the unequal distribution of resources. Claudia Gastrow argues that while Luanda became a massive construction site soon after the civil war as the state and private entities made efforts to restore the broken city, the buildings were inadequate to cater for the growing population of Luanda and the majority remained in the slums.[17] The poor still crowded the slums on the outskirts of the city. In the context of postcolonial Angola, as the poverty-stricken citizens kept being elbowed from the city, these projects exemplified what Thomas Waller terms 'an urbanisation process geared towards providing houses for private investors and the governmental elite, while the majority of the population are imprisoned in poverty'.[18] This might explain why *Kianda* destroys the buildings in Kinaxixi Square, which are symbols of exploitation and marginalization. For Pepetela, the myth of *Kianda* becomes a loaded narrative device for capturing the colonial and postcolonial anxieties of the common people in Angola.

Some critics have read *Kianda*'s return in Pepetela's novel as a sign for Angolans to reject foreign influence and reclaim their values lost through colonization.[19] My reading of *Kianda* in the novel seeks to complicate these ideas. I argue that while the water-spirit trope can metaphorize the desire in Angola for an agency that is predicated on indigenous epistemologies, *Kianda*'s 'return' negates definite resolutions. His representation in the novel as a formless and elusive figure problematizes any such return and, in so doing, complicates the idea of a pristine Angolanness or authentic Angolan experience that is retrievable. I read *Kianda*'s return and chaotic manifestation in the novel as representative of the broken political and socio-economic system in postcolonial Angola. As he triumphantly returns to the sea, *Kianda* leaves behind a large group of protesters who lack a clear way forward. This can indicate Pepetela's refusal to create a messiah out of *Kianda* in recognition of the elusive and ongoing search for meaningful solutions in postcolonial war-torn Angola. Departing from the vindictive and hostile *Kianda*, I now turn to a benign water spirit.

The protective *Sedna* in Lynton Burger's *She Down There* (2020)

In this section, I build on Penny Bernard's work on the role of indigenous knowledge in the protection of the environment.[20] Bernard suggests that because some bodies of water are believed to house different spirits, they become sacred sites where different rituals occur. The sanctification of these bodies of water ensures their protection. Elsewhere, Jauquelyne Kosgei highlights the value of indigenous knowledge in the conservation of marine life through a reading of poetry by Kenya's coastal communities. She argues that because of their dependence on the sea for survival, these communities mostly made up of fisherfolk are in 'possession of unique knowledge and practices that aid in the conservation of the ocean'.[21] In a Zimbabwean context, Collins Garikai Machoko demonstrates that the beliefs in *Njuzu* recognize the sacredness of the natural environment, hence the need for its preservation.[22] This link of water spirits to conservation is especially relevant in this era of unprecedented assaults on the natural world. Thinking with these scholars, we appreciate the importance of indigenous knowledge in preserving the environment, a theme that I explore through my reading of *Sedna*, the water spirit in Burger's *She Down There*.[23]

Drawing on different indigenous beliefs about water, Burger creates a world where 'the sea is inhabited by many supernatural creatures, the underwater people.... Creatures from a time when the veil between humans and other animals was thin.'[24] As a result, the ocean becomes a space that dissolves the hierarchies popular in land-based narratives. In this instance, water allows for certain forms of writing where all creatures are equal and interconnected. In the novel, *Sedna* manifests as a water spirit inclined towards reconciling the relationship between humans and oceans. From the myth of her origin, *Sedna* can be read as both a water spirit and a sea creature. The legend tells how *Sedna* was hacked to pieces and thrown into the ocean by her father for defying the elders and refusing to marry. The parts of her that were thrown into the ocean metamorphose into different sea creatures, explaining why *Sedna*'s first duty is to protect the animals who as an extension, are her offspring. The pain she feels when sea creatures are being hunted down is dramatized in the first chapter of the novel where she fights to save two sea cows from being impaled by poachers. When she fails to save the cows, 'she cries out as if she too has been impaled'.[25] *Sedna*'s heart bleeds not only for the lost sea cows but especially for the divide between humanity and nature. This incident serves as an example of the many fights this water spirit engages in to save the ocean and all its life forms. As I argue elsewhere, *Sedna*'s death, which at first suggests an ending, is transformed into a beginning of new lives, a multi-species turn that explains the interconnectedness of diverse creatures in the novel.[26]

Sedna is described as half-woman, half sea-creature in line with some beliefs concerning water spirits. We read that she was 'forever destined to be the voice of the sea creatures, the one that the Shamans have to dive down to each spring to appease, to ask to release the animals for the summer hunt'.[27] Like most water spirits, she must be appeased and worshipped to keep providing for her followers. In some African novels, nature is shown as being at the mercy of humans, but positioning *Sedna* as nature's voice suggests otherwise. The fact that the shamans must ask *Sedna* to release animals for the people's sustenance shows the reciprocal relationship between nature and humans. *Sedna*'s depiction in the novel not only gives nature agency but also dissolves the line between the natural and the supernatural. The lack of a veil between human and animal spirits in the ocean points to the belief in the existence of a universal consciousness that unites all life and non-life forms. In reconciling the human with the ocean, Burger does not restrict us to the materiality of the ocean but instead unites us as humans with its creatures.

Besides *Sedna*, we have Claire, a character that I read as a contemporary water spirit in the novel. This framing of Claire resonates with William Kamkwamba, a character in Chiwetel Ejiofor's film *The Boy Who Harnessed the Wind* (2019),[28] who I read as a contemporary rainmaker. To save his family from starvation, William defies the odds and builds a windmill. This windmill provides enough power to pump water from underground to irrigate crops. While traditional rainmakers would have performed rituals to attract the rain, the thirteen-year-old boy improvises and turns to the rubbish dump to secure some of the materials he needs to build his windmill. While William turns to books and the dumpsite, Claire relies on her professional skills to save the ocean and its creatures. Claire is a marine biologist who 'feels as comfortable underwater as on land'.[29] Just like *Sedna*, Claire's passion is to understand and protect the ocean and its creatures. She also has deep ancestral links that tie her to water. Her grandmother constantly reminds her that they are sea people. In as much as *Sedna* makes the depths of the ocean her home, Claire's profession as a marine biologist allows her access to the deep sea. She carries the torch of her Haidan ancestors who as 'indigenous peoples regard the inland waters, rivers, wetlands, sea, islands, reefs, sandbars and seagrass beds as an inseparable part of their estate'.[30] Through her job, Claire is involved in research projects that allow her to contribute to the preservation of the ocean and its creatures just as *Sedna* does. Through the figures of *Sedna* and Claire, Burger shows how a change in our attitude towards that which is other-than-human is needed to protect our environment, especially in this period of untenable global warming.

The untameable Rebekkah in Meg Vandermerwe's *The Woman of the Stone Sea* (2019)

In this section, I explore how Meg Vandermerwe's *The Woman of the Stone Sea*[31] draws on the indomitable nature of water spirits to express feminine agency. In this, I think with Henry John Drewal's conceptualization of *Mamiwata* (a central and western African water spirit) as representing a free spirit outside patriarchal social norms.[32] This link between the feminine, water spirits and water bodies is also evident in Flora Nwapa's works where female characters draw strength from certain goddesses of the river.[33] Similarly, Vandermerwe rescues and empowers her female characters by aligning them to water spirits and in so doing provides them with unconventional sanctuary in water. In the novel, the figure of the *Watermeisie* (water maiden) is used to enable female characters like Rebekkah to confound societal expectations and live freely like the water maidens at sea. Rebekkah is a non-conformist who not only challenges her husband Hendrick but also the society at large. Her wilfulness is constantly compared to that of water spirits who are known for their independence and obstinance. We encounter the same trend in Mohale Mashigo's short story 'Manoka' in her 2019 collection *Intruders* where water and the ability to shape-shift into sea creatures liberates and empowers female characters.

The Woman of the Stone Sea draws on the creolized *Watermeisie* tradition which unites Khoisan ideas on water spirits and popular ideas on *Mamlambo* to interrogate the ideas of not only freedom but also of gender equality in post-apartheid South Africa. The novel is set in a small village on the west coast of South Africa. It is the story of Hendrik, a struggling fisherman. His wife Rebekkah relocates to this coastal village from the dry lands of Karoo, a fact that might explain her fascination with water and mermaid stories throughout the novel. She later disappears, never to be seen again, and because of her fascination with water, the villagers believe she was swallowed by the sea. Throughout the narrative, Rebekkah is obsessed with both the idea of mermaids and water. She divulges to Hendrick that '[w]hen I was a girl on the farm, Ouma (grandmother) told me stories. About water maidens. When I was little … even as a teenager, that's what I wanted to be. Beautiful and free in the water like them.'[34] The simile captures Rebekkah's drive throughout the narrative, to chase her desires. When she later disappears and Hendrick travels to her hometown to look for her, Rebekkah's Ouma concludes that '[m]aybe the water maidens took her'.[35] She wonders if 'Hendrick want[s] her to perform the rituals needed to get her back'.[36] This offer by the grandmother to conduct rituals to get Rebekkah back recalls some southern African beliefs where sangomas (traditional healers) appeal to water spirits for the safe return of 'drowned' individuals.[37] With the help of the sangomas, the victim's family performs certain rituals that are accompanied by sacrifices. If the water spirits accept the sacrifices, the person returns from the depths of the waters without harm and at times with the added endowment of powerful healing powers. However, if the procedure is done incorrectly, the family might never see their relative again.

In the novel, Rebekkah is introduced as the beautiful new primary school teacher who sweeps Hendrick off his feet. Her independence and determination to carve her own path sets her apart. Before long, she is known as an inkommer (newcomer) who has no respect for village traditions. Rebekkah's independence sets her apart in a village where everyone tries to oblige societal expectations. She carries this aloof nature into her relationship with Hendrick who desperately tries to pin her down. In most popular imaginaries, the mermaid figure is ever seductive but remains unattainable. We learn from Hendrick's flashbacks that Rebekkah was likewise inaccessible both before and after their marriage: 'She's been swimming. She's wearing an orange costume and she's laughing; but her eyes are like they often were with him, distant and hard.'[38] One can argue that from the beginning she defied the idea of marriage as ownership, as water spirits cannot be owned. Like the water maids she is drawn to, Rebekkah refuses to fully commit to Hendrick after marriage and insists on making her own decisions. When

Hendrick tries to warn her about the dangers of loitering alone in the dark, she firmly tells him, 'I can look after myself. Don't tell me what to do.'[39] Her attitude and behaviour resonate with Phephelaphi, the female protagonist in Yvonne Vera's *Butterfly Burning* (1998). As I argue elsewhere, Phephelaphi is described as a woman who chose her own destinations regardless of the cost.[40] Similarly, Rebekkah puts her needs first when, just like Vera's Phephelaphi, she informs Hendrick that 'I do not want a baby, Hendrick. Not with you or anyone. I'm not going to stop having the injection.'[41] Rebekkah is on birth control measures, an indication of her determination to own her body. Instead of bowing to the reproductive role assigned to them by phallocratic regimes, Phephelaphi and Rebekkah battle to emplace themselves in productive public spaces, the former through her dreams of becoming a nurse and the latter through becoming a teacher. Through this association with water spirits, the female characters struggle for and achieve autonomy over their bodies and lives.

I argue that although Rebekkah marries Hendrick, she remains just as elusive as a mermaid until she vanishes never to be seen again. The day Rebekkah disappears she is seen 'standing, stockstil, up to her ankles in the surf, looking out to the silver horizon'.[42] The narrator stresses that 'everyone knew she liked to swim by herself, even early in the morning, and since women don't just evaporate and since no one saw her leave the village by the small dirt road, it was decided that she must have paddled out and been swept away by a sudden strong current'.[43] Water spirits are known to vanish if disrespected or their abodes disregarded. Read within this frame, Rebekkah's feelings of suffocation with Hendrick's efforts to domesticate her, prompted her disappearance with no trace. From these illustrative attributes, Rebekkah can be likened to the water maids she often spoke about. Growing up in dry Karoo, the boundless sea represented the ultimate freedom for her and, just like Mashigo's Manoka, her escape from patriarchal constraints is tied to the sea.

Conclusion

The entanglements between the human and non-human, land and water – the natural and the supernatural – that one encounters in the texts speaks to many ways of being in these watery southern worlds. I argue that these watery readings are a necessary approach to analyzing southern African literature that transcend the limiting political and historical readings that are popular in literary studies. The water spirits take on diverse roles and assume varied forms. In *The Return of the Water Spirit*, Pepetela deploys the figure of *Kianda* to represent the challenges of postcolonial Angola. The struggle for solutions persists in war-torn Angola mirroring the struggle to pin down *Kianda*, the elusive water spirit in the text. The slipperiness of *Kianda* also speaks to the challenges of reclaiming an authentic Angolan identity to which some critics have linked the figure. Additionally, the recognition of the presence of spirits in water turns water bodies into sacred sites that are revered and preserved. If people take seriously other means of knowing the world (indigenous knowledge systems), conservation efforts can be improved, as we find in *She Down There*. We are left to ponder what the oceans and rivers would be like if we thought of them as sacred waters – perhaps it is not too late to switch to that reverential attitude before all water bodies are desecrated. Lastly, by aligning female characters with indomitable water spirits, we see that instead of being read as victims of patriarchal regimes, characters like Rebekkah can be reread as individuals with some agency, who are not merely at the mercy of patriarchal forces.

Notes

1. Hester Blum, 'The Prospect of Oceanic Studies', *PMLA* 125, no. 3 (2010): 670–7.
2. Kerry Bystrom and Isabel Hofmeyr, 'Oceanic Routes: (Post-It) Notes on Hydro-colonialism', *Comparative Literature* 69, no. 1 (2017): 1–6.
3. Isabel Hofmeyr and Charne Lavery, 'Oceanic Humanities for Blue Heritage', in *The Palgrave Handbook of Blue Heritage*, ed. Rosabelle Boswell, David O'Kane and Jeremy Hills (Cham: Springer International Publishing, 2022).
4. For clarity and emphasis, the names of the water spirits in this chapter will be presented in italics.
5. Luck Makuyane, 'Hydro-colonialism: A Hydro-critical Reading of Three Texts on Kariba' (MA diss., University of the Witwatersrand, Johannesburg, 2021).
6. Mia Couto, *Sleepwalking Land*, trans. David Brookshaw. (London: Serpent's Tail, 2006).
7. Clara Onofre, 'Angola: On the Mermaid Kianda and Other Mythical Beings', Web log. *Global Voices* (blog), 28 October 2018. Available online: https://globalvoices.org/2008/10/28/angola-on-the-mermaid-kianda-and-other-mythical-beings/.
8. Joshua Matanzima, 'Stereotyping, Exploitation, and Appropriation of African Traditional Religious Beliefs: The Case of Nyaminyami, Water Spirit, among the Batonga People of Northwestern Zimbabwe, 1860s–1960s', *Journal of Africana Religions* 10, no. 1 (2022): 72–99.
9. Mapule Mohulatsi, 'Black Aesthetics and the Deep Ocean' (MA diss., University of the Witwatersrand, Johannesburg, 2019).
10. Emily Chow, 'Forging New Selves at the Junction of Times: The Foundation of an Angolan Identity in Pepetela's *The Return of the Water Spirit*', *Projection 1*, no. 1 (2012): 54–62.
11. Blecher, Sara (dir.), *Otelo Burning*. DVD. South Africa: Sara Blecher and Cinga Films, 2011.
12. The manfish figure in 'Protista' shares resemblances with the *njuzu*, both exhibiting traits of mythical water beings. Like the *njuzu*, the manfish transforms the river into an enchanted realm, exerting a captivating influence. Similarly, the manfish possesses the ability to entice individuals into its aquatic realm, mirroring the *njuzu's* reputed lure of victims into their abodes. Although the *njuzu* can be benevolent, offering awards to individuals in certain instances, they also possess the potential for malevolence, as depicted in the story, causing harm or torment to their victims.
13. Charles Mungoshi, *Waiting for the Rain* (London: Heinemann, 1975).
14. Pepetela, *The Return of the Water Spirit*, trans. L. R. Mitras (London: Heinemann, 2002).
15. Ibid., 108.

16. António Andrade Tomás, 'Refracted Governmentality: Space, Politics and Social Structure in Contemporary Luanda' (PhD diss., Columbia University, 2012).
17. Claudia Gastrow, 'Cement Citizens: Housing, Demolition and Political Belonging in Luanda, Angola', *Citizenship Studies* 21, no. 2 (2017): 224–39.
18. Thomas Waller, 'The Blue Cultural Fix: Water-Spirits and World-Ecology in Jorge Amado's *Mar Morto* and Pepetela's *O Desejo de Kianda*', *Humanities* 9, no. 3 (2020): 72.
19. Victor Ogbeide, 'Pepetela's *The Return of the Water Spirit* as a Parable of the Postcolonial Condition in Angola', *European Scientific Journal* 9, no. 35 (2013): 157–69.
20. Penny Bernard, 'Ecological Implications of Water Spirit Beliefs', *USDA Forest Service Proceedings, RMRS-P-27* (2003): 148–54.
21. Jauquelyne Kosgei, 'Indigenous Knowledge and Marine Conservation', *Wasafiri* 36, no. 2 (2021): 71–8.
22. Collins Garikai Machoko, 'Water Spirits and the Conservation of the Natural Environment: A Case Study from Zimbabwe', *International Journal of Sociology and Anthropology* 5, no. 8 (2013): 285–96.
23. Lynton Burger, *She Down There* (Johannesburg: Penguin Random House, 2020).
24. Ibid., 30–1.
25. Ibid., 9.
26. Confidence Joseph, 'Multi-spirited Waters in Lynton Burger's *She Down There*', in *The Palgrave Handbook of Blue Heritage*, ed. Rosabelle Boswell, David O'Kane and Jeremy Hills (Cham: Springer International Publishing, 2022), 141–59.
27. Burger, *She Down There*, 6.
28. The film *The Boy Who Harnessed the Wind* (2019), written and directed by Chiwetel Ejiofor, is set in Malawi. It follows the narrative of a young boy who ingeniously constructs a windmill using discarded materials, aiming to generate electricity for his family and village.
29. Burger, *She Down There*, 20.
30. Sue Jackson and Jon Altman, 'Indigenous Rights and Water Policy: Perspectives from Tropical Northern Australia', *Australian Indigenous Law Review* 13, no. 1 (2009): 27–48.
31. Meg Vandermerwe, *The Woman of the Stone Sea* (Cape Town: Umuzi, 2019).
32. Henry John Drewal, 'Mami Wata: Arts for Water Spirits in Africa and its Diasporas', *African Arts* 41, no. 2 (2008): 60–83.
33. Flora Nwapa, a renowned Nigerian writer, is celebrated as a leading figure in African feminism due to her substantial body of work that offers insights into Igbo customs from a feminine standpoint. Notable works by Nwapa include *Idu* (1970), *This Is Lagos, and Other Stories* (1971), *One Is Enough* (1981), *Never Again* (1975), *Wives at War, and Other Stories* (1980) and *Women Are Different* (1986).
34. Vandermerwe, *The Woman of the Stone Sea*, 32.
35. Ibid., 56.
36. Ibid.
37. Bernard, 'Ecological Implications of Water Spirit Beliefs', 148–54.
38. Vandermerwe, *The Woman of the Stone Sea*, 67.
39. Ibid., 108.
40. Confidence Joseph, 'Of Water and Water Spirits in Southern African Literature' (PhD diss., University of the Witwatersrand, Johannesburg, 2021).

41. Vandermerwe, *The Woman of the Stone Sea*, 93.
42. Ibid., 53.
43. Ibid.

Bibliography

Bernard, Penny. 'Ecological Implications of Water Spirit Beliefs in Southern Africa: The Need to Protect Knowledge, Nature, and Resource Rights'. *USDA Forest Service Proceedings* RMRS-P-27 (2003): 148–53.
Blecher, Sara, dir. *Otelo Burning*. DVD. South Africa: Sara Blecher and Cinga Films, 2011.
Blum, Hester. 'The Prospect of Oceanic Studies'. *PMLA* 125, no. 3 (2010): 670–7.
Burger, Lynton. *She Down There*. Johannesburg: Penguin Random House, 2020.
Bystrom, Kerry, and Isabel Hofmeyr. 'Oceanic Routes: (Post-It) Notes on Hydro-Colonialism'. *Comparative Literature* 69, no. 1 (2017): 1–6.
Chow, Emily. 'Forging New Selves at the Junction of Times: The Foundation of an Angolan Identity in Pepetela's *The Return of the Water Spirit*'. *Projection 1*, no. 1 (2012): 54–62.
Couto, Mia. *Sleepwalking Land*, trans. David Brookshaw. London: Serpent's Tail, 2006.
Drewal, Henry John. 'Mami Wata: Arts for Water Spirits in Africa and its Diasporas'. *African Arts* 41, no. 2 (2008): 60–83.
Gastrow, Claudia. 'Cement Citizens: Housing, Demolition and Political Belonging in Luanda, Angola'. *Citizenship Studies* 21, no. 2 (2017): 224–39.
Hofmeyr, Isabel, and Charne Lavery. 'Oceanic Humanities for Blue Heritage'. In *The Palgrave Handbook of Blue Heritage*, edited by Rosabelle Boswell, David O'Kane and Jeremy Hills, 31–40. Cham: Springer International Publishing, 2022.
Jackson, Sue, and Jon Altman. 'Indigenous Rights and Water Policy: Perspectives from Tropical Northern Australia'. *Australian Indigenous Law Review* 13, no. 1 (2009): 27–48.
Joseph, Confidence. 'Multi-Spirited Waters in Lynton Burger's *She Down There*'. In *The Palgrave Handbook of Blue Heritage*, edited by Rosabelle Boswell, David O'Kane and Jeremy Hills, 141–59. Cham: Springer International Publishing, 2022.
Joseph, Confidence. 'Of Water and Water Spirits in Southern African Literature'. PhD diss., University of the Witwatersrand, Johannesburg, 2021.
Kosgei, Jauquelyne. 'Indigenous Knowledge and Marine Conservation in Oral Poems from the Kenyan Coast'. *Wasafiri* 36, no. 2 (2021): 71–8.
Machoko, Collis Garikai. 'Water Spirits and the Conservation of the Natural Environment: A Case Study from Zimbabwe'. *International Journal of Sociology and Anthropology* 5, no. 8 (2013): 285–96.
Makuyana, Luck. 'Hydro-colonialism: A Hydro-critical Reading of Three Texts on Kariba'. MA diss., University of the Witwatersrand, Johannesburg, 2021.
Marechera, Dambudzo. *The House of Hunger*. London: Heinemann, 1978.
Mashigo, Mohale. *Intruders: Short Stories*. Johannesburg: Picador Africa, 2019.
Matanzima, Joshua. 'Stereotyping, Exploitation, and Appropriation of African Traditional Religious Beliefs: The Case of Nyaminyami, Water Spirit, among the Batonga People of Northwestern Zimbabwe, 1860s–1960s'. *Journal of Africana Religions* 10, no. 1 (2022): 72–99.
Mohulatsi, Mapule. 'Black Aesthetics and the Deep Ocean'. MA diss., University of the Witwatersrand, Johannesburg, 2019.
Mungoshi, Charles. *Waiting for the Rain*. London: Heinemann, 1975.
Nwapa, Flora. *Efuru*. London: Heinemann, 1966.
Nwapa, Flora. *Idu*. London: Heinemann, 1970.

Nwapa, Flora. *Never Again*. Trenton, NJ: Africa World Press, 1975.
Nwapa, Flora. *One Is Enough*. Enugu: Tana, 1981.
Nwapa, Flora. *This Is Lagos and Other Short Stories*. Trenton, NJ: Africa World Press, 1971.
Nwapa, Flora. *Wives at War*. Trenton, NJ: Africa World Press, 1980.
Nwapa, Flora. *Women Are Different*. Trenton, NJ: Africa World Press, 1986.
Ogbeide, Victor. 'Pepetela's *The Return of the Water Spirit* as a Parable of the Postcolonial Condition in Angola'. *European Scientific Journal* 9, no. 35 (2013): 157–69.
Onofre, Clara. 'Angola: On the Mermaid Kianda and Other Mythical Beings'. Web log. *Global Voices* (blog), 28 October 2018. Available online: https://globalvoices.org/2008/10/28/angola-on-the-mermaid-kianda-and-other-mythical-beings/.
Pepetela. *The Return of the Water Spirit*, translated by L. R. Mitras. London: Heinemann, 2002.
Tomás, António Andrade. 'Refracted Governmentality: Space, Politics and Social Structure in Contemporary Luanda'. PhD diss., Columbia University, 2012.
Vandermerwe, Meg. *The Woman of the Stone Sea*. Cape Town: Umuzi, 2019.
Vera, Yvonne. *Butterfly Burning*. Harare: Baobab Books, 1998.
Waller, Thomas. 'The Blue Cultural Fix: Water-Spirits and World-Ecology in Jorge Amado's *Mar Morto* and Pepetela's *O Desejo de Kianda*'. *Humanities* 9, no. 3 (2020): 72.

CHAPTER 12
'ALL WATER HAS A PERFECT MEMORY': IN SEARCH OF DAMBUDZO MARECHERA'S STREAM

Tinashe Mushakavanhu

The river is a principal source in Zimbabwean writer Dambudzo Marechera's early fiction, particularly his first book, *The House of Hunger* (1978), and also in his later mythology. Yet the presence of water in Marechera's writings appears to be underresearched, or ignored, and scholars often treat water references as ancillary to the broader political narrative. The critical discourse around Marechera's writing project has been rendered in a prescriptive nationalist framework which subsumes a great deal else that is interesting about him. This nationalist framework has not only the effect of suppressing what is possible to understand but also forecloses the possibilities of the multiple, layered meanings of his texts, which drew from his varied experiences in both Zimbabwe and Britain, in favour of a precast, monolithic reading. This essay extends and complicates the reading of Marechera, because water stimulates a theoretical formulation of understanding his imaginative impulse of remembering, as articulated by Toni Morrison when she writes about a river of her own:

> … the act of imagination is bound up with memory. You know, they straightened out the Mississippi River in places, to make room for houses and liveable acreage. Occasionally the river floods these places. 'Floods' is the word they use, but in fact it is not flooding; it is remembering. Remembering where it used to be. All water has a perfect memory and is forever trying to get back where it was. Writers are like that: remembering where we were, what valley we ran through, what the banks were like, the light that was there and the route back to our original place. It is emotional memory – what the nerves and the skin remember as well as how it appeared. And a rush of imagination is our 'flooding'. … like water, I remember where I was before I was 'straightened out'.[1]

Upon his expulsion from the University of Oxford in the mid-1970s, Marechera can be seen to 'flood' back to his childhood. In remembering where he came from he was able to recover himself from a process that had 'sent him down' because he refused to be 'straightened out'. He had to go through a form of exclusion that was supposed to be an ultimate humiliation from a select society to which he no longer belonged and had all rights withdrawn. Through the composition of his first book, Marechera drafts a personal philosophy on the act of remembering, based on experiences growing up in a small Rhodesian town. Life stories have a geography too. In writing about his life and where he came from, Marechera was demonstrating that the historical imagination is never completely spaceless. Such tracings are not to tie us to any fixed past. They are, or can be, a creative process of affective mapping.

What happened to Marechera after he left Oxford is murky, but his early work emanates from this crisis. According to him, the book that became *The House of Hunger* was written while he was camping near the River Isis, the name for the Thames as it flows through Oxford. And thus water functions as a source of inspiration from which he emerges as a water body, a *njuzu*, a writer.[2] Owen Kibel,[3] who knew Marechera at Oxford, remembered noticing this spiritual aspect in their interactions:

> He must have been enthralled with the storytelling in Shona before becoming educated in English. The transformation of symbols that are indigenous to African culture, such as the river people, must have given him a cognitive freedom unknown to those from a western culture. A dual universe needed a translator, and he was rapidly becoming adept at using his creative gifts to weave themes back and forth between the two cultures. Like the oft cited example of Joseph Conrad, his different linguistic heritage caused him to have a rare sensitivity to the nuances of the English language.[4]

But in order to become a *njuzu*, one has to be submerged in the water and reappear in a new body and with new powers. *Njuzu* are not supposed to reveal what they discover underwater, or what they're told or who they see. In an interview with Dutch journalist Wim Bossema that has never been published, Marechera describes this submersion, as a form of suicide: 'You can see the departure from the house of hunger as a form of suicide and the rest of the book is what passes through the narrator's mind as he plans for the departure.'[5] From this, Marechera's childhood metamorphoses into a narrative and ideology of writing situated in a specific place of memory. Marechera places only himself next to the river:

> I managed to get myself a tent. I would camp by the River Isis. I wrote most of *House of Hunger* in that tent. My initial impulse was simply one of utter despair. Well, I felt that I had lost everything. There I was in exile, seemingly no future, no nothing. I started asking myself what had happened to my generation. A kind of lost generation feeling.[6]

It is the search for self that partly informs the composition of the book, which leads Marechera to the source, at the head of the stream. The act of remembering, associated with the river, is closely linked to personal identity and experiences as well as the past and familial origins. In other words, Marechera deploys recollections of childhood as a metaphor of creativity and a mode of critical thinking. It's a kind of literary archaeology that embraces certain autobiographical strategies. Memory weighs heavily in what he writes, in how he begins, in what he thinks is significant to tell about himself and where he comes from. The river is a trigger of rememberances. The Rusape River evokes his childhood memories and also brings back the memories of the journey that the narrator initiated when he says, 'I got my things and left'.[7] The river, which is out of sight in the text, is presented as a porous border that conjures and puts into context different historical times as well as geographical and literary spaces.

Marechera's self-romanticization, connected to a river in Oxford, summons another river from which his tale emerges – the Rusape River – a long inland water body in the east of Zimbabwe. This amniotic pull of rivers fascinates Marechera, who delights in the watery inspiration that links the world through memory. His knowledge is almost entirely heuristic but the idea of following a river from its source is a form of mapping his desire to experience life without a filter, through the senses. Set in Vengere – a community that grew along the banks of the Rusape River – this was a society composed mostly of immigrants who worked in the surrounding farmlands owned by white families. The river then continues as a source throughout Marechera's life and work. As an imaginative geography, the Rusape River becomes the product of representation, because water was a central feature in the spiritual practices of the local black Africans in the area where Marechera grew up and was a fundamental component in the cosmological system connecting the living with the dead. For Marechera, geography is important to map parts of his animated selfscapes and open up the tracings of the spatial remains that make us. But Marechera is denied the use of water as a resistant title by his publishers, and his imagination is condemned to a drought-stricken valley, dry, arid land – the house of hunger. Indeed, while he camps by the river, hunger intrudes but it is beyond the physical. It is the slow, meandering streams of nostalgia, the raging currents of conflict and the stagnant waters of social decay. Inadvertently, water, or its absence, becomes a tool of violence, and an archive of destruction, displacement and perennial hunger in Zimbabwean literature produced in the 1970s and 1980s. Hunger has been the defining metaphor of post-independence Zimbabwe, attributed to Marechera, but also his contemporaries including Charles Mungoshi, Musaemura Zimunya, Chenjerai Hove, Stanley Nyamfukudza and Wilson Katiyo. This theme is emphasized, for example, in the first major study of Zimbabwean writers by Musaemura Zimunya, titled *Those Years of Hunger and Drought: The Birth of African Fiction in English in Zimbabwe*, published two years into independence in 1982. In fact, the rhetoric of nature permeates Shona and Ndebele literatures as a grammar of nationalist resistance.

The published title of Marechera's book, *House of Hunger*, throttles a whole generation to a point of no recovery because house of hunger is a fabricated space. By evoking the river in his original title, *At the Head of the Stream*, Marechera was gesturing that he belongs to a fluvial culture associated with the Rusape River. But as is evident in the way Marechera opens his book with scenes of black protest:

> All the black youth was thirsty. There was not an oasis of thought we did not lick dry; apart from those which had been banned, whose drinking led to arrests and such like flea-scratchings.[8]

It is this thirst that permeates throughout the book. *At the Head of the Stream* was discarded and considered 'weak' and unmarketable. This misreading is popularized at a time when Rhodesia is being condemned as a pariah society. Yet, the point of making the river a referential point was because the community Marechera grew up in was built facing away from the riverbed. Another reason was that after Marechera submitted his manuscript to Heinemann, he ended up in prison for possessing cannabis and faced deportation. At this point he is just another aspiring twenty-five-year-old writer yet to publish any significant work. In order to convince the judge about his right to remain, the book became a form of collateral. *The House of Hunger* manuscript was thus presented as evidence, a form of political manifesto that would endanger Marechera if he were to be returned to Rhodesia, a country that was under the vice grip of die-hard white supremacists who had declared unilateral independence. House of hunger, a metaphor in the book, became the dry parched life of Marechera's down-and-out existence and perhaps an important event in his writing career. In a letter to James Currey, his publisher, dated 9 December 1977, he writes:

> But the one thing I am unable to make anyone here believe is that I am an 'author' and that *The House of Hunger* let alone *A Helmet of Darkness* is a reality.... The one thing I certainly hope you will do is make a statement about the nature of *The House of Hunger* in respect of its stance towards white Rhodesia, this is because in my application for political asylum to the Home Secretary I must show and stress the danger to my person of my writings if and when they suddenly choose to deport me to Rhodesia. With your help I can do this.... I know only that I am frantically thinking what countries, what embassies to quickly consider for applying for political asylum if the home office decides to throw the bath water with me in it out into the cauldron of Rhodesia.

Currey suggested to Marechera the title *The House of Hunger*, and Marechera liked the poetics of the new title, as a means to an end. This new title would prove to be a useful defence in Marechera's legal battles as he was fighting against deportation to Rhodesia. His lawyers, Hugh, James, Jones & Jenkins, sent the following letter on the same day (as Marechera's above) to Currey for verification:

> Dear Sir
>
> We act for Mr Marechera in respect of charges to be heard at the Cardiff Magistrates Court on the 15th of December. One of the charges against Mr Marechera is that he is presently an illegal immigrant, his limited leave permit to remain in the United Kingdom having expired on the 2 October 1975.
>
> Mr Marechera could face deportation to this native country i.e. Rhodesia.
>
> Mr Marechera does not wish to return to Rhodesia. He fears for his own safety should he be forced to return to that country.

'All Water has a Perfect Memory'

> Mr Marechera informs us that he has written a book entitled *The House of Hunger* and that he has received from you advances prior to publication of the book.
>
> We understand that the book is controversial in that it related the life of a coloured person under the Smith regime in Rhodesia.

This is the context from which *The House of Hunger* was published. Marechera's creative process and method are buried in the archives. His eccentricity has been promoted instead, making Marechera arguably one of the first celebrity authors from Africa to gain worldwide fame. By re-reading his book in the context of his intended title, *At the Head of the Stream*, we challenge the amnesiac critical discourse. However, to appreciate him, we need to pay due attention to his complex and shifting attitudes towards composition, revision and creative collaboration. Marechera Studies, as has evolved since his death, has not drawn from authorship studies and archival methodologies but relied on a limiting biographical approach as evidenced in the super imposing text, *Dambudzo Marechera: A Source Book of His Life and Work* (1999), which has closed off possibilities of reading Marechera away from its assumed authority. Marechera spent his whole career fighting critics and their persistent hunt for the real in his fictional worlds – something that threatened to dismiss or misrecognize the art of his fiction. Historically, African writers have been beleaguered by the limiting expectation that their work is based purely on the facts of their own lives.

Archival holdings of Marechera's work are dispersed globally, in a combination of major and minor repositories. This is owing to the fact that he deliberately left traces of himself in various places. Even though the idea of Marechera being 'homeless' and unmoored has been popularized, he is not given due credit for actively keeping his own archive, which, in her memoir, Flora Veit-Wild admits to have taken and packed into an empty suitcase:

> You had not written a will but I had the key to your flat. On the day you died I collected all your papers. Some were clipped together; others were still in their envelopes. There was a rejection letter, hastily read, thrown into the cupboard with piles of typed sheets, crumpled clothes, dirty underwear. I rummaged through it all. I shoved everything into a suitcase: notebooks, letters, every bit of paper that bore traces of your writing or that of someone else.[9]

Only through death had Marechera lost control. Alive, he was not credited enough for being his own archivist. The archive remains a matter of debate and contestation and unfortunately remains out of reach to a generation of young Zimbabwean readers and scholars who have been denied access to critically engage with one of their most brilliant writers. In order to access the archive, a Schengen visa to Germany is required, which is never guaranteed, plus funding for flights and accommodation. Marechera studies is a popular genre in the European academy with many dissertations written on the writer, including my own produced at the University of Kent, whereas in his home country, Zimbabwe, young people have to rely on secondary interpretations that ignore the context he writes from. There is a wide divide between the Marechera who is wonderfully told and remembered in anecdotes and the writer subject to critical scrutiny.

What if Dambudzo Marechera had published a book called *At the Head of the Stream* in 1978? It is an important question that has been neglected in Marechera studies and yet it has critical implications in the ways we read or misread Marechera. It is important to interrogate the linguistic and metaphorical implications that a book's title shifts in our readings of it, and in our imaginations. There is no doubt that *The House of Hunger* is a canonical text. Yet, what if its successes are premised on a misreading that began from publication and continued into its various receptions? What if we reframe one of Africa's most iconic twentieth-century literary figures through the unseen histories of his creative process? What if we search again for Marechera's stream and find the connections between the northern and southern rivers that inspired and sustained him?

The erasure of the title *At the Head of the Stream*, arguably, is a form of structural displacement, just as the black people are contained, confined and controlled after being displaced from their magnificent sacred natural setting near the Rusape River. The water people are now homeless, pushed to the verge of destruction. In the 'house of hunger', Marechera was writing from a specific 'place-time'. By situating himself 'at the head of the stream', Marechera was anticipating and attempting to refuse becoming a static figure from a closed time. The author-narrator of Robert Muponde's memoir, *The Scandalous Times of a Book Louse*, writes:

> I cannot think of a better poetic euphemism than that of being considered a Rusape author ... Me? A Rusape Author? I have wondered what it might mean to come from Rusape and the provocation to author from that place-time. Yet the strongest, most adhesive of my personality-forming memories are nested in this town. I have therefore thought about loss as a refrain and a character.[10]

Even though Marechera does not reference the river in specific terms, it is the unsaid backdrop of *The House of Hunger*. Its absence demands its presence. Settler colonialism did not just impose another way of seeing and knowing a place; it imposed another place. The existence of *The House of Hunger* (a product of Heinemann's African Writers Series) is as a result of manipulation and violence, a form of displacement. Colonial hydrology, first through modes of representation and later through infrastructural and administrative acts, changed the narrative of the local people's relationship to water. This fits into the framework Isobel Hofmeyr calls hydrocolonialism because 'water is centrally implicated in imperial and other social orders'.[11] The local people were forced to live in a system which was not designed to serve them, and their voices and lives were marginalized in pursuit of power and profit. Rusape was one of the first outposts for the settler Pioneer Column as they set up shop in the territory they renamed Rhodesia after their principal, Cecil John Rhodes, because of this water body they found and from which they could farm and build their empire.[12] It is a sad tale that the persisting postcolonial geography is now one where the inhabitants of Rusape have perennial water problems and suffer the associated diseases such as typhoid and cholera. But the river became a site for sport and recreation, and therefore facilitated the spectacle of not only white privilege but also power and domination. What is now at the head of the stream?

Muponde opens his memoir with a rhetorical call: 'river, river, where do you take me'? It's a call that echoes in Marechera's writing because 'river cajoles with its stories of plunging, turning, splashing and misting.... It is a Rusape story'.[13] Rusape is defined by the river. The name Rusape was derived from *rusapwe*, which means 'may it never dry'. And there is something contradictory about how Heinemann decided to dry this archival water body in Marechera's fiction and condemned it to the informal settlements, the now famous 'house of hunger', a place of nothing. Colonial settlement near the river began in 1894 with the establishment of a British South Africa Company post on the Rusape River and, as David Mcdermott Hughes describes, 'white owned estates soon traed the major watersheds...'.[14] For the colonialists, settlement always meant displacement. The siting of this colonial outpost was not accidental, but it demonstrated the British Empire's self-proclaimed superiority, maintaining their discursive truth, not only through the domination of people and their cultures but also through the domination of nature – water chief among it. The British, in order to maintain power and the dominance of their truth, needed to subjugate local knowledge. Colonizers saw control of rivers and water systems as a way of controlling local communities and instituting state power. Once they started putting their systems in place, all the rivers dried up. All the wells dried up. There was not a drop of water anywhere.

In these new colonial settlements such as Rusape, the black community was therefore pushed and moved to dry places, where water was turned into beer. Toxic water. *The House of Hunger* opens as follows:

> I got my things and left. The sun was coming up. I couldn't think where to go. I wandered towards the beer hall but stopped at the bottle store where I bought a beer. There were people scattered along the store's wide veranda, drinking. I sat beneath the tall msasa tree whose branches scrape the corrugated iron roofs. I was trying not to think about where I was going. I didn't feel bitter. I was glad things had happened the way they had: I couldn't have stayed on in that House of Hunger where every morsel of sanity was snatched from you the way some kinds of bird snatch food from the very mouths of babes.[15]

Marechera further develops his theory of language and water in *The Black Insider* (1999), in which he offers a brief history of the world through water:

> Language is like water. You can drink it. You can swim in it. You can drown in it. You can wear a snorkel in it. You can flow in the sea in it. You can evaporate and become invisible with it. You can remain standing in a bucket for hours. The Japanese invented a way of torturing people with drops of water. The Portuguese in Angola and Mozambique also used water to torture people. ... It seems inconceivable to think of humans who have no language. They may have invented

gelignite but they cannot do without water. Some take it neat from rivers and wells. Some have it chemically treated and reservoir. Others drink nothing but beer and Bloody Marys and wine but this too is way of taking your water. The way you take your water is supposed to say a lot about you. It is supposed to reflect your history, your culture, your breeding, etc. It is supposed to show the extent to which you and your nation have developed or regenerated. The word 'primitive' is applied to all those who take their alphabet neat from rivers, sewers, and natural scenery – sometimes this may be described as the romantic imagination. The height of sophistication is actually to channel your water through a system of pipes right into your very own lavatory where you shake the hand of a machine and your shit and filthy manners disappear in a roaring water. Being water you can spread diseases like bilharzia and thought. Thought is more fatal than bilharzia. And if you want to write a book you cannot think unless your thoughts are contagious.[16]

For Marechera, the river, which was a source of life, was now forbidden territory, a source of indulgence, a source of civilization. In fact for Marechera, *At the Head of the Stream* exemplified how rivers themselves can be sites of trauma. Rusape River becomes a site and a symbol of economic disparity and social stratification. The reader may not see the river itself in the text because the characters are displaced from it, it is out of focus; instead the reader is forced to witness the violence and life-changing events taking place in the crowded black township. Marechera's memories of and associations with the Rusape River are influenced by its role in the traumatic events that took place there. Thus the river's meaning, like language, is fluid and changes. In the 1960s, when Marechera was growing up, *The Rhodesia Herald* reported:

You can't get more Rhodesian than the Rusape River Boat Race; it's hard-playing fun with just a spice of danger to stiffen the boisterous slapdash nature of the event. Many of the entrants don't treat it as a race at all but as a trip down the river, travelling the way they like with their smokes, drinks and girls.[17]

The Rusape River Boat Race became a mainstay sport in the country that attracted crowds and formalized the displacement of the people who had lived near the river for centuries, and whose livelihoods and cultures were sustained by the river. Vic Mackenzie explains the origins of the boat race, which Marechera and his generation knew about:

The original Rhodesian river race was started in Rusape. It all began as a bet in the Balfour Hotel pub when Solly Ferreira (a Rhodesian army pilot) claimed he could float all the way down the Lesapi River from the Silver Bow bridge to the Chiduku bridge and not fall off his raft (tubes). There are some pretty nasty rapids just before the Crocodile Motel so there were plenty of bet takers. The whole bar emptied one Friday evening to witness Solly's ride down the slimy greasy Lesapi River. Most of them headed for the worst rapids near the Crocodile Motel where they feared or wished Solly would be swept into the swirling abyss. However Solly was a man of impeccable timing. He chose to go down the river after the first really heavy rainstorm where the large volume of water covered the rocks and negated the effect of the rapids. He managed to remain upright on his tube all the way down to the Chiduku bridge and win the bet. We all made our way back to the pub where Solly in typical Ferreira style spent all his winnings on supplying free drinks until the money ran out. Following Solly's epic journey the first race was organised and opened to the public. It ran for a number of years.[18]

In writing about Vengere township in Rusape, Marechera mutes the rowdy noise from the river, which he was old enough to hear and witness. By evoking the river in his original title, as a rivulet, a stream, Marechera was yearning for lost intimacy. Rusape, the river which never stops flowing, is not surprisingly the centre of an important agricultural region. Terence Ranger and Sam Moyo both use the area as a location for their studies on guerrilla warfare, peasant consciousness and the land question in Zimbabwe.[19] The history of the town's employment structure and role as an agricultural and processing centre for the surrounding commercial farm regions confirms its place as an important service region in Rhodesian society. Rusape was exceptional as the locus of the country's most successful peasant maize producers. Against this agricultural prowess, Marechera's fiction is grappling with the geographical consequences of land alienation for the black community. He focuses on the consequences of high unemployment, low education levels, households that in many cases were headed by females, and a high prevalence of prostitution – issues that would manifest and affect his own life too.

The publishing of *The House of Hunger* and the compromises Marechera agrees to become a form of violence in itself that Marechera never forgets. He goes on to protest at the Guardian Fiction Prize ceremony in London where he throws cups and plates at his hosts and accuses them of celebrating his people's poverty. Years later, Marechera told journalist Wim Bossema, 'London wanted me to continue writing House of Hungers all the time. I refused and simply said no. This is why all the books I wrote afterwards were rejected. Each book I write is an experiment.'[20] The tension embedded within the publishing process is a kind of war in which the final, printed version becomes an aggressor against the author's intentions: it is exploitative and plunders and appropriates only what it wants to use. The tyrannical published version of Marechera's book conceals the vulnerability of the author and his subjects and caricatures it instead. Marechera frames his drafts as the living memory of the conflict because they tell everything; in their imperfections they provide the story that without them we could not possibly know. Order is replaced by chaos, and the sacred is profaned. This is the grudge that festers in Marechera, a bitterness and frustration with the publishing system: the Faustian bargain, which he used against Heinemann, over and over, making demands for endless royalties. That is why he laughs in Chris Austen's film, *The House of Hunger* (1983), a documentary commissioned by Channel 4, that when he was detained at Pentonville Prison in London he was asked, who is your next of kin, and he said 'Heinemann. Good god, imagine being buried by Heinemann'.[21] There have been at least eleven editions of *The House of Hunger* published from 1978 to date. Only the Zimbabwe Publishing House edition was released at the height of Marechera's fame to coincide with his return to Zimbabwe in 1982, but the other reproductions have all been for external markets in South Africa, the UK and the US.

The phenomenon of 'Global Marechera' confirms and extends the biases of literary scholarship as modelled on the Western canon. African writers are imagined as objects of study, often read and seen as derivatives of European masters. Thus Marechera is described as the African James Joyce, the African Shelley, the African Kafka which ignores that his work questions traditional ways of understanding the bases of human reality.[22] In order to do that, he looks at specific conditions (Zimbabwe or UK), and to his credit, he innovatively utilizes centuries of history and philosophy from America to Europe, from Asia back to Africa.[23]

To introduce himself as a writer, Marechera adopted the language of the river. William James in *The Principles of Psychology* coined the phrase 'stream of consciousness' in which 'every definite image of the mind is steeped … in the free water that flows around it'.[24] *The House of Hunger* is written in the stream of consciousness technique because it's a style that aligns itself aesthetically with the flow of water that shaped and informed Marechera's imagination. It does not follow a linear progression but meanders like a stream backwards and forwards. The text itself leaps between the past and present and constructs memory as a fluid moving experience. Waves regularly wash over events and thoughts in the text and nearly always suggest the possibility of extinction or death. For Marechera, after his being expelled from Oxford, the Thames and Rusape River became emblems of redemption and renewal, of hope and of escaping from time itself. It was like returning back into the womb, because the Rusape River, as Muponde writes, is

> … the things you look like before you step out of your mother's crevice. I am that without which you cannot become who and what you are. Water. River. Rain. I rain in your tears, when you laugh or cry. I water your fields. I fill your well. If you must live, drink. I am river. Come, boy, don't do that with your legs. You invite water monitors. They like to suckle on a boy's dangles.[25]

In conclusion, Marechera goes to the river to listen to it. He moves between Zimbabwe and Europe in search of himself. The author's geographical dislocation shifts focus of the author's preoccupation from the temporal to the spatial. He finds himself lost in an intercultural journey, which he can only make sense of by writing. Feeling out of place in Oxford, his spirit rests upon the memory of Rusape River, and he tries to identify its reverberations and shadows in all the rivers he comes across. That is why, in a sense, he could only start writing his book facing the Thames. The image of the river, the one before him and the one remembered and imagined, is a figurative geography that is multiple and varied. Without the collegiate affiliation to Oxford that provides him with a sense of home away from home, he feels lost and in loneliness seeks comfort from another river. At the head of the stream. The poetics of the river becomes at the same time a way of connecting the past and the present. Marechera's vision of memory is presented to us in its incompleteness.

Notes

1. Toni Morrison, *Mouth Full of Blood: Essays, Speeches, Meditations* (London: Chatto & Windus, 2019), 243.
2. In Shona folklore, a *njuzu* (merman or mermaid) is an aquatic creature with the head and upper body of a male human and the tail of a fish. They are sometimes associated with perilous events such as floods, storms, shipwrecks and drownings, but also supernatural and magical qualities.
3. Flora Veit-Wild, *Dambudzo Marechera: A Source Book on his Life and Work* (Trenton, NJ: Africa World Press), 167.
4. Letter to Flora Veit-Wild dated 24 March 1991.
5. Wim Bossema, audio interview with Marechera in Harare (1987, not broadcasted).
6. Veit-Wild, *Dambudzo Marechera*, 176–7.
7. Dambudzo Marechera, *The House of Hunger* (London: Heinemann, 1978, 2009), 11.
8. Ibid., 12
9. Veit-Wild, *They Called You Dambudzo* (Johannesburg: Jacana, 2020), 4.
10. Robert Muponde, *The Scandalous Times of a Book Louse* (Johannesburg: Penguin Books, 2021), 10.
11. Isobel Hofmeyr, *Dockside Reading: Hydrocolonialism and the Custom House* (Durham, NC: Duke University Press, 2022), 16.
12. Agnes Andersson, *The Bright Lights Grow Fainter: Livelihoods, Immigration and a Small Town in Zimbabwe* (Stockholm: Stockholm Studies in Human Geography, 2002).
13. Muponde, *The Scandalous Times*, 15.
14. David Mcdermott Hughes, 'Hydrology of Hope: Farm Dams, Conservation, and Whiteness in Zimbabwe', *American Ethnologist* 33, no. 2 (May 2006): 279.
15. Marechera, *The House of Hunger*, 11.
16. Dambudzo Marechera, *The Black Insider* (Trenton, NJ: Africa World Press,1999), 34.
17. Vic Mackenzie, 'The Rusape River Boat Race', *The Rhodesian Herald*, December 1966, 4.
18. Ibid., 5.
19. Terence Ranger, *Peasant Consciousness and Guerrilla War in Zimbabwe: A Comparative Study* (London: James Currey, 1985); and Sam Moyo, *Land Question in Zimbabwe* (Harare: SAPES Trust, 1995).
20. Wim Bossema, audio interview with Marechera, 1987.
21. Chris Austin, *The House of Hunger* [Film] (London: Channel 4, 1983).
22. David Caute, *Marechera and the Colonel: A Zimbabwean Writer & the Claims of the State* (London: Totterdown Books, 2009), 10.

23. Dambudzo Marechera, 'The African Writer's Experience of European Literature', *Zambezia* 14, no. 2 (1987): 99–105.
24. William James, *The Principles of Psychology* (New York: Henry Holt & Company, 1980), 17.
25. Muponde, *The Scandalous Times*, 14.

Bibliography

Andersson, Agnes. *The Bright Lights Grow Fainter: Livelihoods, Immigration and a Small Town in Zimbabwe*. Stockholm: Stockholm Studies in Human Geography, 2002.

Austin, Chris. *The House of Hunger* [film]. London: Channel 4, 1983.

Bossema, Wim. Unpublished interview with Dambudzo Marechera. Harare, 1987.

Caute, David. *Marechera and the Colonel: A Zimbabwean Writer & the Claims of the State*. London: Totterdown Books, 2009.

Hofmeyr, Isobel. *Dockside Reading: Hydrocolonialism and the Custom House*. Durham, NC: Duke University Press, 2022.

Hughes, David Mcdermott. 'Hydrology of Hope: Farm Dams, Conservation, and Whiteness in Zimbabwe'. *American Ethnologist* 33, no. 2 (May 2006): 269–87.

James, William. *The Principles of Psychology*. New York: Henry Holt & Company, 1980.

Mackenzie, Vic. 'The Rusape River Boat Race'. *The Rhodesian Herald*, December 1966, 4–5.

Marechera, Dambudzo. 'The African Writer's Experience of European Literature'. *Zambezia* 14, no. 2 (1987): 99–105.

Marechera, Dambudzo. *The Black Insider*. Trenton, NJ: Africa World Press, 1999.

Marechera, Dambudzo. *The House of Hunger*. London: Heinemann, 1978.

Marechera, Dambudzo. *The House of Hunger*. London: Penguin Modern Classics, 2022.

Morrison, Toni. *Mouth Full of Blood: Essays, Speeches, Meditations* London: Chatto & Windus, 2019.

Moyo, Sam. *Land Question in Zimbabwe*. Harare: SAPES Trust, 1995.

Muponde, Robert. *The Scandalous Times of a Book Louse*. Johannesburg: Penguin Books, 2021.

Ranger, Terence. *Peasant Consciousness and Guerrilla War in Zimbabwe: A Comparative Study*. London: James Currey, 1985.

Veit-Wild, Flora. *Dambudzo Marechera: A Source Book on His Life and Work*. Trenton, NJ: Africa World Press, 1999.

Veit-Wild, Flora. *They Called You Dambudzo*. Johannesburg: Jacana, 2020.

PART IV
SOUNDS, IMAGES AND RESONANCES IN THE FAR SOUTH

CHAPTER 13
THE PLANKTON NET AT THE DOOR: SCOTT'S HUT AND THE POETICS OF 'INTIMATE IMMENSITY'

Joanna Price

> brittle star, krill, salp, weed
>   what's left by ebb or flung
> another story beneath/along
>   our floated, floating stories

In 'Intertidal', Elizabeth Bradfield reflects on the marine life forms that have washed up on a South Georgia beach. The poem is from *Toward Antarctica* (2019), a poetic 'record'[1] of the observations she made on her two recent voyages to Antarctica, where she worked as a naturalist aboard an ecotourist ship. In an earlier collection, *Approaching Ice* (2010), Bradfield wrote about her longing to reach the continent and how it arose from reading about the dreams and experiences of the early polar explorers. Her own stories 'float' upon theirs through her empathic reading of their encounters with place. These explorers' accounts, like Bradfield's poem, sometimes recognize the stories of the small, non-human life forms in the ocean or along the water's edge, that co-exist with their own. Drifting among the organisms Bradfield observes are plankton, whose name derives from the Greek *planesthai*, meaning 'to wander', a root it shares with 'planet'. This etymological link between the minute and the planetary intimates a vital and affective connection, the exploration of which recurs in encounters with Antarctica.

The movement of feelings between Bradfield's two collections illustrates how the affect associated with so-called 'Heroic Age' explorations recurs in the imagination of Antarctica. The explorers' immersion in place there produced affects which circulate both amongst the texts of members of an expedition and between the work of those explorers and that of later writers and artists who visit the southern continent. Whilst the early expeditions are more usually associated with the explorers' encounters with the ice, this chapter traces how the study of plankton on one expedition was part of the imagination of an 'intimate immensity' to which later artists have returned.

The chapter considers some of the feelings evoked in the life writing and photography of R. F. Scott's 1910–13 British Antarctic Expedition and how they are explored by more recent visitors to the continent: New Zealand poet Chris Orsman; New Zealand photographer Jane Ussher; and Hungarian American installation artist Judit Hersko. In the texts of members of Scott's well-documented and much mythologized 'Heroic Age' expedition, feelings of intimacy and absorption appear alongside the patriotic sentiment and imperial ambition for which the expedition is better known. These feelings develop through the men's experience of the physical space they occupy in Antarctica, their relations with each other and their sense of their work, including their scientific research. The study of plankton was one element of the science being conducted on the expedition. It is noted in, but not central to, discussion of the expeditionary work in participants' life writing and photographs. The men's responses to it show, however, that their perception of the scientific work contributed to the affective atmosphere inside the base hut and their embodied response to place.

Scott's hut and the feeling of place

On Scott's expedition, the men's experience of place was shaped by their inhabiting of their base hut – a dwelling on the edge of the largely unknown continent – and their movement through its immediate environs. Scott sought a location for the hut on Ross Island, an area familiar to him from his National Antarctic (*Discovery*) Expedition of 1901–4. He chose 'a shelving beach' on a promontory known on the *Discovery* expedition as 'the Skuary', which he now re-named Cape Evans after his second-in-command, Lt. Edward Evans.[2] It was sheltered by a low ridge and was close to the water's edge at McMurdo Sound, which opened into the Ross Sea, much of which would freeze over in winter. John Wylie notes that in Antarctica, where 'there is no clear boundary between sea and ice', the constant 'mutability' of the environment and 'interactions of sea, ice and land' were a 'source of perplexity and unease' to Scott.[3] He was reassured by the 'sheltered'[4] location of the hut, the 'familiar spatial idiom' of the landscape, as Wylie notes,[5] and the design and construction of the hut itself. The old *Discovery* hut, not far away at Hut Point, had been pre-fabricated in Sydney on the model of an Australian outback bungalow.[6] It was too difficult to heat in Antarctica and the men did not use it as a base, preferring to live on their ship instead. By contrast, the Cape Evans hut, a pre-fabricated wooden construction that Scott had brought from London on the *Terra Nova*, seemed to him, when erected and insulated, to be a comfortable 'house' of 'great proportions' that comprised 'a truly seductive home'.[7]

Scott followed the customary naval model used on ships to divide the interior space into a 'wardroom' for officers and a 'mess deck' for the men. Within this partitioned space, the men lived, worked, slept and were often confined indoors during the darkness of the winter months. Whilst Scott had his own cubicle, and Herbert Ponting, the expedition's photographer, had a darkroom in which he slept, the other men shared sleeping quarters around the walls. The intimacy of the arrangements, whereby the scientists slept alongside their work benches and instruments in the space assigned to their subject, is evoked by Cherry-Garrard's recollection of how, as he lay awake in his bunk at night: 'There was always the ticking of many instruments, and sometimes the ring of a little bell: to this day I do not know what most of them meant.'[8]

The interior spaces of Scott's Cape Evans hut are the subject of some of Jane Ussher's photographs in *Still Life: Inside the Antarctic Huts of Scott and Shackleton* (2010), which

The Plankton Net at the Door

she produced in collaboration with the New Zealand Antarctic Heritage Trust. The hut and its objects have been restored by the Trust with the aim of evoking it as it was during its occupancy on Scott's *Terra Nova* expedition. Objects have been selected for display on site according to their 'iconic' value,[9] as conferred by Ponting's photographs, first-hand accounts of the expedition and other historical documents; or because the Trust deems them 'original and highly significant … in terms of interpreting and understanding the way the site was used by the original expeditions'.[10] Ussher's photographs focus on the detail and texture of objects and surfaces and illuminate dark areas with shafts of light. She believes her photographs, 'in all their gloom … intimacy, and … stillness', convey her sadness at the sense of loss the place evokes, particularly through its association with Scott's last expedition.[11]

Through her selection and placement of the objects she photographs, Ussher further interprets an already-interpreted museal space. Her photographs do several things at once. They document the use in Antarctica of these expeditionary, scientific, domestic or personal items; they capture the aesthetic allure of the textural and previously frozen and abandoned objects; and they evoke the haunting absent presence of the people whose bodies impressed discarded items such as dance shoes, boots and shirts. One object that occurs in several photographs is a plankton net, which Ussher has placed in various areas of the hut, and in composition with different objects. As Derek P. McCormack has observed, reflecting on his study of balloons, 'such simple devices … provide opportunities for thinking about atmospheres – about how they are disclosed, sensed and imagined'.[12] In Ussher's photographs, the plankton net registers, through its presence, position and form, the affective atmosphere of the hut during Scott's expedition and in the present time.

The net hangs alongside the door of the cold porch in two photographs.[13] In one the door is shut and in the other it is ajar, opening into the hut (see Figure 13.1). In both photographs the long, conical shape and whiteness of the net against the dark, scuffed textures of the wooden door draw the eye of the viewer. The net, stained green in parts from use in the sea, guides the eye across the space of the images to the whiteish rope handle on the door between the annex and the cold-porch. The handle, like the scratched door and the shadowed step of the threshold between the porch and the glimpsed interior of the hut, reminds the viewer of how the men would have repeatedly held the handle, pushed the door open with hand or foot, and stepped over the threshold. Through such habitual actions, knowledge of the place they inhabited would have become 'physically inscribed' in them, as Gaston de Bachelard puts it.[14] The proximity of the plankton net to the door also draws attention to how both things, like the porch, serve as a threshold between human and non-human worlds, and between the present of the contemporary visitor and the past of the hut's first occupants. As thresholds, they both separate and connect these worlds.

The affect of Ussher's images of the spaces and objects of the hut arises partly through their resonance with Ponting's portraits of the hut's inhabitants. In one of Ussher's photographs, for example, the large circular hoop of the plankton net hangs on the wall of Scott's cubicle.[15] The bright summer light through the window next to it barely touches

Figure 13.1 Jane Ussher. The first peek through the cold porch into the interior of Captain Scott's last expedition base. Copyright Jane Ussher / Antarctic Heritage Trust.

the net, but it catches the whiteness of the stuffed emperor penguin and the notebook on Scott's desk. The penguin was left in Scott's hut by members of the Ross Sea party of Shackleton's 1914–17 expedition who occupied it subsequently. Nonetheless, Ussher's image of a space of concentration whose subject is now absent recalls Ponting's iconic photograph, 'Captain Scott writing his diary. 7 October 1911'.[16] Through his illumination of Scott at his desk, Ponting conveys his absorption in writing, amidst the expedition paraphernalia, books, clothing and personal items that fill the space.

Ponting is well-known for requiring his Antarctic colleagues to pose, or 'pont' as they called it, in his outdoor photographs. In 'A Portrait in the Wardroom', Chris Orsman reflects on how Ponting's indoor portraits were similarly staged: 'The conversation stops/as this posed, half-candid scene/takes shape under Ponting's/finicky directions.'[17] Ponting intended his photographs to record the expedition for posterity and hoped they would be a commercial resource, raising funds for the expedition and income for himself. His photograph, 'Group in Wardroom of *Terra Nova*. December 1910', suggests how 'the tack of the *Terra Nova* is a stitching – a practising of colonial space', as John Wylie has put it,[18] through its portrayal of a moment in the men's passage southwards from Cardiff via Madeira, Cape Town, Melbourne and New Zealand, to the far south. In the wardroom, as aboard the ship in general, the men occupy a liminal space between home and the little-known land ahead. A portrait of the king hangs on the wall as they crowd into the confined space, sitting or standing around the large wardroom table that dominates it. The setting and their relaxed poses, with some writing in their journals and others resting their elbows amongst the 'clutter of tin plates/and mugs',[19] as well as their casual seafaring attire, all suggest the men's transition from the space of 'civic receptions, banquets, speeches' that accompanied their departure from 'colonial shores'[20] towards their life in Antarctica.

Orsman describes how, like the 'solemn Dutch burghers' of Frans Hals's painting of the Haarlem Militia Company, the men assume a 'resolute air/of good fellowship, /casual gestures of character'.[21] They also rehearse the future disposition of their bodies in their confined Antarctic dwelling: 'They touch elbows around the table/and practise an intimacy to come, /anticipating those regions/where maps and geographies/are bare of natural features.'[22] Orsman's evocation of the men's performance draws out the relationship between intimacy and gesture that is suggested by the common etymological root in the Latin word *intimus*, meaning 'inmost', of 'intimacy' and 'to intimate', meaning 'to make inmost to, hence to make known to'. Like Orsman, Lauren Berlant suggests that this relationship entails a sense of a public:

> To intimate is to communicate with the sparest of signs and gestures, and at its root intimacy has the quality of eloquence and brevity. But intimacy also involves an aspiration for a narrative about something shared, a story about both oneself and others that will turn out in a particular way ... the inwardness of the intimate is met by a corresponding publicness.[23]

Ponting's photographs of the men in the Cape Evans hut suggest their necessary intimacy in its spaces and document their activities and 'shared' sense of purpose for their public back home. Remarking on Scott's cubicle and the items it contained, Ponting notes that Scott 'had created a characteristic environment about him'.[24] Ponting also seeks to 'characterize' his subjects through the spaces and objects amongst which he places them. His photographs often present the men undertaking tasks that typify the role or work they were assigned on the expedition. They are surrounded by the objects they use to conduct the activity, within the small space assigned to them. In the darkness of the winter months, when no natural light entered the hut, Ponting used a magnesium flashlight to illuminate his subjects, thereby accentuating their concentration and evoking the intimacy of the spaces they occupied through contrasts of light and shadow. In these photographs, the men in the hut are absorbed in thinking, dreaming, writing and conducting their work, whether that be scientific, domestic or preparing for expeditions.

From a Bachelardian perspective, Ponting's evocation of these 'intimate' spaces of concentration suggests an 'oneiric house',[25] like the place which 'shelters' our first daydreams and gives rise to our most deeply rooted images and dreams of place. The attributes of the spaces and objects here are learned through what Bachelard calls 'organic habits',[26] the repetition of actions over time so they become imprinted in bodily memory. In Bachelard's view, an 'isolated hut' has an especially oneiric quality because of its 'simplicity' and the 'primitiveness of refuge' it affords.[27] The solitary hut creates a 'concentration of intimacy'[28] and an 'intensity' of inhabitation.[29] Such conditions of sheltered spatial intimacy and psychic intensity are conducive, Bachelard argues, to the imagination of 'intimate immensity'. He explains: 'immensity in the intimate domain is intensity, an intensity of being, the intensity of a being evolving in a vast perspective of intimate immensity'.[30] Such imagination inclines towards the contemplation of grandeur, but it often arises from scrutiny of the miniature, which 'deploys to the dimensions of a universe'.[31]

Like Ponting's photographs, Apsley Cherry-Garrard's book *The Worst Journey in the World* (1922) contributes to a sense of Scott's hut as a dream-like space that shelters dreaming. Written during the nine years after he returned from the continent, it is in part an elegy for Scott and his companions, lost on their return from the Pole. It expresses nostalgic longing for what he regards as the shared ideals of the community on the ice, far from the complexities and materialism of modern Britain and the horrors of the First World War. A sense of the hut as an oneiric refuge is created through the contrast Cherry-Garrard makes between the dream-like companionability of the first winter and the desolation of the second, when Scott and his companions were outside on the ice, missing and presumed dead. During the first winter – when Ponting took most of his photographs of the men indoors – the hut offered the physical and psychical refuge that, according to Bachelard, allows the 'osmosis between intimate and undetermined space'[32] that creates the imagination of 'intimate immensity'. But in the second winter, as the inhospitability of the vast 'undetermined space' outside insisted through the absence of their companions, the fragility of the shelter afforded by the hut and the vulnerability of its boundaries were more apparent. Cherry-Garrard recalls:

> on a bad blizzard night the wind, as it tore seawards over the hut, roared and howled in the ventilator let into the roof: in the more furious gusts, the whole hut shook ... We did not get many nights like these the first winter; during the second we seemed to get nothing else. One ghastly blizzard blew for six weeks.[33]

Edward S. Casey has observed how, according to Bachelard, dwelling in an oneiric house involves a continual exchange between the interior of the body and psyche and 'the outside world [which] becomes part of the being of within (and vice versa)'.[34] Cherry-Garrard's recollection of being bereft in the hut in the second winter underlines the penetrability of mind and body by atmosphere, weather and terrain in the far south. As he records in his diaries for the winter of 1912, the blizzards, more frequent this winter, gave him constant headaches, the lack of light contributed to his depression, and the slowness of the sea to freeze, confining the men indoors, increased his anxiety.[35]

Concluding his narrative, Cherry-Garrard reflects on the criticisms that could be levelled against Scott and his companions. In their defence, he invokes their shared sense of purpose: 'There are many reasons which send men to the Poles, and the Intellectual Force uses them all. But the desire for knowledge for its own sake is the one which really counts and there is no field for the collection of knowledge which at the present time can be compared to the Antarctic.'[36] Eulogistic as Cherry-Garrard's reflection is, the belief that theirs was a 'knowledge-based community'[37] was shared by other members of the expedition, especially Scott, Ponting and the scientists.

Looking for plankton: encounters with ice and sea

Through their activities, the scientists extended their spaces of absorption outdoors, tracing pathways across the ice to make their meteorological and oceanographic observations. Their movements within and around the hut to conduct their scientific investigations formed a 'taskscape', as Tim Ingold has called the production of a landscape through the interconnected activities and movements of the people working within it. Ingold observes: 'It is within the context of this attentive involvement in the landscape that the human imagination gets to work in fashioning ideas about it.'[38] The men's imaginative 'involvement in the landscape' through their response to the scientific work of their colleagues is illustrated by their attention to the activities of the shore-party biologist, Edward W. Nelson. Whilst Scott was critical of what he regarded as Nelson's dilettanteism,[39] he recognized the significance of Nelson's work, being 'to determine the condition under which organic substances exist in the sea'.[40] This work included collecting water samples 'to obtain their salinity values, current measurements, velocity, and direction'[41] and collecting and recording plankton.

Several of the men recalled Nelson working at the 'biological "hole"' he had cut in the sea ice,[42] and around which he built an 'igloo of drifted snow' to protect himself and his equipment.[43] Nelson's work outdoors in all weather reminded his colleagues of the contiguity of their intimate spaces indoors with the extremes of weather and atmosphere outside. Wilson notes, for example: 'Blizzard all day, heavy drift. No going out. Drawing all day ... Nelson was the only one who was out today; he visits his fishing hole whenever he can to break out the newly formed ice.'[44]

Nelson's work with the plankton or 'tow' net is documented by Ponting in two photographs that show him attaching the net to a kite and, with the assistance of Bernard Day, the expedition's motor mechanic, attempting to drop it into the sea then pull it ashore.[45] They conducted this experiment before the sea froze over and it became necessary to trawl for plankton through a hole in the ice. On this occasion, Nelson notes: 'small floating ice crystals choked the net and completely spoilt the catches'.[46] In Ponting's photograph of 'Nelson and Day Landing the Townet. March 15th 1911' (see Figure 13.2), the diagonal line of the pole Day is holding accentuates his position at the intersection of ice, sea and sky. Both men focus on the plankton net that dangles in the snow where it also draws attention to the thresholds they occupy between land and sea.

American nature writer Louis J. Halle writes that the edge between ice and sea in Antarctica 'presents the unique contrast of a lifeless realm with an immediately

Figure 13.2 Herbert Ponting. Nelson and Day landing the townet. March 15, 1911. Copyright Scott Polar Research Institute, University of Cambridge.

adjacent ocean that swarms with the most abundant oceanic life anywhere on earth'.[47] The fascination of expedition members with the life forms both at this edge and in the pelagic waters on the voyage is noted by Cherry-Garrard: 'From first to last the study of life of all kinds was of absorbing interest to all on board, and when we landed in the Antarctic, as well as on the ship, everybody worked and was genuinely interested in all that lived and had its being on the fringe of that great sterile continent.'[48]

Wilson observed the 'astonishing' abundance of the unicellular diatoms[49] and Dennis Lillie, the ship's party biologist, remarked on the increase in size and quantity of the plankton, particularly the diatoms, as the *Terra Nova* 'entered the cold waters of the far south'. Here, 'these minute plants became so numerous as to choke the meshes of the net after it had been fishing only five minutes'.[50] The appearance of the pack ice, too, was affected by the abundance of the diatoms frozen into it, which coloured it 'red orange and yellow everywhere underneath'.[51] The men also noted the vital importance of plankton in the marine food chain and the conditions it needed to survive.

March 1911, when Nelson and Day's activities were recorded by Ponting, is also the occasion of Chris Orsman's poem 'Forelands', in which Orsman considers how others in the party were preoccupied with ice and their 'attempt to read the history of the continent in its natural phenomena'. In mid-March, the geologists returned from an expedition to study the physiography of the landscape, including the ice. Orsman reflects on how the explorers try 'to read/the light of the past/imprisoned in a glacier'.[52] Scott's diary entries in late March and early April record his own preoccupation with the formation of the sea-ice and his conversations about 'ice problems … ice changes and … ice phenomena'.[53] Orsman imagines how, as the onset of winter largely confines the men to the hut and its environs, 'they long to enter/a new world of enraptured seeing, /to feel the steady draw of the horizon'.[54] While the men's exploration of the ice opened vistas of temporal and spatial immensity, the plankton, their object of concurrent enquiry, afforded later scientists and artists what Bachelard might call 'a vast perspective of intimate immensity'.

Plankton and 'the peculiar intimacy of the Anthropocene'

This perspective is explored by Judit Hersko in her speculative narrative essays, artwork and performance lectures about a fictional female Antarctic explorer who becomes fascinated with microscopic plankton. In the 2011 online artwork exhibition 'Anna's Cabinet of Curiosities' and her narrative essays 'Pages from the Book of the Unknown Explorer' (2012) and 'Objects from Anna Schwartz's Cabinet of Curiosities' (2018),[55] Hersko presents the story of the fictional 'Anna Schwartz', who passes as a man to participate in Richard E. Byrd's 1939–41 US Antarctic expedition. While in Antarctica, Anna Schwartz investigates planktonic molluscs. The work includes elements from Hersko's own life as well as that of her mother, a Hungarian photographer and cinematographer. Photographs of her mother provide the image of Schwartz. In this speculative life writing, 'Anna Schwartz' provides a fictional narrative connection between Hersko's own familial story and historical people and events, particularly as they pertain to Antarctica and the scientific investigation of plankton.

Central to Hersko's aesthetics is a fascination with the intimate, including the domestic, the familial and the miniature. In her narrative, Anna Schwartz discovers the work of women miniaturists and album-makers who innovatively adapted domestic and familial traditions to represent and project their lives. They include the Victorian artist Kate Edith Gough, who pasted cut-out photographs of herself and others onto familiar or remote painted settings, often to absurd effect.[56] Hersko adapts this collage technique to insert women into a history of 'heroic age' Antarctic exploration from which they were absent. In *Anna's Cabinet*, for example, she creates images that place Anna in the foreground of both Birdie Bower's desolate photograph of Scott and his companions at the Pole and a still of the *Terra Nova* on the ice, from Ponting's 1933 film *90° South*. In her exploration of the far south, Hersko is drawn to the minute and invisible in the non-human world. Both 'Pages' and 'Anna's Cabinet' include drawings of pteropods – planktonic sea snails – from a report on the scientific findings of the HMS *Challenger*, which conducted extensive investigations into marine organisms on its voyages in the 1870s. Hersko locates Schwartz's Antarctic investigations in Scott's *Terra Nova* hut, which Hersko visited in 2008 on the US National Science Foundation Antarctic Artists and Writers Program. Her photograph of the wardroom and its objects (see Figure 13.3)[57] accompanies the narrative about Schwartz's examination of pteropods under a microscope in Ponting's darkroom. It draws the eye to the open door of Ponting's room and the darkness beyond and evokes the absence not only of the explorers who inhabited the hut but also of women from Antarctica and Antarctic history in that period.

As Lisa Bloom has argued, Hersko's depiction of Anna Schwartz's preoccupation with the minute pteropods contrasts with 'the heroic scale of male exploration narratives and images'[58] But Hersko's photograph of Scott's hut also recognizes the intimacy of its spaces and the allure of its objects. Her treatment of one of those objects, the plankton net, exemplifies her fascination with the intimate. Her photographs of Anna Schwartz's 'invisible drawings' on the plankton net, and of Schwartz's 'self-portrait with snow crystals and planktonic snails',[59] resonate with the accounts of Scott's party of their own attention to the miniature and their appreciation of the 'beautiful silk fabrics' of the nets,[60] which 'phosphoresced beautifully from transparent *Siphonophora*' in the moonlight,[61] and of the ice-crystals in Nelson's net.

Hersko re-creates the plankton net in another set of photographs that explore and extend the feelings associated with Scott's hut in the writing and photographs of the men on the expedition. In 'Anna's Invisible Objects', Hersko, inspired by the objects in the hut, has created a sculpture of icy-white objects where the embroidered and diaphanous plankton net hangs alongside objects including a translucent paper vase inscribed with a wedding photograph of Kathleen and R. F. Scott and a 'paper replica' of Schwartz's Jewish aunt's candy jar. In another photograph, this sculpture is presented alongside a

Figure 13.3 Judit Hersko, *Scott's* Terra Nova *Hut with Herbert Ponting's darkroom*, 2009. Courtesy of the artist.

photograph of her aunt, where Schwartz stands alongside this aunt, who perished in the Holocaust (see Figure 13.4). Hersko's inclusion of these two images that foreshadow familial loss suggests a critique of modernity, whose suppressions of 'nature' and the human – especially female – body she has explored in her earlier work.

In staging her work in Scott's hut, Hersko draws on intimate spaces and objects that *already* connote grief. Her incorporation of the pteropods in her artwork and narrative extends this affective matrix to encompass the connections between the human and the non-human and the microscopic and the planetary. 'Pages' is a work of mourning for Hersko's mother, who died shortly after Judit's return from Antarctica. It also visually represents the findings of her collaborators, scientists researching the effects of ocean acidification, caused by the ocean's absorption of increasing amounts of atmospheric carbon dioxide. One effect is to inhibit the shell-formation of planktonic molluscs. The demise of these creatures would endanger the marine food chain, and, like the decrease of phytoplankton and krill due to the reduction of the sea-ice that supplies their nutrients, would lead to the Southern Ocean becoming 'a sea full of vanishings', as Melanie Challenger has put it.[62] Hersko's incorporation of plankton in her work invites us to reflect on the effects of anthropogenic climate change and the consequent loss of species. 'Pages' and 'Anna's Cabinet' include, for example, photographs of sculptures in which casts of pteropod shells are embedded in the silicone rubber bearing Schwartz's portrait (see Figure 13.5). Through these images, Hersko makes minute or invisible creatures visible and their loss grievable. She allows us to imagine what David Farrier has

Figure 13.4 Judit Hersko, Anna's Cabinet (detail). 2011. Courtesy of the artist.

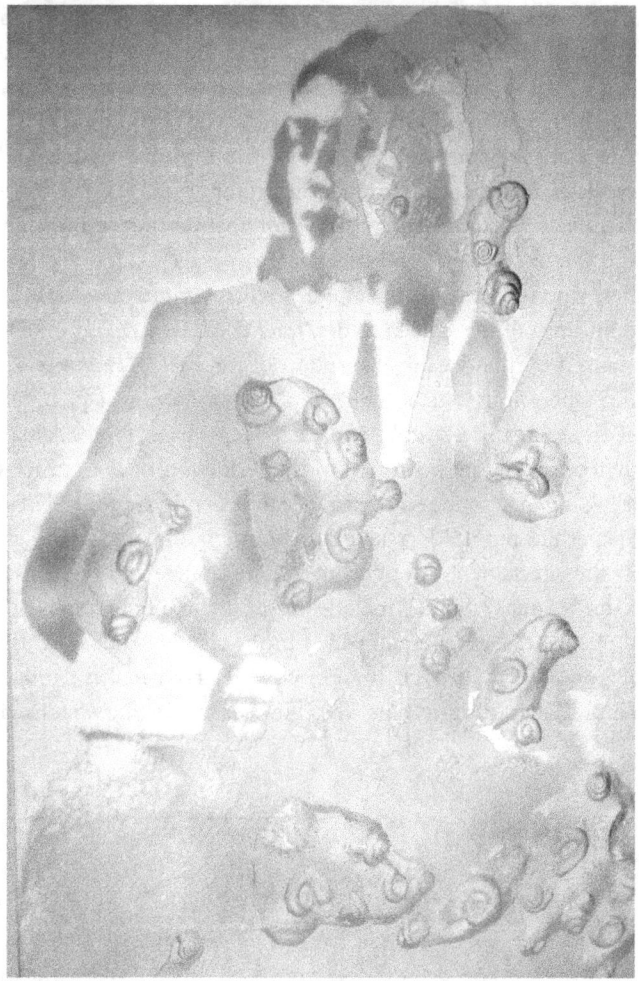

Figure 13.5 Judit Hersko, *Portrait of Anna Schwartz*. 2008. Courtesy of the artist.

called 'the peculiar intimacy of the Anthropocene'[63] as it is manifested in the 'confluence' of the microscopic, the human and the planetary. Hersko's sculpture brings together many elements: the history of Antarctic exploration and women's absence from it, as figured by 'Anna Schwartz'; mid-twentieth-century Jewish migration, of which her mother, who escaped the Second World War Holocaust, was part; and the deeper time of the evolution and potential destruction of plankton. It also connects changes occurring in the Southern Ocean to human activity elsewhere.

As she sails through the Southern Ocean on her return voyage from Antarctica, Elizabeth Bradfield composes a 'Letter Home' to 'America'. Cognizant of the contradictions between her environmentalism and the journey in 'a diesel-powered boat', as well as the consumerist lifestyle that awaits her in America, she hopes nonetheless to return home 'better able to make new connections and see from new perspectives'.[64] In her encounters with Antarctica, both in person and through her reading of others' narratives, 'the vast, raw place was made of intimate moments. Tenderness even.'[65] It is through an attention to the 'intimate' in the 'vast' that Bradfield hopes we will be more able to understand and care for Antarctica and its connections to the planet. The imaginative responses to the study of plankton considered in this chapter reveal a poetics that connects the microcosmic to the planetary in the life writing and photographs of visitors to the southern continent from the early expeditions to the present day.

Notes

1. Elizabeth Bradfield, *Toward Antarctica* (Pasadena, CA: Boreal Books, 2019), 13.
2. Apsley Cherry-Garrard, *The Worst Journey in the World* (1922; repr., London: Pimlico, 2003), 86–7.
3. John Wylie, 'Becoming-icy: Scott and Amundsen's South Polar Voyages, 1910–1913', *cultural geographies* 9, no. 3 (2002): 254.
4. Robert Falcon Scott, *Journals: Captain Scott's Last Expedition*, 1913, ed. Max Jones (Oxford: Oxford University Press, [1913] 2008), 76.
5. Wylie, 'Becoming-icy', 254.
6. David L. Harrowfield, *Icy Heritage: Historic Sites of the Ross Sea Region* (Christchurch, NZ: Antarctic Heritage Trust, 1995), 34.
7. Scott, *Journals*, 97 and 96.
8. Cherry-Garrard, *The Worst Journey*, 193.
9. Antarctic Heritage Trust, *Conservation Plan: Scott's Hut, Cape Evans, British Antarctic Expedition 1910–1913, Ross Island, Antarctica* (Christchurch, NZ: Antarctic Heritage Trust, 2004), 87.
10. Ibid., 87–8.
11. Jane Ussher, *Still Life: Inside the Antarctic Huts of Scott and Shackleton* (Millers Point, NSW and London: Murdoch Books, 2010), 17.
12. Derek P. McCormack, *Atmospheric Things: On the Allure of Elemental Envelopment* (Durham, NC and London: Duke University Press, 2018), 215.
13. Ussher, *Still Life*, 120 and 121.
14. Gaston, Bachelard, *The Poetics of Space*, trans. M. Jolas (New York: Penguin, [1964] 2014), 36.
15. Ussher, *Still Life*, 177.
16. Herbert G. Ponting, *The Great White South, or With Scott in the Antarctic*, ed. Beau Riffenburgh, Liz Cruwys and Jonathan Jeffes (London: Discovery Gallery, [1921] 1999), 167.
17. Chris Orsman, 'A Portrait in the Wardroom', in *South* (London: Faber and Faber, 1999), 18, lines 11–14.
18. Wylie, 'Becoming-icy', 253.
19. Orsman, 'Portrait', 18, lines 8–9.
20. Wylie, 'Becoming-icy', 253.

21. Orsman, 'Portrait', lines 19–21.
22. Ibid., lines 24–8.
23. Lauren Berlant, 'Intimacy: A Special Issue', *Critical Inquiry* 24, no. 2 (1998): 281.
24. Ponting, *The Great White South*, 166.
25. Bachelard, *The Poetics of Space*, 37.
26. Ibid., 36.
27. Ibid., 50.
28. Ibid., 57.
29. Ibid., 52.
30. Ibid., 210.
31. Ibid., 176.
32. Ibid., 245.
33. Cherry-Garrard, *The Worst Journey*, 193.
34. Edward S. Casey, *The Fate of Place: A Philosophical History* (Berkeley and Los Angeles, CA and London: University of California Press, 1998), 293.
35. Apsley Cherry-Garrard, Diary, MS 599/4; BJ Diary, 23 October to 30 October 1911 up to 26 September 1912 [Cape Evans, 23 to 30 October 1911, 29 January to 22 February 1912 and 2 May to 26 September 1912], 1 volume, holograph, Scott Polar Research Institute, University of Cambridge. See, for example, entries for Wednesday 8 May 1912, Tuesday 25 June 1912 and Saturday 24 August 1912.
36. Cherry-Garrard, *The Worst Journey*, 597.
37. Jessica O'Reilly, *The Technocratic Antarctic: An Ethnography of Scientific and Environmental Governance* (New York: Cornell University Press, 2017), 14.
38. Tim Ingold, *The Perception of the Environment: Essays on Livelihood, Dwelling and Skill* (Abingdon, Oxon: Routledge, 2011), 207.
39. Scott, *Journals*, 465.
40. Ibid., 223.
41. Edward Wilson, *Diary of the 'Terra Nova' Expedition to the Antarctic 1910–1912*, ed. H. G. R. King (New York: Humanities Press, 1972), 186.
42. Ponting, *The Great White South*, 178.
43. Cherry-Garrard, *The Worst Journey*, 196.
44. Wilson, *Diary*, 168.
45. Herbert G. Ponting, 'Nelson Attaching Townet to Kite. March 15th 1911'. Photograph. Scott Polar Research Institute, University of Cambridge. Available online: https://www.spri.cam.ac.uk/picturelibrary/catalogue/article/p2005.5.332/; and Herbert G. Ponting, 'Nelson and Day Landing the Townet. March 15th 1911'. Photograph. Scott Polar Research Institute, University of Cambridge. Available online: https://www.freezeframe.ac.uk/collection/photos-british-antarctic-expedition-1910-13-ponting-collection/p2005-5-333.
46. E. W. Nelson, 'Marine Biology – Winter Quarters 1911–1913', in *Scott's Last Expedition*, vol. 2, ed. Leonard Huxley (New York: Dodd, Mead and Company, 1913), 335.
47. Louis J. Halle, *The Sea and the Ice: A Naturalist in Antarctica* (London: Michael Joseph, 1974), 215.
48. Cherry-Garrard, *The Worst Journey*, 6–7.

49. Wilson, *Diary*, 75.
50. D. G. Lillie, 'Summary of Biological Work Carried Out on Board the *Terra Nova*, 1910–1913', in *Scott's Last Expedition*, vol. 2., ed. Leonard Huxley (New York: Dodd, Mead and Company, 1913), 331.
51. Wilson, *Diary*, 75.
52. Orsman, 'Forelands', *South*, 54, lines 21–3.
53. Scott, *Journals*, 156.
54. Orsman, 'Forelands', 55, lines 47–9.
55. Judit Hersko, *Anna's Cabinet of Curiosities*, 2011. Online exhibition at: https://www.lanfrancoaceti.com/portfolio-items/judit-hersko-mep/; Judit Hersko, 'Pages from the Book of the Unknown Explorer', in *Far Field: Digital Culture, Climate Change and the Poles*, ed. Jane D. Marsching and Andrea Polli (Bristol and Chicago: Intellect, University of Chicago Press, 2012), 61–75; and Judit Hersko, 'Objects from Anna Schwartz's Cabinet of Curiosities', in *Future Remains: A Cabinet of Curiosities for the Anthropocene*, ed. Gregg Mitman, Marco Armiero and Robert S. Emmett (Chicago: University of Chicago Press, 2018), 182–90.
56. Hersko, 'Objects', 183.
57. Hersko, *Anna's Cabinet* and 'Pages', 67.
58. Lisa E. Bloom, 'Planetary Precarity and Feminist Environmental Art Practices in Antarctica', *Journal of Postcolonial Writing* 56, no. 4 (2020): 556.
59. Hersko, *Anna's Cabinet*.
60. Scott, *Journals*, 224.
61. Griffith Taylor, *With Scott: The Silver Lining* (London: Forgotten Books, [1916] 2018), 262–3.
62. Melanie Challenger, *On Extinction: How We Became Estranged from Nature* (London: Granta, 2011), 164.
63. David Farrier, *Anthropocene Poetics: Deep Time, Sacrifice Zones, and Extinction* (Minneapolis and London: University of Minnesota Press, 2019), 16.
64. Bradfield, *Toward Antarctica*, 149.
65. Ibid., 147.

Bibliography

Antarctic Heritage Trust. *Conservation Plan: Scott's Hut, Cape Evans, British Antarctic Expedition 1910–1913*, Ross Island, Antarctica. Christchurch, NZ: Antarctic Heritage Trust, 2004.
Bachelard, Gaston. *The Poetics of Space*, translated by M. Jolas. New York: Penguin, [1964] 2014.
Berlant, Lauren. 'Intimacy: A Special Issue'. *Critical Inquiry* 24, no. 2 (1998): 281–8.
Bloom, Lisa E. 'Planetary Precarity and Feminist Environmental Art Practices in Antarctica'. *Journal of Postcolonial Writing* 56, no. 4 (2020): 556.
Bradfield, Elizabeth. *Toward Antarctica*. Pasadena, CA: Boreal Books, 2019.
Casey, Edward S. *The Fate of Place: A Philosophical History*. Berkeley and Los Angeles, CA and London: University of California Press, 1998.
Challenger, Melanie. *On Extinction: How We Became Estranged from Nature*. London: Granta, 2011.
Cherry-Garrard, Apsley. *The Worst Journey in the World*. London: Pimlico, [1922] 2003.
Farrier, David. *Anthropocene Poetics: Deep Time, Sacrifice Zones, and Extinction*. Minneapolis and London: University of Minnesota Press, 2019.

Halle, Louis J. *The Sea and the Ice: A Naturalist in Antarctica*. London: Michael Joseph, 1974.

Harrowfield, David L. *Icy Heritage: Historic Sites of the Ross Sea Region*. Christchurch, NZ: Antarctic Heritage Trust, 1995.

Hersko, Judit. 'Objects from Anna Schwartz's Cabinet of Curiosities'. In *Future Remains: A Cabinet of Curiosities for the Anthropocene*, edited by Gregg Mitman, Marco Armiero and Robert S. Emmett, 182–90. Chicago: University of Chicago Press, 2018.

Hersko, Judit. 'Pages from the Book of the Unknown Explorer'. In *Far Field: Digital Culture, Climate Change and the Poles*, edited by Jane D. Marsching and Andrea Polli, 61–75. Bristol and Chicago: Intellect, University of Chicago Press, 2012.

Ingold, Tim. *The Perception of the Environment: Essays on Livelihood, Dwelling and Skill*. Abingdon, Oxon: Routledge, 2011.

Lillie, D. G. 'Summary of Biological Work Carried Out on Board the *Terra Nova*, 1910–1913'. In *Scott's Last Expedition*, vol. 2., edited by Leonard Huxley, 328–34. New York: Dodd, Mead and Company, 1913.

McCormack, Derek P. *Atmospheric Things: On the Allure of Elemental Envelopment*. Durham, NC and London: Duke University Press, 2018.

Nelson, E. W. 'Marine Biology – Winter Quarters 1911–1913'. In *Scott's Last Expedition*, vol. 2, edited by Leonard Huxley, 335. New York: Dodd, Mead and Company, 1913.

O'Reilly, Jessica. *The Technocratic Antarctic: An Ethnography of Scientific and Environmental Governance*. New York: Cornell University Press, 2017.

Orsman, Chris. 'A Portrait in the Wardroom'. In *South*. London: Faber and Faber, 1999.

Ponting, Herbert G. *The Great White South, or With Scott in the Antarctic*, edited by Beau Riffenburgh, Liz Cruwys and Jonathan Jeffes. London: Discovery Gallery, [1921] 1999.

Scott, Robert Falcon. *Journals: Captain Scott's Last Expedition*, edited by Max Jones. Oxford: Oxford University Press, [1913] 2008.

Taylor, Griffith. *With Scott: The Silver Lining*. London: Forgotten Books, [1916] 2018.

Ussher, Jane. *Still Life: Inside the Antarctic Huts of Scott and Shackleton*. Millers Point, NSW and London: Murdoch Books, 2010.

Wilson, Edward. *Diary of the 'Terra Nova' Expedition to the Antarctic 1910–1912*, edited by H. G. R. King. New York: Humanities Press, 1972.

Wylie, John. 'Becoming-icy: Scott and Amundsen's South Polar Voyages, 1910–1913'. *cultural geographies* 9, no. 3 (2002): 249–65.

CHAPTER 14
THE MUSICAL LIVES OF MAWSON'S MEN
Carolyn Philpott

When Douglas Mawson and the men of the Australasian Antarctic Expedition (AAE) were preparing for their epic journey to the far south in late 1911, they packed not only essential scientific equipment, food and clothing supplies but also a surprisingly diverse array of musical instruments. Their surviving diaries from the expedition, as well as their later published accounts, mention various wind instruments such as a flute, piccolo and mouth organ; a mandolin; an autoharp; an accordion; a piano (which stayed on board the ship, the *Aurora*); and a portable pump organ that was transported to the main hut at Cape Denison and which is now housed at the Mawson's Huts Replica Museum in Hobart, Tasmania (see Figure 14.1).[1] The men also took with them hymn books and gramophones with numerous records.

With extremely cramped conditions aboard the *Aurora* and limited space in the prefabricated huts they planned to erect in Antarctica, the decision to take these items suggests that the men anticipated music playing an important role in their lives during the AAE.[2] This is perhaps not so surprising, however, when considered within the context of the times. Like many middle-class Australians of their day, various members of the AAE were proficient amateur singers and several also played one or more musical instruments; music was thus a prominent part of their home lives that they were unwilling to forgo in Antarctica. The many references to composing, performing and listening to music in the men's diaries and published narratives of the AAE provide ample evidence that they enjoyed music at regular intervals through their days in Antarctica, as well as called on it in both times of celebration and hardship.

Drawing on historical records – including diaries, musical items and the AAE's 'newspaper', the *Adelie Blizzard* – this chapter explores the role of music in the lives of Mawson's men during their journey to and time in Antarctica. In particular, it reveals how they used music to fill space and mark time during the expedition and how they (ironically) adapted northern music and traditions to suit their own experiences as 'Southern' men and to aid their survival in the far south.

Music in routine expeditionary life

The AAE's men participated in music making from the earliest days of the expedition, when enduring a rough journey across the Southern Ocean aboard the *Aurora*. At this point, they were mostly strangers, but they soon found themselves connecting during evening singalongs in the ship's saloon, a practice which drew on naval traditions and

Figure 14.1 The AAE's original pump organ, as it sits today in the Mawson's Huts Replica Museum in Hobart, Tasmania. Photo: Carolyn Philpott, with permission from the Mawson's Huts Foundation.

simultaneously established a routine that would continue once they reached Antarctica. Sometimes their singalongs on the *Aurora* included piano accompaniment, although this was not without its challenges. For example, according to the diary of biologist and artist Charles Harrisson, a 'concert' held on the evening of 9 December 1911 featured Frank Wild singing various songs, with 'all joining in the chorus[es]', and with 'Dr McLean at the piano, but both musician and music stool made occasional excursions across the saloon when the old boat took an extra roll'.[3] Reflecting many years later on this early part of the expedition, the AAE's biological collector and taxidermist Charles Laseron wrote, 'It was now we began to really know one another, for in the evenings, after the day's toil was done, we yarned and sang to our hearts' content.'[4]

The men continued to enjoy the evening singalongs once they had constructed and moved into the AAE's two continental bases: the main base at Cape Denison, where eighteen men, including Mawson, lived for the first year, and a smaller party for a second

The Musical Lives of Mawson's Men

year; and the Western Base, which was located nearly 2,500 kilometres west of the main base, on an ice shelf, and was home to eight expeditioners for a year.

At the main base at Cape Denison, the men regularly enjoyed listening to the gramophone and holding singalong sessions from dinnertime onwards, especially during the first year of the expedition (see Figure 14.2). Sometimes these sessions lasted for hours, and on occasion, one or more of the men would accompany the singing on an instrument or play purely instrumental music.[5] Several of the men also formed a makeshift instrumental ensemble known as the 'Adélie Land Band', which gave a number of impromptu performances during the AAE's first winter in Antarctica. As Mawson noted in his diary on 6 June 1912: 'In the evening the Adélie Land Band strikes up.... [The] men crawl out of their beds all eager to be in it.'[6] The following evening, the AAE's chief medical officer and bacteriologist, Dr Archibald McLean, recorded in his diary: 'The Adelie Band had a practice tonight ... [We] finished up with Auld Lang Syne.'[7] Stillwell's diary entry from the same day indicates that Frank Hurley, the expedition's official photographer, organized the band and that 'Correll with his piccolo was foremost. ... Tin drums and metal triangles were to the fore and the whole effect was not unmusical'.[8]

As these diary extracts suggest, musical activities were particularly popular with the expeditioners during the long, dark and extremely cold winter months in Antarctica.

Figure 14.2 Frank Hurley, 'A winter evening at the hut' (1911), National Library of Australia, http://nla.gov.au/nla.obj-136188901. Used with permission.

Music was also integral to the celebration of birthdays and other special occasions, such as midwinter day, most of which were marked by more formal evening dinners and entertainment. Most of the music that Mawson's men enjoyed in the far south was familiar to them from their home lives (and, ironically, originated from the northern hemisphere), such as excerpts from Gilbert and Sullivan operettas, especially *The Mikado*; popular classical music; music hall songs; ragtime music; and hymns.[9] As McLean's diary entry above intimates, the musical evenings at the main base typically finished with the singing of 'Auld Lang Syne', which the men also sang at other times prior to parting company, such as before embarking on sledging journeys.

Once the novelty of their existing musical resources wore off, however, several of the expeditioners began to compose new songs (or at least new lyrics for pre-existing tunes) that reflected their own experiences. This soon became a favourite pastime: Laseron notes that 'Even Mertz [who was Swiss and not fluent in English] ... became infected with the popular craze of songwriting.'[10] Laseron's AAE diary and papers, as well as those of the expedition's chief magnetician, Eric Webb, include multiple sets of original song lyrics written by various members of the party and mention some occasions on which the songs were performed.[11]

Some of the men's original lyrics, such as 'Aurora Australis', penned by McLean, are patriotic and even imperialistic in nature; this particular song features lines such as 'We're a pure Australian crowd' and 'We'll be conquerors of Adelie Land'.[12] However, even though the title 'Aurora Australis' immediately informs the listener of the song's southern provenance through its reference to the southern lights, Laseron notes that the lyrics should be sung to the tune of 'The Lord High Executioner' from Gilbert and Sullivan's *The Mikado*.[13] While at first the combination of Australian references in the lyrics and an English tune might seem awkward, this operetta was very popular among the AAE's men, most of whom would have considered themselves British subjects, as well as Australians, at the time.[14] Further, the first verse's mention of unfurling the 'Union Jack' in this 'unknown land' reveals that the men were acutely aware of their role in assisting with the expansion of the British Empire into the far south.[15] In this way, music could serve to reinforce the significance of their conquests, enabling, in Elizabeth Leane's words, 'the men to proclaim their activities as legendary'.[16]

Composing and performing original songs also provided much-needed diversion and entertainment, facilitated the release of pent-up emotions, helped with boosting team morale and bonding, and afforded the men a creative means of recording their experiences for later personal or public consumption. Many of the newly composed song lyrics are humorous, with 'intensely personal' references to one or more expedition members.[17] For example, the lyrics for a song titled 'Only a Leaf', which Webb recorded in his Sledging Diary and Laseron kept a copy of inside the cover of his main diary, poke fun at McLean and his efforts in the kitchen by describing him as 'a new unconventional Cook', who 'rose from the ranks of those that cook crook'.[18] The lyrics, which the men note were sung to the tune of the British music hall song 'Sue, Sue, Sue', then go on to provide a witty parody of the expedition's doctor, as the second chorus illustrates:

Stew! Stew! Stew! Just take a spoonful or two,
Stew! Stew! Stew! Curried seal's very nice with a
    little boiled rice,
So Do! Do! Do! Ah, why do you look so blue?
For if with you it don't agree,
You can bring it up you see,
with Ugh! Ugh! Ugh![19]

The verse that follows shifts the focus to the men's experiences of sledging but continues in a similar comic vein:

Sledging is crook on the icy plateau,
Wind 70 an hour and at 30 below,
My cheeks and my ears frostbitten have been,
And frostbites were many on my never-been-seen,
Bites on my fingers – and bites on my toes,
Bites on my – Oh yes! – and also my nose.[20]

While music making and listening were predominantly evening activities during the early months of the expedition, it was not long before they filtered into other times in the men's days as well, becoming part of their expeditionary routines. For example, the men at the main base soon began using their gramophone as a daily morning alarm clock, as Hurley wrote in his diary:

At 7.30am the night watchman winds up the gramophone and selects a record according to his mood. A towel is thrust into the horn to subdue the tune to pianissimo. Gentle strains fall on the ears of the … sleepers [who] stir and turn in their bunks. It is pleasant to play in the day with harmony – it invariably closes with song.[21]

Additionally, every Sunday when at the main base, the men sang familiar hymns from home at church services, often accompanied by Frank Stillwell on the pump organ.[22] Again, these hymns most likely would have originated from Britain, reinforcing for many of the men their dual identities as British subjects and Australians who were serving both the motherland and their homeland through their roles in the far south. These regular Sunday services no doubt formed an important part of the men's weekly routine and simultaneously provided a marker of time passing.

Similarly, the Western Base Party enjoyed music at regular intervals. They did not have much space in their hut, nor as many musical instruments as the main base party; however, the Western Base Party did have a gramophone and some records, which they soon knew 'by heart' and that they would sing along to.[23] Harrisson's diary entry from 26 April 1912 gives an indication of types of recordings at their disposal, which again seem to have been largely of northern-hemisphere provenance:

> The gramophone plays a great part in our home. There are a few comic songs (that I'm deadly sick of!), but many fine selections. 'Reminiscences of Offenbach' (played by band of Coldstream Guards) [is] one of the best. Then there's 'Gems from Maritana' [and] 'Tis known to all' (from Daughter of the Regiment) ....[24]

Unlike at the main base, where the composition of original songs seems to have provided an antedote to the men becoming 'sick of' particular recordings, the Western Base members do not appear to have invented their own songs or lyrics. Instead, they relied much more heavily on their gramophone to fill the space of the hut and pass the time. Celebratory dinners for birthdays, midwinter and anniversaries were 'accompanied throughout by music on the gramophone'[25] and, as at the main base, the Western Base Party used their gramophone as a morning alarm. According to the meteorologist Morton Moyes:

> We were soon in a routine. We took it in turns to be 'cook' for the day. The duties included ... preparing breakfast which was announced by starting the gramophone, when we would wake to the voice of Harry Lauder singing 'John, John, John, go and put your little trousers on'.[26]

This latter song was not only a highly appropriate selection because it encouraged the men to get up and organized for the day, but it was also another example of a south-north connection: it was composed by an Australian, Richard Isaac Banks (1878–1915), who became a famous vaudeville and music-hall performer under the name of Billy Williams.

The Western Base Party also enjoyed regular Sunday church services, with several different hymns sung each week by all members of the group, occasionally accompanied by the geologist Arch Hoadley on the autoharp.[27] They also routinely played the hymn 'God be with you till we meet again' on the gramophone before departures on sledging trips.[28]

Exceptional musical occasions

Music also proved useful when the men experienced extreme hardship. For example, during a sledging journey to lay food depots in August 1912, Morton Moyes and five of his companions from the Western Base endured, in his words, 'a period of great discomfort' when they became caught in a blizzard, narrowly avoided an avalanche and were reduced to just one tent for six men.[29] In desperation, they dug a small trench in the ice, '12 feet by 8 feet and 3 feet deep', which they covered with the remaining tent, anchored with sledges and large blocks of ice, and then huddled inside for 'almost five days of extreme discomfort'.[30] It was not long before they became wet through from ice melting around their bodies. Nevertheless, they made the best of the situation. According to Moyes:

No one outside would have realised the discomfort. ... [At] times a passer-by – if there had been one – would have thought that a musical festival was in progress. Frank Wild, an old sea-dog, had a wide knowledge of sea shanties and we soon learned them .... It was surprising to find what a number of hymns were known and with a further assortment of excerpts from grand opera, all tastes could be satisfied.[31]

Moyes recalled that everyone joined in the singing, which occupied 'the greater part' of each day, meaning that 'the miserable conditions did not affect the spirit in the trench'.[32]

Just a couple of months later, Moyes again turned to music for comfort when he was left alone in the Western Base hut while his companions undertook a sledging journey. Expecting to be 'alone for a few days only', he busied himself with cleaning and other duties, but as weeks began to pass, he became increasingly concerned that 'the whole party had perished' and anxious that he would be left 'surviving like the last leaf on a branch'.[33] As time went on, he began to find the silence surrounding him 'oppressive and unnerving'.[34] He listened to music on the gramophone in an attempt to fill the empty space of the hut and lift the 'heavy burden of silence that gave no peace'.[35] Coincidentally, when his comrades finally returned – almost nine weeks after they had left – it was music that signalled their arrival: they broke Moyes's silence by singing a song as they sledged into base. As Moyes later recalled:

Then came the day when I felt the solitude had at last beaten me. As I sat writing up my journal, I thought I heard a sledging song, one of those rollicking ditties we used to sing to boost our morale. I stood up, alarmed by the fancy, shaking with a sense of confusion. I'm going dippy, I thought. This is it. I stared stupidly about me. I heard the singing again, as faint and elusive as the far-off note of a bugle.[36]

He hurried outside the hut and when he saw his friends sledging towards him, he was so 'overcome with joy' that he stood on his head.[37]

Sledging itself could be a gruelling, as well as tedious, activity and the AAE's men composed several original sledging songs to motivate and distract themselves while man-hauling heavy sledges across the icy plateau. One of these songs in particular, the 'Southern Sledging Song', encouraged some of the main base's men on 'through many trials and tribulations' and they sang it at full volume when sledging into base.[38] The lyrics of the 'Southern Sledging Song' were composed by Hurley, who had undertaken a sledging journey toward the South Magnetic Pole with Webb and engineer Robert 'Bob' Bage during the summer of 1912–13.[39] Travelling for several hundred miles across the desolate plateau, the men entertained themselves by singing and inventing songs while out on the march, as well as while relaxing in their tent. Webb recorded sixteen pages of lyrics in his Sledging Diary, including several sets relating directly to their sledging journey, such as 'The Merry Sledgers', 'Tramp, Tramp, Tramp' and the 'Southern Sledging Song'.[40] The lyrics of the 'Southern Sledging Song' are highly motivational and project a strong sense of group identity as the men tackle the inhospitable icescape: 'Hauling, toiling, tireless on we tramp … It has to be done, so we make of it fun/We men of the Southern Trail.'[41] Through the line 'We men of the Southern Trail', in particular, Hurley suggests that he and his companions now identify closely with – and even *belong* to – the far south. The sledging song, as a type of work song that facilitates teamwork through rousing lyrics and a regular beat that promotes synchronization of movements, is closely related to the sea shanty, another genre of northern-hemisphere provenence that emerged from maritime traditions. Mawson's men would have been familiar with this popular type of sailor's work song, especially as Frank Wild (a former member of the British Merchant Navy and Royal Navy) was known to regularly sing them and most likely did so aboard the *Aurora*.[42] It is fitting, therefore, that Hurley set the lyrics of the 'Southern Sledging Song' to a popular sea song known as 'Sailing, sailing', which similarly makes light of hard physical work and also speaks of returning 'home again' after a perilous journey.[43] For Hurley and his fellow sledgers, 'home' no doubt referred to the main base hut, as well as their homes further north. The melody of this song is in a major key and has a relatively

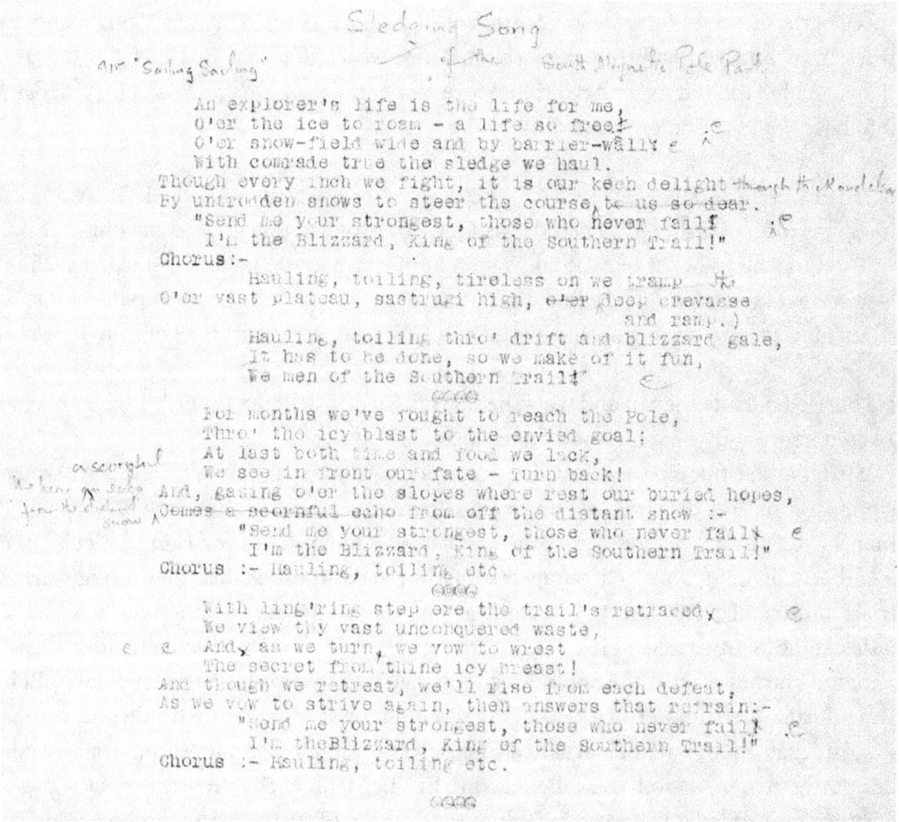
Sledging Song

An explorer's life is the life for me,
O'er the ice to roam - a life so free!
O'er snow-field wide and by barrier-wall!
With comrade true the sledge we haul.
Though every inch we fight, it is our keen delight
By untrodden snows to steer the course, to us so dear.
"Send me your strongest, those who never fail!
I'm the Blizzard, King of the Southern Trail!"
Chorus :-
Hauling, toiling, tireless on we tramp
O'er vast plateau, sastrugi high, o'er deep crevasse and ramp.)
Hauling, toiling thro' drift and blizzard gale,
It has to be done, so we make of it fun,
We men of the Southern Trail!"

For months we've fought to reach the Pole,
Thro' the icy blast to the envied goal;
At last both time and food we lack,
We see in front our fate - Turn back!
And, gazing o'er the slopes where rest our buried hopes,
Comes a scornful echo from off the distant snow :-
"Send me your strongest, those who never fail!
I'm the Blizzard, King of the Southern Trail!"
Chorus :- Hauling, toiling etc

With ling'ring step ere the trail's retraced,
We view thy vast unconquered waste,
And, as we turn, we vow to wrest
The secret from thine icy breast!
And though we retreat, we'll rise from each defeat,
As we vow to strive again, then answers that refrain:-
"Send me your strongest, those who never fail!
I'm theBlizzard, King of the Southern Trail!"
Chorus :- Hauling, toiling etc.

Figure 14.3 The 'Southern Sledging Song' as printed in *The Adelie Blizzard*, with notes likely made by McLean. Courtesy of the Australian Polar Collections, South Australian Museum, Adelaide.

small pitch range, making it appropriate for amateurs to sing whilst undertaking physical labour, whether at sea or while hauling sledges across ice. The AAE's men were obviously very proud of the 'Southern Sledging Song'; it was published as the opening item in the first issue of their 'newspaper', *The Adelie Blizzard* (see Figure 14.3).

The main base party created a rather exceptional musical occasion of a different kind on 12 October 1912, when they staged what is believed to be the first 'opera' on the Antarctic continent. Titled *The Washerwoman's Secret*, this original work was developed and performed by a 'musical society' established by several members of the party, known

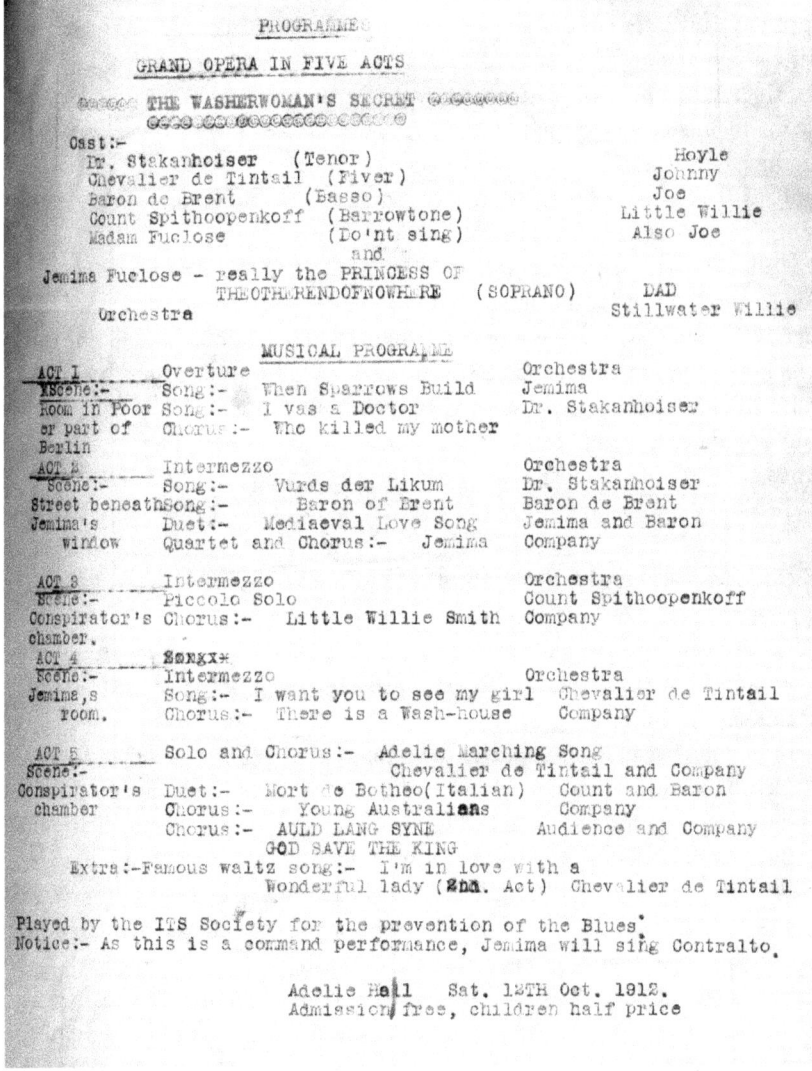

Figure 14.4 Original programme for *The Washerwoman's Secret*. Courtesy of the Australian Polar Collections, South Australian Museum, Adelaide.

as the 'Its Society for the Prevention of the Blues'.[44] The group advertised the performance as a 'Grand Opera in Five Acts' and from the men's diaries, it is clear that it was grand in length (at two-and-a-half hours in duration), if not subject matter.[45] Laseron, who designed the opera's scenario, described the work as a 'tragedy ... with a complicated and highly dramatic plot'.[46] The surviving programme from the event (Figure 14.4) and the men's diary entries, however, indicate that the work was comic in nature and more like a burlesque.[47] The cast members were given humorous names: McLean (who the other men nicknamed 'Dad'), for example, acted as 'Jemima Fuclose – really the PRINCESS OF THEOTHERENDOFNOWHERE', a name that appears to mock the AAE's assistant collector, John Close, as well as refer to their remote location.[48] As the 'leading lady', McLean took advantage of the spotlight and kept the audience laughing hysterically by dressing as a woman with 'beautiful golden hair' and makeup made from watercolour paints, singing in a high-pitched voice and performing several awkward 'love' scenes.[49] While the main storyline did not directly relate to the men's Antarctic experiences, the programme nevertheless included an 'Adelie Marching Song' and a chorus titled 'Young Australians' (see Figure 14.4). Moreover, within some songs there were humorous references to various expedition members.

Overall, the performance seems to have both entertained the men and boosted their morale after a long and challenging winter: Laseron noted in his diary that the opera was 'a howling success, and the audience laughed from beginning to end', meaning that they had 'managed to extract some fun from this God forsaken hole'.[50] Mawson also considered the event 'an immense success', recording that it 'ended in a patriotic song voicing our determination to keep our spirits up notwithstanding the unparalleled weather, and to do our upmost', after which they 'all retired wearied with laughter'.[51]

Final observations and conclusions

As the examples here have illustrated, music played several important roles in the daily lives of the Australasian Antarctic Expedition's men. Initially used primarily for entertainment in the evenings as a way of filling the space of the hut and passing the time, music soon began to be employed in various functional ways at other hours as well. It regularly bookended their days: drawing them out of sleep in the mornings, as well as helping them to unwind after a full day of work. In a place where extended periods of either daylight or darkness threatened to disrupt their circadian rhythms, music became a valuable marker of time, lending a sense of structure and routine to their lives. The Sunday services they held regularly, in which music played a central part, no doubt also served as markers of time – in this case, weeks – passing.

Music also functioned as an effective means of boosting morale, expressing facets of their identity and facilitating connections. As several examples discussed above have shown, engaging in musical activities such as listening, composing and performing (especially comic songs) seems to have formed part of their strategy for surviving emotionally in the far south. By adapting northern music and traditions into a southern context (through their newly composed song lyrics in particular), they could project their identity as 'Southern' men who were serving lands to the north (Britain and Australia) through their duties in the far south. Music also provided a powerful means of connecting the expeditioners with each other through shared experiences and of connecting their lives in Antarctica with their lives back at home. As is evident from their diaries, listening to or performing familiar music often provoked memories of their home lives, as well as helped them to create a home-away-from-home in Antarctica. Additionally, listening to or performing sacred music could help the men to feel a sense of connection to the Divine and to lift their spirits, especially in times of hardship. Music also proved beneficial as a motivational tool, especially their newly composed sledging songs, which directly assisted them with the difficult task of man hauling.

While the AAE's main achievements were of course scientific and exploratory in nature, considering the expedition through the lens of music nevertheless reveals much about the personalities of Mawson's men and their daily lives in the far south. As this research has uncovered, some of the men – especially Correll, Harrisson, Hunter, Hurley, Laseron, McLean, Moyes, Stillwell, Webb and Wild – were particularly musical, regularly engaging in the activities of music listening, creating and/or performing. Mawson himself, however, does not appear to have actively participated in music creation or performance during the AAE, although he did enjoy listening to the others' music making.[52] In this way, this research contributes to recent scholarly efforts to shed more light on other members of the AAE, rather than continuing to focus the spotlight entirely on its leader.[53] Simultaneously, the surviving musical materials from the AAE, especially the examples of northern music that they adapted for their own purposes, provide insights into how Mawson's men viewed themselves: as steadfast, as well as larrikin, 'Southern' men who were ultimately risking their lives in a quest to 'conquer' the far southern continent for both their homeland and motherland.

Notes

1. Charles Harrisson, *Mawson's Forgotten Men: The 1911–1913 Antarctic Diary of Charles Turnbull Harrisson*, ed. Heather Rossiter (Sydney: Murdoch Books Australia, 2011), 29, 137; Frank Stillwell, *Still No Mawson: Frank Stillwell's Antarctic Diaries 1911–13*, ed. Bernadette Hince (Canberra: Australian Academy of Science, 2012), 101, 119; Douglas Mawson, *Mawson's Antarctic Diaries*, ed. Fred Jacka and Eleanor Jacka (Sydney: Allen & Unwin, 1988), 89; Kylie Quinn, 'Life on Board SY Aurora', Australian Antarctic Program. Available online: https://www.antarctica.gov.au/about-antarctica/history/exploration-and-expeditions/australasian-antarctic-expedition/crew-life-on-board-aurora/; Jack Hoadley, *Antarctica to Footscray: Arch Hoadley* (Melbourne: Sid Harta, 2010), 89; Charles Francis Laseron, *South with Mawson: Reminiscences of the Australasian Antarctic Expedition, 1911–1914* (London: G. G. Harrap & Australasian Pub. Co., 1947), 59.

2. Morton Moyes, *The Aura of the Antarctic: Antarctic Recollections of Captain Morton Moyes* (Adelaide: Peacock Design & Print, 2014), 6; Hoadley, *Antarctica to Footscray*, 63.

3. Harrisson, *Mawson's Forgotten Men*, 5–6.

4. Laseron, *South with Mawson*, 32.
5. See Stillwell, *Still No Mawson*, 59, 61, 66, 101, 119.
6. Mawson, *Mawson's Antarctic Diaries*, 89.
7. Archibald McLean, 7 June 1912, in Dr Archibald Lang McLean Diaries, 2 December 1911–26 February 1914, kept while a member of the Australasian Antarctic Expedition, 1911–14, State Library of New South Wales, ML MSS 382/1, item 2.
8. Stillwell, *Still No Mawson*, 93.
9. Laseron, *South with Mawson*, 89, 92. While most of the AAE's members had homes in the Australasian region, a few travelled south from the northern hemisphere, including Frank Wild, Belgrave Ninnis, Xavier Mertz and Francis Bickerton.
10. Ibid., 113.
11. Charles Laseron, Diaries (2), 21 November 1911–24 February 1913, kept while a member of the Australasian Antarctic Expedition, 1911–14, together with related papers, 1911–12, State Library of New South Wales, ML MSS 385; Eric Webb, Sledging Diary, 10 November 1912–11 January 1913, kept on the Australasian Antarctic Expedition, 1911–14, State Library of New South Wales, MSS 2895/1. See also Laseron, *South with Mawson*, 97–8; 112–14.
12. Laseron, Diaries, ML MSS 385, item 1. Adélie Land is part of the approximately 4,000 miles successfully explored during the AAE.
13. Ibid.
14. Laseron, *South with Mawson*, 89.
15. Laseron, Diaries, ML MSS 385, item 1.
16. Elizabeth Leane, *Antarctica in Fiction: Imaginative Narratives of the Far South* (Cambridge: Cambridge University Press, 2012), 124.
17. Laseron, *South with Mawson*, 99.
18. Webb, Sledging Diary.
19. Ibid.
20. Ibid.
21. Frank Hurley, *Argonauts of the South: Being a Narrative of Voyagings and Polar Seas and Adventures in the Antarctic with Sir Douglas Mawson and Sir Ernest Shackleton* (London: G. P. Putnam's Sons, 1925), 51.
22. Stillwell, *Still No Mawson*, 58.
23. Moyes, *Aura of the Antarctic*, 18.
24. Harrisson, *Mawson's Forgotten Men*, 108.
25. Hoadley, *Antarctica to Footscray*, 103.
26. Moyes, *Aura of the Antarctic*, 9.
27. Ibid.; Jack Hoadley, *Antarctica to Footscray*, 89.
28. Harrisson, *Mawson's Forgotten Men*, 111.
29. Moyes, *Aura of the Antarctic*, 11–12.
30. Ibid., 12.
31. Ibid.
32. Ibid., 23.
33. Ibid., 14, 108.

34. Morton Moyes (as told to G. Dovers and D. Niland), 'Season in Solitary', *Walkabout* 30, no. 10 (1964): 21.
35. Ibid., 23.
36. Ibid. For more on silence and solitude in Antarctica, see Carolyn Philpott and Elizabeth Leane, 'Silent Continent? Textual Responses to the Soundscapes of Antarctica', *ISLE: Interdisciplinary Studies in Literature and Environment* 29, no. 4 (2022): 1030–54.
37. Moyes, *Aura of the Antarctic*, 108.
38. Hurley, *Argonauts of the South*, 93.
39. Carolyn Philpott and Elizabeth Leane, 'Making Music on the March: Sledging Songs of the "Heroic Age" of Antarctic Exploration', *Polar Record* 52, no. 267 (2016): 710.
40. Webb, Sledging Diary.
41. Ibid.
42. Philpott and Leane, 'Making Music on the March', 699.
43. Ibid., 712.
44. Laseron, *South with Mawson*, 110.
45. Laseron, Diaries, ML MSS 385, item 2; McLean, 12 October 1912, Dr Archibald Lang McLean Diaries, ML MSS 382/1, item 2.
46. Laseron, *South with Mawson*, 110.
47. Programme for *The Washerwoman's Secret*, Australian Polar Collections, South Australian Museum; Dr Archibald Lang McLean Diaries, ML MSS 382/1, item 2.
48. Elizabeth Leane to Carolyn Philpott, 17 February 2013, email correspondence.
49. Laseron, *South with Mawson*, 111; Cecil Thomas Madigan, *Madigan's Account: The Mawson Expedition*, trans. J. W. Madigan (Moonah: Wellington Bridge Press, 2012), 269; Laseron, Diaries, ML MSS 385, item 2.
50. Laseron, 12 October 1912, Diaries, ML MSS 385, item 1.
51. Douglas Mawson, *Home of the Blizzard* (Adelaide: Wakefield Press, 1996), 131; Mawson, *Mawson's Antarctic Diaries*, 121.
52. This is evident from Mawson's writings, as well as those of other AAE members, and aligns with Paquita Mawson's claim that during her husband's younger years, he had not been particularly interested in performing music, despite his mother's skills as a singer and performer. Paquita Mawson, *Mawson of the Antarctic: The Life of Sir Douglas Mawson F.R.S. O.B.E.* (London: Longmans, 1964), 21, 24.
53. Other examples include Heather Rossiter's edited version of Charles Harrisson's diary (referenced above); David Jensen's *Mawson's Remarkable Men: The Personal Stories of the Epic 1911–14 Australasian Antarctic Expedition* (Sydney: Allen & Unwin, 2015); and Elizabeth Leane, Ben Maddison and Kimberley Norris's article 'Beyond the Heroic Stereotype: Sidney Jeffryes and the Mythologising of Australian Antarctic History', *Australian Humanities Review* 64 (2019): 1–23.

Bibliography

Harrisson, Charles. *Mawson's Forgotten Men: The 1911–1913 Antarctic Diary of Charles Turnbull Harrisson*, edited by Heather Rossiter. Sydney: Murdoch Books Australia, 2011.

Hoadley, Jack. *Antarctica to Footscray: Arch Hoadley*. Melbourne: Sid Harta, 2010.

Hurley, Frank. *Argonauts of the South: Being a Narrative of Voyagings and Polar Seas and Adventures in the Antarctic with Sir Douglas Mawson and Sir Ernest Shackleton*. London: G. P. Putnam's Sons, 1925.

Jensen, David. *Mawson's Remarkable Men: The Personal Stories of the Epic 1911–14 Australasian Antarctic Expedition*. Sydney: Allen & Unwin, 2015.

Laseron, Charles Francis. *South with Mawson: Reminiscences of the Australasian Antarctic Expedition, 1911–1914*. London: G. G. Harrap & Australasian Pub. Co., 1947.

Leane, Elizabeth. *Antarctica in Fiction: Imaginative Narratives of the Far South*. Cambridge: Cambridge University Press, 2012.

Leane, Elizabeth, Ben Maddison and Kimberley Norris. 'Beyond the Heroic Stereotype: Sidney Jeffryes and the Mythologising of Australian Antarctic History'. *Australian Humanities Review* 64 (2019): 1–23.

Madigan, Cecil Thomas. *Madigan's Account: The Mawson Expedition*, translated by J. W. Madigan. Moonah: Wellington Bridge Press, 2012.

Mawson, Douglas. *Home of the Blizzard*. Adelaide: Wakefield Press, 1996.

Mawson, Douglas. *Mawson's Antarctic Diaries*, edited by Fred Jacka and Eleanor Jacka. Sydney: Allen & Unwin, 1988.

Mawson, Paquita. *Mawson of the Antarctic: The Life of Sir Douglas Mawson F.R.S. O.B.E.* London: Longmans, 1964.

Moyes, Morton. *The Aura of the Antarctic: Antarctic Recollections of Captain Morton Moyes*. Adelaide: Peacock Design & Print, 2014.

Moyes, Morton (as told to G. Dovers and D. Niland). 'Season in Solitary'. *Walkabout* 30, no. 10 (1964): 20–3.

Philpott, Carolyn, and Elizabeth Leane. 'Making Music on the March: Sledging Songs of the "Heroic Age" of Antarctic Exploration'. *Polar Record* 52, no. 267 (2016): 710.

Philpott, Carolyn, and Elizabeth Leane. 'Silent Continent? Textual Responses to the Soundscapes of Antarctica'. *ISLE: Interdisciplinary Studies in Literature and Environment* 29, no. 4 (2022): 1030–54.

Quinn, Kylie. 'Life on Board SY Aurora', Australian Antarctic Program. Available online: https://www.antarctica.gov.au/about-antarctica/history/exploration-and-expeditions/australasian-antarctic-expedition/crew-life-on-board-aurora/.

Stillwell, Frank. *Still No Mawson: Frank Stillwell's Antarctic Diaries 1911–13*, edited by Bernadette Hince. Canberra: Australian Academy of Science, 2012.

CHAPTER 15
SIGNALS FROM THE SOUTH: DECODING THE LIFE OF AN ANTARCTIC WIRELESS OPERATOR
Elizabeth Leane

On a hill on the outskirts of the regional Australian town of Ararat sit a group of buildings that look like they were purpose-made for the set of a horror film. The site of the Aradale Psychiatric Hospital – first constructed in the Victorian period as the Ararat Lunatic Asylum – is a jumble of decaying structures and broken windows, dominated by a run-down mansion and its formerly stately gardens. The combination evokes a sense of past grandeur and present ruin. Closer to the centre of town is an older, more foreboding building, its high, dark stone walls topped by barbed wire. This is J-Ward, the separate maximum-security wing of the asylum, a converted Victorian gaol where the 'criminally insane' were housed. Decommissioned in the early 1990s, both sites are now open to regular tour groups. One story that occasionally features on the tours is that of Sidney Jeffryes, a wireless operator and one-time member of the 1911–14 Australasian Antarctic Expedition led by Douglas Mawson. In early 1913, Jeffryes succeeded in sending and receiving wireless messages across the Southern Ocean between Antarctica and Australia for the first time, an achievement that was hailed in media headlines across the country. Yet just over a year later, Jeffryes had been committed to Ararat asylum, and thence to J-Ward, where he lived in obscurity until his death in 1942.

In this chapter, I lay out my attempts to decipher fragments of Jeffryes's life and afterlives, focussing particularly on the role of communication across distance: spatial, temporal and emotional. Jeffryes's feat of sending and receiving radio messages between the two southern continents had national significance, but it exacted an enormous personal toll. While Antarctica was not the root cause of Jeffryes's mental illness – which was very likely what we would now call schizophrenia – the pressures that surrounded his efforts to connect across the Southern Ocean had a significant effect on when and how his illness unfolded. Jeffryes's life was, I argue, an inherently southern life, in that his fate was entirely bound up in this inaugural electromagnetic coupling of the two southernmost continents.

A wireless life: Connecting continents through radio

Born in mid-1884 in what was then the colony of Queensland, Sydney, Harry Jeffryes (he would later spell his first name 'Sidney') entered a British Empire in which concepts of distance and time had been transformed by a series of technological developments – in transport, industrial machinery and printing and communications technologies.[1] Wired telegraph had already revolutionized long-distance communication by the time Jeffryes was born – indeed, he grew up in a household that was literally inseparable from this technology. During his early childhood, his father had worked as a wired telegraph officer in or near Toowoomba,[2] eventually becoming the postmaster at the rural town of Allora, where the family very likely lived in a residence attached to the Post Office building.[3] So Jeffryes was raised in a world of letters, messages, telegrams and transmissions.

While Jeffryes's childhood was surrounded by the infrastructure of wired telegraphy, his early adult life coincided with the heyday of wireless technology.[4] He was three years old when radio waves – a form of electromagnetic (EM) radiation – were discovered, and he had turned seventeen when Guglielmo Marconi successfully transmitted the first message by wireless telegraphy across the Atlantic in 1901.[5] By this time, public demonstrations of wireless technology had already occurred in Australia, although the first official wireless transmission (across Bass Strait from Victoria to Tasmania) was not sent until 1906, and the construction of a series of coastal stations began in late 1910.[6] These changes brought into being a new profession: the wireless operator. Due to a couple of high-profile maritime disasters in which wireless played a key role, this newly emerging role was from at least 1909 'fixed in the public mind' as a 'heroic' one.[7]

Jeffryes appears to have quickly taken advantage of the opportunity to join this glamorous new profession. His movements in the very early years of the century are somewhat hazy. An 'S. Jeffreys'/'Sidney Jeffreys' (born 'abt' 1885/1886) was working as an apprentice clerk within the traffic division of the Queensland railways between 1901 and 1906, a role that would likely have involved exposure to wired telegraphy.[8] An 'S. E. Jeffryes' was working as a telegraphist in New South Wales in 1909.[9] Both are likely to have been the Sidney Jeffryes of interest here. Whatever the case, by 1911 Jeffryes was working as a shipboard operator for the Australasian Wireless Company – continuing the family tradition, although now in the new wireless medium.

At the same time that Jeffryes was gaining proficiency as a wireless officer, Douglas Mawson – geologist, explorer and veteran of Ernest Shackleton's *Nimrod* expedition (1907–9) – was considering the advantages of using the new technology to connect Antarctica and Australia. Such an idea had been first mentioned in the Australian press in late 1907, as an aspirational possibility for Shackleton's expedition.[10] In 1908 the concept arose again, with the aptly named *Daily Telegraph* (Sydney) arguing that wireless communication with Antarctica would give great assistance to meteorology in Australia. The newspaper foresaw an added advantage: 'what would surpass in interest a daily report from that region of snow and ice of [the *Nimrod* explorers'] experiences and discoveries … ?'[11] Hopes that Robert Falcon Scott's second expedition, which departed in 1910, might take a device to communicate with New Zealand also came to nothing, with the British explorer considering the weight of the equipment too much of an obstacle.[12] When Mawson began announcing plans to lead his own expedition, then, he was aware that incorporating wireless would be an innovative and exciting step, which would in turn help to attract financial support for his venture.

By early 1911, when Mawson was publicly campaigning to lead an Australian expedition to Antarctica, he was emphasizing the need for it 'to have wireless equipment at any cost'.[13] Not coincidentally, at around the same time, Hugh Denison, newspaper magnate and director of the Australasian Wireless Company, donated a thousand pounds to the expedition (the location of the main base, Cape Denison, would be named after him).[14] The wireless plans drew frequent positive comment in the press, although as the departure time drew near, the need to make good on this promise was causing Mawson the 'most anxiety' of any aspect of the expedition.[15] Eventually the Australasian Wireless Company agreed to sell Telefunken wireless sets to Mawson with the promise to buy them back on his return at half the original cost of 650 pounds each.[16] So, when the expedition departed at the end of that year, it included equipment sufficient for two wireless stations – one at the main base in Antarctica and a relay station at the subantarctic Macquarie Island.[17] The expedition secretary Conrad Eitel told the press at this time that 'it is to the wireless equipment that the … expedition looks for the greatest results'.[18]

The value of the wireless was not only scientific and logistical but also geopolitical. Both wired and radio telegraphy, alongside steam-based transport and new printing technologies, were part of the 'increasingly more complicated global webs and circuits of the expanding empire'.[19] Britain's 'postal and telegraphic services', noted a member of parliament in the late 1880s, possessed 'a cohesive force' that other empires lacked.[20] Moreover, as Elleke Boehmer (see Note 19, 12) has observed, the imperialist sentiments which the telegraph both enabled and enacted were readily transferred to a nationalist context in Britain's colonies. So, while Britain was looking to use the telegraph to bind together the colonies to its south, the southern continent of Australia in turn had colonial aspirations even further south, in which telegraphic connectivity again played a part. Certainly Mawson's aspirations in Antarctica were explicitly territorial and economic, and he emphasized the unique claim Australia had on the region: 'lying within wireless telegraphic distance of our borders, the Antarctic continent ha[s] a special call upon the Australian people'.[21] Mawson's choice of words is significant here: in telegraphy, to 'call' was to contact via that technology, so the explorer's language evokes the idea of Antarctic already 'calling' – sending messages – to Australia. As Ben Maddison, Kimberley Norris and I have argued elsewhere, 'Mawson's vision relied on the idea that Eastern Antarctica would become part of the newly formed Australian nation, with the wireless being the primary mechanism that sutured the continents together'.[22] A lot was riding, then, on the success of the wireless and hence the efforts of the wireless operators in Antarctica and Macquarie Island.

In early October 1911, Jeffryes called on Mawson in person in Adelaide, to apply for a position as wireless operator on his Antarctic expedition. He is likely to have read about Mawson's plans in the newspapers earlier that year. They certainly would have caught his eye, as he was already pushing limits in his new profession. In late September 1911, the media reported his claim to a new long-distance transmission record for a ship wireless on the Australian coast (Adelaide to Suva, Fiji); and in late October a second record – this time for the greatest Southern Hemisphere overland distance between ships – was announced.[23] His visit to Mawson occurred between the appearance of these two reports. Mawson had already appointed engineer Walter Hannam as the operator for the continental base but continued to be 'anxious' about the wireless's success and unsure about Hannam's 'actual operating experience'.[24] He passed Jeffryes's name to Hannam twice, emphasizing the former's strength of character ('a very decent sort of man', 'a very good man as a man'), and suggesting that although too small to be a sledger, he might be suitable for Macquarie Island, or as a backup continental operator.[25] Hannam, however, overlooked Jeffryes, choosing another shipboard wireless operator, Arthur Sawyer, for Macquarie Island. The expedition departed in December 1911, without Jeffryes on board.

Despite Mawson's promise of regular reports, nothing was heard from Antarctica via the wireless for many months. Back in Australia, the support team was highly concerned about the apparent failure of the equipment in Antarctica. Eitel sent a telegram to Mawson's former mentor, geologist Edgeworth David, in early 1912 saying that the wireless was a 'complete fiasco'.[26] Accusatory letters were dispatched to the Australasian Wireless Company, which had supplied the main apparatus, and Denison defended the company, pointing out among other things that Hannam's 'knowledge of the wireless was purely elementary'.[27] Eitel considered the success of the wireless so important to the expedition that he proposed to charter a ship immediately to take down replacement equipment.[28] This came to nothing, however, and it was not until September 1912 that anything was heard from Antarctica. Hannan managed to get a few messages through to Macquarie Island around that time but received nothing, so he was unaware of this success. His struggles with the wireless were in part due to the weather conditions: Mawson had inadvertently established his base on what the men quickly discovered to be one of the windiest places on Earth. To what extent the wireless struggles were due to the windy location, the equipment, Hannam's 'elementary' skills or simply the challenge of using such new technology in such a remote and extreme place is unlikely ever to be known. But for Hannam, there was little consolation; Mawson told him that the wireless was the 'biggest failure' of the expedition.[29] The timing was particularly poor, as this was the year of the *Titanic* disaster, in which wireless was popularly considered to have played a 'heroic role'.[30]

When the relief ship travelled down to Antarctica at the end of 1912 to take the expedition members home, Jeffryes volunteered to join what was assumed to be a roundtrip, taking with him a 'duplicate set of receiving apparatus' in the hopes of making good on Mawson's original vision.[31] When the ship arrived in Antarctica in early 1913, however, a sledging party led by Mawson had not returned by the scheduled time, and the vessel eventually had to depart without them. Five men from the 1912 group remained behind to wait for the missing sledgers, which meant staying another whole year in the south. The wireless was repaired, the masts re-erected and extended, crystals replaced and equipment moved from the cold workshop into the warmer – and now relatively empty – living area.[32] The 1912 wireless operator Hannam, however, was keen to come home, and Jeffryes agreed to take his place. For any early twentieth-century person, accepting a place in an Antarctic expedition was a momentous decision, but Jeffryes had little clue just how much it would derail his career and his life.

'One of the heroes goes insane': The winter of 1913

The year that followed was not an easy one, and initially the wireless was a bright spot in an otherwise tedious and melancholy period. Mawson had staggered home shortly after the ship left, barely alive himself and bringing the news that his two sledging companions were dead. The six men from the original group were thus faced with an unexpected year in the south while dealing with the deaths of two much-beloved friends, for which Mawson, as leader of the sledging party, was in some sense responsible. At least one of the men, meteorologist Cecil Madigan, voiced his resentment of his leader frequently in his diary. As the only newcomer to this small group of men tied together by communal grief as well as a year already spent in the south, Jeffryes faced a difficult situation by any estimation.

Despite the interpersonal and physical challenges, Jeffryes quickly established radio contact with Macquarie Island and even occasionally Australia and began regularly sending and receiving messages. Madigan believed that the success of the wireless was at least partly due to Jeffryes's personal equipment: 'Jeffryes has a very sensitive crystal … [whereas] Hannam's crystal does not give anything.'[33] The Australian press, while not blaming Hannam for the previous year's problems, gave Jeffryes full credit for the 1913 success. In an article sub-headed 'Wonderful wireless work', the *Argus* newspaper noted that from the time Jeffryes took over, 'the apparatus has achieved a triumph'.[34] Similarly celebratory articles appeared in newspapers across the country.

In the south, however, difficulties mounted. Operating the wireless was by Mawson's admission 'very tedious and nerve-racking work'.[35] Jeffryes had to keep strange hours because reception was best at night. This meant he slept a lot during the day (to Mawson's annoyance) and did not venture outside as much as the others. Even with this late-night schedule, various atmospheric phenomena created frequent interference. The homesick men were keen to send and receive news via the wireless – Madigan considered messages 'oases in [a] desert', and the men would wait eagerly not only for the global news, which brought novelty to their monotonous existence, but also to hear from and contact family and friends. Mawson, however, prioritized expedition business and publicity, thus generating resentment and putting extra pressure on Jeffryes, the sole channel through which news flowed between the two continents. In early June, one of the wireless masts blew down, temporarily stopping all communication and putting an extra burden on Jeffryes to rectify the situation. This is the point from which Jeffryes's life, and the dynamics of the expedition, changed irrevocably.

In early July, in the middle of the dark Antarctic winter, Jeffryes began to act strangely. Taking a comment Madigan made about Arthur Conan Doyle's novel *The Hound of the Baskervilles* as a personal slight, the radio operator became enraged and later attacked his companion. From this time on, Jeffryes behaved in a paranoid and reclusive manner, believing the other men were out to kill him, warning Mawson of an impending murder, refusing to wash himself or his clothes, storing his own urine on a shelf, hanging a sheet around his bed and muttering to himself. These symptoms are all consistent with a diagnosis of what is now termed schizophrenia, a condition which can be triggered by stress.[36] In the early twentieth century, however, this illness was only just beginning to be recognized; the expedition doctor, Archie McLean, instead gave the broad diagnosis of 'delusional insanity'.[37] The following months were difficult for all the men as Jeffryes's condition waxed and waned but never disappeared. His initial offer to resign from the expedition was rejected by Mawson, who scoffed that such an idea was anyway ridiculous when he could not leave the hut.[38] More importantly, Jeffryes was the only person with requisite wireless experience; once the mast was re-erected, he was needed to maintain contact with the outside world. Nonetheless, Mawson grew increasingly uneasy about his reliability, particularly after he caught him sending out a message to Macquarie Island that the other men were 'unwell' (this did not arrive, although Mawson could not have known that).[39] In early October, despite his previous protestations, Mawson officially dismissed Jeffryes from the expedition. This expulsion was of course administrative rather than literal: the men continued to live uneasily with Jeffryes until the relief ship arrived, landing them back in Adelaide, South Australia, in late February 1914.

At this point, things got even worse. Although he had continued to behave unusually on the voyage home and took no part in the welcoming celebrations, Jeffryes was allowed to board a train alone to his home in distant regional Queensland. He did not arrive but was found starving and ragged in the Victorian bush around a week later, claiming that Mawson had hypnotized him. Almost exactly a year after his success with the wireless had been hailed throughout the land, Jeffryes again hit the press across the country, but for very different reasons. 'One of the heroes goes insane', ran one headline, with others terming the event 'A Sad Case' and a 'Pathetic Episode'.[40] Such images were in stark contrast to the 'heroic tradition' of the wireless officer current at the time.[41] They threatened to cast doubt not only on Mawson's leadership but also the whole discourse of white masculine resilience and endurance in extreme cold environments on which polar (both north and south) exploration relied. Mawson went into damage control, publicly distancing himself from Jeffryes, whom he emphasized he had 'not chosen' when he first applied in late 1911; suggesting – despite protests from Jeffryes's family and the absence of diary evidence – that the man 'was not as strong as he might have been' from the time he arrived in the far south; and claiming that the wireless operator had been 'normal' on the voyage home.[42] Meanwhile, Jeffryes was quickly consigned to the asylum system, never to re-emerge.

'[M]y will became suddenly magnetic': EM radiation and the noisy mind

Talking to reporters after his discovery in the bush, Jeffryes appears to have highlighted two causes for his problems: Mawson had hypnotized him and 'The solitude of the ice ... had got on his nerves.'[43] Encouraged by Mawson's own confirmation that 'the weather conditions in Adelie Land are very trying', the papers leapt on the second explanation, with headlines such as 'Solitude of the Ice', 'Victim of the Frozen South', and 'The Lonely Antarctic' all laying the blame for Jeffryes's mental condition on his year spent in the far south.⁴⁴ But Jeffryes other, seemingly more delusional, comment – that the expedition leader had hypnotized him – might actually provide a better clue to the factors that contributed to his psychosis.

Jeffryes's belief that Mawson had hypnotized him stretched back at least to September 1913, when in a letter to his leader he wrote that 'I have been continuing my duties for the past two weeks under the influence of a hypnotic spell under which you have found it encumbent [sic] to place me to avert a calamity'.⁴⁵ In a later letter, written while in the Ararat Hospital for the Insane (as it was then called), Jeffryes provided a retrospective account of what happened in midwinter 1913:

> I ... fell into a magnetic spell. My will & all my faculties remained exactly as they were before, and the change which I actually felt traverse my brain & which it seemed to strengthen, exposed my thoughts & feelings to all & sundry, in the hut. The fact is, that my will became suddenly magnetic and I am in a permanent state of mental thought transference, telepathy, or whatever you chose [sic] to call it.⁴⁶

Having dealt for many months with the stresses of detecting and deciphering electromagnetic signals, Jeffryes began to think of his own mind as some form of wireless, broadcasting messages to the world at large. At one point after Jeffryes's illness became apparent, Madigan wrote in his diary that 'Morsing seems second nature to him';⁴⁷ ironically, Jeffryes seems to have naturalized his wireless operating ability, imagining his brain as a device for detecting electromagnetic signals. Other documents reinforce the role of the wireless in his breakdown: not long after his first symptoms appeared, he wrote to a friend that 'My endeavours to make a success of the wireless here has lead [sic] to my being murdered in its interests.'⁴⁸ In letters to Mawson he accused the other men of jealousy 'at a very early stage of the starting of the wireless' and alludes to tension about his having taken over Hannam's role.⁴⁹ One of his paranoid letters – telling a friend that he was being 'hounded to death' by the other expeditioners – was written in the back of a book from the expedition library, entitled *Electricity in the Service of Man*.⁵⁰ Everything about Jeffryes's illness, it seems, was entangled with electromagnetism.

This entanglement did not cease on Jeffryes's return to Australia. A superintendent at Ararat Hospital for the Insane noted that at times his patient would become 'preoccupied', acting as if he was 'receiving wireless messages'. The medic concluded that 'the Polar experience had made a very marked – possibly indelible – mental impression [on Jeffryes], owing ... chiefly to worry in connection with the receiving, or failure to receive, messages so faint as to be at times indecipherable'. Even in the asylum then, Jeffryes remained mentally in the far south, manning the wireless. There are many signs that it was not – or at least not only – the isolation, darkness and cold of the far southern winter that affected Jeffryes so badly but also his dedicated yet often fraught efforts to invisibly connect the two southern continents.

That Jeffryes's delusions focused both on the wireless and on thought transference should come as no surprise. From the outset, telegraphy, wired and wireless, was associated with the paranormal, including communication with the dead, mesmerism and telepathy.⁵¹ These ideas were not restricted to spiritualists, but extended into the scientific community. British physicist Oliver Lodge, the first person to demonstrate wireless telegraphy in public, 'repeatedly supported the link between wireless and telepathy'.⁵² Lodge believed the concept of the ether – a postulated invisible fluid filling the universe, sometimes likened to an ocean, and thought to be necessary for the propagation of radio and other electromagnetic (EM) waves – might also explain otherwise mysterious psychic phenomena. 'By conceiving of thoughts as a form of radiation', writes Anthony Enns, 'scientists began to describe consciousness as a wireless receiver and transmitter'.⁵³ Jeffrey Sconce suggests a melancholy aspect to such ideas: unlike wired technology, which involved physical connection between communicators, wireless was disembodied, imagined as 'a lonely realm of distant and estranged consciousnesses, a vast ocean where the very act of communication reminded the operator of his or her profound isolation'. Communicating by wireless, he suggests, was like being an explorer navigating the 'unfathomable depths' of this ocean, 'a journey traversed primarily across mysterious expanses of silence and static'.⁵⁴ Coming of age at a time when this discourse around wireless was at its height, and then operating across the roughest ocean while located in the most isolated community in the world, Jeffryes eventually came to conflate his own estranged consciousness with wireless technology. His hypnotized mind and magnetized will expressed an identification with his role as Antarctic wireless operator that had gone to extremes.

Jeffryes's afterlives

Once removed from his role as an Antarctic wireless operator, it seems, Jeffryes gradually shifted away from his fixation on hypnosis and thought transference. By 1915, his delusions had taken on an increasingly religious dimension. He developed a messiah complex and later became obsessed with the Freemasons. His role in the expedition, as the first person to successfully establish two-way communication between Antarctica and Australia, largely vanished from public view. By the time he died of a cerebral haemorrhage, his identity had been forgotten – his profession on his death certificate is listed as 'labourer', his parentage 'not known'.⁵⁵ He was buried in an unmarked grave in the local cemetery. And just as he was removed from society, Jeffryes's achievements were largely written out of Australian Antarctic – and wireless – history. Even in the twenty-first century, it is still not unusual to see Hannam rather than Jeffryes promoted as 'Radio's Polar Pioneer'.⁵⁶

Jeffryes is not, however, entirely without afterlives. One way he is remembered is through the buildings where he spent the second half of his life: Aradale asylum and the nearby J-Ward. His photograph and story figure on an interpretative panel in a cell in J-Ward, which, as mentioned at the start of this chapter, is now open to tour groups. Unsurprisingly, both J-Ward and Aradale do a good trade in dark tourism. While Jeffryes is hardly the most sensational of the patients to have lived in the facility, he occasionally features in the ghost tours, producing at least one report of the spirit of the wireless operator communicating with guides and tourists from the beyond, in Morse code.[57] Telegraphy, especially wireless telegraphy, was associated not only with telepathy but also communication with the dead – the coded taps of the wireless key in morse having their equivalents in the table-rapping messages of the séance.[58] That Jeffryes should still, in the early twenty-first century, reportedly be sending messages in Morse across a divide greater than the Southern Ocean seems strangely fitting. Over a hundred years after the expedition, and eighty years after his death, the Antarctic radioman is still – it seems – tapping out coded messages from the remotest regions imaginable.

*

The prospect of decoding Jeffryes's life is daunting. While there are numerous documents covering his time in Antarctica and its immediate aftermath, his early life is barely recorded, and the copious and untidy records of the asylum offer only oblique and occasional glimpses into his post-Antarctic existence. Unlike many other expeditioners, Jeffryes kept no diary – at least none has surfaced – and the dozen or so letters he wrote all date from the period during which he was suffering from psychosis and give little insight into his professional achievements. His records are full of coding errors: all parts of his name – particularly his unusually spelled surname – were constantly misspelled or mis-transcribed in official documents. From the perspective of the twenty-first century, Jeffryes's life, like the airwaves, is characterized by 'mysterious expanses of silence and static'.[59] But to leave this life untold is to refuse its challenge to the narrative of heroic masculine achievement that has largely dictated the shape of far southern exploration stories and lives,[60] and also to overlook a history of far southern communication that stretches back over a century.

Questions of information and interpretation become particularly pressing for a subject who spent his life – and apparently also his afterlife – trying to send and receive messages. If a radioman snatching faint coded messages from the ether can be likened to a spirit communicating from beyond the grave, this metaphor also works in reverse: the process of researching or writing a life is one of detecting signals from the noise of the archives. Perhaps the past, in this case, is not a foreign country but rather an ice-covered continent, and the intervening decades are a cold ocean – continuous, encircling, rough and deep – over which signals, however distorted, attenuated and noisy, are occasionally received.

Notes

1. Clare Pettitt, '"The Annihilation of Space and Time": Literature and Technology', in *The Cambridge History of Victorian Literature*, ed. Kate Flint (Cambridge: Cambridge University Press, 2012): 550–72.
2. Birth certificate of Sydney Harry Jeffryes, born 20 July 1884, Registrar of Births, Deaths, Marriages and Divorces, Queensland, 1884/c/2721.
3. Allora Historical Society, Pers. Comm., 11 February 2023.

4. 'Wireless' was the term initially used to describe the new technology, in contrast to 'wired' telegraphy. However, in 1906, the international community agreed on 'radio' as a more accurate term, although the older term continued to persist (Lewis Coe, *Wireless Radio: A Brief History* [Jefferson, NC, and London: McFarland, 1996], 3). The terms are used interchangeably in this chapter.
5. Sungook Hong, *Wireless: From Marconi's Black Box to the Audion* (Cambridge, MA, and London: MIT Press, 2010), xii.
6. Ann Moyal, *Clear Across Australia: A History of Telecommunications* (Melbourne: Thomas Nelson, 1984), 108–12.
7. Coe, *Wireless Radio*, 6–7.
8. 'Index for Queensland Railway Employees 1889–1940', *Ancestry Library* Available online: https://www.ancestrylibrary.com.au (accessed 4 March 2022).
9. *Commonwealth Gazette*, 17 April 1909, 951.
10. 'Wireless Telegraphy', *Observer* (Adelaide), 7 December 1907, 40.
11. 'Wireless from the Fleet', *Daily Telegraph*, 8 August 1908, 8.
12. 'Antarctica', *Observer*, 18 September 1909, 35; 'Southward Ho!', *Evening News* (Sydney), 18 October 1910, 5.
13. 'Polar Research', *Observer*, 28 January 1911, 39.
14. 'Antarctic Exploration', *Argus*, 17 January 1911, 7.
15. 'Mawson's Millions', *Daily Telegraph*, 6 October 1911, 9.
16. Hugh Denison, Letter to Conrad Eitel, 13 February 1912, Australian Polar Collection, South Australian Museum, 143/2AAE.
17. A receiving station had been planned for another continental base, but missing parts meant that it never eventuated. Douglas Mawson, *Home of the Blizzard: Being the Story of the Australasian Antarctic Expedition, 1911–1914*, vol. 2 (London: Heinemann, 1915), 64.
18. 'Antarctica', *Daily Telegraph*, 4 December 1911, 9.
19. Elleke Boehmer, 'Circulating Forms: The Jingo Poem at the Height of Empire and Beyond', *English Language Notes* 49, no. 1 (2011): 11–27, at 12. See also Daniel R. Headrick, *The Tentacles of Progress: Technology Transfer in the Age of Imperialism, 1850–1940* (New York and Oxford: Oxford University Press, 1988), 98.
20. Headrick, *Tentacles*, 97.
21. 'Mawson Expedition', *Argus* (Melbourne), 9 November 1912, 7.
22. Elizabeth Leane, Ben Maddison and Kimberley Norris, 'Beyond the Heroic Stereotype: Sidney Jeffryes and the Mythologising of Australian Antarctic History', *Australian Humanities Review* 64 (2019): 1–12, at 6.
23. 'Shipping News', *Advertiser* (Adelaide), 19 September 1911, 8; 'Wireless', *The Express and Telegraph* (Adelaide) 20 October 1911, 2.
24. Douglas Mawson, Letter to Walter Hannam, 19 October 1911, State Library of New South Wales, MLMSS 171/14.
25. Ibid., 14 October 1911, 19 October 1911.
26. T. W. Edgeworth David, Letter to Orme Masson, 9 February 1912, Australian Polar Collection, South Australian Museum 143/2AAE.
27. Hugh R. Denison, Letter to Conrad Eitel, 13 February 1912, Australian Polar Collection, South Australian Museum 143/2AAE.

28. Conrad Eitel, Letter to Dr Ward, 9 February 1912, Australian Polar Collection, South Australian Museum 143/2AAE.
29. Walter Henry Hannam, Diary, 10 September 1912, State Library of New South Wales, MLMSS 384/2.
30. Hong, *Wireless*, x. See also Jeffrey Sconce, *Haunted Media: Electronic Presence from Telegraphy to Television* (Durham, NC and London: Duke University Press, 2000), 73.
31. J. K. Davis, quoted in 'Australasian Antarctic Expedition', *The Mercury* [Hobart], 25 December 1912, 5.
32. John Gillies, 'Building a Replica of the Wireless Set Used by Douglas Mawson's 1911 to 1914 Australasian Antarctic Expedition and Notes on the Installation and Operation of the Wireless System', unpublished pamphlet, n.d. Available via the Mawson's Huts Foundation.
33. Cecil Madigan, *Madigan's Account: The Mawson Expedition: The Antarctic Diaries of C.T. Madigan 1911–1914*, transcribed by Julia W. Madigan (Hobart: Wellington Bridge, 2012), 354.
34. 'Icebound Explorers', *Argus*, 9 April 1913, 13.
35. Mawson, *Home of the Blizzard*, 136.
36. Leane, Maddison and Norris, 'Beyond the Heroic Stereotype', 10.
37. Archibald Lang McLean, Diary, 11 July 1913, State Library of New South Wales, MLMSS 382.
38. Douglas Mawson, four-page note concerning Jeffryes's resignation and condition, undated and unaddressed, South Australian Museum, Australian Polar Collection, 177AAE.
39. Douglas Mawson, handwritten note among Adele Land wireless logs, 3 September [1913], South Australian Museum, Australian Polar Collection, 35AAE/2.
40. Respectively, *Clarence and Richmond Examiner*, 19 March 1913, 6; *Barrier Miner* (Broken Hill), 19 March 1914, 4; *Sydney Morning Herald*, 14 March 1914, 21.
41. Coe, *Wireless Radio*, 26.
42. 'Lonely Antarctic', *Sydney Morning Herald*, 14 March 1914, 21.
43. Ibid.
44. *Darling Downs Gazette*, 16 March 1914, 5; *Advertiser*, 16 March 1914, 8; *Sydney Morning Herald*, 14 March 1914, 21.
45. Sidney Jeffryes, Letter to Douglas Mawson, 21 September 1913, South Australian Museum, Australian Polar Collection, 177AAE.
46. Sidney Jeffryes, Letter to Maisie Eckford, 14 July 1914, State Library of New South Wales, MLMSS 7064.
47. Madigan, *Madigan's Account*, 406.
48. Sidney Jeffryes, Letter to Mrs G. Fox, 13 July 1913, Australian Polar Collection, South Australian Museum, 177AAE.
49. Sidney Jeffryes, Letters to Douglas Mawson, 18 July 1913, 27 July 1913, South Australian Museum, Australian Polar Collection, 177AAE.
50. Sidney Jeffryes, Incomplete Letter to Mrs Fox, 13 July 1913, written on back flyleaf of *Electricity in the Service of Man: A Popular and Practical Treatise on the Applications of Electricity to Modern Life*, by R. Mullineux Walmsley, State Library of New South Wales, Mitchell Library 621.3/14.
51. See, for example, Sconce, *Haunted Media*, particularly ch. 2; Richard Noakes, 'Thoughts and Spirits by Wireless: Imagining and Build Psychic Telegraphs in America and Britain,

circa 1900–1930', *History and Technology: An International Journal* 32, no. 2 (2016): 137–58; Anthony Enns, 'Psychic Radio: Sound Technologies, Ether Bodies and Spiritual Vibrations', *Senses and Society* 3, no. 2 (2008): 137–52.
52. Simone Natale, 'A Cosmology of Invisible Fluids: Wireless, X-Rays, and Psychical Research around 1900', *Canadian Journal of Communications* 36 (2011): 268.
53. Enns, 'Psychic Radio', 138.
54. Sconce, *Haunted Media*, 14, 65.
55. Death certificate of Sydney Jeffreys [*sic*], died 16 October 1942, Registrar of Births, Deaths and Marriages Victoria, 28915/1942.
56. Mike Smyth, 'Radio's Polar Pioneer', *Critical Comms*, 17 April 2013. Available online: https://www.criticalcomms.com.au/content/industry/article/radio-rsquo-s-polar-pioneer-831744600.
57. Aradale Ghost Tours – Ararat Lunatic Asylum, 16 May 2021, 28 February 2922, *Facebook*. Available online: https://www.facebook.com/profile/100064370572379/search/?q=jeffryes; David Waldron, pers. comm., 16 May 2021.
58. Noakes, 'Thoughts and Spirits', 138–9.
59. Sconce, *Haunted Media*, 65.
60. As my colleagues and I have observed elsewhere (Leane, Maddison and Norris, 'Beyond the Heroic Stereotype', 16) the affront that Jeffryes's mental illness posed to the stereotype of the polar explorer was played out in a larger scale in the impending war, during which 'shell shock' similarly challenged the image of the soldier. For a contemporaneous narrative dealing with mental illness, institutionalization and silencing, see Kate Kennedy's biography of First World War poet Ivor Gurney: *Dweller in Shadows: A Life of Ivor Gurney* (Princeton, NJ: Princeton University Press, 2021).

Bibliography

Boehmer, Elleke. 'Circulating Forms: The Jingo Poem at the Height of Empire and Beyond'. *English Language Notes* 49, no. 1 (2011): 11–27.
Coe, Lewis. *Wireless Radio: A Brief History*. Jefferson, NC and London: McFarland, 1996.
Enns, Anthony. 'Psychic Radio: Sound Technologies, Ether Bodies and Spiritual Vibrations'. *Senses and Society* 3, no. 2 (2008): 137–52.
Headrick, Daniel R. *The Tentacles of Progress: Technology Transfer in the Age of Imperialism, 1850–1940*. New York and Oxford: Oxford University Press, 1988.
Hong, Sungook. *Wireless: From Marconi's Black Box to the Audion*. Cambridge, MA and London: MIT Press, 2010.
Kennedy, Kate. *Dweller in Shadows: A Life of Ivor Gurney*. Princeton, NJ: Princeton University Press, 2021.
Leane, Elizabeth, Ben Maddison, and Kimberley Norris. 'Beyond the Heroic Stereotype: Sidney Jeffryes and the Mythologising of Australian Antarctic History'. *Australian Humanities Review* 64 (2019): 1–12.
Madigan, Cecil. *Madigan's Account: The Mawson Expedition: The Antarctic Diaries of C. T. Madigan 1911–1914*, transcribed by Julia W. Madigan. Hobart: Wellington Bridge, 2012.
Mawson, Douglas. *Home of the Blizzard: Being the Story of the Australasian Antarctic Expedition, 1911–1914*, vol. 2. London: Heinemann, 1915.

Moyal, Ann. *Clear Across Australia: A History of Telecommunications*. Melbourne: Thomas Nelson, 1984.

Natale, Simone. 'A Cosmology of Invisible Fluids: Wireless, X-Rays, and Psychical Research around 1900'. *Canadian Journal of Communications* 36 (2011): 263–75.

Noakes, Richard. 'Thoughts and Spirits by Wireless: Imagining and Build Psychic Telegraphs in America and Britain, circa 1900–1930'. *History and Technology: An International Journal* 32, no. 2 (2016): 137–58.

Pettitt, Clare. '"The Annihilation of Space and Time": Literature and Technology'. In *The Cambridge History of Victorian Literature*, edited by Kate Flint, 550–72. Cambridge: Cambridge University Press, 2012.

Sconce, Jeffrey. *Haunted Media: Electronic Presence from Telegraphy to Television*. Durham, NC and London: Duke University Press, 2000.

Smyth, Mike. 'Radio's Polar Pioneer'. *Critical Comms*, 17 April 2013. Available online: https://www.criticalcomms.com.au/content/industry/article/radio-rsquo-s-polar-pioneer-831744600.

CHAPTER 16
REMOTE IMAG(IN)ING THE ANTARCTIC: LIFE WRITING AND THE RESONANT PAGE
Elizabeth Lewis Williams

Prelude

I have been trying to explore Antarctica without actually going there. Even now, the continent is hard to reach, not just because of distance or weather but because opportunities are restricted to scientific research, adventure travel or tourism – and a journey can feel difficult to justify when some estimates of carbon emissions per passenger trip (for cruises) are as much as 4.14 tons per person.[1] Antarctica is also difficult to see – this continental manifestation of the farthest south often disappears at the bottom of maps or under the globe, and a feature of crossing the Antarctic Convergence is the enshrouding fog. My motivation for these virtual travels arose because I wanted to understand my father's life when he worked there between 1959 and 1965. He died young, leaving an unpublished (and to his children, unknown) book about the continent with this invitation: 'try to imagine you were actually taking part in this book, actually living the events, seeing the sights, hearing the sounds – and the silence...'[2] In the absence created by his death, I answered him through poetry. I crossed the vast distance in time and space, between my writing and his living, to join him on the page. We became 'faraway close' – that experience of 'distant proximity' given such immediacy by Lockdown which Elleke Boehmer explores in her work about 'southing'.[3]

Recently, remoteness was replaced by presence, at least in terms of Antarctica. I was fortunate enough to be offered the chance to give lectures and readings on a large cruise ship which made three consecutive visits to the Antarctic Peninsula. I experienced an uncanny sense of travelling backwards out of memory into its place of origin. As I looked at Port Lockroy (where my father worked) through binoculars, I was struck by the fact that even here, so close, an act of imagination was required to make landfall. Had I visited the museum and Post Office, the same would be true if I were to see the place as it was. Each visit to the Peninsula felt different and, surrounded by the Ice,[4] I reflected on the potential of both ice and the white page to hold together so many layers of time and experience in one place in a way that a singular journey cannot do.

Remote imag(in)ing

Antarctica's unique qualities make it an ideal subject for poetry. Intellectually conceived before it was discovered, it remains an imagined as well as a material continent. Visually, it is almost entirely covered in ice. The optical phenomena associated with ice means that it is often difficult to tell the material entity from its reflection in the water, or clouds in the sky. The nature of ice itself, which both preserves and transforms, lends itself to metaphor.[5] Poetry, too, is material and conceptual. Words on the page, felt in the speaking mouth and the listening ear, can give voice to people and places distant in time and space, echoing the way in which remote sensing machines allow an Antarctic scientist to hold together deep time with the present moment, or hear the sounds of auroral space within the confines of a hut. This chapter considers a particular kind of life writing, of people and place, which takes as its starting point the remoteness of the southernmost continent, and the distance across which it is often imaged and imagined, drawing parallels between place and page, remote sensing devices and the poetic imagination, to explore the possibilities of poetic form and a multi-media installation to enable a remote experience of Antarctica. The most familiar understanding of remoteness is linked to its origin in the Latin word *remotus*, past participle of *removere* (to remove) which entered English through the Middle English meaning, 'far apart'. All too often, the place (or idea) from which it is removed is somewhere in the northern hemisphere, if not European, at least shaped by a European consciousness, and freighted, therefore, with political and economic bias. Take Greenwich Mean Time. Because of the economic dominance of the US which employed Greenwich as the basis for its national time zone system, and because in the late nineteenth century 72 per cent of the world's commerce depended on sea-charts which had Greenwich as the Prime Meridian, measurements of latitude and time (according to the clock) were centred on London.

Remoteness is temporal as well as spatial. Travel companies, according to cultural anthropologist Owe Ronström, see remoteness beginning at a point more than three hours away[6] and such places are often seen as locations where time operates differently, or where the past is in some way preserved in the present. The social anthropologist Edwin Ardener, for example, describes a number of paradoxes associated with remoteness, one of which is that *'Remote areas are full of ruins of the past'*.[7] These relics of former modes of living – such as the Highland Clearances – were also the physical traces of structures of thought which had impacted on the world, and a further indication that remoteness is conceptual (he cites the romantic depiction of Gaeldom) or a state of mind (his own experience in the Cameroons). Ronström develops this idea by suggesting that remoteness is 'an intensively multi-relational phenomenon'.[8] In addition, he argues, a definition of remoteness

> will further have to consider how [it] is produced by movements and perspectives, by how connections are set up and how boundaries are drawn and crossed. It will also have to consider remoteness in terms of words, concepts, and metaphors; of imageries, affects, and figures of thought; and, lastly, how all these relational dimensions mould as one naturalised totality.[9]

This 'naturalised totality' is a complex mesh of individual, social, physical and conceptual relations. An embodied experience of remoteness has at its centre point the observer in a particular place and time, spatially and sensorily immersed in a remote place. A remote experience, however, suggests the observer is removed or distant from what is being experienced and needs to employ other means to engage with the place (or time) across the distance. Ronström's shift from spatial and temporal conditions in the material world to a consideration of language and affect suggests that conceptual remoteness is a linguistic construct and can therefore be bridged by language. This has a particular significance for life writing which by its nature sees the writer temporally and spatially removed from their subjects.

Antarctica is remote in the extreme. It is at the farthest point on the globe, on the other side of a climatic and geographic boundary, the Antarctic Convergence, which ensures that its temperatures are lower than at equivalent latitudes in the north. Sensory experience of the continent is necessarily muffled by thick protective clothing, which exposes as little of the body as possible to the climate, or mediated by remote sensing devices. The Antarctic imaginary also embodies the conceptual nature of remoteness. The speculated continent took visual form in maps with a southern landmass of one shape or another drawn in, monsters and all, to counterbalance the landmasses to the north.[10] The cartographic representation of a body changing shape and disappearing briefly[11] before taking its current form is a biography of sorts. The life of the continent emerges in a sequence of maps which also demonstrate that before its existence had been proven, it was simply *Nondum Cognita* – not yet fully known. The title of John Speed's world map, published in London in 1627 – 'A New and Accurat Map of the World Drawne according to ye truest Descriptions latest Discoveries & best observations yt have beene made by English or Strangers'[12] – demonstrates the way in which accounts, linguistic constructs, were given parity with scientific observations – and that a representation of something believed, but not proven, to be true could be considered 'accurat'. This mixture of real and fantastic geography is perhaps most clearly seen in Joseph Hall's *Mundus alter et idem*. His world map – in which regions such as Crapulia (a land of drunkards and gluttons) is located to the south of the Cape of Good Hope – satirizes both human society and the idea that the world can be truly represented on a map.[13] Even so, as Hiatt also points out, in Hall's time, *Terra Australis Nondum Cognita* was a unique expression of 'the signifying potential of unknown land'[14] – unseen but conceptually understood.[15]

Antarctica, considered as land, remains unknown in at least one experiential sense. It is covered in ice hundreds of metres thick. Remote imaging has determined the nature of the land under it – the heights of mountains, where there are valleys, and where the land actually lies below sea-level, but when standing on the ice, the land beneath has to be imagined as well as imaged. This is just one of the ways in which Antarctica epitomizes many of the paradoxes of remoteness. The geographer Yi Fu Tuan described the collapse of the near (homeplace) and far (alien space) which eliminates the middle-distance zone of the homespace in extreme locations of desert and ice.[16] The more hostile or remote the conditions, the more intimately thrown together were (and are) the people within the homeplace. In an Antarctic hut, especially in the early days of inhabiting the continent, men were often confined indoors by weather or winter darkness, with little private space, and the alien landscape outside could penetrate the walls of the hut, or the tent, in the form of snow or ice. In addition, these small places of habitation and work were, and are, at the centre of questing across space and time, meeting points of evidence for continental drift detected in the rocks, hundreds of thousands of years of climate history in the ice, and the movements of the upper atmosphere.[17] Personal time represented by quotidian routine abuts the very different sense of ice time, or geological time, or space time enabled by remote sensing technologies.

Representations of Antarctica become bound up with the nature of representation itself. Just as the actual and the conceptual are collapsed in cartographic depictions of Antarctica, a similar effect can be seen in writing about the continent. In his essay 'The Uses of Antarctica', the cultural critic and writer Francis Spufford notes

> Antarctica has constantly vanished *into* writing, into the act of representation itself, as if being there and describing being there had collapsed into each other ... to travel across the whiteness is to inscribe it, very frequently; footprints have often recalled the other kind of printing. Here, the possibility of Antarctica becomes the possibility of saying anything, anything at all, on an empty page.[18]

A photograph taken at Halley Bay on the Brunt Ice shelf in 1969 shows a flat icescape written over by the movement of people and machines. The buildings of this remote research station are invisible under the snow: the only indication of their existence is in a series of 'surface installations'. Parts of the sky have the same texture as the snow, and the areas of bright white on the horizon are icebergs, thrown above the sea line as a result of an optical illusion. There are objects positioned in an arrangement which appears random without the code which will unlock the connections between them. The anthropologist Tim Ingold returns repeatedly to different ways of reading both the landscape and the printed page, citing medieval commentators who compared reading to wayfaring, and the surface of the page to an inhabited landscape.

> The reader, in short, would *inhabit* the world of the page, proceeding from word to word as the storyteller proceeds from topic to topic, or the traveller from place to place.[19]

The icescape shown in the photograph suggests 'the empty page' referred to by Spufford, written on by human activity, with the buried base like the vanished continent, invisible under the writing which signifies its presence. To understand the image, or the text, the reader is required to *inhabit* the world of the writer. To exist within the page as well as within the world requires an act of imag(in)ation.

The resonant page

For Samuel Taylor Coleridge, whose *Rime of the Ancient Mariner* was the first English-language poetic journey to Antarctica, the imagination was more than a fanciful activity of the mind; it was an essential component of being alive.

> The primary imagination I hold to be the living power and prime agent of all human perception, and as a repetition in the finite mind of the eternal act of creation in the infinite I AM.[20]

Coleridge was well-read in philosophy and psychology. As a non-conformist and a poet, for him the created world, like a page of poetry, was inscribed by the language of God. The imagination, he believed, is a capacity which is shared by everyone to a greater or lesser extent; what he terms the secondary imagination is still a '*vital*' power, a process which 'dissolves, diffuses, dissipates, in order to re-create'.[21] It allows the sensations of the body to be combined with thought, to produce a realized conception, to write a poem. It is this sense of signals received by the senses, transformed by the mind and transmitted through the poem, which recalls the radio transmitters and the remote sensing machines of the Antarctic world.

Poems are written landscapes, ready for sounding. In 'This Limetree Bower, My Prison', Coleridge takes the reader on a journey, following his friends on a walk which he himself is unable to take because he was injured. As he details their route, from the bower which he thinks of as a prison, arranging his words as he follows them in his mind, 'A delight/Comes sudden on my heart, and I am glad/As I myself were there'.[22] His response is emotional and physical as well as cerebral. Rather than creating an image in his mind, he is able to be in one place and experience another through his imagination.

Poems may be written, but they are descendants of an oral tradition; their architecture is sonic. Charles Stankievech's description of fieldwork as part of the commentary for an exhibition on Magnetic Norths, is apposite here.

> a landscape need not be natural and the architecture may not always be a traditional shelter or sculpture, but can be composed of sonic material, electromagnetic fields, light fluctuations, or relationships.[23]

In *The Rime of the Ancient Mariner*, Coleridge gives us a figure of the listener in the form of a wedding guest, captured both physically and in his imagination by the old sailor's words: he 'cannot choose but hear'.[24] He experiences the Antarctic world through the sound of the words:

> The ice was here, the ice was there;
> The ice was all around:
> It cracked and growled, and roared and howled,
> Like noises in a swound.[25]

Here the repetitions, and the reported sounds of ice under pressure, which echo and rhyme and repeat as the Mariner relives the increasing horror of the experience, provide a soundscape which mirrors the apparent limitlessness of the ice both for the character in the poem and the listener.

Another spoken aspect of poetry which evokes the peculiar collapse of temporalities in Antarctica – particularly when written in the first person – is what Jonathan Culler refers to as the iterable 'now' of poetic time.[26] The reader of the poem speaks with their own voice, breathing into the poet's words and, if there is a narrative voice, inhabiting that voice, too. The lyric 'I' is a kind of summoning which allows the present moment of speaking to sound out the moment of writing, which could be centuries past, breaking down the boundedness of the individual in an echo of the way snow penetrates the walls of a hut, or frost bites the skin.

The poems which follow demonstrate some of the ways in which sound, voice and the deployment of words on the page evoke the Antarctic experience which I have imagined from a distance. In Antarctica, dedicated as it is by the terms of the Antarctic Treaty, to peace and to science, the dominant activities of scientific investigation (and staying alive) impact on the way language is heard.[27] The first group of poems is taken from my collection *Erebus*, based on personal and archival stories of scientists, including my father. They were written a long time after his death, and from the northern rather than the Southern Hemisphere. I had not been to Antarctica when I wrote them; the physical journeys I made were to the British Antarctic Survey archives in Cambridge. Many of these records are numeric, graphic, instrumental – but there are traces of embodied experience scribbled in the margins and sounding between the lines, as well as recorded in audio and on film. Such historic material, from an Antarctica remote in time and space, stands in for primary sense data. It is recombined in the imagination and transmitted through the imagery, sounds and structure of the poems to enable the reader to inhabit a particular Antarctic place and time.

The first three poems are taken from a sequence called 'The Practical Application of Ionospherics'. They explore my father's experience of remoteness (and of mine from him) through his research as an ionosphericist and his attempts at radio communication with home. The second three poems are taken from an extended sequence 'Met Obs' which, like 'The Practical Application of Ionospherics', sets the scientific work of meteorological observation in its environmental and social context. The short prose poems include fragments from the base journals,[28] shown in italics. The curator-poet, collecting data and responding to signals in both personal and institution archives, appears in the margins of the sequence (though not here), both influencing, and influenced by, the forms and language throughout.

Remote imaging, meteorological observations and radio communication become metaphors for relationship: with the self, with others and with the planet. The machines become prosthetic sensors allowing us to see and to imagine across. They record signals which are interpreted by people who inhabit that environment, and then transmitted to people on the other side of the planet – if the conditions are right. Language, made up of units of sound, can be visually represented in different ways – letters and words, as code, as cut-out text, as light – and broken down as a result of environmental interference. The gap between word and thing, speaker and audience, writer, readers and text can be emphasized by the layout of words on the page, or the deliberate juxtaposition of different forms of code. Recalling Ronström's definition of remoteness as a 'multi-relational phenomenon', I suggest that to experience the Antarctic world of the page is to place the emphasis on 'in', to sense a remote life within the sonic world of language.

The second group of poems moves towards a different consideration of the relationship between remote sensing and the imagination. They posit the Indigenous shaman as ecologist, scientist and poet. Here the vital power described by Coleridge is experienced by the man becoming shaman, sensing the history of the world through rocks and snow; it is the quality that allowed Keats to fly with the nightingale, and takes the form of the jaguar, shamanic spirit guide, whose movement and breath unspools time and turns the fossils in the museum – part of the written life of earth – back into trees. They ask, too, how far removed from this mythological world view the science of remote sensing actually is. As the writer Jean McNeil said when talking about the atmospheric record trapped in the ice, 'Through analysing this data, scientists become augurers.'[29] Their machines and their minds, like those of the shaman and poets, travel across time and space in order to gather data which will allow them to tell a story about the world.

The final part of this chapter looks at an installation based on my poem *Deception Island*, a textual and sonic evocation of place through voice, where a replica of the refuge hut from Portal Point on the Antarctic Peninsula becomes a portal into the life of a remote sub-Antarctic island.

***

Life Writing and the Southern Hemisphere

I

Calling the Antarctic[30]

28th May 1959

Dear Mrs. Lewis,

    She smoothes her coat, checks the mirror,

In March,

    Margaret?

an invitation **from the BBC**

    traces age lines on her face. Picks a hat -

explaining our plans for a series of weekly broadcasts

    Are you ready? Margaret?

"Calling the Antarctic"

    For a second time, she clips the letter

    (proposing coffee) and amended script

local news does lend colour and interest

    into a neat black bag, just right for London,

the time allotted to each family group is two minutes,

    We don't want to miss the train.

on Sunday, 28th June!

    breathes in deeply, out again,

    joins her husband at the door

    her daughters at the station,

    and at Bush House, Strand, WC2,

11 a.m. (our time)

    will record a message to her son.

    'Hello, George, this is

(i)

Flying somewhere. Already flown?

No amount of playing back could make it tell.

28th March 1959
Beastie and the timer up the shoot nobody has the correct time

People are required to man the machine.
Radio waves in pulses sound the universe:
their journeys timed
show distance through delay –
figures plotted on graphs, photographic traces
record the movements of the upper atmosphere.

Like Eudoxus
constructing a model of concentric rings
he describes the layers:
troposphere, ionosphere (F1, F2, D and E)

> *When there isn't a sun to irradiate,*
> *there isn't an ionosphere (as such)*
>   *off which*
> *they can transmit our messages.*

15th December 1952

Geoffrey, Robby and myself went ashore… to inspect the base hut, and to declare the base reopened. Simultaneous thrill of arrival and sting of cold; what matter a door broken by *persons unknown,* the hollowness of empty rooms, and a scattering of boxes islanded by meltwater and rain? Time to sweep floors, light fires, make our presence felt.

Life Writing and the Southern Hemisphere

Codes (2)

State of Sea

5 = Rough

> I counted 94 fag ends per square foot
> on the floor by the electronic equipment. Apart from the fact

6 = Very Rough

> it should be forbidden because of the fire risk,
> it's a disgusting habit.
> One person here hasn't washed his socks
> for 16 months.

> *To go day after day without washing and then make bread.*

9 = Phenomenal.

Sympathetic Light

The sun has not risen
for 90 days, and the snow
is falling outside the hut.

I cannot take you in my arms,
or press the skin above your heart
with my ear. My love,

you are wholly invisible,
even your scent has vanished
under fathoms of ice.

But I am not a pit pony
stalled in the dark until
my sight has withered

or a man who has hauled
a sledge across the ice so long
his eyes have forgotten to focus.

A flower blossoms in my eye
a black pool widening
with its winter use.

I am alert, tuned to the dark,
watching as firefly dots
leap from an angled mirror

to scribe with red light
a pattern on photopaper
which speaks your shock:

the collision of tectonic plates
felt in the hunched frames
of seismometers,

on the other side of the earth.
My love, I do not know you yet,
but over such a measurable distance

I listen for your heart
with my eyes in the dark.

II

Fenriskjeften[31]

       Wolf's jaw
at the end of the world;

mountains, saw-toothed,
stretch into wolf-leer.

     *

    In orbit,
    small metal bodies

    catch the sun
    on panelled wings,

    send messages
    in radio waves

    to readers waiting
    at their screens

    to animate data,
    take its pulse.

     *

Dwarves in their fastness
renew their netting

from the sky's tears,
and a glacier's groan,

from the beard of the wind,
and the roots of mountains.

     *

    Ice veined like trees,
    seeps into livid deltas.

Sea-levels rise, charted
in lines of serrated colour
like teeth in an opening jaw.

*

Massed in the Dry Valleys,
Olympus opposes Asgard.

Where are the gods of the south?

*

    Satellite eyes
           check ice
over wolf tongue
           check ice
cut by wolf fang
           check bindings
on the wolf god
at the end of the world.

Becoming Shaman

The Painters have dispersed.
Their marks are burning
on the rock walls
above the forest canopy.

                Inside mother mountain,
                his skin is breached by darkness,
                his edges dissolving into the drip of water,
                the soft, brief rush of bat,
                a memory of footsteps
                travelling outwards

where rain remembers smoke
from fires which have cooled, voices
which have scattered, ashes
which have lost their fire.

                Cold, this point of fear
                which clamps him to the stone
                whilst his mind dissipates
                and his heart slows
                to the pulse of earth.

Birds fly out of their names
trailing lines across the air
electric with connection,
calling.

                He is unbodied, falling from himself,
                over the abyss, becoming wings
                without flight.

In the forest, blood roots
reach outwards, leaves sound
the descent of rain.

                The mountain speaks
                a language of rending
                and the drip of water becomes river
                becomes sea and he
                above it and within it
                a receiver

of waves
of sound
beating
on skin
stretched with longing
over eons

continents slumbering
through shifting dreams:
the Earth's tectonic symphony
scored in ripples and knuckles of stone

waves
of sound
beating
on skin

as flakes
of light
fall
into the mountain
like snow.

The Last Forests in Antarctica

Pawprints on the floor of the gallery,
a mist of breath on the glass.
In the cabinet,
the stones are silent.

Jaguar blinks,
    exhales
and the glass evaporates, vanishing
in a rustle of leaves.

Through a shimmer of sea smoke,
jaguar prowls,
    listening backwards
through wraiths of snow,
to the shush of sledge,
and the creak of feet,
    circling
through scattered vowels
and trailing consonants,
    marking
the crack of hammer,
and the split of rock.

Jaguar leaps,
    winding time
backwards from the opened book
to a leaf falling
through dappled light.
Nothofagus, Southern Beech.

On the shelves, petrified vertebrae
grow back into tree, ferns
unfurl, become green.

Poised at the window,
Jaguar blinks.
    Leaves
are covered, pressed,
ghosted by a weight
of silt and clay.

In a rustle of blinds,
the last forests in Antarctica
vanish into stone.

Remote Imag(in)ing the Antarctic

Coda: Deception Island installation[32]

The installation *Deception Island* was designed to take its audience on a journey described by my father (generalized as 'a man') which also creates a polyvocal life of the island. It plays with the sensory resonances of language and poetry within an actual space in order to activate the imagination as defined by Kathryn Yusoff and Jennifer Gabrys – 'a way of seeing, sensing, thinking, and dreaming the formation of knowledge which creates the conditions for material interventions *in* and political sensibilities *of* the world'.[33] As with Coleridge's definition, they see imagination as an active, *creative* power which has a potentially transformative effect.

A replica of the Reclus Hut offered a perfect home for the installation: a small refuge inside which the paradoxes of life in a remote place could be experienced. The metaphoric and the literal coincide in Portal Point (the name of the location on the Antarctic Peninsula where the original hut was built). The hut is an intimate domestic space.[34] The alien snowscape which penetrated the hut in the form of ice is represented in the projection of a film on one of the windows, a montage of archival film footage from 1945 to 1967, echoing both the mixed temporalities of the Antarctic experience, and the operation of memory. Here, remoteness can be experienced as a 'multi-relational phenomenon'; going into the hut allows the audience to physically enter the world of the poem.

On the page the poem completes a broken circle, echoing the island's shape, beginning and ending with the passage through Neptune's Bellows. The reader follows the traveller, eyes crisscrossing the page with the shapeshifting witch, the unstable curator of the material. Voices from past and present sound out through the spaces on the page,

the whiteness doing '*the work of time*',[35] as the poet Glyn Maxwell described it. Poetic form, as well as word sounds, adds to the resonance. In the short extract above, from the beginning of the poem, Basalt speaks in iambic pentameter, a metre fragmented by the ocean in a brief exchange which echoes their epic combat. All the forms embody an essential aspect of the characters and their situation: the young whale sings in the form of a ballad; the whalers and scientists in overlapping fragments of prose; a glacier in a compressed block of unpunctuated text. The selection of actors to speak the voices in the recording took these soundings one stage further: the texture and timbre of individual voices was carefully balanced for overall impact.

Archival recordings and an original composition, employing, for example, the frequencies of whale song adapted for the cello and the human ear, completed the soundscape, and the audio was heard through headphones for the maximum immersive effect. Feedback written after the experience suggested the audience felt they had been on a journey: 'Transporting … A great time-travelling journey to the South … Still returning to Norwich…' The installation gave form to the poetic page; entering the sonic landscape created a sense of physical travel and enabled the remote imag(in)ing of the life of this remote Antarctic island.

Notes

1. G. Li, W. Li, Y. Dou and Y. Wei, 'Antarctic Shipborne Tourism: Carbon Emission and Mitigation Path', *Energies* 15 no. 21 (2022): 7837, 8.
2. A. G. Lewis, *Years on Ice: Life in Antarctica 1958–1965* (Poland: Amazon Fulfilment, 2019), xi.
3. Elleke Boehmer, 'Faraway Close', *English Academy Review* 38, no. 1 (2021): 68.
4. I have capitalized *Ice* here following the title of Stephen Pyne's book, and also to indicate the way in which the ice personifies the continent itself.
5. An interesting political instance of this quality can be seen in the way that the Antarctic Treaty (by which the continent is governed) 'freezes' a variety of sometimes overlapping claims. This means that differing national concepts of the continent coexist with its material reality.
6. Owe Ronström, 'Remoteness, Islands and Islandness', *Island Studies Journal* 16, no. 2 (2021): 283.
7. Edwin Ardener, *The Voice of Prophecy: And Other Essays*, rev. edn. (Oxford and New York: Berghahn Books, 2007), 218.
8. Ronström, 'Remoteness, Islands and Islandness', 272.
9. Ronström, 'Remoteness, Islands and Islandness', 272.
10. Referencing the age of discovery, Ardener suggested that the 'remote was actually compounded of "imaginary" as well as "real" places; yet they were all of equal conceptual reality or unreality before the differences were revealed'. Ardener, *The Voice of Prophecy*, 213.
11. Stephen Pyne commented that 'Cook's greatest discoveries did not reveal new lands so much as they defined the dimensions of the known coastlines and erased whole continents of a hypothetical geography'. S. J. Pyne, *The Ice* (London: Phoenix, 2004), 74.

12. *A New and Accurat Map of the World Drawne According to Ye Truest Descriptions Latest Discoveries & Best Observations Yt Have Beene Made by English or Strangers. 1651.* n.d. Available online: https://www.raremaps.com/gallery/detail/82139/a-new-and-accurat-map-of-the-world-drawne-according-to-ye-tr-speed.
13. Alfred Hiatt, *Terra Incognita: Mapping the Antipodes before 1600* (London: The British Library, 2008), 251.
14. Ibid.
15. In *Antarctica in Fiction: Imaginative Narratives of the Far South* (New York: Cambridge University Press, 2012), Elizabeth Leane detailed the many ways in which the imagined continent has been depicted in literature, both before and after its discovery.
16. Yi-Fu Tuan, 'Desert and Ice: Ambivalent Aesthetics', in *Landscape, Natural Beauty and the Arts*, ed. S. Gaskell and I. Kemal (Cambridge: Cambridge University Press, 1993), 139–57.
17. Francis Spufford, 'The Uses for the Southern Continent in Twentieth-Century Culture', in *Imagining Antarctica: Cultural Perspectives on the Southern Continent*, ed. Ralph Crane, Elizabeth Leane and Mark Williams (Hobart, Tasmania: Quintus, 2011), 21.
18. Spufford 'The Uses for the Southern Continent in Twentieth-Century Culture', 24.
19. Tim Ingold, *Lines: A Brief History* (Abingdon: Routledge, 2016), 94.
20. Samuel Taylor Coleridge, *Biographia Literaria*, ed. George Watson (London: J. M. Dent and Sons, 1987), 167.
21. Ibid.
22. Samuel Taylor Coleridge, *The Oxford Authors: Samuel Taylor Coleridge*, ed. H. J. Jackson (Oxford: Oxford University Press, 1985), 40.
23. Charles Stankievich, *Magnetic Norths*. 2010. Concordia University, Montreal. Available online: http://ellengallery.concordia.ca/piste-de-reflexion/les-nord-magnetiques/?lang=en.
24. Coleridge, *The Oxford Authors: Samuel Taylor Coleridge*, 47.
25. Ibid., 48.
26. Jonathan Culler, 'The Language of Lyric', *Thinking Verse* IV i (2014): 160–76, 172–3.
27. I have explored this idea much more fully in my thesis *The Magnetic Observatory: An Exploration of Scientific and Poetic Measure in Antarctic Poetry* (2019).
28. A record of life on base: weather, creatures noted, work carried out, and other incidental observations is kept throughout the year for every British research station.
29. Jean McNeil, *Ice Diaries: An Antarctic Memoir* (Toronto: ECW Press, 2016), xii.
30. In 1955 the BBC initiated a weekly programme 'Calling the Antarctic'. As part of the programme, a two-minute personal message was broadcast each week from London to a different man overwintering in the Antarctic. As my father collected ionospheric data, measuring the impact of solar flares on the ionosphere (and therefore on radio and radar transmissions), his family were planning their message. It took his mother three months to arrange the recording. Recognizing the need to show both the factual basis of the poem and its imagined situation, I have combined snippets from letters sent to my gran (my historic data, if you like) with invented text.
31. This is the name given to a group of mountains in East Antarctica's Drygalski Mountain Range. Part of Norway's Antarctic territory, they are named after Fenris, or Fenrir, in Norse mythology. This wolf son of Loki was destined to break free from his chains and, in the great battle at the end of the world, kill Odin and swallow the ocean and the sky. There are plenty of characters in the myths of southern Indigenous navigators – Selk'nan, Yaghan, Maori. It is telling that their names do not feature prominently in an Antarctic cartography largely drafted by northern people.

32. https://storymachines.co.uk/portfolio/deception-island/.
33. Jennifer Gabrys and Kathryn Yusoff, 'Imagination and Climate Change', *WIREs Climate Change* 2 no. 4 (2011): 516;
34. It was dismantled and moved to Port Stanley in the Falkland Islands where it is now housed in a museum.
35. Glyn Maxwell, *On Poetry* (London: Oberon Books, 2012), 13.

Bibliography

Ardener, Edwin. *The Voice of Prophecy: And Other Essays*, rev. edn. Oxford and New York: Berghahn Books, 2007.
Boehmer, Elleke. 'Faraway Close'. *English Academy Review* 38, no. 1 (2021): 67–8.
Coleridge, S. T. *Biographia Literaria*, edited by George Watson. London: J. M. Dent and Sons, 1987.
Coleridge, S. T. *The Oxford Authors: Samuel Taylor Coleridge*, edited by H. J. Jackson. Oxford: Oxford University Press, 1985.
Culler, Jonathan. 'The Language of Lyric'. *Thinking Verse* IV i (2014): 160–76.
Gabrys, Kathryn, and Jennifer Yusoff. 'Imagination and Climate Change'. *WIREs Climate Change* 2 no. 4 (2011): 516–34.
Hiatt, Alfred. *Terra Incognita: Mapping the Antipodes before 1600*. London: The British Library, 2008.
Ingold, Tim. *Lines: A Brief History* Abingdon: Routledge, 2016.
Leane, Elizabeth. *Antarctica in Fiction: Imaginative Narratives of the Far South*. New York: Cambridge University Press, 2012.
Lewis, A. G. *Years on Ice: Life in Antarctica 1958–1965*. Poland: Amazon Fulfilment, 2019.
Lewis Williams, E. *Deception Island*. Norwich: Story Machine, 2021.
Lewis Williams, E. *Erebus*. Norwich: Story Machine, 2022.
Li, G., W. Li, Y. Dou, and Y. Wei. 'Antarctic Shipborne Tourism: Carbon Emission and Mitigation Path'. *Energies* 15, no. 21 (2022): 7837.
Maxwell, Glyn. *On Poetry*. London: Oberon Books, 2012.
McNeil, J. *Ice Diaries: An Antarctic Memoir*. Toronto: ECW Press, 2016.
A New and Accurat Map of the World Drawne According to Ye Truest Descriptions Latest Discoveries & Best Observations Yt Have Beene Made by English or Strangers. 1651. n.d. Available online: https://www.raremaps.com/gallery/detail/82139/a-new-and-accurat-map-of-the-world-drawne-according-to-ye-tr-speed.
Pyne, S. J. *The Ice*. London: Phoenix, 2004.
RMG. 'What Is the Prime Meridian – and Why Is It in Greenwich'? n.d. Royal Museums Greenwich. Available online: https://www.rmg.co.uk/stories/topics/what-prime-meridian-why-it-greenwich. (accessed 18 February 2023).
Ronström, Owe. 'Remoteness, Islands and Islandness'. *Island Studies Journal* 16, no. 2 (2021): 270–97.
Spufford, Francis. 'The Uses for the Southern Continent in Twentieth-Century Culture'. In *Imagining Antarctica: Cultural Perspectives on the Southern Continent*, edited by Ralph Crane, Elizabeth Leane, and Mark Williams, 17–30. Hobart, Tasmania: Quintus, 2011.
Stankievech, Charles. *Magnetic Norths*. Concordia University, Montreal, 2010. Available online: http://ellengallery.concordia.ca/piste-de-reflexion/les-nord-magnetiques/?lang=en.
Tuan, Yi-Fu. 'Desert and Ice: Ambivalent Aesthetics'. In *Landscape, Natural Beauty and the Arts*, edited by S. Gaskell and I. Kemal, 139–57. Cambridge: Cambridge University Press, 1993.

PART V
EMBODYING THE SOUTH

CHAPTER 17
THE FUGITIVE LIVES OF DAVID STUURMAN
Sarah Comyn and Porscha Fermanis

In the 1780s, while still a teenage boy, the Khoi resistance leader David Stuurman was apprenticed to several Dutch farmers in Gamtoos in the Eastern Cape of South Africa. The missionary Johannes van der Kemp reported on Stuurman's mistreatment, noting that he was tied to a wagon, beaten with a *sjambok* and left in the sun after salt was rubbed into his wounds.[1] By the 1790s, Stuurman and his brother Klaas had deserted their positions of bondage and enfleshment at various Cape Dutch farms, joining the Xhosa peoples during the second Xhosa War (1789–93) before escaping to Baviaanskloof in the heart of the Kouga Mountains, where they lived as *drosters* (or escaped slaves and servants) in the self-described Gonaqua or Gamtoos Nation. This was the first of Stuurman's many escapes from conditions of subjection and unfreedom, and the beginning of a series of fugitive existences in precarious maroon communities, as he moved in and out of Dutch and subsequently British carceral systems following British control of the Cape Colony in 1795 and then more permanently in 1806.[2]

Unfolding within the interstices of two southern colonial worlds as well as within more explicitly Indigenous spaces of alliance, Stuurman's life foregrounds the tensions between the determinism of captivity, the agency of escape and the more liminal status of fugitivity, a status occupying a complex non-place between freedom and unfreedom, personhood and property, civil life and social death. As Fred Moten has argued in relation to the emergence of a Black radical tradition, fugitivity is not a concept restricted to a literal flight from slavery but rather a much more capacious category in which freedom and unfreedom perpetually coexist in persons who refuse to remain within the structural position of social death.[3]

For Moten, fugitive subjecthood largely aligns with self-recognition and the condition of becoming: '[T]he moment in which you enter into the knowledge of slavery, of yourself as a slave, is the moment you begin to think about freedom … the moment at which you become a fugitive.'[4] In other words, it is only when an enslaved person self-consciously recognizes their own oppression that fugitivity becomes a lived reality, moving the subject from bondage, conscription and silence to flight, marronage and voice.[5] Yet fugitivity can also work to mitigate the putative relationship between voice and autonomous individual subjectivity by allowing for the un-individuated experiences of collective struggle. Here the complex, multiple meanings of fugitivity emerge more clearly, for like many other fugitives Stuurman rarely speaks directly in the historical record. And like so many unvoiced Indigenous lives from the southern peripheries, his life story is fractured, plural, shadowy and fleeting, recorded either in those colonial sources that document his incarcerations or in acts of advocacy by white European missionaries and philanthropists.

What are we to make of those fugitive persons who do not conform to the ideal voice of that most northern or Euro-American of constructs: the self-possessed, literate liberal subject? What, indeed, are we to make of those who leave behind little or no record of voice at all, even that of reported or indirect speech? Writing from within the framework of subaltern studies that emerged from the Global South, Gayatri Spivak has long cautioned against uninterrogated celebrations of voice, testimony and literacy, warning that the 'staging of the world in representation – its scene of writing ... – dissimulates the choice of and need for "heroes," paternal proxies, agents of power'.[6] In extending subaltern studies to encompass diasporic or transnational Blackness, Paul Gilroy, too, has argued that we must 'recognize the anti-discursive and extralinguistic ramifications of power at work in shaping communicative acts', noting that in many cases there may be no 'grammatical unity of speech to mediate communicative reason' beyond the act of insurgency or flight itself.[7]

As our assemblage of Moten, Spivak, and Gilroy's theorizing intimates, challenges to intellectual production generated in the Global North emerge not just from places and/or social identities with 'deep prior experiences of subjection' but also from the dynamic clustering of different forms of subaltern and Indigenous knowledge.[8] How, then, should we understand Stuurman's discursively unstable and largely unvoiced episodes of flight in between scenes and sites of punitive constraint? As historical impasses or 'unarchivable' gaps in the written archive? Or as part of the process of 'effacement through disclosure', since Stuurman's individual life story is also part of the larger, collective fugitivity of a marooning and specifically Indigenous body politic, a quest for justice, land reclamation and sovereign self-determination that has since been characterized as a form of 'Khoi nationalism'?[9]

In her research into the life of perhaps the best-known Khoi woman of the nineteenth century, Sarah Baartman, Pamela Scully provides one answer to these questions in advocating for what she calls a 'peripheral vision', describing how she 'gave up the search for the "whole subject" and instead sought ways to acknowledge incompleteness'. Like that of his Gonaqua compatriot and indeed of so many other ultimately unknowable lives transported to or taken from the far south, Stuurman's life is revealed only via a '"perpetual transition" through the intersections of other phenomena and other subjectivities'.[10] Yet if, as Meg Samuelson has argued, the story of Baartman's exhibited body has largely been deployed to signify 'a nation recovering from a traumatic past', Stuurman has played a different role in South Africa's ongoing process of nation-making. While he, too, has been recognized as 'an ancestor to the post-apartheid nation', Stuurman has become 'a living symbol, in death, of the power of democracy' and national unification.[11] In other words, Stuurman's role in national memory in present-day South Africa rests both on his anti-colonial resistance and on his part in strengthening local alliances between Khoi and Xhosa.

This chapter understands Stuurman's life as both distinctively southern in its fugitivity and incompleteness and as one fashioned in many respects by the norms and values of the Global North, thereby inviting us to view the north/south hemispheric divide as a metaphor for other presumptive dichotomies such as white/Black, enslaved/Indigenous and voiced/unvoiced. In the absence of unmediated auto-representations, we argue that Stuurman's plural and fragmented life – his fugitive *lives* – require fugitive modes and methods of reading that cut across or act aslant to these dichotomies. Like the fragment in the archive, the fugitive existence is a '"disturbance", a contradiction … in the self-representation of that particular totality and those who uncritically uphold it'.[12] Moreover, fugitivity encourages what Tina Campt has characterized as 'creative practices of refusal, nimble and strategic practises that undermine the category of the dominant'. To read *for* fugitivity resists the desire for those coherent narratives, exemplary lives and interiority models of life writing so often imposed upon southern lives by northern writers in favour of life stories that are 'more fractious than cumulative, more a space of catachresis than catharsis', as well as being attentive towards the recursive, unsettled and contingent possibilities that fugitivity offers.[13]

The first part of this chapter provides an analysis of extant accounts of Stuurman's life by white European missionaries and humanitarians, examining the unnatural history of how it was repackaged as a life of exemplification shaped by the demands of the abolitionist movement, with its simultaneous acknowledgement, neutralization and pacification of Indigenous resistance. Moving on from our consideration of the geopolitics of northern knowledge formation, the second part imagines Stuurman's incarcerations on Robben Island as potentially radical moments of African solidarity, as well as connecting Stuurman's movement across south-south carceral spaces to a longer, inter-generational narrative of resistance and identity formation within racialized carceral settings in South Africa. The final part considers Stuurman's afterlives and legacies as a symbol of Indigenous resistance and unification in post-apartheid South Africa, including poems and performances by Amanda Lois Stone and other contemporary Khoi revivalists, whose work points to the importance of oral and community-based projects in complicating the more sanitized scene of official commemoration. In each case, we see Stuurman as a distinctively southern figure, in the sense that his life stories resist conversion into the Global North's normative exempla and thus capture the ambivalent resonances of southern difference and incompleteness.

An exemplary life

The best-known account of Stuurman's life was written by the Scottish poet and abolitionist Thomas Pringle in his *Narrative of a Residence in South Africa* (1834). The *Narrative* repeats much of Pringle's 1828 essay in the *New Monthly Magazine*, 'The British Government at the Cape of Good Hope – Treatment of the Natives', which in turn relies heavily on John Barrow's account of the Stuurman brothers in his *Travels into the Interior of South Africa* (1801, 1806), as well as drawing on the testimony of 'a gentleman who knew the circumstances well and had been a personal witness of many of them'.[14] This 'personal witness' was most likely the Bethelsdorp missionary Johannes van der Kemp, although eyewitness accounts by van der Kemp and his successor, James Read Sr, must themselves be understood as profoundly mediated by the need to downplay Indigenous resistance for a British audience.[15] Curiously, Pringle's *Narrative* also refers to Saxe Bannister's *Humane Policy* (1830) and John Philip's *Researches in South Africa* (1828) for further supporting evidence, even though these accounts had themselves largely relied on Pringle's *New Monthly* essay.

This circuitous pattern of citation and self-citation within several interconnected and mutually authenticating texts reveals not only Stuurman's archival fugitivity but also the extent to which such accounts attempt to centre the white humanitarian actor in the position of witness and benevolent intervenor, although it is unlikely that Pringle or any other interlocutor besides the Bethelsdsorp missionaries had ever met Stuurman in person. Complicating these layers of repetition even further is Matthew Shum's view that 'there are strong reasons to believe that, writing in the abolitionist spirit of 1834, [Pringle] retrospectively adjusts passages in the *Narrative* to reflect views he did not have at the time', creating an image of himself as 'proselytiser for the humanitarian causes represented by the missionaries'.[16] Using sentimental frameworks geared towards a British metropolitan audience, Pringle's poetry in *African Sketches* (1834) is noted for his occupation of Indigenous perspectives through the speakers of poems such as 'The Bechuana Boy' and 'The Song of the Wild Bushman'. Given the centrality of Stuurman's case to Pringle's image as humanitarian proselytizer, it is surprising that Stuurman does not feature in any of Pringle's poems, although Pringle does ventriloquize a fellow Indigenous resistance fighter, the Xhosa prophet Makhanda Nxele (c. 1780–1820), in the poem 'Makanna's Gathering'.[17] As a living, petitioning subject, Stuurman was perhaps beyond Pringle's ventriloquizing ambitions, potentially creating an unreadable or uncomfortable disturbance in Pringle's poetic record of Indigenous representation.

Responding to Stuurman's transportation to Botany Bay in Australia where he laboured in convict gangs, Pringle's *Narrative* includes a footnote crediting himself with drawing Stuurman's plight to the attention of Richard Bourke, governor of the Cape Colony from 1826 to 1828 and of New South Wales from 1831 to 1837, whose own attempts at intervention in Stuurman's case rely on the authenticating patterns of humanitarian narrative citation discussed above.[18] From Cape Town, Bourke writes to Governor Darling in New South Wales in August 1828 'soliciting his intervention' on behalf of Stuurman, noting that as 'I have reason to believe that this man's case was rather a hard one, [...] I venture to ask your Excellency to allow him a Ticket of Leave to enable him to work for his own benefit in the hope, after a short time he may obtain a Pardon and be permitted to return to his own Country'.[19]

Stuurman's own (though very likely transcribed) petition for pardon to Darling in December 1828 repeats the summation of his case as a 'hard one'. Denying he was sentenced to life, Stuurman argues that his 'sentence was Seven Years Transportation, which has now expired about twelve months, therefore, I think it a hard case, because I cannot speak the language sufficiently fluent to make myself readily understood' (Figures 17.1a and b).[20] Stuurman's reference to his disfluency in English suggests that, to the extent he spoke a language other than his Indigenous one, he was Dutch or Afrikaans-speaking, thereby navigating the demands of multiple linguistic worlds. The confusion over Stuurman's actual sentencing is repeated in official colonial correspondence until Darling's intervention in February 1829: 'Let the Principal Superintendent of Convicts be instructed to prepare a Ticket of Leave in his favor and to inform David Steerman [sic] accordingly.'[21] Although Stuurman earned his ticket of leave, he was to die a year before Bourke arrived in New South Wales and was able to inform him of his pardon. Stuurman was buried in the Roman Catholic quarter of the Devonshire Street Cemetery in Sydney, which was subsequently resumed to make way for the Sydney Central Railway Station.[22]

The textual debates about Stuurman's sentencing reveal the colonial networks and bureaucracy that simultaneously work to represent and efface him. While it is tempting to characterize Stuurman's petition to Governor Darling and his later pardon as a moment in which the southern fugitive speaks and disrupts the white imperial archive – potentially a moment of 'life writing as political and legal supplication' – the criminal pardon is 'a strikingly imperial instrument'.[23] Like other imperial forms, 'petitioning was a mechanism for state-centralization, institution-building and the bureaucratization of state-power' that inculcated 'subjects as supplicants'.[24] The petition could therefore reinforce imperial institutionalization and disempower the petitioner as much as it could encourage dissenting voices. At the same time, the campaigning role of Stuurman's wives and children (who were held in 'abject servitude' as indentured servants following his sentence) should not be underestimated. Saxe Bannister notes that a memorial was presented by his children to the then governor of the Cape Colony, Sir Lowry Cole, 'praying that their father may be restored to his home'; and one of Stuurman's wives unsuccessfully petitioned Queen Victoria on his behalf.[25]

Yet if Stuurman's life-record in the white, imperial archive is marked by belatedness and failed intervention, he is also proleptically constructed as an exemplary, if malleable, colonial rebel. Pringle's epitaph for Stuurman as 'The Last Chief of the Hottentots' in his *Narrative* points to the resurrecting recitation of Stuurman's life that will be repeated throughout the nineteenth and twentieth centuries (and even into the twenty-first), as Stuurman is continually re-invoked in relation to other insurgencies and humanitarian causes.[26] Pringle begins this pattern when he draws parallels between the circumstances of the indentured Khoi and the Atlantic slave trade, while Saxe Bannister emphasizes that Stuurman's case is 'as much deserving mercy, as those of the Scottish Jacobites'.[27] In 1879 the Australian novelist Marcus Clarke would resurrect Stuurman as the 'last Hottentot chieftain' at a crucial moment in the Anglo-Zulu war; and Stuurman was once again invoked at the turn of the century as a means of condemning Boer brutality while Australia was involved in fighting the 1899–1902 Anglo-Boer war.[28]

A carceral life

Pringle's rehabilitation of Stuurman as the 'Last Chief of the Hottentots' attempts to rescue him from a formless mob of fugitives, raiders, criminals and convicts, and to reconstruct him as a more marketable and sympathetic figure whose exemplary character

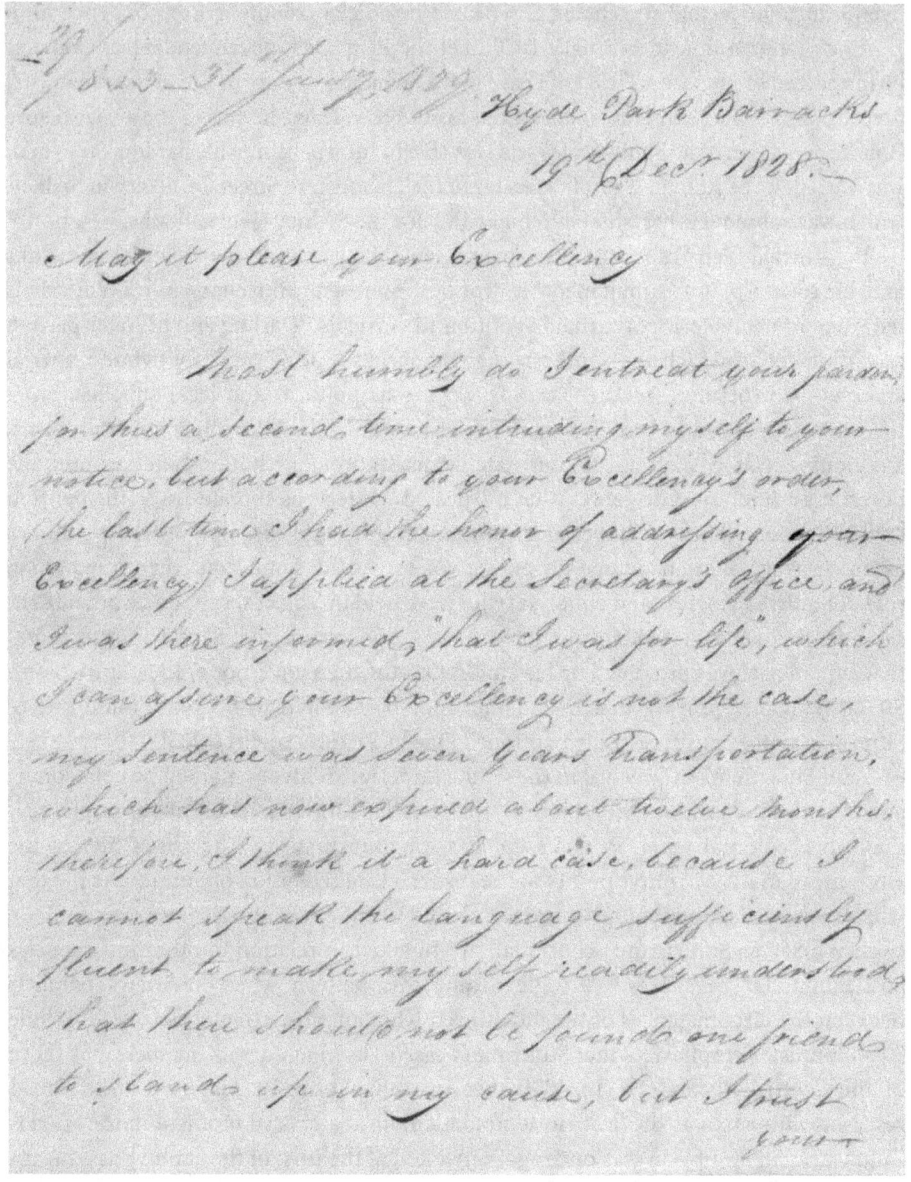

Figure 17.1a David Stuurman to Governor Darling, 19 December 1828, MHNSW – StAC: NRS 905 [4/2015] 29/853. Used with permission.

is shaped both by the nobility of his struggle and by the unlikelihood of his success. In white humanitarian accounts, Robben Island is either rarely mentioned or emerges as a site of injustice where political prisoners are held without any prospect of release, one that allows campaigning advocates such as Pringle to argue for the need for a more universal culture of civil rights across the British Empire. Robben Island was certainly

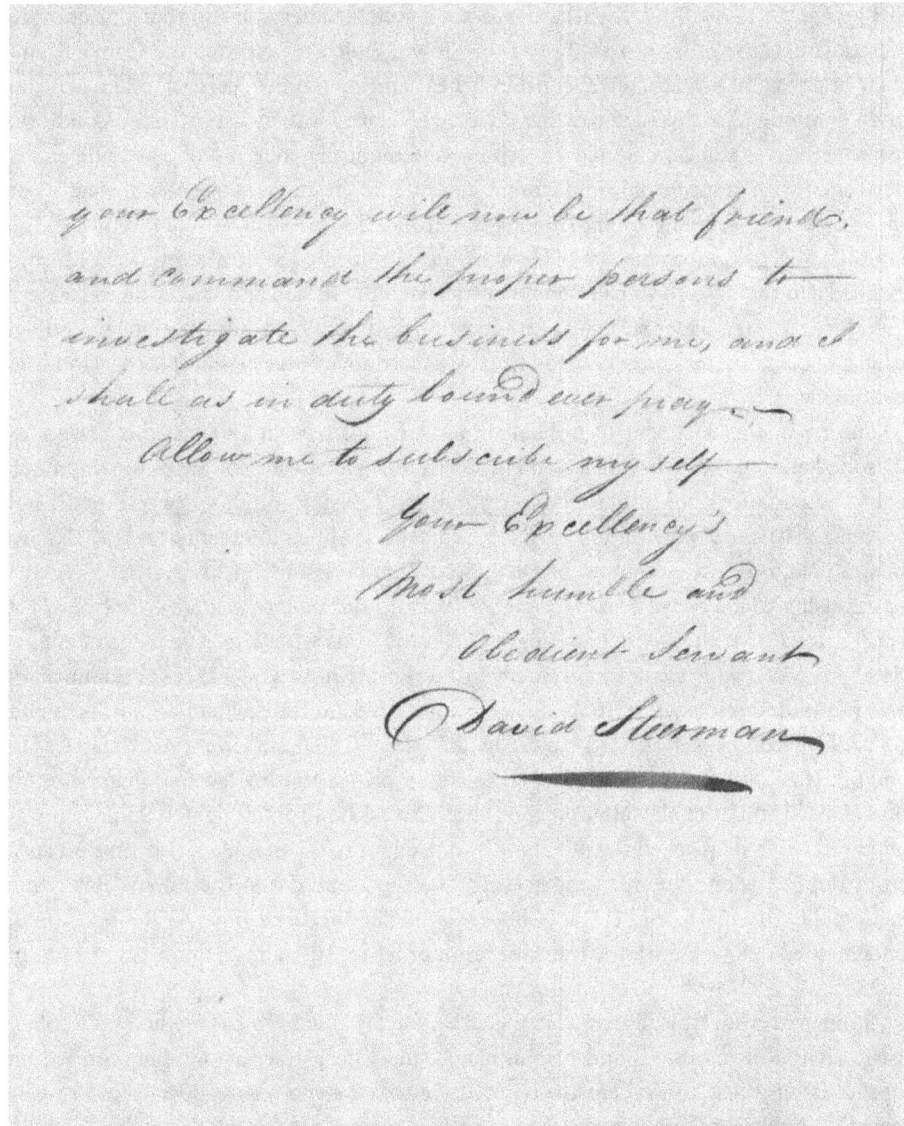

Figure 17.1b David Stuurman to Governor Darling, 19 December 1828, MHNSW – StAC: NRS 905 [4/2015] 29/853. Used with permission.

an important site for Indigenous confinement during the pacification of the Cape in the early years of the frontier wars. As Harriet Deacon has put it, 'one can map the expansion of the colonial frontier in South Africa by tracing the origins of political prisoners who were sent to Robben Island.'[29]

Unsurprisingly, Robben Island was a hub for anticolonial sentiment and activity, both within and outside prison walls. Governor Benjamin D'Urban recognized as much in

1837 when he argued that the island was not a suitable alternative to transportation to Australia because of its proximity to Cape Town, which meant that 'the Convicts and their Friends and acquaintances constantly hear and sometimes see, each other, and can often communicate'.[30] Well aware that collective identity was an important precondition for effective resistance, colonial governors systematically sought to break Indigenous networks, with transportation playing a key role in the process of natal alienation or the irrevocable severing of Indigenous ties to land, kin and local communities. The liquidization of Stuurman's life – from an identity formed within land-based kinship networks in the Eastern Cape to one that traversed the Indian and Pacific Oceans – was therefore part of a wider strategy of pacification and political neutralization, as Robben Island became increasingly embedded in south-south routes of slavery, coercion and confinement.[31]

Stuurman was first sent to Robben Island without trial in 1809 on the charges of 'Disobedience to the Field Cornet' and the catch-all legal category of 'Suspicious conduct' after objecting to Khoi military conscription and refusing to relinquish escaped Khoi servants, slaves and other fugitives from his *kraal* or farming settlement near Bethelsdorp mission station.[32] In December of 1809, Stuurman and some of his men escaped the island using whale boats, making their way back to the Eastern Cape, where by 1811 it was reported that they were participating in cattle raids with Xhosa near the Gamtoos River. In 1819, after some involvement in the Fifth Xhosa War (1818–19), Stuurman was recaptured and sent to Robben Island for the second time, where he was likely put to work in conditions of hard labour in the island's shell and limestone quarries. In August 1820, Stuurman again escaped during a prison mutiny led by Johan Schmidt and Hans Trompetter, the latter of whom was also a Khoi frontier fighter. Stuurman was captured when he reached the mainland and tried for his crimes. As a two-time escapee from Robben Island, he was sentenced to life imprisonment in the Botany Bay penal settlement. On 16 December 1820, he was sent, for the third time, to Robben Island and chained to a wall until the transportation order to Australia could be carried out in 1823.[33]

Stuurman is not typically associated with Robben Island. In Xhosa mythology, Robben Island is known as the 'Island of Makhanda', the Xhosa warrior-prophet who led an unsuccessful attack on Grahamstown in 1819 (and is the eponymous speaker of Pringle's poem).[34] As Nelson Mandela writes in *Long Walk to Freedom* (1994), 'I first heard about the island as a child. Robben Island was well known among the Xhosa after Makanna … was banished there…. The memory of [Makhanda's] loss is woven into the language of my people who speak of a "forlorn hope" by the phrase "*Ukuza kuka Nxele*."'[35] While Mandela does not mention Stuurman and later refers to Autshumato, a seventeenth-century Khoi chief, as 'the first and only man to ever escape from Robben Island', Stuurman is nonetheless imbricated in the longer history of political imprisonment and resistance Mandela memorializes in his invocation of Makhanda, since Makhanda was on Robben Island at the same time as Stuurman and drowned during the escape led by Schmidt and Trompetter.[36]

The role of political imprisonment in forming – and sustaining – strategies for resistance and activism has a long history in South Africa.[37] In the record of resistance to apartheid, Robben Island is a spiritual site of pilgrimage and suffering, as attested by stories like Mtutuzeli Matshoba's 'A Pilgrimage to the Isle of Makana' (1979). Prisoners were well aware that they were entering a space of exceptional symbolic significance, a 'place of martyrs' but also a 'university' or place of learning.[38] While we have no way of knowing whether Robben Island was a politically formative experience for Stuurman or if he continued to build on those coalitional alliances between Khoi and Xhosa at which he had excelled on the frontier, the very design of the 1820 escape plan suggests that he did. As a prisoner of war, Makhanda was held separately from other political prisoners on Robben Island, but freeing Makhanda was high on the escapees' agenda: instead of making their way directly to the island's harbour, the fourteen men took a risky detour to release Makhanda.[39] In restoring Stuurman to the pantheon of political prisoners on Robben Island, it therefore becomes possible to imagine his incarceration as part of a longer tradition of radical southern Indigenous alliance building. As Julia Wells has put it, on Robben Island in 1820 'two generations of resistance coming from two different ethnic groups found themselves in identical circumstances'.[40]

Remembering a life

In recent years, Stuurman has been officially commemorated as a figure of resistance in South Africa, one who can provide a prehistory to apartheid resistance and thus to national self-making. While his body may remain buried under the Sydney Central Railway Station, a spiritual repatriation of Stuurman took place in June 2017, involving a ceremony in Sydney and then a second ceremony at the Sarah Baartman Heritage Centre in Hankey (the original site of Stuurman's *kraal*). The incorporation in the Sydney ceremony of the southern African Buffalo Thorn (colloquially known as the *wag-'n-bietjie* or 'wait-a-bit' tree) with its forward and backwards facing thorns, fittingly embodies Stuurman's fugitive lives – at once caught by and defying the structures of captivity, at once reshaping past and future narratives. Crucially, Stuurman's repatriation was framed by the National Heritage Council as part of a narrative of 'unification in the country'.[41] His alliance with the Xhosa and his refusal to allow his people to be recruited into British militia forces have been celebrated as an important prelude to Black and Pan-African resistance movements to apartheid but they also emphasize the longer history of dispossession enacted by settler colonists in southern Africa.

Stuurman's incorporation into the teleological narrative of South Africa's journey towards democracy is evident from his immortalization as a life-sized bronze statue in the controversial travelling Long March to Freedom Monument (Figure 17.2).[42] At the time of writing, the monument is currently on display at Centurian City in Cape Town, but it can also be viewed virtually and has recently become available for world touring, emphasizing Stuurman's mobility and adaptability as a symbol of Black and Indigenous

Figure 17.2 David Stuurman Statue at the National Heritage Monument in Pretoria, South Africa [currently touring].

resistance.[43] Flanked in the monument by his brother Klaas, Stuurman is troublingly positioned almost directly behind the statue of the missionary, van der Kemp. Although this positioning is demonstrative of a particular historical chronology of protest, it also reflects the mediated *re*-presentation of Stuurman through missionary and other philanthropic accounts discussed above. Stuurman's story and legacy have nonetheless been repurposed as part of a process of writing a new history of South Africa, one that prioritizes Black and Indigenous histories and does not view the resistance to apartheid atrocities in isolation.

More significant, perhaps, than the official state commemorative acts of Stuurman – such as the Monument or the renaming of the Port Elizabeth airport as the Chief Dawid Stuurman International Airport – are the ways in which Stuurman's afterlives resonate across the symbolic and cultural activism of what has been termed 'Khoisan Revivalism'.[44] The Khoi poet and singer Amanda Lois Stone (affectionately known locally as the Khoi Nooi, or Khoi Girl) has written a poem in tribute to 'Oom Dawid Stuurman' (Uncle Dawid Stuurman), which she has performed nationally at a number of festivals. Relating her own experience of living in racialized South Africa, Stone speaks of the inspiration of her poem as a complex process, one that in many ways embodies what Javier Ernesto Perez theorizes as 'performing marronage'. Drawing on the work of Black feminist Zenzele Isoke's approach to 'speaking flesh', Perez argues that a 'process of interior intersubjectivity … open[s] the opportunity to "sing with the ancestors, write with the spirits, and dance with ghosts both in this world and foreign to it"'.[45]

Stone was first inspired to write a poem about Baartman on hearing Diana Ferrus's performance of her famous petition poem 'I Have Come to Take You Home' (1998), and she subsequently had a spiritual experience in which she saw visions of Baartman in her dreams.[46] After performing her Baartman poem at the first Khoisan Indaba at Kimberley, Stone had a second visitation in which a figure asked her to 'please write about Oom Dawid Stuurman'. Admitting that at the time she knew nothing about Stuurman's life, Stone's explanation of the origins of her poem situates her afterlife of Stuurman as forming a cultural genealogy of resistance with Baartman and beyond, as her poetry also memorializes 'Krotoa', the famous Khoi translator for the Dutch East India Company and niece of Autshumato.[47]

Stone's poem captures Perez's theory that '[p]oetry is hospitable to … fugitive narratives' because it allows for different narrative trajectories of running *to*, *with* and *from*.[48] Building on Ferrus's poem which opens with an evocation for Baartman to remember and therefore return *to* her homeland, Stone's 'Oom Dawid Stuurman' imagines Stuurman's rightful place as *in* the homeland from which he was severed by incarceration and transportation, seeing his 'signs' in the rocks and hearing his feet still 'stomping':

Oom Dawid Stuurman,
Ek sien nog steeds jou tekens teen die rots
Dis jou eie sprokies verhaal, in jou eie taal
Oom Dawid Stuurman se,
'Meskien sal iemand een dag verstaan'

Uncle Dawid Stuurman
I still see your signs against the rock
It is your own fairy tale story, in your own language
Uncle Dawid Stuurman says,
'Maybe one day someone will understand'[49]

Significantly, Stone imaginatively restores Stuurman's voice, his fluency and his own language in a form of anti-colonial cultural and linguistic repatriation that invokes a communal 'Chorus of voices':

Oom Dawid Stuurman se
Maar nou wil ek net in my eie Afrika's grasbed rus
... met die lied van my Khoimens
Stemmekoor wat se, al ons vyande staan beskaam

Uncle Dawid Stuurman says
But now I just want to rest in my own African grave
... with the songs of my Khoimens
Chorus of voices saying, all our enemies are put to shame.

Recalibrating the fugitive life as at rest in an African grave, Stone rejects the carceral and imperial structures that either muted or ventriloquized Stuurman's voice and instead restores a chorus of 'fugitive speech acts'.[50] Her reclamation of Stuurman's fugitive life is therefore one that simultaneously attempts to lay him to rest and celebrates the very fugitivity that characterizes his political consciousness. Indeed, it is his very resistance to northern patterns of exemplification that make Stuurman an (un)exemplary southern figure, for what is southerness but a quality, state or consciousness of ontological difference that perpetually resists the naturalization of difference – a state that both embraces Indigenous roots and acknowledges the powerfully fragmented nature of those roots? As the Khoi poet Zenzile Khoisan cannily writes of Khoi resistance and survival in 'Claiming Roots': 'Yet, the white man did not know/ there's a stubborn resistance in feigned surrender/ there's still currency in fragments of tongues.'[51]

Notes

1. For this account of Stuurman's life, see V. C. Malherbe, 'David Stuurman: "Last Chief of the Hottentots"', *African Studies* 39, no. 1 (1980): 47–64.
2. On South Africa's ongoing tradition of maroon fugitivity, see Javier Ernesto Perez, 'The Maroon as Abolitionist: On Fugitivity and Gangs in Cape Town', in *The Routledge International Handbook of Penal Abolition*, ed. Michael J. Coyle and David Scott (Abingdon: Routledge, 2021), 96–105.
3. See, for example, Fred Moten, *Stolen Life* (Durham, NC: Duke University Press, 2018). Following Orlando Patterson, Moten uses the term 'social death' to refer to conditions of extreme powerlessness and loss of social identity.
4. Fred Moten, *Black and Blur* (Durham, NC: Duke University Press, 2017), 76.
5. For this reading of Moten, see Martha Feldman, 'Fugitive Voice', *Representations* 154, no. 1 (2021): 10–22.
6. Gayatri Chakravorty Spivak, 'Can the Subaltern Speak?', in *Marxism and the Interpretation of Culture*, ed. Cary Nelson and Lawrence Grossberg (London: Macmillan, 1988), 264.
7. Paul Gilroy, *Black Atlantic: Modernity and Double Consciousness* (Cambridge, MA: Harvard University Press, 1994), 57.

8. Raewyn Connell, *Southern Theory: The Global Dynamics of Knowledge in Social Science* (Cambridge: Polity Press, 2007), 65.
9. Achille Mbembe, 'The Power of the Archive and Its Limits', in *Refiguring the Archive*, ed. Carolyn Hamilton et al. (Norwell, MA: Kluwer Academic Publishers, 2002), 20; Gayatri Chakravorty Spivak, *A Critique of Postcolonial Reason: Towards a History of the Vanishing Present* (Cambridge, MA: Harvard University Press, 1999), 310. On Khoi nationalism, see, for example, Elizabeth Elbourne, 'Freedom at Issue: Vagrancy Legislation and the Meaning of Freedom in Britain and the Cape Colony, 1799–1842', *Slavery and Abolition* 15, no. 2 (1994): 114–50.
10. Pamela Scully, 'Peripheral Visions: Heterography and Writing the Transnational Life of Sara Baartman', in *Transnational Lives: Biographies of Global Modernity, 1700–Present*, ed. Desley Deacon, Penny Russell and Angela Woollacott (London: Palgrave Macmillan, 2010), 28–9, 34–5; Desley Deacon, Penny Russell and Angela Woollacott, 'Part I: Writing Lives Transnationally', in *Transnational Lives*, 13.
11. Meg Samuelson, *Remembering the Nation, Dismembering Women? Stories of the South African Transition* (Pietermaritzburg: University of Kwazulu-Natal Press, 2007), 5; Scully, 'Peripheral Visions', 33.
12. Gyanendra Pandey, 'Voices from the Edge: The Struggle to Write Subaltern Histories', in *Mapping Subaltern Studies and the Postcolonial*, ed. Vinayak Chaturvedi (London: Verso, [1995] 2000), 296, cited in Benjamin Miller, 'Fragments in the Archive: The Subaltern Protests of Charles Never', *Journal of Australian Studies* 45, no. 4 (2021): 493.
13. Tina M. Campt, *Listening to Images* (Durham, NC: Duke University Press, 2017), 22; Anjali Arondekar, *For the Record: On Sexuality and the Colonial Archive in India* (Durham, NC: Duke University Press, 2009), 171, cited in Miller, 495.
14. Thomas Pringle, 'The British Government at the Cape of Good Hope', *New Monthly Magazine and Literary Journal: Part I* (London: Henry Colburn, 1828), 168.
15. Van der Kemp acknowledged that the Khoi leaders were disappointed by his neutrality during the frontier wars. James Read Sr, too, downplayed the active role played by Khoi on the eastern frontier. On these pacification narratives, see, for example, Elizabeth Elbourne, *Blood Ground: Colonialism, Missions, and the Contest for Christianity in the Cape Colony and Britain, 1799–1853* (Kingston, ON: McGill-Queens University Press, 2002), 143, 148, 368–9.
16. Matthew Shum, *Improvisations of Empire: Thomas Pringle in Scotland, the Cape Colony and London, 1789–1834* (London: Anthem Press, 2020), 4.
17. Thomas Pringle, *The Poetical Works of Thomas Pringle* (London: Edward Moxon, 1838), 3–8, 11–12, 35–45.
18. Thomas Pringle, *Narrative of a Residence in South Africa*, new ed. (London: Edward Moxon, 1835), 259–60.
19. Richard Bourke to Governor Darling, 5 August 1828, MNHSW – StAC: NRS 905 [4/2015] 29/853.
20. David Stuurman to Governor Darling, 19 December 1828, MNHSW – StAC: NRS 905 [4/2015] 29/853.
21. Governor Darling, Memorandum for the Colonial Secretary, 11 February 1829, MNHSW – StAC: NRS 905 [4/2015] 29/853. The misspelling of Stuurman's name here is the result of a phonetic spelling of the Dutch or Afrikaans pronunciation of Stuurman.
22. Tony Voss, 'South Africa in Sydney'. Available online: http://sanationalsociety.co.za/wp-content/uploads/2020/06/South-Africa-in-Sydney-by-Tony-Voss.pdf. Stuurman's remains may have been relocated to Bunnerong Cemetery.

23. Penny van Toorn, 'Indigenous Australian Life Writing: Tactics and Transformations', in *Telling Stories: Indigenous History and Memory in Australia and New Zealand*, ed. Bain Attwood and Fiona Magowan (Crows Nest, NSW: Allen & Unwin, 2001), 1–20 (8); Caitlin Adams, 'Thinking the Empire Poor: Plebian Petitions for Clemency in Britain and New South Wales', *History Australia* 19, no. 3 (2022): 433.

24. On the imperial instrumentality of petitions, see Rohit De and Robert Travers, 'Petitioning and Political Cultures in South Asia: Introduction', ed. Rohit De and Robert Travers, *Modern Asian Studies* 53, no. 1 (2019): 9; and Richard Huzzey and Henry Miller, 'Colonial Petitions, Colonial Petitioners, and the Imperial Parliament, ca. 1780–1918', *Journal of British Studies* 61 (2022): 263.

25. Saxe Bannister, *Humane Policy; or Justice to the Aborigines* (London: Thomas and George Underwood, 1830), 55.

26. Pringle, *Narrative*, 259.

27. Bannister, *Humane Policy*, 55.

28. Marcus Clarke, 'Stuurman, Brothers-Patriots and Hottentots', *Sydney Morning Herald*, 6 May 1879, 7. On the invocation of Stuurman, see Kristyn Harman, *Aboriginal Convicts: Australian, Khoisan, and Maori Exiles* (Sydney: University of New South Wales Press, 2012), 161–2.

29. Harriet Deacon, 'Patterns of Exclusion on Robben Island, 1654–1992', in *Isolation: Places and Practices of Exclusion*, ed. Alison Bashford and Carolyn Strange (London: Routledge, 2003), 154.

30. D'Urban to Glenelg, 14 February 1837, TNA CO48/171 (also in Cape Archives GH23/11/16), cited in Clare Anderson, 'Convicts, Carcerality and Cape Colony Connections in the 19th Century', *Journal of Southern African Studies* 42, no. 3 (2016): 436.

31. Anderson, 'Convicts, Carcerality and Cape Colony Connections', 430. On transportation as a strategy to break Indigenous resistance, see L. C. Duly, '"Hottentots to Hobart and Sydney": The Cape Supreme Court's Use of Transportation, 1828-38', *Australian Journal of Politics and History* 25, no. 1 (1979): 39–50. On liquidization as a metaphor to describe the condition of global mobility, see Zygmunt Bauman, *Liquid Modernity* (Cambridge: Polity Press, 2000).

32. In 1802, Governor Francis Dundas had granted Stuurman and his brothers a *kraal*, primarily as a buffer from attacks on Dutch farms by Xhosa tribes but also as a means of fomenting antagonism between the Khoi and Xhosa peoples.

33. On Stuurman's escape, see Harriet Deacon, 'The British Prison on Robben Island 1800–1896', in *The Island: A History of Robben Island 1488–1890*, ed. Harriet Deacon (Cape Town: David Philip, 1996): 42–3; Julia C. Wells, *Rebellion and Uproar: Makhanda and the Great Escape from Robben Island, 1820* (Pretoria: Unisa Press, 2007); and Malherbe, 'David Stuurman', 47–64.

34. Like Stuurman, Makhanda was the subject of eulogistic life histories by Pringle and other humanitarians. See, for example, Pringle, *Narrative*, 307.

35. Nelson Mandela, *Long Walk to Freedom: The Autobiography of Nelson Mandela* (London: Little, Brown and Company, 1994), 327–8.

36. Ibid., 328. On Mandela's investment in Makhanda, see also Julia C. Wells, *The Return of Makhanda: Exploring the Legend* (Pietermaritzburg: University of KwaZulu-Natal Press, 2012), 6.

37. Daniel Roux, 'Writing the Prison', in *The Cambridge History of South African Literature*, ed. David Attwell and Derek Attridge (Cambridge: Cambridge University Press, 2012), 545.

38. Ibid., 552, 555.

39. Wells, *The Return of Makhanda*, 215–39.

40. Julia C. Wells, 'Discovering the Spirit of Makhanda: Dreamer or Hero', 2 July 2022, n.p. Available online: http://www.makana.gov.za/history-culture/discovering-the-spirit-of-makana/.
41. National Heritage Council Briefing on the David Stuurman Project, 17 April 2013. Available online: https://pmg.org.za/committee-meeting/15692/.
42. For an account of some of the controversies surrounding the monument, see Marnell Kirsten, 'The March Continues: A Critique of the Long March to Freedom Statue Collection Exhibited in Century City', *Image & Text* no. 34 (2020): 1–16.
43. The Monument can be viewed virtually at: https://www.longmarchtofreedom.co.za/Home/StatuesNames.
44. On 'Khoisan revivalism' see, for example, Lorenzo Veracini and Rafael Verbuyst, 'South Africa's Settler-Colonial Present: Khoisan Revivalism and the Question of Indigeneity', *Social Dynamics: A Journal of African Studies* 46, no. 2 (2020): 259–76; and Rafael Verbuyst, *Khoisan Consciousness: An Ethnography of Emic Histories and Indigenous Revivalism in Post-Apartheid Cape Town* (Leiden: Brill, 2022).
45. Javier Ernesto Perez, '"They Still Call Us *Drosters*": Performing the Memory of Marrons and Slavery with Formerly-Incarcerated Men in Cape Town', *Research in Drama Education: The Journal of Applied Theatre and Performance* 26, no. 3 (2021): 447. See also Zenzele Isoke, 'Black Ethnography, Black (Female) Aesthetics: Thinking/Writing/Saying/Sounding Black Political Life', *Theory & Event* 21, no. 1 (2018): 148–68.
46. Ferrus's poem was instrumental in achieving the repatriation of Baartman's remains and was read as part of the bill passed to repatriate Baartman in 2002.
47. Origins of the poem recounted by Stone in correspondence with the authors.
48. Perez, '"They Still Call Us *Drosters*"', 448.
49. Transcript and translation kindly provided by the author, Amanda Lois Stone, and reproduced here with permission.
50. Perez, '"They Still Call Us *Drosters*"', 448.
51. Zenzile Khoisan, 'Claiming Roots', in *There Are No More Words: A Collection of Poems* (Cape Town: Uhuru Design Studio, 2018), 58–9, cited in Verbuyst, *Khoisan Consciousness*, epigraph, n.p.

Bibliography

Adams, Caitlin. 'Thinking the Empire Poor: Plebian Petitions for Clemency in Britain and New South Wales'. *History Australia* 19, no. 3 (2022): 430–49.

Anderson, Clare. 'Convicts, Carcerality and Cape Colony Connections in the 19th Century'. *Journal of Southern African Studies* 42, no. 3 (2016): 429–42.

Arondekar, Anjali. *For the Record: On Sexuality and the Colonial Archive in India*. Durham, NC: Duke University Press, 2009.

Bannister, Saxe. *Humane Policy; or Justice to the Aborigines*. London: Thomas and George Underwood, 1830.

Bauman, Zygmunt. *Liquid Modernity*. Cambridge: Polity Press, 2000.

Campt, Tina M. *Listening to Images*. Durham, NC: Duke University Press, 2017.

Connell, Raewyn. *Southern Theory: The Global Dynamics of Knowledge in Social Science*. Cambridge: Polity Press, 2007.

De, Rohit, and Robert Travers. 'Petitioning and Political Cultures in South Asia: Introduction', special issue. *Modern Asian Studies* 53, no. 1 (2019): 1–20.

Deacon, Desley, Penny Russell, and Angela Woollacott. 'Part I: Writing Lives Transnationally'. In *Transnational Lives: Biographies of Global Modernity, 1700–Present*, eds Desley Deacon, Penny Russell and Angela Woollacott., 13–14. London: Palgrave Macmillan, 2010.

Deacon, Harriet. 'The British Prison on Robben Island 1800–1896'. In *The Island: A History of Robben Island 1488–1890*, ed. Harriet Deacon, 33–56. Cape Town: David Philip, 1996.

Deacon, Harriet. 'Patterns of Exclusion on Robben Island, 1654–1992'. In *Isolation: Places and Practices of Exclusion*, ed. Alison Bashford and Carolyn Strange, 153–72. London: Routledge, 2003.

Duly, L. C. '"Hottentots to Hobart and Sydney": The Cape Supreme Court's Use of Transportation, 1828–38'. *Australian Journal of Politics and History* 25, no. 1 (1979): 39–50.

Elbourne, Elizabeth. *Blood Ground: Colonialism, Missions, and the Contest for Christianity in the Cape Colony and Britain, 1799–1853.* Kingston, ON: McGill-Queens University Press, 2002.

Elbourne, Elizabeth. 'Freedom at Issue: Vagrancy Legislation and the Meaning of Freedom in Britain and the Cape Colony, 1799–1842'. *Slavery and Abolition* 15, no. 2 (1994): 114–50.

Feldman, Martha. 'Fugitive Voice'. *Representations* 154, no. 1 (2021): 10–22.

Gilroy, Paul. *Black Atlantic: Modernity and Double Consciousness.* Cambridge, MA: Harvard University Press, 1994.

Harman, Kristyn. *Aboriginal Convicts: Australian, Khoisan, and Maori Exiles.* Sydney: University of New South Wales Press, 2012.

Huzzey, Richard, and Henry Miller. 'Colonial Petitions, Colonial Petitioners, and the Imperial Parliament, ca. 1780–1918'. *Journal of British Studies* 61 (2022): 261–89.

Isoke, Zenzele. 'Black Ethnography, Black (Female) Aesthetics: Thinking/Writing/Saying/Sounding Black Political Life'. *Theory & Event* 21, no. 1 (2018): 148–68.

Khoisan, Zenzile. 'Claiming Roots'. In *There Are No More Words: A Collection of Poems.* Cape Town: Uhuru Design Studio, 2018.

Kirsten, Marnell. 'The March Continues: A Critique of the Long March to Freedom Statue Collection Exhibited in Century City'. *Image & Text* 34 (2020): 1–16.

Malherbe, V. C. 'David Stuurman: "Last Chief of the Hottentots"', *African Studies* 39, no. 1 (1980): 47–64.

Mandela, Nelson. *Long Walk to Freedom: The Autobiography of Nelson Mandela.* London: Little, Brown and Company, 1994.

Mbembe, Achille. 'The Power of the Archive and its Limits'. In *Refiguring the Archive*, edited by Carolyn Hamilton et al., 19–28. Norwell, MA: Kluwer Academic Publishers, 2002.

Miller, Benjamin. 'Fragments in the Archive: The Subaltern Protests of Charles Never'. *Journal of Australian Studies* 45, no. 4 (2021): 491–506.

Moten, Fred. *Black and Blur.* Durham, NC: Duke University Press, 2017.

Moten, Fred. *Stolen Life.* Durham, NC: Duke University Press, 2018.

Pandey, Gyanendra. 'Voices from the Edge: The Struggle to Write Subaltern Histories'. In *Mapping Subaltern Studies and the Postcolonial*, edited by Vinayak Chaturvedi, 281–99. London: Verso, [1995] 2000.

Perez, Javier Ernesto. 'The Maroon as Abolitionist: On Fugitivity and Gangs in Cape Town'. In *The Routledge International Handbook of Penal Abolition*, edited by Michael J. Coyle and David Scott, 96–105. Abingdon: Routledge, 2021.

Perez, Javier Ernesto. '"They Still Call Us *Drosters*": Performing the Memory of Marrons and Slavery with Formerly-Incarcerated Men in Cape Town'. *Research in Drama Education: The Journal of Applied Theatre and Performance* 26, no. 3 (2021): 442–60.

Pringle, Thomas. 'The British Government at the Cape of Good Hope'. *New Monthly Magazine and Literary Journal: Part I.* London: Henry Colburn, 1828.

Pringle, Thomas. *Narrative of a Residence in South Africa*, new ed. London: Edward Moxon, 1835.

Pringle, Thomas. *The Poetical Works of Thomas Pringle*. London: Edward Moxon, 1838.

Roux, Daniel. 'Writing the Prison'. In *The Cambridge History of South African Literature*, edited by David Attwell and Derek Attridge, 545–63. Cambridge: Cambridge University Press, 2012.

Samuelson, Meg. *Remembering the Nation, Dismembering Women? Stories of the South African Transition*. Pietermaritzburg: University of Kwazulu-Natal Press, 2007.

Scully, Pamela. 'Peripheral Visions: Heterography and Writing the Transnational Life of Sara Baartman'. In *Transnational Lives: Biographies of Global Modernity, 1700–Present*, edited by Desley Deacon, Penny Russell and Angela Woollacott, 27–40. London: Palgrave Macmillan, 2010.

Shum, Matthew. *Improvisations of Empire: Thomas Pringle in Scotland, the Cape Colony and London, 1789–1834*. London: Anthem Press, 2020.

Spivak, Gayatri Chakravorty. 'Can the Subaltern Speak?', In *Marxism and the Interpretation of Culture*, edited by Cary Nelson and Lawrence Grossberg, 271–313. London: Macmillan, 1988.

Spivak, Gayatri Chakravorty. *A Critique of Postcolonial Reason: Towards a History of the Vanishing Present*. Cambridge, MA: Harvard University Press, 1999.

van Toorn, Penny. 'Indigenous Australian Life Writing: Tactics and Transformations'. In *Telling Stories: Indigenous History and Memory in Australia and New Zealand*, ed. Bain Attwood and Fiona Magowan, 1–20. Crows Nest, NSW: Allen & Unwin, 2001.

Veracini, Lorenzo, and Rafael Verbuyst. 'South Africa's Settler-Colonial Present: Khoisan Revivalism and the Question of Indigeneity'. *Social Dynamics: A Journal of African Studies* 46, no. 2 (2020): 259–76.

Verbuyst, Rafael. *Khoisan Consciousness: An Ethnography of Emic Histories and Indigenous Revivalism in Post-Apartheid Cape Town*. Leiden: Brill, 2022.

Voss, Tony. 'South Africa in Sydney'. Available online: http://sanationalsociety.co.za/wp-content/uploads/2020/06/South-Africa-in-Sydney-by-Tony-Voss.pdf.

Wells, Julia C. *Rebellion and Uproar: Makhanda and the Great Escape from Robben Island, 1820*. Pretoria: Unisa Press, 2007.

Wells, Julia C. *The Return of Makhanda: Exploring the Legend*. Pietermaritzburg: University of KwaZulu-Natal Press, 2012.

CHAPTER 18
RECOVERING A BIOGRAPHY OF A SOUTHERN CITY, BULAWAYO
Isaac Ndlovu

Melina Rorke's *Melina Rorke: Her Amazing Experiences in the Stormy Nineties of South Africa's Story Told by Herself* (1939) has been read as an autobiography-cum-travelogue,¹ which, while 'compounded of fact and fiction, [the] historical framework around which the biography is woven is … sound'.² The author was born Melina da Fonseca in 1867, the daughter of Travers da Fonseca, who had been 'appointed Consul to Portuguese East Africa in the early 1880s',³ at 'a time when the eyes of the whole world were fixed greedily on Africa'.⁴ Rorke spent her childhood at Delagoa Bay before attending the Dominican Convent School in Cape Town. It is from Cape Town, at the age of fourteen, that she claims to have eloped with and married Frederick Rorke, 'the hero of the victorious visiting [rugby] English team'.⁵ Soon after, she accompanied her husband and his team on a tour of South African cities. Later, in the diamond town of Kimberley, where Rorke's family was then residing, she claims that her husband breaks his neck during a rugby match, dying instantly. But by this time, Rorke was already pregnant. In 1893, at the age of eighteen, now with a toddler son, she alleges to have accompanied her older brother, Sebastian, on an adventurous trip, first to Fort Victoria (now Masvingo) and to Bulawayo, both in Zimbabwe. She built a home and settled in colonial Bulawayo, where historical records suggest she spent fourteen years.⁶ Contrary to her claims, historical sources indicate that she went to Lobengula's territory with her husband already having three children, two sons and a daughter. Her husband, Frederic Rorke, went to Australia in 1897 and never came back. Rorke obtained a divorce in 1899. It is assumed that she stayed on in Bulawayo and migrated to the United States of America in 1908, where she became an actress.

De Haan states that life writing is directed 'to literary-theoretical research concerned with ethical questions associated with the construction of … identity evident in personal sources'.⁷ Trying to recover and reconstruct an accurate biography of a city from a contested autobiography such as Rorke's text presents complications related to factuality and the way in which knowledge is produced. The process requires 'the practice of intellectual humility that engenders a different way of seeing, listening, relating within knowledge ecologies'.⁸ This modesty is implied in Achille Mbembe's anxiety about an African scholarship that uncritically blames everything that goes wrong in Africa on western modernity and its knowledge-making processes.⁹ Mbembe also highlights the 'false belief that only autochthonous people' can produce 'a legitimate scientific discourse on the realities of the continent'.¹⁰ Although Mbembe does not emphasize that knowledge production in and on Africa has been overly exposed to Euro-American epistemologies, his insights explain my seemingly paradoxical choice of a text by a white female with northern affiliations. The recovery of Bulawayo's biography from Rorke's life writing helps us 'see the "North" and "South" as relational categories, mutually constitutive, and entangled'.[11]

Recovering a biography of a southern city from this contested text is an opportunity to engage with the concept of 'hubris of the zero point' – the illusion that knowledge-making has no geo-political location.[12] Through an analysis of Rorke's text, set in the violent early colonial period of southern Africa, this chapter constructs a partial biography of a particular time and perspective on a southern city's 'life' whose colonial history holds clues on how colonization and colonial difference can be re-assessed in ways that show the uneven epistemological entanglements of the south and north that still prevail today. Writing a southern city's life through the 'northern' lens of a white woman is a refusal to see decolonial thinking as a project of complete disengagement with western epistemologies. Instead it is a de-linking to re-link, in ways that acknowledge the need to consider the geo-politics of knowledge production. Thus, this discussion is alert to 'the geography and biography of knowledge',[13] that is, the recognition that epistemology and knowledge production about the self, others and place are always linked to identity and location. Owing to our vantage point in history and shifts in social paradigms, Rorke's text allows a simultaneous writing and reading of Bulawayo's life through and against her perspective.

Banality and aura of Bulawayo

In the late nineteenth century, during the scramble for Africa when Rorke embarks on her journey to Bulawayo from Kimberley, southern Africa had had white settlers for centuries. Rorke insists that she accompanies her older brother Sebastian (Bassy) to Bulawayo on a gold-seeking expedition just before the outbreak of the Anglo-Ndebele war of 1893. Sebastian, we are told, had heard 'about the possibility of finding gold in Bulawayo [because the] same reefs that held the rich deposits in Jo'burg supposedly cropped out again near Bulawayo'.[14] Pre-colonial Bulawayo was imagined as a place where fortunes could be made as in Johannesburg.[15] About going to Bulawayo, Rorke writes that they were going to 'strike north in Lobengula's territory'[16] and calls this part of southern Africa the 'almost unknown heart of Africa' reachable by going 'through forests, across mighty rivers, over mountains'!'[17]

Today, Bulawayo is the second largest city in Zimbabwe, formerly Rhodesia and Southern Rhodesia.[18] Within the wider global capitalist landscape, Bulawayo is an ordinary city, however; during the period Rorke narrates, it featured in the big political debates of European metropolises. Rorke's autobiographical enterprise 'make[s] manifest the peculiar aura of' Bulawayo, as Benjamin might have written.[19] Benjamin argues that 'the destruction of the aura … extracts sameness even from what is unique'.[20] Something similar can be observed in conjunction with the banality and aura of Bulawayo tantalizingly captured in Rorke's narrative.

In terms of population density, Bulawayo was the only place with some semblance of pre-colonial town status before Rhodes's invasion of Zimbabwe in 1890. Additionally, though Bulawayo 'was visited regularly by traders and the emissaries of Cecil Rhodes' as late as 1893,[21] King Lobengula had preserved the traditional architecture of his capital, a rejection of European culture, since the Ndebele people had had close to a half-century of contact with Europeans at this point. When, as Rorke writes, Rhodes's army, led by his friend Leander Starr Jameson, destroyed Bulawayo, Rhodes retained the town's name.[22] Rhodes also built the new colonial town on the ruins of the old, effacing the precolonial town but also using it as a foundation for the new. Alexander Davis in *The Directory of Bulawayo and Handbook to Matabeleland 1895–1996* has the following entry for 22 September: 'Mr. Rhodes ordered the building of a commodious dwelling-house upon the site of the old King's Kraal.'[23] Rhodes thus tapped into the aura of old Bulawayo by making the colonial town visible through the partial presence of the old. Marking the permanent colonization of this southern place, today Rhodes and Jameson are buried at World's View, at Matobo Hills,[24] 35 kilometres to the south-west of Bulawayo, while Ndebele King Lobengula's burial place remains unknown. The refusal by the chiefs to disclose Lobengula's burial place suggests that the invisibility of burial sites was normative among the Ndebeles. Where Rhodes was keen on making colonial Bulawayo visible by building on the ruins of the old, he also partly achieved the invisibility that Lobengula intended by burning his capital. Similarly, Rorke uses both the pre-colonial and early colonial towns to achieve autobiographical visibility but also unintentionally constructs the visibility of this southern city, a process that facilitates the recovery of its biography.

Rorke articulates and silences multiple exclusions during her stay in Bulawayo because she was both part of the white colonizers and a victim of colonial patriarchy, thus her text participates in the construction of 'inactive silence' regarding black colonial residents.[25] For example, when Bulawayo was under siege during the Anglo-Ndebele Uprising of 1896-7, Rorke boasts of shooting a Ndebele soldier, whom she claims was about to kill her sister-in-law, never pausing to introspect. Inadvertently, Rorke's comments corroborate historical records showing early resistance to colonial domination by Bulawayo black residents.[26] Through this action, Rorke undercuts her subsequent construction of the residents either as absent, silent or acquiescent to colonial rule and exploitation. Although Rorke establishes herself as fighting against white patriarchy, hers is a struggle which fails to incorporate Bulawayo's black residents, who are 'excluded and invisibilized' by her narrative's enacting colonial violence.[27] What Rorke can see and articulate is mediated by the hegemonic colonial paradigm.

Rorke's text reveals and constructs early colonial Bulawayo as a contact zone. For Mary Louise Pratt, contact zones are 'social spaces where cultures meet, clash, and grapple with each other, often in contexts of highly asymmetrical relations of power'.[28] It is the 'authority of presence' or being in Bulawayo during a moment of violent colonial transition, which gives traction to Rorke's account.[29] The historical events that Rorke claims to have witnessed or participated in include the defeat of Lobengula's much larger army by about 700 white soldiers and their black collaborators in 1893, the destruction of pre-colonial Bulawayo and Lobengula's fleeing and disappearance, the founding and rapid development of colonial Bulawayo, the doomed Jameson Raid (1895), the Ndebele uprising of 1896–7 and the Anglo-Boer War (1899–1902). Additionally, the narrative is buoyed by Rorke's claim to be among the first white females in colonial Bulawayo. All these events capture a social space under contestation.

The black labourers who participated in the rapid building projects at which Rorke marvels are only available as curiosities for her constructions of the self. For example, she relates a fantastical story of rats that were 'as large as small cats' that infested the young town.[30] She writes:

When excavating was finally started for the Bulawayo Club rats swarmed out of the earth in such enormous numbers that workmen fled in terror, all except one unfortunate man who stumbled and fell. A few minutes later when the other workmen missed him and went back to see where he was they found nothing left but his skeleton.[31]

This nameless workman feeds into colonial imagination of southern places as replete with danger from which the white subject is shielded. Significantly, black residents had known how to survive and thrive in this place before their violent displacement and colonial destruction of the area's ecological balance.

Notably, Rorke never saw pre-colonial Bulawayo because Lobengula ordered that his capital be razed to the ground as Rhodes's army advanced.[32] This was an act of admitting defeat, and yet of defiance as well as a military strategy. Rhodes's victorious army was hoping to acquire shelter and other resources. Lobengula also denies Rhodes the symbolic victory that comes from capturing a vanquished king and his articles. Since Lobengula's Bulawayo had vanished when Rorke finally settled there, the reader only gets a glimpse of the townscapes from Bassy, who had visited the town on an earlier occasion. Apparently, the 'headquarters of the great Matebele chief Lobengula',[33] Rorke's expression, did not have 'the variety of things' that white people needed.[34] Bassy tells his sister, who is eager to go straight to Bulawayo without going round Fort Victoria, 'that Bulawayo was just an exaggerated replica of the kraals [they] had passed, a collection of mud and wattle huts'.[35] Bassy's dismissive and condescending observation also reveals that contrary to Rorke's earlier imaginations, there were villages along their route and not just forests, rivers and mountains.

While still on their way to Fort Victoria, en route to Bulawayo, Rorke learns that Rhodes has concocted an excuse for attacking Bulawayo. She claims that she was displeased with Rhodes's boundless imperialism while 'Bassy was excited at the prospect of a good scrap [since] it would simplify things greatly to have the English in formal possession of the territory'.[36] Vaughn-Williams shows that Lobengula was aware of the precarity of his position and the colonial threat to his kingdom and had stationed 'impis (armies) along the borders of [his] country to prevent parties of white people from coming in'.[37]

Lobengula's border policing proved ineffective and Rorke reports that after Lobengula's retreat, Rhodes 'hurried to Bulawayo [wanting] the new town of Bulawayo to be laid on the ruins of the old one [and subsequently throwing] open the whole country to land entry, giving every soldier and officer the same rights – to a farm of six thousand acres, a mineral right of twenty acres, and an equal share in the king's cattle, two hundred and fifty thousand head'.[38] The matter-of-fact reporting of the plunder of Bulawayo's resources is striking. In an entry of 4 August 1894, Davis observes: 'Claim rights, loots, and farm rights, appear to be the staple conversation [among white settlers]. *Everyone has Rights* except the Matabele, a strange reversal of affairs in Matabeleland.'[39] Describing the city of fifty years after 1893, Yvonne Vera says for black residents, 'Bulawayo [was] not a city for idleness. The idea [was] to live within the cracks. Unnoticed and unnoticeable, offering every service but with the capacity to vanish when the task required [was] accomplished.'[40] Thus, while Rorke's narrative provides an insight into colonial material pillage, Vera's novel exposes the violence of colonial rule on the bodies and minds of black residents.

Entering Bulawayo: Fulfilling a secret ambition

Rorke's 'own secret ambition' was to be 'the first white woman to enter the new town of Bulawayo'.[41] Meanwhile, Jameson had 'issued orders that no one was to go to Bulawayo until he gave them permission; the town was a smouldering ruin, and the presence of women and children at that time was almost undesirable.'[42] Rorke goes to Bulawayo anyway and becomes the only unmarried white woman amid young men 'with baggy trousers, ragged shirts, and hard, calloused hands'.[43] Although she focuses on proving that she was one of the first white women to witness pre-colonial Bulawayo's replacement with European civilization, she also reveals that colonialism happened at cultural and epistemological levels due to her text's effacement of black voices in its reproduction of colonial knowledge of southern places. Although constructing herself as a marginalized colonial woman, Rorke's depiction of white men as the only ones responsible for Bulawayo's new way of life, and her narrative's silences about black people's participation, inscribe her into the dominant masculine colonial worldview which her text tries to debunk.

Entering the town for the first time, Rorke claims to be despondent and conflicted about what she sees. She says that as she went

> through the ruins of old Bulawayo – the ruins consisting solely of dead bushes, scorched trees, and occasionally blackened fire-stones [she noticed that] heavy rains had washed away the soot and ashes, and nature had already started to cover the scars with verdant green. Nothing was left to remind the traveller that he was trespassing on ground once sacred to one of the mightiest of African kings.[44]

Similarly, about the destruction of the 1870 established Bulawayo, Father Croonenberg, in his diary entry of 28 August 1881, writes that after its being burnt down, Bulawayo 'will leave no ruins behind, no traces of its ephemeral existence'.[45] There is an assumption here that the Ndebeles held Western notions of towns and cities. However, Ndebele people seem to have sought permanence elsewhere and not in the durability of their physical structures. In the Ndebele cosmology, Bulawayo was relocatable and did not cease to exist in 1881 and 1893.[46]

Rorke describes new Bulawayo as 'a few scattered beehive huts and squat, oblong buildings disfiguring the slopes of a barren, windswept hill'.[47] The town does not fit Rorke's idea of a white town because it 'is almost the same, but not quite' a replica of a black settlement, to reverse Bhabha's assertion that 'colonial mimicry is the desire for a reformed, recognizable Other'.[48] Rorke describes how Jameson took them on a tour of the town as soon as they arrived. She reports: 'Dr Jameson's short legs fairly twinkled as he led us along the wide … main street pausing occasionally to let Bassy marvel at the amount of work that had been accomplished during his absence'.[49] This is what Rhodes wanted: 'the streets were all to be wide enough for a bullock-cart to turn in; trees – thousands of them – were going to be planted; every house was going to have its own big garden; the railway was going to be brought north to meet the needs of the city'.[50] A mere four years after the establishment of the new town, the railway reached Bulawayo. The railway irreversibly opened Bulawayo to colonial modernity. In narrating these events that involved an exploited 'army of native workers',[51] Rorke employs distancing narrative strategies to give the impression that she did not share Rhodes's vision by using metaphors of disease to refer to it. She talks of people being 'infected by Mr Rhodes' visions' about the new Bulawayo.[52] Thus, Rorke's detailing of the rapid development of new Bulawayo is coloured by her attempt to recuse herself from colonial violence.

Bulawayo: A nexus of Southern and Northern epistemologies

Meanwhile, Rorke employs nostalgia as a strategy which aligns her with the subaltern residents of Bulawayo. She says that as Jameson was excitedly showing Bassy the developments in the town, she was 'busy fighting back her disappointment'.[53] She is 'depressed by the fate of the stalwart Zulus, who for generations had trod the very ground on which [she] was walking'.[54] Through the description of this internal conflict, Rorke reveals that biographical texts resist singularity and authorially imposed coherence. The pre-colonial Bulawayo that Rorke is depressed about only existed in her imagination, because the town had always been in a state of interregnum existence, pausing for a while between each cycle of destruction. This suggests that the Bulawayo that had always been, still is in some forms, despite the destruction and erasure.

However, in 1893, the Bulawayo that was rising would be Rorke's Bulawayo, a town that embraces a different kind of continuity. Just after it was announced that Bulawayo was not going to be a second Johannesburg, Rorke declares: '[M]y interests now were all bound up in Bulawayo, and I should have felt that I had abandoned a friend in trouble had I left the town in its dark hour.'[55] The romanticized personification of the town indicates the depth of Rorke's attachment to the new social life that Bulawayo offered to a single woman far away from the patriarchal constraints of Kimberley. She writes:

> In spite of all the newcomers I was still the only eligible white woman in the town, and the result was that my little house was under perpetual siege, though nothing was farther from my plans than becoming a wife again.[56]

When her brother mentions the possibility of their going back to Kimberley, Rorke says:

> I was afraid that if I went back at that time I should find myself marooned in Kimberley, and, having tasted the joys of managing my own home, the freedom of being my own mistress, I was unwilling to risk their loss.[57]

The repetition of 'I' and 'my' in the passage celebrates how Bulawayo was an escape from patriarchal control and womanhood constraints of her time. Bulawayo becomes 'a native place "bettered" by western intervention'.[58] Her earlier sympathy with the conquered and displaced Bulawayo residents is incorporated as a strategy to humanize her self-narrations. Rorke seems oblivious that she achieves location in Bulawayo through the dislocation of others, proving true that 'narratives of location are also narratives of dislocation and alterity'.[59]

Ironically, the organizing principle of Rorke's self-narration is that her stay in Bulawayo is an interval. Like Bulawayo, Rorke undergoes the process of breaking and reconstruction. Bulawayo, like the Cape Town convent, and Kimberley, ultimately become too small to contain her aspirations. Her departure from Bulawayo is foreshadowed by a statement she makes just before leaving for England to train as a nurse and actor. She claims she had planned to return to Bulawayo and marry a gentleman named Billy Saddler after her training but also admits that it became clear to Saddler that 'upon going to England and becoming an actress it was obvious that [she] couldn't be contented in Bulawayo'.[60] To explain her leaving Bulawayo, Rorke fabricates the mysterious death of Saddler on the day of her return from England. Training as a nurse and actor in London prepares the reader for Rorke's exiting Bulawayo. However, she is conflicted about her departure:

> It was something of a wrench to leave Bulawayo, for the whole town turned up to speed Edgar (Rorke's son) and me on our way, but I had made up my mind this time that nothing would prevent me from going on stage.[61]

Although Rorke quits Bulawayo, her narrative has ensured that Bulawayo as seen through her eyes lives on as readers relive its townscapes through the pages of her text.

Conclusion

Rorke's text offers glimpses of both late pre-colonial and early colonial Bulawayo, enabling the reader to (re)imagine the town through the eyes of a white female who considered herself to be on the borderline of colonial violence and openly adopts a subversive feminist stance against white patriarchy. Rorke's resort to fabrications do not simply highlight the challenge identified by Levi of whether it is possible to 'put down in writing an individual's life',[62] but also the difficulty of adopting unsanctioned ways of apprehending historical truth in life narratives. Since Rorke claims a geographical vantage point and presents a sanitized picture of her stay in Bulawayo, it is in the slippages of her text that the life of early colonial Bulawayo can emerge. By recovering a biography of Bulawayo from Rorke's narrative, it is possible 'to let [a place] forgotten by History with a capital H speak'.[63] Rhodes's insistence to build the colonial city on the ruins of the old can be read metaphorically to argue that recovering a biography of a southern city through and against Rorke's perspective creates a palimpsest of city and texts, north and south colliding and meshing but with each geo-epistemic site remaining in sight. The contending principles of town/city conception that are evident in Rorke's text reveal that the pre-colonial town was founded on principles of impermanence and invisibility while the colonial town was guided by the idea of permanence and visibility.

The biography of Bulawayo that emerges from Rorke's text is incomplete. Today, this partial knowledge, its geopolitics and its locatedness and embodied-ness are what those interested in a liberated humanity advocate to those involved in knowledge production. Although those in the south loathe the coloniality of power still exerted by the north, they find the north alluring in many ways.[64] Similarly, northern citizens are increasingly dissatisfied with their ways of being in the world, and some are turning to the south for alternatives because 'rationality and technology have not completely managed to overcome all obstacles to human freedom'.[65] Rorke tries to escape patriarchal constraints and resolve her colonial contradictions by writing a narrative that is neither factual nor fictional, a text that shows that her stay in Bulawayo also anticipates her departure. The city of Bulawayo also inhabited and inhabits this zone of permanent impermanence. This imposed and self-imposed precarity, which always anticipates departure, also marks departure as incomplete.

Notes

1. Daymond and Smit call Rorke's text an autofiction. Margaret J. Daymond, 'Freedom, Femininity, Adventure and Romance: The Elements of Self-Representation in *Melina Rorke Told by Herself*, in *Southern African Writing: Voyages and Explorations*, ed. G. V. Davis (Amsterdam, Atlanta: Rodopi, 1994). Lizette Smit, 'Gender Tensions, Taboos and Textual Acts in Melina Rorke's Autofiction', *Life Writing* 19, no. 1 (2020): 81–97.

2. Melina Rorke, *Melina Rorke: Her Amazing Experiences in the Stormy Nineties of South Africa's Story Told by Herself* (London: George G. Harrap & Company, 1939), n.p.
3. Ibid., 10.
4. Ibid.
5. Ibid., 12.
6. Ibid., 4.
7. Binne De Haan, 'The Eclipse of Biography in Life Writing', in *Theoretical Discussions of Biography: Approaches from History, Microhistory, and Life Writing* (revised and augmented edition), ed. Hans Renders and Binne Haan, 177–94 (Leiden and Boston: Brill, 2014), 178.
8. Michelle M. Lazar, 'Politics of the "South": Discourses and Praxis', *Discourse & Society* 31, no. 1 (2020): 9.
9. Achille Mbembe, 'Getting Out of the Ghetto: The Challenge of Internationalization', *CODESRIA Bulletin* 3 & 4 (1999): 5.
10. Achille Mbembe, 'African Modes of Self-writing', *Public Culture* 14, no. 1 (2002): 239.
11. Lazar, 'Politics of the "South"', 6.
12. Santiago Castro-Gómez, *Zero-Point Hubris: Science, Race, and Enlightenment in Eighteenth-Century Latin America* (London: Rowman & Littlefield, 2021).
13. Sabelo J. Ndlovu-Gatsheni, 'Decoloniality as the Future of Africa', *History Compass* 13, no. 10 (2015): 492.
14. Rorke, *Melina Rorke: Her Amazing Experiences*, 116.
15. Johannesburg was founded in 1886 upon the discovery of gold in the area. Cecil John Rhodes is one of the few British imperialists who became extremely rich by exploiting the mineral resources of these southern places.
16. Rorke, *Melina Rorke: Her Amazing Experiences*, 78.
17. Ibid., 79.
18. The name 'Rhodesia' commemorates Rhodes, who acquired this territory and declared it a British colony.
19. Walter Benjamin, 'Central Park', in *Selected Writings*, ed. H. Eiland and M. W. Jennings (Cambridge, MA: Harvard University Press, 2003), 173.
20. Walter Benjamin, 'The Work of Art in the Age of Its Technological Reproducibility', in *Selected Writings*, ed. H. Eiland and M. W. Jennings, 251–83 (Cambridge, MA: Harvard University Press, 2003), 256.
21. Rorke, *Melina Rorke: Her Amazing Experiences*, 117.
22. Bulawayo is an IsiNdebele word, a language spoken in southern Zimbabwe, which means one who is killed or a place of killing if the prefixes 'KoBulawayo' or 'KwaBulawayo' are added.
23. Alexander Davis, *The Directory of Bulawayo and Handbook to Matabeleland 1895–1996* (Bulawayo: Books of Zimbabwe, [1896] 1981), 27.
24. The Matobo Hills have saved as burial places, shrines and sacred places for indigenous people. When Rhodes instructed in his will to be buried in this place, he was inserting himself into a long line of spiritual guardians of the land.
25. Abena P. A. Busia, 'Silencing Sycorax: On African Colonial Discourse and the Unvoiced Female', *Cultural Critique* 14 (1989–90): 86.
26. Terence Ranger, *Revolt in Southern Rhodesia, 1896–97: A Study in African Resistance* (London: Heinemann Educational Books Limited, 1967).

27. Sylvia Wynter, 'Unsettling the Coloniality of Being/Power/Truth/Freedom: Towards the Human, After Man, Its Overrepresentation – An Argument', *The New Centennial Review* 3, no. 3 (2003): 261.
28. Mary Louise Pratt, 'Arts of the Contact Zone', *Profession* (1991): 34.
29. Anthony Chennells, 'The Authority of Presence: Reading Judith Todd's *Through the Darkness* as Diary', *Journal of Literary Studies* 25, no. 1 (2009): 106.
30. Rorke, *Melina Rorke: Her Amazing Experiences*, 145.
31. Ibid., 146.
32. In his diaries, Father Croonenberg, who arrived in Bulawayo in 1878 and was still there in 1893, reports that the deliberate setting alight of the Ndebele capital was done after every ten to twelve years. For example, he reports one such destruction on 15 September 1881 of the settlement founded in 1870. Ironically, when Lobengula was forced to set Bulawayo on fire in 1893, it was also due for ritual destruction because it was already twelve years old.
33. Rorke, *Melina Rorke: Her Amazing Experiences*, 116.
34. Ibid., 117.
35. Ibid. Fort Victoria is where Rhodes's Pioneer Column had established the first white settlement in 1890.
36. Ibid., 122.
37. H. Vaughan-Williams, *A Visit to Lobengula in 1889* (Glasgow: University Press Glasgow, 1947), 15.
38. Rorke, *Melina Rorke: Her Amazing Experiences*, 136.
39. Davis, *The Directory of Bulawayo*, 26.
40. Yvonne Vera, *Butterfly Burning* (New York: Farrar, Straus and Giroux, [1998] 2000), 6.
41. Rorke, *Melina Rorke: Her Amazing Experiences*, 137.
42. Ibid., 130.
43. Ibid., 138.
44. Ibid.
45. The Rhodesiana Society, *Diaries of the Jesuit Priests 1879–1881* (Salisbury: Rhodesia Publishing Co., 1959), 81.
46. Pathisa Nyathi, *Traditional Ceremonies of AmaNdebele* (Gweru: Mambo Press, 2001); and Terence Ranger, *Bulawayo Burning: The Social History of a Southern African City, 1893–1960* (Oxford: James Currey, 2010).
47. Rorke, *Melina Rorke: Her Amazing Experiences*, 138.
48. Homi Bhabha, 'Of Mimicry and Man: The Ambivalence of Colonial Discourse', *Discipleship: A Special Issue on Psychoanalysis* 28 (1984): 126.
49. Rorke, *Melina Rorke: Her Amazing Experiences*, 139.
50. Ibid., 136.
51. Ibid.
52. Ibid.
53. Ibid., 139.

54. The Ndebeles of southern Zimbabwe are an offshoot of the Zulu kingdom. Mzilikazi, the founder of the Ndebele kingdom, had once been a chief under Tshaka before their fallout in 1821, leading to Mzilikazi's northward trek, finally settling with his people in 1840 in modern day Zimbabwe.
55. Rorke, *Melina Rorke: Her Amazing Experiences*, 154.
56. Ibid., 149.
57. Ibid., 154.
58. Andrea Feeser, 'Constance Fredericka Gordon Cumming's "Picturesque" Vision: A Christian, Westernized Hawai'i, in *Issues in Travel Writing: Empire, Spectacle, and Displacement*, ed. Kristi Siegel (New York: Peter Lang Publishing, 2002), 102.
59. Floya Anthias, 'Where Do I Belong? Narrating Collective Identity and Translocational Positionality', *Ethnicities* 2, no. 4 (2002): 492.
60. Rorke, *Melina Rorke: Her Amazing Experiences*, 230.
61. Ibid., 231.
62. Giovanni Levi, 'The Uses of Biography', in *Theoretical Discussions of Biography Approaches from History, Microhistory, and Life Writing Revised and Augmented Edition*, ed. Hans Renders and Binne Haan (Leiden and Boston: Brill, 2014), 62.
63. Ibid., 87.
64. Aníbal Quijano, 'Coloniality of Power, Eurocentrism, and Latin America', *Nepantla: Views from South* 1, no. 3 (2000): 533.
65. Ndlovu-Gatsheni, 'Decoloniality as the Future of Africa', 492.

Bibliography

Anthias, Floya. 'Where Do I Belong? Narrating Collective Identity and Translocational Positionality'. *Ethnicities* 2, no. 4 (2002): 491–514.
Benjamin, W. 'Central Park'. In *Selected Writings*, edited by H. Eiland and M. W. Jennings, 161–99. Cambridge, MA: Harvard University Press, 2003.
Benjamin, Walter. 'The Work of Art in the Age of Its Technological Reproducibility'. In *Selected Writings*, edited by H. Eiland and M. W. Jennings, 251–83. Cambridge, MA: Harvard University Press, 2003.
Bhabha, Homi. 'Of Mimicry and Man: The Ambivalence of Colonial Discourse'. *Discipleship: A Special Issue on Psychoanalysis* 28 (1984): 125–33.
Busia, Abena P. A. 'Silencing Sycorax: On African Colonial Discourse and the Unvoiced Female'. *Cultural Critique* 14 (1989–90): 81–104.
Castro-Gómez, Santiago. *Zero-Point Hubris: Science, Race, and Enlightenment in Eighteenth-Century Latin America*. London: Rowman & Littlefield, 2021.
Chennells, Anthony. 'The Authority of Presence: Reading Judith Todd's *Through the Darkness* as Diary'. *Journal of Literary Studies* 25, no. 1 (2009): 98–114.
Davis, Alexander. *The Directory of Bulawayo and Handbook to Matabeleland 1895–1996*. Bulawayo: Books of Zimbabwe, [1896] 1981.

Life Writing and the Southern Hemisphere

Daymond, Margaret J. 'Freedom, Femininity, Adventure and Romance: The Elements of Self-Representation in *Melina Rorke Told by Herself*'. In *Southern African Writing: Voyages and Explorations*, edited by G. V. Davis, 1–15. Amsterdam, Atlanta: Rodopi, 1994.

De Haan, Binne. 'The Eclipse of Biography in Life Writing'. In *Theoretical Discussions of Biography Approaches from History, Microhistory, and Life Writing* (revised and augmented edition), edited by Hans Renders and Binne Haan, 177–94. Leiden and Boston: Brill, 2014.

Feeser, Andrea. 'Constance Fredericka Gordon Cumming's "Picturesque" Vision: A Christian, Westernized Hawai'. In *Issues in Travel Writing: Empire, Spectacle, and Displacement*, edited by Kristi Siegel, 85–108. New York: Peter Lang Publishing, 2002.

Lazar, Michelle M. 'Politics of the "South": Discourses and Praxis'. *Discourse & Society* 31, no. 1 (2020): 5–18.

Levi, Giovanni. 'The Uses of Biography'. In *Theoretical Discussions of Biography Approaches from History, Microhistory, and Life Writing* (revised and augmented edition), edited by Hans Renders and Binne Haan, 61–74. Leiden and Boston: Brill, 2014.

Mbembe, Achille. 'African Modes of Self-writing'. *Public Culture* 14, no. 1 (2002): 239–73.

Mbembe, Achille. 'Getting Out of the Ghetto: The Challenge of Internationalization'. *CODESRIA Bulletin* 3 & 4 (1999): 1–10.

Ndlovu-Gatsheni, Sabelo J. 'Decoloniality as the Future of Africa'. *History Compass* 13, no. 10 (2015): 485–96.

Nyathi, Pathisa. *Traditional Ceremonies of AmaNdebele*. Gweru: Mambo Press, 2001.

Pratt, Mary Louise. 'Arts of the Contact Zone'. *Profession* (1991): 33–40.

Quijano, Aníbal. 'Coloniality of Power, Eurocentrism, and Latin America'. *Nepantla: Views from South* 1, no. 3 (2000): 533–80.

Ranger, Terence. *Bulawayo Burning: The Social History of a Southern African City, 1893–1960*. Oxford: James Currey, 2010.

Ranger, Terence. *Revolt in Southern Rhodesia, 1896–97: A Study in African Resistance*. London: Heinemann Educational Books Limited, 1967.

The Rhodesiana Society. *Diaries of the Jesuit Priests 1879–1881*. Salisbury: Rhodesia Publishing Co., 1959.

Rorke, Melina. *Melina Rorke: Her Amazing Experiences in the Stormy Nineties of South Africa's Story Told by Herself*. London: George G. Harrap & Company, 1939.

Smit, Lizelle. 'Gender Tensions, Taboos and Textual Acts in Melina Rorke's Autofiction'. *Life Writing* 19, no. 1 (2020): 81–97.

Vaughan-Williams, H. *A Visit to Lobengula in 1889*. Glasgow: University Press Glasgow, 1947.

Vera, Yvonne. *Butterfly Burning*. New York: Farrar, Straus and Giroux, [1998] 2000.

Wynter, Sylvia. 'Unsettling the Coloniality of Being/Power/Truth/Freedom: Towards the Human, After Man, Its Overrepresentation – An Argument'. *The New Centennial Review* 3, no. 3 (2003): 257–337.

CHAPTER 19
FROM THE FAR BANK: *TWO-BODY PROBLEM* IN THE SOUTH
Louis Rogers

It's strange – or more exactly, estranging – to read your own words. To write this chapter, I have been rereading a play that I wrote in 2018. I had a pretty good idea at that time of what it was about: the themes and ideas I wanted to explore, the characters and situations I'd come up with. But reading the play now, six years since writing it and four since it was last performed, I see the interests, images and atmospheres that slipped past or through my immediate intentions. Most of all, I see that the play is really about all of this: the ways certain forms of communication, instrumental to one end, can involve or conceal others.

In *Two-Body Problem* I tried to stage a character's experience of a kind of inadvertent life writing. The play is performed by one actor playing one character who speaks, apparently, to the audience.[1] This character announces they will be giving a lecture covering a recent research trip. This lecture gradually becomes more and more like a narrative, and what is meant to be an impersonal recounting of facts starts to reveal her personality, fears and uncertainties. Set on Deception Island, off the Antarctic peninsula, the play is also concerned with how place and location define expression – with a physical and geographic, as well as textual, notion of speaking 'from' and 'to'. This geographic concern maps on to a more immediate spatial one: that of the theatre.

In this essay, I return to *Two-Body Problem* to trace the ways the play relates to its far-southern setting in its exploration of some of the dynamics and practices of life writing. I discuss how the play responds to *Frankenstein* (1818), the novel whose anniversary it was commissioned to mark: in particular, that text's idea of the far north, against which my play faces the far south, and its use of epistolary and dialogic forms, in answer to which I used the academic lecture and the monologue. I take two influences on my play, Jenny Diski's memoir *Skating to Antarctica* and J. M. Coetzee's novel *Elizabeth Costello*, as points of comparison for its interests in geography, biography, travel, research and the ways writing is shaped by occasions, commissions and physical situations. These point the way to a concluding reflection on how life writing and a far-southern setting relate to the context of the theatre, and the kinds of self-revelation – for character and author – that might be permitted at this nexus.

Two-Body Problem was written on commission for the Museum of the History of Science in Oxford, when in 2018 the Museum was looking to stage a performance in its basement laboratory to mark the bicentennial of Mary Shelley's *Frankenstein*. The abiding image the novel had left me with was of its two central characters – Dr Frankenstein and his creature – locked in relentless pursuit across the ice of the far north, each both tortured and defined by the other's existence in a thrilling – in fact, horrific – vision of research and creation. We encounter this image through the eyes, or more specifically the prose, of Captain Walton, an explorer leading an expedition to the north. Walton's ship gets trapped in the ice and encounters an exhausted Dr Frankenstein. The letters he writes home to his sister, which in the fiction of the novel are its literal text, grow to include the full first-person accounts of Frankenstein and then the creature.

The polar image of creature and creator in pursuit, and Walton's freighted and fated expedition which gives the book its frame, marked *Frankenstein* in my mind as a novel of the north. The north in *Frankenstein* is the furthest frontier of human knowledge, resilience and ambition: a setting that dramatizes the promethean hubris that is the novel's stated concern (*Frankenstein, or: The Modern Prometheus*). The far south of today seemed a rich variation on this. Antarctica is in a related but different way strongly associated with research: the site of many long-term geographic, zoological and meteorological projects. It is a largely untamed wilderness but also an organized and carefully regulated territory where national borders jostle in surreal rearrangement – France beside Australia, a Norwegian island off the coast of Chile. Today's Antarctica is far removed from the individualistic romanticism in and against which Shelley wrote. Everyone is in Antarctica for a stated reason and generally as a smaller part of a bigger operation. Tourism there is expensive and always in groups. Solo explorers not so far from the nineteenth-century mould do still undertake journeys across it, but even they are monitored.

I wanted to explore the less simple reality of the south against fantasies of what it might represent to the north. Instead of the fearsome blank expanse of the North Pole in which *Frankenstein* opens, I thought of accounts of Antarctica as various, noisy, odorous, colourful, as a place where people work, where they speak languages like Spanish and English, where they go for dinner and write poems, where they are busy and bored.[2] Antarctica is on the one hand scientific, institutional, even bland, and on the other haunted by danger, isolation, extreme weather and ghost stories.

As an extension of this duality, I set the play within the form of an academic lecture, a textual setting which similarly proposes a kind of functionality haunted by other possibilities – those of narrative, personality, performance or subjectivity. I was inspired by the dialogic and intentional forms of address that make up Shelley's novel – Walton's letters, and in turn Frankenstein's and the creature's addresses. I hear a tension within these: the way Frankenstein's and the creature's narratives are designed to make a case for their speaker; the way Walton's confidence, misgivings and judgements infiltrate his reports to his sister. Beneath a claim to objective factuality are undercurrents of personality, of life. The premises for my own experiment were, then: in place of the north, the south; in place of the novel-as-letters, the play-as-lecture.

And so, *Two-Body Problem* begins with a scholar of the history of science arriving on stage to deliver a lecture on galvanism. The lecturer, named Lynne, explains that she will introduce its history and run through some of her current research, which relates to a recent trip to Antarctica. Launching into the basics, she mentions its (to her, overemphasized) association with Mary Shelley's *Frankenstein*. Seeming to digress, she moves on to her research trip. The lecture gradually slips into narration, and into the present tense, as she describes the trip arising from an unsolicited email inviting her to join a research team on Deception Island, Antarctica, for unclear reasons. Lynne ignores the invitation at first but, antagonized by professional rivalries, eventually replies, and ends up on her way to Antarctica. She is not sure who is inviting her and paying for the trip, what specialisms of hers are in demand or what the research project is about. She evades her own knowledge of this not-knowing.

Lynne travels via Chile and, in her increasingly immersed retelling, we catch up with her in Punta Arenas waiting for a boat to Antarctica. She catches a tourist cruise ship to the Antarctic, and a Zodiac takes her from the boat to Deception Island. There she is met by a Chilean woman named Ines. (At this point the actor, or maybe Lynne, is inhabiting or playing this second character.) Ines takes her to an anonymous-looking research station and promises her hosts will come to explain everything soon.

Throughout this journey, Lynne has been rereading *Frankenstein* to prepare for an inter-disciplinary seminar which she is obliged to teach. She is preoccupied by the image at the beginning of the novel of Dr Frankenstein's years-long chase after his creature. Lynne is disturbed by this image of being bound to your creation, pursued and in pursuit, in a way she wasn't when she was younger. She describes scientific research as a similar, bleakly irresolvable pursuit, in which every discovery gives way to new questions. She describes a physics problem called the two-body problem, in which one must measure the motion of two objects locked in motion and in isolation, affecting only each other with no other forces at play.

At the research base, Lynne suffers sleepless nights because of an uncoverable window that lets light stream in all the summer night. In this sleepless state the noises surrounding her, of machinery, ice and animals, slip beyond recognition. Instead of a white expanse, she discovers Antarctica to be overfull of sensory stimulation. In place of dark mystery is bright insistence.

As Lynne waits, her fear builds. She gets lost inside the base, finding only locked doors and bland meeting rooms. Finally, she is met by Dr Clavel, an assistant to the research leader. It is intimated that some product of their research has escaped on the island and that the researchers have been caught up trying to recover it. This seems to be the reason Lynne has been contacted. The work being undertaken is in the realm of the 'transhumanist' projects which real private companies undertake with the frank aim of overcoming death.[3] Through the veneer of Lynne's increasingly challenged incredulity, we learn that bodies and parts of bodies are being stored in cryogenic storage dewars at this site, waiting for science to catch up with them. Some type of newly formed and animated body seems to have broken out and is now being hunted across the ring-shaped island by the leader of the research project.

After dismissing Dr Clavel's claims, Lynne lies awake again, and late at night momentarily sees a face at her window. Nerves finally frayed, she flees the station. On the shore she sees a huge figure, anonymous under snow gear, about to pilot a Zodiac. She boards and escapes Deception Island with the unspeaking person and sees, as they depart, a white emergency flare released from the station against the white night sky.

If the play started by asserting a settled fictive setting, in which the audience too were implicated as the lecture's audience, by the end we are unsure if Lynne is at home or abroad; in a lecture theatre or in an Antarctic lab or, at some level, in her own head; whether she travelled back north or is still south.

The play is based around a series of corresponding tensions between opposing categories: call them poles. Lynne thinks of herself as a rational and scientifically minded person but finds herself more and more susceptible to irrational suggestions of terror and fantasy. She takes a pragmatic, even deflationary view of the project of scientific research, while others she encounters conceive of it as a heroic individual crusade. Antarctica is a place where the humdrum businesses of science and tourism are carried out but is also rich in myth and strangeness (aspects brought on stage by Lynne's brother, with whom she speaks on the phone, and who, unlike her, associates the place with its eery histories of thwarted expeditions). As an audience, we are watching a lecture but also an entirely embodied performance. We are in the far south, on Deception Island, and also in a lecture theatre in the northern hemisphere (the play is written so as to entertain the idea that wherever it is performed is its literal setting).

Where there is uncertainty between these poles, there is dramatic tension. As a writer, I was drawn to these practically as engines for suspense and interest as much as thematic poignance. I wanted to further the tension in *Frankenstein*'s letters and dialogues: one kind of writing – circumscribed, intentional, directed – becoming another – unruly, betraying, suggestive. I used the heightened forms of academic, science-adjacent writing, with its expectations of objectivity, rigour and factuality, and of the lecture, with its connotations of formality, impersonality and professionalism. Lynne wrestles with the outrageousness of what she is having to relate, struggling to keep control of a story that exceeds reasonable bounds. It is this struggle which gives her away as a character, which lets tension and pathos into what is meant to be a factual lecture. Another way of describing this dynamic could be as literal writing – putting pen to paper, leaving a note, preparing a lecture, writing home – giving rise to writing of a more figurative, conceptual kind – cognizing, symbolizing, mythicizing, narrativizing, self-fashioning.

I drew on a range of references as I developed these ideas. Two texts in particular stand out as sources. Jenny Diski's *Skating to Antarctica* (1997) is a work of memoiristic nonfiction tracking a journey to the far south and reflecting on Diski's personal history, in particular her relationship with her mother. J. M. Coetzee's *Elizabeth Costello* (2003) is a novel about a celebrated Australian writer travelling the world to hear and deliver lectures. These are both texts set in the Southern Hemisphere: Diski is a traveller from the north to the south, while Costello travels from south to north as well as south to south. This geography is essential to the texts' explorations of personal history, familial connections and the origins and stability of identity.

Skating to Antarctica is established as a kind of anti-travel writing. The author-character Diski introduces herself as inveterately indolent and disinclined to adventure, restlessness and all the other motivations familiar to the male European mode of travel writing which she quietly refutes. She does not set out to Antarctica with ideas of history or grand metaphor to explore but for petty, personal reasons, albeit laced with a kind of literalized symbolism: a longing for oblivion and obsession with whiteness, both autodiagnosed as originating in her time spent in psychiatric wards as a teenager. In this sense, she is ultimately disappointed: Antarctica, when she gets there by cruise ship, is vivid and rambunctious. She finds a more redolent oblivion in her anonymous cabin on the ship, in which she relishes holing up.

The far south, contrary to expectations, is variously and awkwardly real. Diski savours this kind of disappointment: 'I am not averse to disappointment. It has its own special pleasures. Disappointment is the hidden agenda within fantasy, a nugget for the *afficionado* who might trick up the bland negativity of the word by sliding alphabetically towards *disjunction* and *disparity*.'[4] I liked the idea of this real south as a further inversion of *Frankenstein*'s symbolic north. I also liked the idea of a less than purposeful, tentative journey against the brazen, pathbreaking ambition of Walton's. In Diski I found a likable, irritable, sharp, retiring and unromantic protagonist, remote in every sense from the tragic individual at the centre of *Frankenstein*.

Most of all, I found an intriguing disquietude in the way her life story was transmitted, sharing pagination with a travelogue, inside a self-conscious piece of writing and publishing. The trip to Antarctica forms one thread of the book while the other comprises a memoir of Diski's childhood and her relationship with her now estranged, and possibly deceased, mother. The two are interwoven without overlap, understood to be coeval but never explicitly connected. What is at first a travelogue turns out also to be life writing; the first seems to facilitate or occasion the second. In a gesture typical of Diski, she foregrounds the commissioning and production of the text: 'The book I was going to write about the trip, and my mother, was to be my first full-length non-fiction, it had been agreed.'[5] Writing fits into a frank chain of causality as a profession, a habit and a means of access; an answer to her originating question, 'How can I get to Antarctica?'[6]

Elizabeth Costello, like Diski, is an atypical literary traveller. The novel *Elizabeth Costello* opens as she arrives in Pennsylvania to collect a literary prize. Much is made of her age and ungainliness and tiredness as she traipses around the globe. When she receives an opportunity to speak on a cruise ship travelling from Christchurch to Cape Town, though, it is 'an offer she cannot refuse'.[7] Like Diski, she longs to see the Antarctic – 'those vast horizons, that barren waste'.[8] She has her own idea of a kind of oblivion, which, in its own ways, will not be met. In Pennsylvania, on the cruise ship and later in Amsterdam, Costello is employed to give lectures. These occasions for speaking form the structure of the novel and the core of several chapters (styled as 'Lessons'). Wherever she goes, people are anxious to hear what Elizabeth thinks – she is a major writer – but are usually disappointed. She talks about realism and animal rights rather than her most famous novel. The ideas in *Elizabeth Costello* – those held by and explored in depth in her lectures – are always framed, and often made ironic, by the circumstances of their delivery. In one representative moment at the podium, 'She is not sure, as she listens to her own voice, whether she believes any longer what she is saying.'[9]

Coetzee problematizes the idea of 'pure' ideas, portraying them as inescapably situated in time, context and company. His peripatetic novel also suggests they may be shaped by places. Costello is a writer of the south – an Australian – navigating a contemporary environment of globalized, anonymous locations: airports, hotels, cruise ships, universities. In Coetzee's telling, these are not so much places where geographic identity disintegrates as places where tenacious geographic identities butt surreally against each other: a wristwatch set aside on a bedside table in Pennsylvania still runs on Canberra time; a Nigerian author and an Australian author reencounter each other some miles off the Ross Ice Shelf in the Antarctic Sea. The novel invites the reader to consider how ideas are inflected by the relationship between countries and hemispheres – by geopolitics, colonial hangovers, literary heritages, jetlags – and, in finer geography, by the relationship between speaker and audience within a lecture hall: the pressures of expectation, reputation, overheated or overcooled rooms, unfamiliar acoustics, a speaker's fee, an impending dinner with the provost.

It is interesting that both these texts preoccupied by the ways writing and thinking are occasioned – in terms of context, company, geography, time and financing – have earlier iterations in different circumstances. *Elizabeth Costello*'s first appearance was in two lectures Coetzee was invited to give at Princeton; not unlike Elizabeth Costello surprising her audience with a lecture on animal rights, Coeztee surprised his audience with (to all appearances) a short story about an Australian writer named Elizabeth Costello. Earlier rumblings of Costello's ideas about animals can also be found in texts by Coetzee, such as an essay for the 'Food' issue of *Granta* written from Texas: another commission, another location, another readership, another set of conventions to meet or thwart.[10]

Skating to Antarctica meanwhile was preceded by an article Diski published in the *London Review of Books*, which recounts much the same narrative with a subtle variation.[11] In the book, as the cruise finally approaches the Antarctic continent, bad weather looks liable to prevent the passengers from making landfall. Diski delights in the idea of coming all the way and not arriving, and of being the only person to know whether she did. Ultimately, she does not make clear whether she 'arrived'. This fading out forms the book's climax in concert with the emergence of inversely concrete information about her mother (that she has died) which Diski had been evading discovering. In the *LRB* article, however, Diski does arrive: she sets foot on the ground at Hope Bay, into a crevasse hidden by snow which seems to offer 'an assurance … that I am where I am'. To ask which telling is the true version would not be irrelevant but would miss the sense that one suits (is *true to*) the form of the long-form personal essay while another functions in the larger frame of the book. Each is shaped by its telling. Indeed, the realization ultimately drawn out in the book version of *Skating* is self-reflexive: that 'there are infinite ways of telling the truth, including fiction, and infinite ways of evading the truth, including non-fiction'.[12]

The lineages of both texts reflect an idea of writing as work, as situated in the world, emphasizing the way the texts in their final forms embody these concerns. The south is a setting in these texts not just for events but for writing: it is where Costello speaks, and while in the north is perceived as speaking 'from'; where Diski travels under the influence of instinct, and where she untangles some of her own life story. The way both play with and ironize their forms – a 'full-length non-fiction' in which the author knowingly excludes information; a novel made of 'Lessons' full of prolix philosophizing

– echoes this sense of situation. I wanted to capture this quality of double embodiment in *Two-Body Problem* – a text bound to its location in the world and in itself, one in which the unfolding, the writing itself, is the drama.

Elizabeth Costello begins by invoking the 'problem' of 'how to get us from where we are … to the far bank'. This 'far bank' is, we take it, fiction. This idea of farness then reverberates through the book: again as 'the far territory' of fiction, and then in a question Costello is asked by a journalist about writing, as an Australian, from the 'the far edges'.[13] Gesturing through the interviewer to one provincializing association of the south with farness, *Elizabeth Costello* finds a richer resonance in this condition. It dramatizes distances between places and people as tensions inherent to communication, understanding expression as always between two defined and real locations – rather than between a firm (e.g., northern) point and a vague, extending (e.g., southern) horizon – just as it understands expression as always between a speaker and a listener (or writer and reader).

Diski also uses the south to remind of the locatedness of writing. Where a different European travel writer might see in the far south an emptiness ripe for interpretation and mythologizing, Diski finds astringent reality at the other end of her world. *Skating to Antarctica* describes not a revelation facilitated by a symbolic extremity but rather a pragmatic wrangling with reality, the interrelation of knowledge and uncertainty, memory and speculation, fact and fiction, involved in understanding one's life. It understands life writing (even life) as one of Diski's relishable disappointments. It is a book preoccupied by another kind of distance – distance from one's family, from one's life, from one's self – which, like in *Elizabeth Costello*, is ultimately vindicated as a way of knowing rather than an impediment to it.

In *Two-Body Problem*, the remoteness and the realness of the south are used as a source of some horror. If in *Frankenstein* the far north was the terrifying, shapeless, infinite of human capability, I wanted to explore the differently terrifying idea of tangible, observable reality. I explored the horror of one's creation having a kind of mundane, intractable existence, a mute agency: a factuality. (*Elizabeth Costello* has some of this: Costello's popular first novel seems to lead a persistent independent life years after she wrote it, and Elizabeth too can seem a recalcitrant, unruly creation of Coetzee's, never more so than when she wanders unexpectedly into his subsequent novel, *Slow Man* [2005].)

I also wanted to use the south to dramatize and – by the play's end – confuse notions of where the text was speaking 'to' and 'from'. Like the letters that constitute *Frankenstein*, the performance of *Two-Body Problem* (the words spoken by Lynne to the audience) is given a fictional reason for being in itself. It always refers to the dialogic set-up that is its premise, spatialized in the theatre, between the single performer and (experientially, grammatically) singular audience. These are the essentials of theatre: director Peter Brook's description of the most basic 'act of theatre' was: 'a man walks across [an] empty space whilst someone else is watching him'.[14] I did not register until after we finished performances how the title of *Two-Body Problem* evokes this famous formulation, but the connection is salient: I was trying to draw on something inherent to theatre in my one-person play, highlighting – staging – the way the character's performance is affected by the fact of audience and their spatial relation. The title of the play also references the two-character paradigm at the heart of *Frankenstein*. With a one-woman show, I wanted to evoke the two-person drama of *Frankenstein*, summoning up with one actor the spectre of the absent, anticipated second. (When I pitched the play to the Museum, the commissioners' first question was 'When will we see the monster?')

The dialogic situation is a source of drama and, for my character, anxiety, but in *Two-Body Problem*, and in Diski's and Coetzee's texts, I see liberating potential too. If we think about writing, especially any kind of life writing, through the dialogic, polar formulations of north–south, performer–audience, speaker–listener (if we think about it as a two-body problem), it could show itself to be an enabling, revelatory situation – far more than a claustrophobic entrapment. It could instantiate what Arabella Kurtz describes in psychoanalysis – another formalized, spatialized type of dialogue – in conversation with Coetzee: 'a theory of human interrelatedness, a theory of relationships that emphasises … how people need other people to understand, and indeed in order to learn to be, themselves'.[15] A listener helps us understand ourselves by making us a speaker; the north takes form with respect to the south; an audience makes your walk into a performance. In these frameworks action becomes expression.

Along all the lines I have described, *Two-Body Problem* is unavoidably a piece of life writing of my own. I wrote it immediately after returning to the town I was born in, Oxford, after six months in Buenos Aires, during which I also travelled in Patagonia as far south as Punta Arenas, with its mottled grey skies, cormorants, lumpen statues, distant tankers, sushi restaurants, its postcards showing Antarctica Chileno. In Buenos Aires, the jacaranda trees, the warm November nights, my friend's kind relatives, the blatant and obscured colonial history all made me think about the latitudinally close place where my own family has roots, a few generations deep. Sentences and thoughts in the play overlap with my diaries as well as parts of emails I sent friends, postcards I sent home and texts I wrote before and since under other auspices. It is a piece of reasonably extravagant fiction, but as I began by observing, it is also inevitably a product of my own self – a fact so obvious it barely needs stating, yet strange, if I think about it, and a little ghostly.

I have reflected above on ideas and questions behind my play *Two-Body Problem* – some which I was cognisant of trying to work into my writing, others which become clearer with distance, and when the play is placed in conversation with other texts which I am in the useful position of knowing were especially meaningful to its writer. The far south, with its associations with scientific projects and exploration, historic and present, provided a rich setting for a narrative about research and creation. These associations also laid the foundations for exploring how selfhood and self-understanding might be tied to creation, and specifically the way a self might be discerned and even illuminated among the tissue of writing – or any form of expression – meant to be impersonal. This slippage between forms, and the ways such forms are occasioned, are illuminated by Diski's and Coetzee's genre-confounding texts. As in these books, the geography of the south in the play underpins the sense in which the communication it depicts is situated between a 'from' and 'to'. These dialogic models of south–north and speaker–listener are dramatized by the performer–audience dynamic of a one-person show, which draws an ambivalent attention to its form. *Two-Body Problem* presents a drama of self-estrangement as a character contends with her own performance. Taking it in the company of influences which suggest a wary but vindicating sensitivity for remoteness, I am also encouraged to consider the possibility of engaging such a process more or less deliberately, of seeing self-estrangement as a means to life writing: writing to become an other, or a creature; to see oneself from the far bank.

Notes

1. Martha Skye Murphy played this part in all performances and was extensively involved with developing the character in rehearsal.
2. Among my sources for this picture of Antarctica were the two texts discussed in detail below, especially Jenny Diski's *Skating to Antarctica*, as well as conversations with people who had overwintered on Antarctica, researchers at the Scott Polar Research Institute in Cambridge, scholars of Captain Scott and others.
3. My key reference for the realities of this was Mark O'Connell's book *To Be a Machine* (London: Granta, 2017).
4. Jenny Diski, *Skating to Antarctica* (London: Virago, 1997), 7.
5. Diski, *Skating to Antarctica*, 220.
6. Ibid., 5.
7. J. M. Coetzee, *Elizabeth Costello* (London: Vintage, 2003), 36.
8. Ibid., 35.
9. Ibid., 39.
10. J. M. Coetzee, 'Meat Country', *Granta* 52 (winter 1995).
11. Jenny Diski, 'A Feeling for Ice', *London Review of Books* 19, no. 1 (2 January 1997).
12. Diski, *Skating to Antarctica*, 220.
13. It is recalled a final time toward the novel's close as 'the far side of the gate', suggesting some form of afterlife in the book's allegorical penultimate chapter.
14. Peter Brook, *The Empty Space* (London: Penguin, [1968] 2008), 9.
15. J. M. Coetzee and Arabella Kurtz, *The Good Story* (London: Penguin, 2015), 175.

Bibliography

Brook, Peter. *The Empty Space*. London: Penguin, [1968] 2008.
Coetzee, J. M. *Elizabeth Costello*. London: Vintage, 2003.
Coetzee, J. M. 'Meat Country'. *Granta* 52 (winter 1995): 41–52.
Coetzee, J. M., and Arabella Kurtz. *The Good Story*. London: Penguin, 2015.
Diski, Jenny. 'A Feeling for Ice'. *London Review of Books* 19, no.1 (2 January 1997). Available online: https://www.lrb.co.uk/the-paper/v19/n01/jenny-diski/a-feeling-for-ice.
Diski, Jenny. *Skating to Antarctica*. London: Virago, 1997.
O'Connell, Mark. *To Be a Machine*. London: Granta, 2017.

CHAPTER 20
MOGAU GRACE
Khutso Mabokela

The story Mogau Grace imaginatively reflects on my painful experiences as a South African woman born in the mid-1980s. It weaves and braids the story of my life with those of my maternal grandmother who died in my arms when I turned thirty, my mother who had me out of wedlock when she was twenty and the description of the township of Mankweng near Polokwane in the Limpopo Province of South Africa where I grew up and still live. Combining autobiographical and biographical material of marginalized women and a place that shaped me, the piece thinks through multiple southern-ness by depicting the typical emotional and physical violence that an ordinary South African township woman encounters. The story provocatively and playfully employs the motifs of god(s) and dream(s) to capture my inability to fully grasp my life's experiences in relation to my aspirations. Through the story, I contemplate how my unfulfilling romantic relationships and experience of gang rape have affected me and the way I respond to the world.

1994. Amazing grace. Mandela becomes god. The black god. Worshipped by all. The University of the North in Mankweng was to become the University of Limpopo. Steadily blackening. The great imperceptible out migration of white lecturers and support staff. The university becoming chimney coloured. Mankweng is reborn as a university township. The Grahamstown of Limpopo. The Stellenbosch of the far north. Minus Rhodes. Without Afrikaners. Malectures is born. The lecturers' own patch in Zone 1. The avalanche of in migration of black instructors. Equipped with bookish education and residing near the university. Polokwane is 30 kilometres. Too far away. Only white lecturers had viewed it as nearby. The elite Malectures developed fast and was designed for upper civil servants and university lecturers. There was goodwill from the moneyed white world and Mandela was not radical. His defiance had been tamed when his choppers were surgically removed. Slow slicing. Twenty-seven years in the inner sanctuary of white gods' violence had led to a steady damascene process. South Africa was big enough for everyone. South Africa belongs to all its residents. Amandla! The fist of worship limps in the air. Its muscles tortured by the relentless microscopic venom from white fangs.

Like Mandela, I became a god. A tiny powerful god. Mandela discovered his godship in the holy of holies of apartheid's iron chambers. I became a god by falling in and out of love. The brutality of men turned into a rock. Solid rock god. When adolescence becomes a trickle. Adolescents are believers, says one clever person. Their rebellion and fearlessness are an expression of deep belief. My burning adolescent romance was belief. I believed in love. In unity and completeness. In absolutes. Like Mandela of the fifties and sixties. He fell in love with freedom, and when he came out of prison, South Africa had become big enough for all. I fell into rebellious love and when I emerged, I was Mandela. Transformed by prison bonds. My thighs bare and bloodied, my adolescent belief flaccid at half-mast. Dead inside. Killed by manacles of romance.

Lovers die and get killed. Gods are not lovers and do not fall in or out of love. Gods thrive on worship and being worshipped. I am a god now because I don't fall in love, and I am nobody's lover. They all hide their faces in reverence when they discover the god I am. That I don't die. That I died and lived again. That they killed me. That I love and give love even to those who don't deserve it. That I am powerful. Uncontrollable. Controlling. Dictatorial, loving dictator. That things must be done my way because I want it that way.

I am a desired god. Making others desire. Levinas was correct: 'Desire is absolute if the desiring being is mortal and the Desired invisible.' A beautiful woman is a god, invisible. Men desire my approval. They worship me. My slightly plagiarized formulation: Worship is absolute if the worshipping beings are men and the worshipped is me. In their thousands. I thrive on their supplications. Their petitions expand my divinity. I listen to them all. I answer a few. The ones that serve my purpose and match my will. That is what gods do, they cannot be dictated to. Gods need all prayers, but they are not obliged to indulge everyone. I must be wanted. Exclusively so. I want devoted men. Worshippers. Me alone they should adore. I lose power with one missed adoration.

A god is worshipped best when dead; that is why gods must die. I became god when my god died. She died in my arms. It is when you embrace the death of god that you start living. A flash of power and an instant of absolute powerlessness. A moment of invisibility for both her and myself. As she disappeared, I was shrouded with godliness. The death of god is a liberating moment and tears mark liberty, a release from the clutches of visibility. Watering the seed that gives birth to another god. When I germinated, sprouted, I produced luscious shoots. Dispensed love and ceased desiring. I became love.

Gods must be killed. Rendered imperceptible. I was slain by my worshippers and those who desired me absolutely. I died for desire so I could be desired. Gods are multiplied by death. I became a multiplicity. They splayed me. They knifed. Outside. Inside. On top. Underneath. Behind. In front. I became a wound. Multiple scars. A mutilated me. I wasn't afraid of dying. Either way I was dead. Whether I lived or died. My survival was my death. Death served me. I didn't perish. Like an animal. Animals can't be gods. They don't imagine and lack anticipation and retrospection. I flash backwards and forwards. Sideways I illuminate. Imperfectively.

Gods must have messengers. Spokespersons and puppets to render the invisible visible through words. Oh gods! As your worshipper-spokesperson, inspire me to inscribe and describe you into being. Blow your impelling breath into these fingers. Fingers that will create you in words. Stimulated by the invisible mind made visible by these very creative movements. Make me your chief creator through these graphic signs. Posterity must know of your mortality immortalized thus. Your immortality mortalized. Of your immorality moralized. Your moralized immorality. Of your beauty beautified. Beautified beauty. Let your beauty inspire a written refrain that will proclaim the creatorship of your creation. You are better worshipped when nailed thus to the pages of this ditty. Your nailer and spreader over the pages to come, let me be. Let me be your irreverent worshipper violator as your presence vanishes in this tale. For 'violence is writing'. A subjugation of emotions. Not their outlet. Chopping and grinding your being into a thousand particles. Myriads of symbols. Millions of signs to confound decipherers. Countless tracks that throw the tracker into a muddy dizzying eddy. Leaving only a swirling silhouette. An absence. A hole. A gap. An abyss for the reader to trip into. And never to recover balance.

Dreams

My dreams reveal that I know more than I am aware. They laugh at my conscious knowledge by exposing how much I know without knowing it. I fear this vast knowledge disclosed in my dreams. It's like being forced into a murky pool during a dark night. I feel a compulsion to tell this story. I am not in control. I cannot choose my dreams. Stories choose me. And when I tell them, I call them my stories. They are dreams. Unruly. Coming on their own.

I dream when I am awake as much as I do when sleeping. I forget most of my sleeping dreams. Only a few lurk until morning. When awake, my thoughts are my dreams. I don't conjure them up. They come unbidden. My thoughts tell me I am god and that I can recall them anytime I want to. But this is a dream. It's like a dream telling you: you are dreaming. One very clever guy said that we invent our friends in our dreams and immediately forget about it. He says we then proceed as if we are dealing with real persons, not those we have invented. The dreams I dream when I sleep and the dream I dream when awake continuously tell me I am in charge. But how can I when I know so much without knowing it?

Dreams are an imposition. I don't dream but I am one big dream. I don't choose my dreams, they come unbidden. Some gently, and others violently. Take my life. I didn't choose me. Things that happened to me. Most of them at least. I am a dream that just came. How can I control what came on its own? It takes whatever direction that it plotted for itself when it decided to come. Since coming to know I have thoughts, I have been one giant rolling dream ball. Getting bigger with each passing day as other dreams attach themselves to the original dream. Me.

I did not apply for me to come. But I came anyway. Some call me a gift. This is to sanitize dreams. I am a dream. However, I must forget this and imagine I am a gift. That there is meaning to everything. Unreproducible. Like a dream. I can't will myself to re-dream a dream. I can't undream myself out of the dream I am. Dream myself out of dreams, undoing the nightmare of natality, reversing conception, forgetting that I have been repeatedly entered, opened and closed and opened again, like a dilapidated South African township taxi. Carrying men with violent dreams to their dreamy comings. Only undreaming violence can achieve such because violence is the annihilation of dreaming. The undoing of dreams. Of life. To dream is to live. Stories are what make life and an untold life has not been lived. Life is inscribed in dreaming. Storytelling. A narrative.

My first love was not a dream. It was not dreaming. The muteness of my first love was violence. No story can be told of my first love. It didn't impose itself. I invited it in. I reproduced it again and again. Dreams come once. On their own. Singular. If I dream one dream twice, I dream. If I imagine telling the same story twice. I dream. Only violence repeats itself. Non-language is cyclical. Death repeats itself the same way. Language is a dream. Try telling a story twice and it mutates. Dreaming is living. Living is only done once. Living is unrepeatable. When you attempt replication, repetition, you get a mutant. Duplication is a non-life. It is a copy. Unoriginal. A violent image. A nightmare.

I was twenty and I met Mpilo. I dreamt him into existence and forgot he was my creation. For over two years, I kept the duplicating machine going. With the same results. I tried photocopying. Still no success. The colour copier gave me stunning copies. Close inspection revealed disappointing results. An original cannot be coaxed into existence from a copy. No matter how colourful. I had created him perfect. The imperfections were his. For two years, his obsessive and confessed cheating never led me to uncreate him. Undream him. Creations, like dreams, have a way of having minds of their own. I dreamt us faithful to each other. Giving us beautiful kids. Producing happy dreams together. I kept up with the dreams. He churned nightmares. The crevices of my dreams were there for him to inscribe his dreams. Our dreams. Instead, he kept piling hallucinations upon our dreams. Heaping violence into the delicate crannies of my dreams. His was a non-story. A no narrative. Beastly dumbness. After a dreamy two years, I deleted him. I muted my dreams. I shed my old skin and dreamt I had emerged renewed. I believed I was strong and invisibly invincible, rising from the ashes of my muted dreams.

Then Lufu rushed into my dreams. New love made me defiant. Dagga. Marijuana. Alcohol. Bliss. Nirvana. Lufu gave me all and more. I am possessed. My mother strongly disapproves and threatens to disown me. She chucks me out of the house. 9 pm. I have Lufu. I walk to Lufu's house. Into his arms. He will embrace me. Undo mother out of my existence. Township darkness lurks with prowling young men. Five accost me. I am defiant. This my hood. From childhood. I am not afraid of darkness. Of dark man. I fight with womanly courage. I am no match for the horny horns of excited young men. I become fair game. They knife. They poke. They thrust. Others close my mouth. Others spread my thighs. Ripping me open. As they take turns to mount and dismount. As they enter and exit. I die. They kill me. This is not a dream. It's death.

Big worshipped worshipper

Many years later I am resurrected. I am god. I start dreaming again. I am alive. I live. Gods always get what they want. Well, almost. My energies are pervasive but targeted. I knew this instinctively, but I got the opportunity to test this theory in a massive way. I had long passed the period of blissful waiting. Childhood. And the torturous believer stage. I am now an apprentice god. I am at university and just completed the first year of my MA degree. It is early in the year, and it is re-registration time for continuing post-graduate students. And the rest. But I neither had a bursary nor sponsorship in the previous year. I have stayed on campus, nevertheless. I have accumulated a combined debt for my tuition and accommodation fee that I can never dream of paying off on my own. The condition for continuing with my second year is that I must pay.

We are standing in long winding queues despite our indebtedness. Hoping against all hope that we would be allowed to register although we owe the university thousands. I am hoping that my good course work marks in the previous year will persuade some humane clerk to break institutional financial protocols and register me anyway. I am hoping to be served by some male clerk. I have seen them become blissful children when gods show face and flash hallowed smiles. Hoping against all common sense that they will be the ones to kill gods. I use this to the full. What is the use of having teeth if you are only going to drink milk?

Those with or without debt are all scrambling in the queues. Call it indefatigable African optimism. Then something wondrous happens. As I turn around in despair, I see a potential worshipper passing by with bodyguards, followers and all. A meat eater. No milk for that one. The teeth are too mature. 'I wonder how it would be like. To be worshipped by a god.' I dream. An expressed word, even to oneself, is a wish. It is more than a wish. It has magical force of self-propulsion to self-fulfillment if uttered by a trainee god. Words are actions. Actions have consequences.

Every place has a god. This god that I was now fixated on owned the university or almost and many other places besides. Gods inhabit multiple places and accumulate imperceptible invincibility through a multitude of worshippers. That is why gods are always wrestling each other for places. The fight for worshippers is real. Worshippers make gods. Gods get power from worshippers. Gods must dominate many places and peoples, as I was to learn soon. My words had expressed a wish to dominate a god of gods. God's commanding determination is irreversible. It always yields desired results. But what if gods' conflicting determinations converge? A storm. A cyclone. Destruction.

I captured the god. He settled my debt, and I was registered. I was ecstatic. The celebrations were premature. I had hoped to conquer god. Kill him. Give him heirs and secure my future. The god was averse to physical contact. His horn of salvation was limp. Overused to a point of uselessness. Dead. But the demands for nudes came with thunder and lightning like a storm over the city of gold. The god was hoping to revive his reign and raise his horn by gorging young worshippers' bodies. With his eyes. In all their desperate naked glory. For me, the effects were worse than the gang rape. I was asphyxiated to a point of breathlessness. Unable to delete the god or the permanent me that now filled his smartphone. Providing a private perverted feast for the women eater.

Adagio Mankweng

Outsiders see a blank, a uniformity when they look at Mankweng. It is homogeneous bliss and a place of waiting, a holding place. That is how I experienced it as a child. I thought nothing of it. There was nothing to think about. Children do not think. Children do not see place and don't fight for it. As a child, I saw Mankweng without seeing it. I felt it without feeling it. It touched me without me touching it. Its smells shaped me without me smelling them. Being in a womb must feel like that. Involuntarily meticulously crafted and being there without being there. Sheltered. Without a will.

Before the age of thirteen, Koko was my place. My womb. I had the unusual position of being both first and last born. Not as being the last child. I have siblings. Mother tells me that she sheltered me for nine months before she knew who I was. Later, I realized she continued to do so for seventeen years. Before I knew who I was. Like harbouring a stranger. Protected by a stranger. The outcome is unpredictable. My relationship with mother needs Freud. It's a dream. A statement uttered in jest. Why am I Koko's child although Mama sheltered me so long? And continues to protect me so. There must have been, there must be, an emotional absence. A gap. Snapped synapses. Aborted affection between strangers. It needs suturing with unremembered chains of love.

Mama was born in the vexed and vexing sixties in the laid-back rural area of Ga-Kgatla, a holding space for unwilling worshippers of the system. Pass laws. White gods were losing grip but keen on consolidating it. Worshippers were restive and agitated. Bent on worshipping other gods. There is no middle ground when it comes to worship. Voluntarily or under compulsion, you do it. Gods don't believe in democracy, and freewill has consequences either way. Willing worshippers must do the will of gods and dissenters must be punished.

1960. Sharpeville. White gods clash with dissenting black worshippers and sixty-nine are sacrificed. Many more escape the altar but have sizzling missiles lodging in or piercing through their skins. Tattooed. Branded. Marked for life. Emotional and psychological scarification and sclerotization the lot of all escapees, bystanders and perpetrators. The best of historians have their heads spinning trying to document the sixties. History is pitiable because it relies on facts. Where facts are absent, they must be invented since gaps are intolerable. The large-scale tragedy against blacks was a necessity to the birth of South Africa. There is no unity without catastrophe since terror unifies, and divides. Division and self-centredness can also be born of feelings of peace and security. Gods also gather and scatter worshippers.

Mama moved to Mankweng when she was about ten. The town was much smaller back then, packed with dissenting grumbling worshippers. Most people in Zone 1, the Mondlana Section, knew each other by name for they were brothers and sisters. Brutalized worshippers are united androids. Their violation overrides their internal differences. Ubuntu is a counter move. A coercion camouflaged as a way of life. Another viciousness. A god. Indiscernible. Indomitable. Umuntu must conform or be cast out from abantu. Few choose to be brutes. So, Ubuntu prevails.

I don't expect my mother to tell me about her childhood in the late sixties. Full nothingness is childhood. Filled by others. Others who were not children themselves. Childhood is unknowable. Piaget tried. Only to come up with suppositions. Mere gestures. With his children's childhoods passing by undented. Etched with a big question mark. For children are no mere imitators. They are additions. They add and complicate to the amusement and puzzlement of their coaches.

Koko tells me that my mother was a beautiful and well-loved child in the sixties and early seventies. The late seventies ushered in adolescence and Mama became an ardent believer. A worshipped worshipper. Worshippers are sheltered. In a blissful womb. Ubuntu saved her. Teenagers don't die but gods get killed. As soon as she turned nineteen, Mama met a god worshipped by many. Mama's god was a wordsmith, a radio man who charmed prospective worshippers with a liquid voice and sugary tongue. Oily sweetness as to the ears of young women and everywhere else. Mama was determined to make that smoothness lubricate only her ears and send willed chills through her body. Beauty and determination have killed many arrogant gods and transmogrified them into dumb grunting mutes. The death of gods created me. It is when gods die that I come to life, making me a big new god.

The mutual death of gods created life in the mid-eighties. Mankweng in the 1980s. South Africa and townships on fire. Sacrifices everywhere. The acrid and angry incense of burning tyres. Gods are fond of smoke of cremated screaming mutilated worshippers. New gods must be resurrected from tyre cinders. Pitch black. To relinquish their godship, white gods wanted human sacrifice. To allow black gods to be born, they demanded white ashes from incinerated black bodies. I come to life when gods are dying and when gods get killed. I was there but absent in the eighties. Childhood memories are supplements. Extensions of other people's presences. The mid- and late eighties come to me in blurred black and white flashing pictures. Part of the generation of the freedom bound. The Joshuas. Moses had to die and be buried by God. Rendered invisible to be better worshipped.

Mama talks of her death and of her god in staccatos and forced downloads. The bandwidth is limited. It's Africa. Ubuntu prevails. Certain matters are not for babies' ears. Babies can hear music but can't sing. They only sing later in imitation of their teachers. But they don't produce originals. The original is always lacking, demanding to be augmented. In vain Ubuntu tries to prevail on children to sing the original and stop them from chanting their parents' deaths. That should always remain visibly invisible. The speakable unspeakable.

Mankweng is a universe. To its residents. Those who were born and have died there are like tiny insects on a patch of grass at the back of Koko's place which has been my home since birth. Most of Mankweng's residents are born there and carry out the business of being infants, babies, children, adolescents, adults and parents right there. The occupation of living and the inevitable process of ageing and the event of death all occur there on that tiny patch. It's a world where battles are fought, lost and won. Transitional life ceremonies are planned and executed right there. There are gods and worshippers, and gods fight for devout worshippers and rebellious worshippers are subdued and tamed.

Travelling to distant greener patches in other yards is a mission that must be carefully planned and carefully thought in advance. Border jumping is unthinkable. There are razor wired and electrified fences and gates manned by muscled and heavily armed guards. Intrusion, infringement can lead to death. Without proper entry ceremonies one better stay at home or risk being torn to pieces attempting a futile forceful entry. Most are compelled to stay at home within Koko's patch. Patching for the rest of their lives.

Adolescents refuse to stay put on Koko's patch because they are energetic eccentrics. They are believers. Other patches must be explored and conquered. Their patch must be supplemented and patched. To hell with entry and exit rites. We will right the wrongs of grown-ups. Grown-ups with their myopic rules and regulations. In their imaginations they see dangers everywhere. They imagine armed merciless border guards who are ready to extort and maim intruders. It's their strategy of making us stay on their dry patch. Adolescents are believers keen on patching up the world, wanting to mend it for and with love.

The greener the patch, the bigger the killer insects. Armed with incisors ready to slice you in half. Or if you barely escape you will be oozing blood from all vital organs. Effecting a lingering death caused by a thousand cuts. Mankweng, Zone 1, the elite area is subdivided into two patches, the Mondlana and Malectures. Mondlana derives its power from tradition. It's the oldest and everything began there, a point of origin. All orientations are taken from there. The ancestors of Mankweng and their descents stay there, and Koko's house is here. Even in townships, respect accrues to those who belong to the oldest lineages. They become the de facto chiefs, chieftains and gods. They are tradition and repositories of all kinds of memories, especially the ones relating to catastrophe. It is recalling calamities that makes a community. Those who remember them; the custodians of tragic memories are owed respect. The community would disintegrate without them so they must stay put content with their spiritual riches. Self-respected and self-protecting. Self-venerating and sometimes despised. The Mondlanas. The Mondlana patch was occupied by the lower service staff of the university during the University of the North days. The Mondlanas became royals among the black people because they worked alongside white people. Royalty through association and I too became royal.

Mankweng. Mondlana. Zone 1. Disjointed visions of Koko holding my little hand. The crèche was only 500 metres from home. Koko loves me. Loved. Only lovers hold hands, but enemies sometimes kiss. Connecting and connected. Forced intimacy. Love speaks more eloquently when it is mute and when it articulates itself in signs and gestures. That is how Koko and I loved each other. Words came later as inferior supplements. My Koko's last born and for nine years the only child. Mogau Grace.

Koko

Moses says anything after seventy is extra time and with extraordinary stamina eighty but glutted with pain and nostalgia. He spoke from experience for he was given fifty extra and he was oversupplied with drama, rebellion and rebelliousness. The slaves he freed never wanted freedom. They preferred meat, fish from the Nile, cucumbers, garlic and leeks. Nostalgia sanitizes the past and makes the present unbearable and the future unthinkable. But gods want worshippers. So, Moses forced them through water, womblike, over the mountain and the desert to the plains of Moab. However, the majority only caressed the thresholds of Canaan and two out of the millions of the original dissenting worshippers licked honey and drank milk of the promised land. The rest finding a permanent abode on the altar of starvation, disease, divine disasters and lack of extra time. Unlike Moses's abundance, Koko was given threescore and fifteen years.

Koko was always Koko to me and it strikes me now how young she was when I was born. Nine shy of threescore. I have a lot of worshippers who are older than that! The woman eater is in fact much older. Was much older when he consumed me. When I killed him. When we both died. Or almost. Koko was just thirty-eight when Ntatemoholo died. That young. She had barely started living already with six children. I always wondered why Koko never remarried. Now I realize that it was because of all the children. A woman with a lot of kids repels potential worshippers. No matter how beautiful. Men are like male lions. Given an opportunity they would kill the offspring of another man. They still kill without killing. Koko decided to keep her children alive. Koko opted for death rather than live without her kids and so she died before sixty.

She came back to life as god. Lutheran. Over four hundred years of rebellion. Salvation equals divine grace. No papas. Just God and the Bible. Her favourite hymn to Him:

'Amazing grace, how sweet the sound'

1 Amazing grace, how sweet the sound,
That saved a wretch like me!
I once was lost, but now am found;
Was blind, but now I see.
2 'Twas grace that taught my heart to fear,
And grace my fears relieved;
How precious did that grace appear
The hour I first believed!
3 Through many dangers, toils, and snares
I have already come;
'Tis grace has brought me safe thus far,
And grace will lead me home.[1]

John Newton's exclamatory statement of redemption and re-conversion penned in 1772 at sea as a captain of a slave ship. A flash of redemption converted him into an abolitionist and humanist. He became a friend of Wilberforce through the amazing grace of god. This tune was perfected by slaves in the American South. It was sung before the 'I have a dream' by Martin Luther King and after Mandela's release from prison. Through the turbulent sea of life, Koko was kindness itself because of God's grace. In the stormy arranged marriage and tempestuous widowhood she remained charity personified, insisting that thinking of others is the best way of thinking of oneself. As far as I remember, our home was Park Station. Marabastad Taxi Rank. Where destinations begun, arrivals multiplied hastily, and departures executed with great reluctance. Grace carried Koko in the seventies as a lonely but resolute young widow with half a dozen of young ones all under seventeen. Koko worked methodically without rest to provide for her big young family. Never shouting when in pain. Never lacking anything essential but always frugal. Everything is from god and everything is god. Koko was godly content.

Koko is my teacher. Only those who have lived can die and only those who have died can live. I am alive because I have died several times. Those who have not lived, fetuses, babies and young children, don't die. They simply expire. Like machines, they cease operating without having lived. I live because I am in touch with ancestors. I am an ancestor because Koko died in my hands. Koko died because she had lived, and she lives because she died. Koko lives through me, and she lives in me. I live in Koko, and she is truly there. I was born the day Koko died.

Acknowledgements

For constructive interest, creative advice and intellectual and moral support, my sincere thanks are to my 'dude', Isaac Ndlovu.

Note

1. 'Amazing Grace' was written by John Newton in 1772 and published in 1779 in Newton's and Cowper's *Olney Hymns*, page 53.

INDEX

abolitionists *see* Newton, John ('Amazing Grace'); Pringle, Thomas
Aboriginal people (Australia)
  indigenous languages 14, 18–19, 22, 54, 59–60
  The Town Grew Up Dancing: The Life and Art of Wenten Rubuntja (Rubuntja) 53, 54, 55, 58–60, 61
abyssal lines 67, 69–70, 72
abyssal metaphors 71–2, 73, 74–5
Adelie Blizzard 194, 195
'Adélie Land Band' 189
Adivasi people 53, 57
  see also Mayilamma: The Life of a Tribal Eco-warrior
Afrikaaps language 19
Aguirre Cerda, Pedro 40
Alberdi, Juan Bautista (*Memoria descriptiva sobre Tucumán*) 106–7
Albrow, Martin 123
Alfred and Emily (Lessing) 28–9
'Amazing Grace' (Newton) 287
amity lines 69, 70, 73
Andaman and Nicobar Islands, Indian Ocean tsunami (2004) 132–5, 136
Andrews, Joseph (*Journey from Buenos Aires*) 106
Angola 146, 148, 163
  in *The Return of the Water Spirit, Kianda* 147, 148, 152
'Anna's Cabinet of Curiosities' (Hersko) 179, 180, 181, *181*
'Anna's Invisible Objects' (Hersko) 180, *181*
Antarctica
  connectedness to South America (fiction from Argentina and Chile) 42, 43–4, 103, 105, 109
  isolation, European narratives of 103, 104, 109
  nature/humanity, dual qualities of 270
  and the poetry of Elizabeth Bradfield 171, 182–3
  remoteness 215–18, 220–1, 233, 275
  scientific projects and exploration, associations with 270, 276
  The Rime of the Ancient Mariner (Coleridge) 218, 219
  in *Two-Body Problem* (Rogers) 269, 270, 271, 272
  see also Australasian Antarctic Expedition (AAE, 1911–14); British Antarctic Expedition (1910–13); Chilean Antarctic Expedition (1947); Lewis Williams, Elizabeth; *Skating to Antarctica* (Diski); Southern Ocean

Antártica: una visión gráfica del continente helado (*Antarctica: A Graphic View of the Frozen Continent*) (Coloane) 45–6
Antártica (Chilean Antarctic Institute) 45
Anthropocene 1, 131, 136, 182
Aotearoa/New Zealand 13, 14, 25, 26, 27, 30–4, 116
apartheid, resistance to 247, 248
Aradale Psychiatric Hospital (Ararat Hospital for the Insane) 201, 207, 208–9
Arctic Ocean 104
Ardener, Edwin 216
Argentina
  Antarctica, connectedness with (non-fiction travel narratives) 103, 105–9
  Antarctica, tensions with Chile 40, 41
  conceptions of the literary south (Coetzee) 115, 116, 118, 121, 122
  San Martín National University (UNSAM) 115, 119, 125
Arrernte language, representation (in *The Town Grew Up Dancing*) 54, 59–60
as-told-to life narratives 53, 55
  see also Mayilamma: The Life of a Tribal Eco-warrior; *Town Grew Up Dancing, The: The Life and Art of Wenten Rubuntja* (Rubuntja)
At the Head of the Stream (as the original title for Marechera's *The House of Hunger*) 159–60, 161, 162, 164, 165
At the Mountains of Madness (Lovecraft) 104
Aurora 187
'Aurora Australis' (McLean) 190
Austen, Chris (*The House of Hunger*, 1983 film) 165
Australasian Antarctic Expedition (AAE, 1911–14)
  musical instruments 187, *188*
  music for motivation and comfort 192–5, *194*, 197
  music in routine expeditionary life 187–92, *189*, 196
  opera (*The Washerwoman's Secret*) 195–6, *195*
  wireless telegraphy and Jeffryes 201, 202–6, 208
  see also Mawson, Douglas
Australia
  conceptions of the south (Coetzee and Heine) 115, 116, 117, 118, 122, 124
  dilly (dhili) bags 15–18, *16*, *17*
  Indigenous languages 14, 18–19, 22
  as part of the economic north 53, 123
  'southern' forms of life writing (*yarning*) 3

Index

The Town Grew Up Dancing: The Life and Art of Wenten Rubuntja (Rubuntja) 53, 54, 55, 58–60, 61
   see also Australasian Antarctic Expedition (AAE, 1911–14)
autobiography see Frame, Janet; Lessing, Doris; *Los pasos del hombre: Memorias* (*The Footsteps of Man: Memories*) (Coloane); *Mayilamma: The Life of a Tribal Eco-warrior*; *Melina Rorke: Her Amazing Experiences in the Stormy Nineties of South Africa's Story Told by Herself* (Rorke); *Mogau Grace* (Mabokela); *Town Grew Up Dancing, The: The Life and Art of Wenten Rubuntja* (Rubuntja)
autotopographical objects 27–8, 30, 31, 34
   Alfred Tayler's prosthetic leg 28–30
   George Frame's war souvenirs 28, 30–4

Baartman, Sarah 240, 249
Bachelard, Gaston de 173, 175–6
Bage, Robert 'Bob' 193
Balfour, Graham 74
Banks, Richard Isaac ('John, John, John, go and put your little trousers on') 192
Bannister, Saxe (*Humane Policy*) 242, 243
Barnes, David Perry 41
Barrow, John (*Travels into the Interior of South Africa*) 241
baskets see dilly (dhili) bags
Bauman, Zygmunt 123
'Becoming Shaman' (Lewis Williams) 230–1
Benet, Juan 120–1
Benjamin, Walter 258
Berlant, Lauren 175
Bernal, Martin 72
Bernard, Penny 149
'Between My Father and the King' (Frame) 32–3
Bhabha, Homi 262
Bianchini, Federico (*Antaiártida: 25 días encerrado en el hielo* (*Antarctica: 25 Days Locked Up in the Ice*)) 109
Big Oil (Nigeria) 82, 84–5, 86, 87, 88
Black Insider, The (Marechera) 163–4
Blecher, Sara (*Otelo Burning*) 147
Bloom, Lisa 180
blue hemisphere 1
blue water novels 138–9, 140
Boehmer, Elleke
   birth of niece 21
   Empire, the National, and the Postcolonial, 1890–1920 2, 20–1, 27
   'The Father Antenna' 22 n. 4
   on J. M. Coetzee 117
Bolsonaro, Jair 92

Borges, Jorge Luis 117, 120, 121, 122
Bose, Sugata (*A Hundred Horizons*) 133
Bossema, Wim 158, 165
Bourke, Richard 242
Bower, Birdie 179
Bradfield, Elizabeth (*Toward Antarctica*)
   'Intertidal' 171
   'Letter Home' to 'America' 182–3
Brazilian Northeast 91–2, 93, 94, 95–6, 97, 98
Britain
   Antarctic claims 40, 46, 104, 105, 108, 110 n. 6
   British writers and Argentinian Antarctic writings 105, 106, 107, 109
   and oil (in Nigeria) 84, 86
   Saro-Wiwa family 83
   see also British Antarctic Expedition (1910–13); British Empire
British Antarctic Expedition (1910–13) 171
   and Hersko's narrative artwork 171, 179–81, *180*, *181*
   scientific investigations 171, 177–9
   Scott's *Terra Nova* base hut 172–7, *174*, 179–80, *180*, *181*
   wireless equipment 202
British Empire
   Andaman and Nicobar islands 132
   British identity of the Australian explorers (AAE, 1911–14) 190, 191
   Cape Colony (and Stuurman) 239, 241, *244–5*, 242–6, 247
   New Zealand (in Frame's autobiographical writing) 25, 26, 27, 30–4
   white settlement promotion schemes 26–7
   wireless technology 203
   see also British Antarctic Expedition (1910–13); Southern Rhodesia (British colony)
British Empire Exhibitions (Wembley, 1924, 1925) 25, *26*
Brown, Bill 33
Bulawayo, representation in *Melina Rorke: Her Amazing Experiences in the Stormy Nineties of South Africa's Story Told by Herself* (Rorke) 257, 258–63, 264
Burger, Lynton (*She Down There*) 145, 149–50, 153

'Cabo de Hornos (Cape Horn)' (Coloane) 42
Calderón Le Joliff, Tatiana 41
'Calling the Antarctic' (Lewis Williams) 222–3
Campos, Marcio D'Olne 3
Campt, Tina 241
Cape Colony/Cape of Good Hope (and Stuurman) 239, 241, *244–5*, 242–3, 247
Cape Evans (*Terra Nova*) base hut 172–7, *174*, 179–80, *180*, 181

Index

Cape Horn (Coloane) 39
'Captain Scott writing his diary. 7 October 1911' (Ponting) 174
carbon emissions 181, 215
Cardone, Ignacio 104–5
cartographic thinking *see* metaphorical cartography
cartography, maps of Antarctica 217, 235 n. 31
Casanova, Pascale 115, 118, 119, 120–1, 122
Casey, Edward S. 176
Castro, Ines E. de 95
Castro, Josué de 91, 92–3, 93–4, 95, 96, 98, 99
Catelli, Nora 121
Ceitelis, Jack 45
Chakrabarty, Dipesh 136, 137
Challenger, Melanie 181
Cherry-Garrard, Apsley (*The Worst Journey in the World*) 172, 176–7, 178
Chile
    and Coetzee's conception of 'the south' 115, 118, 121
    Coloane and Chilean Antarctic Expedition (1947) 39–47
    fiction from (connecting South America with Antarctica) 42, 43–4, 103, 105, 109
    and the south as a literary region 116, 121, 124
Chilean Antarctic Expedition (1947) 40, 41, 42–7
Chilenos en la Antártica (*Chileans in the Antarctic*) (Vila Labra) 43
'Chronicling the Devastation' *see* 'Town by the Sea, The' (Ghosh)
Clarke, Marcus 243
climate change
    carbon emissions 181, 215
    and the 'centrality of the improbable' in fiction 131, 137, 138, 139, 140
    Chakrabarty on 136, 137
    Ghosh's non-fiction life writing 132–5, 136, 137, 138
    India 131
    new styles of humanities research 145
    unequal distribution 136
Coca-Cola, Plachimada dispute 56, 57
'Codes (2)' (Lewis Williams) 226
Coetzee, J. M.
    Elizabeth Costello 117, 269, 272, 273–4, 275
    'Global South', terminology 2, 123
    Hispanic south 115, 116, 117–18, 119–20, 121–5
Cohen, Margaret 131, 138, 139
Coleridge, Samuel Taylor
    on imagination 218–19, 221, 233
    The Rime of the Ancient Mariner 218, 219
    'This Limetree Bower, My Prison' 219
Cole, Teju 13
Collen, Lindsey (*Mutiny*) 137

Collins, Michael 20
Coloane, Francisco
    background 39
    Coloane's Antarctic writings 40, 42–7, 103, 108
colonialism
    and abyssal lines 70, 72
    anti-colonialism (Lessing and Frame's autobiographical writing) 27, 30, 32
    hydrocolonialism 162
    legacies of and the 'authoritative life' 3
    linguistic and epistemological impositions 14, 19, 163
    and neocolonialism (Nigeria) 84, 85, 86, 87, 88
    and the north/south paradigm 2, 56, 123, 131
    postcolonial betrayal, protest against (South African literature) 145, 146, 147, 148, 152
    postcolonial India 53, 132–3
    quilombo settlements 97
    seafront settlement 134
    see also British Empire; Portuguese Empire; Southern Rhodesia (British colony)
Comaroff, Jean (*Theory from the South*) 118, 119
Comaroff, John L. (*Theory from the South*) 118, 119
Comyn, Sarah 2–3
Conditions of Life of the Working Classes of Recife (Castro) 93
Connell, Raewyn (*Southern Theory*) 118, 119
Los conquistadores de la Antártida (*The Conquerors of Antarctica*) (Coloane) 40, 42, 43–4, 45, 46
Conrad, Joseph 13, 16, 139, 158
contact zones 2, 259
copyright 60–1
Couto, Mia (*Sleepwalking Land*) 146
Covid-19, faraway closeness (Boehmer) 2, 20
crafted objects *see* dilly (dhili) bags
Cremonte, Néstor 107
criollismo genre 42
Croonenberg, Father (Jesuit missionary) 261–2, 266 n. 32
Culler, Jonathan 220
Currey, James 160
cyclones 136, 137–8, 139

Dar es Salaam, University of 94
Davis, Alexander 259, 261
Day, Bernard 177, *178*
Deacon, Harriet 245
de Castro, Ines E. *see* Castro, Ines E. de
de Castro, Josué *see* Castro, Josué de
Deception Island (Lewis Williams) 221, 233–4
Deception Island, *Two-Body Problem* (Rogers), setting for 269, 271, 272
De Haan, Binne 257
Denison, Hugh 203, 204

291

Index

Díaz, Emilio (*Relatos antárticos* (Antarctic Narratives)) 108
dilly (dhili) bags 15–18, *16*, *17*
Diski, Jenny (*Skating to Antarctica*) 269, 272–3, 274, 275, 276
distant proximity/faraway closeness (Boehmer) 19–21, 215
Dorfman, Ariel (*Death and the Maiden*) 116
Dos lecciones de Elizabeth Costello (Coetzee, trans. Barra) 115
Douglas, Oronto 86
Drabinski, John 73, 75
Drake Passage 42, 45, 103, 109
dreaming tracks 22n9
Drewal, Henry John 150
Dunn, Edward John 67, 72, 74
D'Urban, Benjamin 245–6
Dussel, Enrique 91

Eagle, Mary 60
Echeverría, Esteban 105
Eitel, Conrad 203, 204
Ejiofor, Chiwetel (*The Boy Who Harnessed the Wind*) 150
Elizabeth Costello (Coetzee) 117, 269, 272, 273–4, 275
Enns, Anthony 208
En Viaje (magazine) 41, 42, 44
environmental themes
    Antarctica, twentieth-century fiction 105
    Brazil's Northeast 92
    Big Oil and Ken Saro-Wiwa (Nigeria) 82, 84, 85
    Coloane's nonhuman agenda 40, 45, 46, 47
    environmental justice life writing 54, 56–7, 58, 60
    indigenous knowledge 14, 149, 153
    'Letter Home' to 'America' (Bradfield) 182
    and water spirits in southern African literature 145, 146, 149–50
    see also climate change
Erebus (Lewis Williams) 220, 222–9
Escribiendo el Sur Profundo (Writing the Deep South) project 116–17, 124
etymologies, southern 14, 18–19

Falkland Islands/Islas Malvinas 103, 107
farness
    Antarctica, remoteness of 215–18, 220–1, 233, 275
    faraway closeness/distant proximity 19–21, 215
    northern perspective of the Southern Hemisphere 1, 14
    object and word biography 22
    sound of (radio) 2, 13
Farrier, David 181–2

Faulkner, William 120, 121
feminine agency, water spirits in southern African literature 150–2, 153
feminism *see* women
'Fenriskjeften' (Lewis Williams) 228–9
Fermanis, Porscha 2–3
Ferreira, Solly 164–5
Ferrus, Diana ('I Have Come to Take You Home') 249
'15th December 1952' (Lewis Williams) 225
Fifth Xhosa War (1818–19) 246
First World War
    Alfred Tayler's prosthetic leg and wartime memories 27, 28–30
    George Frame's war-mementoes 30–4
    myths of imperial glory 31
    resettlement schemes 25–7
    Rhodesia Native Regiment 28
Fontanarrosa, Roberto 103, 108
'Forelands' (Orsman) 178–9
Frame, Alexander 25
Frame, George Samuel 25, 26, 27, 28, 30–4
Frame, Janet 27, 28, 29–30, 31, 34
    'Between My Father and the King' 32–3
    Intensive Care (1970) 32
Frankenstein (Shelley) 269–70, 271, 272, 273, 275, 276
Freire, Paulo 3
Furtado, Celso 95

Gabrys, Jennifer 233
Garba, Tapji 72
García, Pedro Andrés (*Sierra de la Ventana*) 106, 107
Gastrow, Claudia 148
Gervasoni, Carlo 106
Ghosh, Amitav, non-fiction life writing 131, 132–9, 140
Gilbert and Sullivan operettas 190
Gilroy, Paul 240
Giokoo incident (May 1994) 86
Glissant, Édouard 72, 73, 74, 75
globalization, Coetzee's exploration of 122–3, 124
Global North
    Antarctica, European narratives of isolation 103, 104, 109
    Argentine travel writing, influences on 105–6, 107, 109
    Australia 53, 123
    Big Oil (in Nigeria) 82, 84–5, 86, 87, 88
    climate change, impact distribution 136
    exemplary narratives, appropriation of southern lives 241–5
    globalization as a northern construct 123, 124
    indigenous texts, alignment of 53, 56, 57

Index

intellectual production, conventions of 118, 119–21, 122, 166, 240, 241, 257–8
and modernity 118
musical influences (Australasian Antarctic Expedition, 1911–14) 190, 191–2, 194, 196, 197
northern-ness in *Frankenstein* (Shelley) 270, 273, 275
and place names in the Southern Hemisphere 19, 21
terminology 2–3
see also Britain; colonialism
Global *Northeast* 99
Global South
and an anti-colonial critique (Lessing and Frame) 27
Big Oil (Nigeria) 82, 84–5, 86, 87, 88
climate change 131, 136, 137
economic disadvantage and coloniality 2, 56, 123, 131
India, inclusion of 53
Indian Ocean 131
seafront settlement 134
self-governing Indigenous literature 53, 54–61
terminology 2–3
in *The World Republic of Letters* (Casanova) 118
water and spirituality 145
Goeman, Mishuana 55
Gomba, Obari 4, 67
Gomes, Bethânia 96
Gonzalez, Jennifer A. 27–8
González, Jorge 46
Great Derangement, The (Ghosh) 131, 132, 136–8, 139
Green, Jenny 54, 59–60
Greenwich Mean Time 216
Grovogu, Siba 2, 27
Guillén, Mauro 122–3
Gusinde, Martin 43

Haag, Oliver 60
Haesbaert, Rogério 92
Halle, Louis J. 177–8
Halley Bay research station 218
Hall, Joseph (*Mundus alter et idem*) 217
Hannam, Walter 203–4, 205, 208
Haraway, Donna 99
Hardt, Michael 123
Harrisson, Charles 188, 191, 197
Hayes, Patrick 3
Heine, Jorge 116–17, 118, 124
Heinemann's African Writers Series 162, 163, 165–6
Hersko, Judit, fictional narrative of 'Anna Schwartz' 171, 179–81, *180*, *181*

Hiatt, Alfred 217
Hicks, Dan 67
Hoadley, Arch 192
Hofmeyr, Isabel 3, 132–3, 145, 162
Holger, Vice-admiral Immanuel 40
Horta, Luis 44
House of Hunger, The (Marechera) 147, 158–60, 161, 162, 163, 164, 165–6
Howkins, Adrian 41, 43
Hughes, David Mcdermott 163
Hughes-Warrington, Marnie 18
human beings
human interrelatedness (Coetzee) 276
and nature 136, 145, 147, 149–50, 152, 218
nonhuman agenda (Coloane) 40, 43, 45, 46–7
'transhumanist' projects (in *Frankenstein* and *Two-Body Problem*) 270, 271, 275
humanitarians *see* Newton, John ('Amazing Grace'); Pringle, Thomas
Humboldt, Alexander von 106
Hungry Tide, The (Ghosh) 136
Hunt, J. Timothy 85
Hurley, Frank 189, *189*, 191, 193, 197
'hydrophasia' 131

India
Andaman and Nicobar Islands, tsunami (2004) 132–5, 136
Delhi tornado 132, 138
indigenous Adivasi life writing 53–4, 55–8, 60, 61
Plachimada dispute 56, 57
'voice of the Global South' 131
Indian Ocean
climate-related events 131–40
water spirits 146
Indigenous people
abyssal lines and metaphors (ostrich-egg water carrier and stick chart) 67, *68*, 70, 71, 72, 73, 74
crafted objects (dilly/dhili) bags 15–18, *16*, *17*
in European abolitionist texts 241, 242, 243
hydrocolonialism 163
knowledge systems and environmental protection 14, 149, 153
languages 14, 18–19, 22, 54, 59–60
Mayilamma: The Life of a Tribal Eco-warrior 53–4, 55–8, 60, 61
Town Grew Up Dancing, The: The Life and Art of Wenten Rubuntja (Rubuntja) 53, 54, 55, 58–60, 61
water spirits 146, 148, 149, 150, 151, 153
worlding the south 3
Yahgan (Patagonia) 43–4, 45, 47
see also Khoisian people

Index

'El inglés de Lockroy' (Coloane) 46
Ingold, Tim 177, 218
In the Shadow of a Saint (Wiwa) 81, 82, 83–4, 85, 87–8
'Intertidal' (Bradfield) 171
Irmer, Georg 67, 72, 74
Isis River 158
'Island of Makhanda' *see* Robben Island
Islas Malvinas/Falkland Islands 103, 107

Jameson, Leander Starr 259, 261, 262
James, William 166
Jeffryes, Sidney
    Australasian Antarctic Expedition (AAE) career 203–6
    birth 201
    death 201, 208
    early career 202
    mental illness 201, 205–7, 208, 209
    remembrance of 208–9
Justo, Liborio 103, 108
J-Ward (Aradale Psychiatric Hospital) 201, 208

Kariba Dam (Zambezi River) 146
Kemp, Johannes van der 239, 241
Kenya, indigenous knowledge and environmental protection 149
Kesavan, Mukul 136
Khoisan, Zenzile 250
Khoisan people
    Baartman, Sarah 240, 249
    languages of 14, 19
    water spirits 146, 151
    see also Stuurman, David
Kianda (water spirit) 146, 147, 148, 152
Kibel, Owen 158
Klare, Michael 87
Komo, Dauda Musa 84, 85, 86
Kosgei, Jauquelyn 149
Kurtz, Arabella 276

language
    conceptual remoteness 216–17
    Indigenous languages 14, 18–19, 22, 54, 59–60
    see also metaphors
Lanuza, José Luis 105, 107
Laseron, Charles Francis 188, 190, 196, 197
'Last Forests in Antarctica, The' (Lewis Williams) 232
Lavery, Charne 145
Leane, Elizabeth 41, 103, 105, 109, 190
Lessing, Doris 27, 28–30, 31, 32, 33
    Alfred and Emily 28–9
Lestido, Adriana (*Antártida negra: Los diarios (Black Antarctica: The Diaries)*) 109

Levi, Giovanni 264
Lewis, A. G. 215
Lewis Williams, Elizabeth
    background 215
    'Becoming Shaman' 230–1
    Deception Island 221, 233–4
    indigenous shaman figure 221
    'The Last Forests in Antarctica' (Lewis Williams) 232
    'Met Obs' sequence of poems 220, 226–9
    'Practical Application of Ionospherics' sequence of poems 220, 222–5
life writing
    abolitionist repackaging (*Narrative of a Residence in South Africa* (Pringle)) 241, 242, 243
    bridging space-time gaps 14, 19–21, 22, 217
    and climate change (Ghosh's non-fiction life writing) 132–5, 136, 137, 138
    defining the genre 3
    environmental justice life writing 54, 56–7, 58, 60
    ethical questions (De Haan) 257
    as redress (Ken Wiwa) 87–8
    Two-Body Problem (Rogers) 276
    see also as-told-to life narratives; autobiography; novels; objects; photography; poetry; travel writing
Lillie, Dennis 178
Limpopo, University of 279
Lobengula (Ndebele King) 259, 260–1
Lodge, Oliver 208
Long March to Freedom Monument (National Heritage Monument, Pretoria, also touring) 247, *248*
Lovecraft, Howard Phillips (*At the Mountains of Madness*) 104

Mabokela, Khutso (*Mogau Grace*) 279–88
McCormack, Derek P. 173
McDonald, Peter D. 117
Machoko, Collins Garikai 149
Mackenzie, Vic 164
McLean, Archibald (Archie) 188, 189, 190, 196, 197, 206
McNeil, Jean 221
Madigan, Cecil 205, 207
Mafezzini, Ángel (*Un viaje a las montañas blancas (A Journey to the White Mountains)*) 108
Maier, Karl 82
'Makanna's Gathering' (Pringle) 242
Makhanda (Makanna) Nxele 242, 246
Mamiwata (water spirit) 150
Mamlambo (water spirit) 147, 151
Mandela, Nelson 246, 279

Index

Mann, Guillermo 40
Marechera, Dambudzo
    asylum application 160–1
    linguistic heritage 158
    nationalist readings 157
    Oxford University, expulsion from 157–8, 166
    The Black Insider 163–4
    The House of Hunger 147, 158–60, 161, 162, 163, 164, 165–6
Marshall Islands 67, *68*, 74
Martin, Anne 18
Mashigo, Mohale ('Manoka' in *Intruders*) 151
Massey, Doreen 91, 92, 98
Matabeleland *see* Bulawayo
Mawson, Douglas
    on the 'Adélie Land Band' 189
    on the grand opera 196
    remote identification (letter from his wife, Paquita) 20
    wireless telegraphy and Jeffryes 202–3, 204, 205, 206, 207
    see also Australasian Antarctic Expedition (AAE, 1911–14)
Mawson, Francisca Adriana (Paquita) 20
Mawson's Huts Replica Museum (Hobart, Tasmania) 187, *188*
Maxwell, Glyn 234
Mayilamma: The Life of a Tribal Eco-warrior 53–4, 55–8, 60, 61
Mbembe, Achille 257–8
Il meglio di Francisco Coloane (The Best of Francisco Coloane) 39
Melina Rorke: Her Amazing Experiences in the Stormy Nineties of South Africa's Story Told by Herself (Rorke) 257, 258, 259–60, 261, 262–3, 264
Menchu, Rigoberta 3, 56
metaphorical cartography (amity and abyssal lines) 69, 70, 71, 72, 73
metaphors
    abyssal 71–2, 73, 74–5
    Global South (underdevelopment and coloniality) 2, 99
    hunger and post-independence Zimbabwe 159
    ice 216
    language and water 163
    north/south hemispheric divide 240–1
    pampas grass, and the sea (Argentinian fiction and travel writing) 105, 106–7, 109
    prostheses 29, 30
    telegraphy 208, 209
    theory of 71
    water spirits (southern African literature) 145–6, 148
    writing and landscape 218

Middle Passage 73
Middleton, Paul 87
Mississippi River (Toni Morrison) 157
Mogau Grace (Mabokela) 279–88
Mohulatsi, Mapule 146
Morrison, Toni 157
MOSOP *see* Movement for the Survival of the Ogoni People
Moten, Fred 239
Movement for the Survival of the Ogoni People (MOSOP) 82, 85, 86
Moyes, Morton 192–3, 197
Moyo, Sam 165
Mundy, Colleen 18
Mungoshi, Charles (*Waiting for the Rain*) 147
Muponde, Robert (*The Scandalous Times of a Book Louse*) 162, 163, 166
Museum of the History of Science (Oxford) 269

Narrative of a Residence in South Africa (Pringle) 241–2, 243
Nascimento, Beatriz 91, 92–3, 96–7, 98, 99
National Antarctic (Discovery) Expedition (1901–4) 172
National Heritage Monument (Pretoria) *248*
Ndebele people, representation in *Melina Rorke: Her Amazing Experiences in the Stormy Nineties of South Africa's Story Told by Herself* (Rorke) 259–60, 261, 262, 263
Negri, Antonio 123
Nelson, Edward W. 177
Nelu, Chief 74
neocolonialism (Nigeria) 84, 85, 86, 87, 88
neoliberalism 71
Neruda, Pablo 39, 41, 120, 121
Netzloff, Mark 69
Newton, John ('Amazing Grace') 287
New Zealand 13, 14, 25, 26, 27, 30–4, 116
New Zealand Antarctic Heritage Trust 173
Nicobar and Andaman Islands, Indian Ocean tsunami (2004) 132–5, 136
Nigeria 81–2, 83, 84–7, 88
90° South (Ponting) 179
njuzu (water spirits) 147, 149, 158
nonhuman life
    and artistic engagement with Scott's *Terra Nova* hut 171, 173, 179, 181–2
    nature and human beings 136, 145, 147, 149–50, 152, 218
    nonhuman agenda (Coloane) 40, 43, 45, 46–7
north *see* Global North
Northeast, Brazilian 91–2, 93, 94, 95–6, 97, 98
northern hemisphere *see* Global North
North Pole 270
'Northropocene' 2

Index

novels
    Antarctica (Coloane) 40, 41, 42, 43–4, 45, 46, 103, 108
    Antarctica in European and US fiction 103, 104, 105
    blue water novels 138–9, 140
    climate change and the 'centrality of the improbable' 131, 137, 138, 139, 140
    creative writing and faraway closeness 20
    Elleke Boehmer 20, 21
    Flights (Tocarczuk) 13
    The Hungry Tide (Ghosh) 136
    Intensive Care (Frame) 32
    literary *Weltanschauung* in Faulkner's novels 120, 121
    water spirits in southern African literature 145, 146, 147–53
    see also short stories
Nwapa, Flora 150
Nxele *see* Makhanda (Makanna) Nxele
Nyamimyami (river god) 146
Nyerere, Julius 94

objects
    autotopographical objects 27–34
    dilly (dhili) bags 15–18, *16*, *17*
    object biography 22
    ostrich-egg water carrier 67, *68*, 70, 71, 73, 74
'Objects from Anna Schwartz's Cabinet of Curiosities' (Hersko) 179
oceanic south 131–40
    see also Southern Ocean
Oglesby, Carl 2
Ogoni region (Nigeria) 81, 82, 83, 84, 85–7, 88
Okonta, Ike 86
Okuntimo, Paul 86
Onetti, Juan Carlos (*A Brief Life*) 121
'Only a Leaf' 190–1
'Oom Dawid Stuurman' (Stone) 249–50
oral traditions
    Coloane's retelling 43–4
    copyright ownership 60–1
Orsman, Chris 171, 174, 175, 178
Overseas Settlement Committee 26

'Pages from the Book of the Unknown Explorer' (Hersko) 179, 181
Palmares 96
pampas grass, and the sea (Argentinian fiction and travel writing) 105, 106–7, 109
paratexts
    Mayilamma: The Life of a Tribal Eco-warrior 53–4, 55, 56–7, 58
    The Town Grew Up Dancing 58–60

Pariyadath, Jothibai 54, 58, 60
Parmar, Pooja 57
Los pasos del hombre: Memorias (*The Footsteps of Man: Memories*) (Coloane) 40, 46
Patagonia 39, 41, 43–4, 103, 107, 109, 276
Paterson, Mary 25
Peel, Michael 86
Peers, Laura 15, 67
Pepetela (*The Return of the Water Spirit, Kianda*) 145, 147–8, 152
Perez, Javier Ernesto 249
Philip, John (*Researches in South Africa*) 242
Phillips, Jock 31
photography
    Halley Bay on the Brunt Ice shelf (1969) 218
    Scott's *Terra Nova* base hut *see* Ponting, Herbert; Ussher, Jane, photography of
Piñero, Sergio (*El puñal de Orión*) 105, 107–8
Pitt Rivers Museum (Oxford) 15–18, *16*, *17*, 67, *68*, 70, 72, 74
place names 19, 21
Plachimada dispute 56, 57
plankton
    collection of (accounts by members of Scott's expedition) 177, 178, *178*
    in Hersko's artwork 179–80, 181, *181*, 182
    'Intertidal' (Bradfield) 171
    plankton net 173–4, *174*, *178*, 180, *181*
Poe, Edgar Allan Poe (*The Narrative of Arthur Gordon Pym of Nantucket*) 103, 104
poetry
    Antarctica, remote imag(in)ing 215–18
    Bradfield, Elizabeth 171, 182–3
    Coleridge, Samuel Taylor 218, 219
    indigenous knowledge and conservation 149
    Lewis Williams, Elizabeth 105, 222–3, 224, 225, 226, 227, 228–9, 230–1, 232
    Pringle, Thomas 242
    resonant page 218–20
    Stone, Amanda Lois 248–50
Ponting, Herbert
    darkroom of 172, 180, *180*
    90° South 179
    and 'A Portrait in the Wardroom' (Orsman) 174, 175
    and Ussher's photography 173
'Portrait in the Wardroom, A' (Orsman) 174, 175
Portuguese Empire 73, 91, 147, 148, 163
Pratt, Mary Louise 259
Prieto, Adolfo 105, 106–7
Pringle, Thomas
    African Sketches 242
    Narrative of a Residence in South Africa 241, 242, 243, 244

Index

prosthetics 28–30, 32, 33, 34
El puñal de Orión (*Orion's Dagger*) (Piñero) 105, 107–8
Puwar, Nirmal 2

quilombos 96–7, 98

radio communications
   Antarctic exploration 202–3, 203–4, 205
   and the British Empire 203
   and Jeffryes' mental illness 201, 205–7, 208, 209
   Los conquistadores (Coloane), setting for 42, 43
   and poetry 219, 220, 224, 228
   sound of southern farness 2, 13
   supernatural associations 208, 209
radio operators 202, 206
   see also Jeffryes, Sidney
Rangarajan, Swarnalatha 54, 56–7, 58
Ranger, Terence 165
Read Sr., James 241
Reclus Hut (Portal Point) 233
remote identification 20, 22
remote sensing/imaging machines 216, 217, 218, 219, 220, 228–9
Return of the Water Spirit, Kianda, The (Pepetela) 145, 147–8, 152
Rhodes, Cecil 259, 260, 261, 262
Rhodesia (unrecognized state of)
   in the work of Marechera 158, 159, 160–1, 163–5
   see also Southern Rhodesia (British colony); Zimbabwe
Rime of the Ancient Mariner, The (Coleridge) 218, 219
Rivers State Internal Security (RSIS) 85–6
Robben Island 241, 244–7
Rogers, Louis (*Two-Body Problem*) 269, 270–2, 275–7
Rojo, Grínor 41, 43
Ronström, Owe 216, 220
Rorke, Melina (*Melina Rorke: Her Amazing Experiences in the Stormy Nineties of South Africa's Story Told by Herself*) 257, 258, 259–60, 261, 262–3, 264
Rowse, Tim 59, 60
RSIS *see* Rivers State Internal Security (RSIS)
Rubuntja, Wenten (*The Town Grew Up Dancing: The Life and Art of Wenten Rubuntja*) 53, 54, 55, 58–60, 61
Rulfo, Juan (*Pedro Páramo*) 121
Rusape River 159, 162–3, 164–5, 166
Rusape River Boat Race 164–5
Ruta, Carlos 119

Said, Edward 99
SAIIA (South African Institute of International Affairs) seminar 116
Samuelson, Meg 1, 2, 6, 131, 240
Santos, Boaventura de Sousa 67, 69, 70, 71, 73
Santos, Milton 91, 92–3, 94–6, 98, 99
Sapir, Edward 14
Sarlo, Beatriz 117
Saro-Wiwa, Ken 56, 81, 82, 83, 84, 85, 86, 87
Schmidt, Johan 246
Schwarz, Bill 26
Sconce, Jeffrey 208
Scott, Robert Falcon *see* British Antarctic Expedition (1910–13)
Scott's *Terra Nova* base hut 172–7, *174*, 179–80, *180*, 181
Scott's *Terra Nova* Hut with Herbert Ponting's darkroom (Hersko) 179–80, *180*
Scully, Pamela 240
sea fiction 138
sea level rise 131, 134, 145
sea views/seafront settlement 134, 137
Sedna (water spirit) 149–50
Shackleton, Ernest (*Nimrod* expedition, 1907–9) 202
Sharpeville massacre 284
She Down There (Burger) 145, 149–50, 153
Shelley, Mary (*Frankenstein*) 269–70, 271, 272, 273, 275, 276
Shell plc. 82, 85, 86
Shona language 158
short stories
   'Between My Father and the King' (Frame) 32–3
   by Coloane, Francisco 39, 42, 46
   by Marechera, Dambudzo 147, 158–60, 161, 162, 163, 164, 165–6
   'Father Antenna, The' (Boehmer) 22 n. 4
   'Manoka' (Mashigo) 151
   see also novels
Shum, Matthew 242–3
Silva Maturana, Raúl 40
Skating to Antarctica (Diski) 269, 272–3, 274, 275, 276
skin names 58
slavery 72, 73, 239
Slovic, Scott 55, 56
Slovo, Joe, letter to his daughter 87
'slow violence' (environmental damage) 56
Smith, Jean 27
Sobchack, Vivian 30
song-lines 22n9
Sorentino, Sara-Maria 72
Soria, Alberto (*La vida en la Antártida* (Life in Antarctica)) 108–9

Index

South Africa
   conceptions of the south (Coetzee and Heine) 115, 116, 117, 118
   water spirits 146, 147, 151
   see also Stuurman, David
South African Institute of International Affairs (SAIIA) seminar 116
South America
   Antarctica, connection with 42, 43–4, 103, 105–9
   Coetzee's Hispanic South 115–25
   Coloane and Chilean Antarctic Expedition (1947) 39–47
South Australian Museum (Adelaide, Australia) 194, 195
Southern Hemisphere
   blue hemisphere 1
   distance and faraway-ness 1, 13–14
   northern perspectives, dominance of 1, 2–3
   wildlife 1
   see also Global South; Indigenous people; individual places
Southern Ocean
   climate change 181
   connectedness with South America (in Argentinian fiction and travel narratives) 103, 105–9
   farness, associations of 13
   navigators 21
   in Poe's fiction 104
   telegraph communications 201
Southern Rhodesia (British colony)
   British Empire Exhibitions (Wembley, 1924, 1925) 25, *26*
   Bulawayo (representation in *Melina Rorke: Her Amazing Experiences in the Stormy Nineties of South Africa's Story Told by Herself*, Rorke) 257, 258–63, 264
   in Lessing's autobiographical narratives 25–6, 28–30, 32, 33
   Rusape, settlement of 162, 163
   see also Rhodesia (unrecognized state of); Zimbabwe
'Southern Sledging Song' 193–5, *194*
South Georgia 103, 107, 108, 171
South Polar regions *see* Antarctica
Spanish Empire 43, 44, 73
Speed, John (world map) 217
Spivak, Gayatri 240
Spufford, Francis 218
Stankievech, Charles 219
Stevenson, Alice 67
stick chart 67, *68*, 70, 71, 73, 74
Still Life: Inside the Antarctic Huts of Scott and Shackleton (Ussher) 172–3

Stillwell, Frank 189, 191, 197
Stone, Amanda Lois ('Oom Dawid Stuurman') 248–50
'stream of consciousness' 166
Stuurman, David
   commemoration of 243, 247, *248*, 247–50
   early life 239
   fugitivity 239, 240, 241, 243, 248, 249–50
   in *Narrative of a Residence in South Africa* (Pringle) 241, 242, 243, 244
   petitions for pardon *244–5*, 242–3
   Robben Island, imprisonment and escape 241, 246, 247
   transportation to Australia 242–3
Stuurman, Klaas 239, 248
subaltern studies 240
Suu Kyi, Aung San 88
Sweet, Ryan 29, 30
'Sympathetic Light' (Lewis Williams) 227

Tara, Obed 134–5
Tasmania
   dilly (dhili) bags 15, 17–18, *17*
   first official wireless transmission 202
   Mawson's Huts Replica Museum (Hobart, Tasmania) 187, *188*
Tasmanian Museum and Art Gallery (Hobart) 17–18
Tayler, Alfred 25–6, 27, 28–30, 33–4
Tayler, Emily 25, 26, 29, 30
telegraph 201–2
   see also radio communications
telepathy
   imaginative identification 13, 20, 21, 22
   and telegraphy 208, 209
Terra Australis Nondum Cognita 217
Terra Nova base hut 172–7, *174*, 179–80, *180*, 181
Thames River 158
The Boy Who Harnessed the Wind (Ejiofor) 150
'This Limetree Bower, My Prison' (Coleridge) 219
Tierra del Fuego 14, 39, 41, 43, 103, 107, 109
Tierra del Fuego (Coloane) 39
Tocarczuk, Olga (*Flights*) 13
Tonga people 146
tornadoes 131, 132, 136, 137, 138
tourism 215
'Town by the Sea, The' (Ghosh) 132–5, 136
Town Grew Up Dancing, The: The Life and Art of Wenten Rubuntja (Rubuntja) 53, 54, 55, 58–60, 61
'transhumanist' projects (in *Frankenstein* and *Two-Body Problem*) 270, 271, 275
translation work (*The Town Grew Up Dancing*) 59–60

Index

travel writing
    Coloane's reflections on 43
    connecting South America with Antarctica 105–9
    En Viaje (travel magazine) 41, 42, 44
    European point of view 3
    Melina Rorke: Her Amazing Experiences in the Stormy Nineties of South Africa's Story Told by Herself (Rorke) 257, 258, 259–60, 261, 262–3, 264
    Skating to Antarctica (Diski) 269, 272–3, 274, 275, 276
Trompetter, Hans 246
'Tsunami of 2004, The' *see* 'Town by the Sea, The' (Ghosh)
tsunamis 132–5, 136, 138, 139
Tuan, Yi-Fu 217
Tuck, Eve 72
'28th March 1959' (Lewis Williams) 224
Two-Body Problem (Rogers) 269, 270–2, 275–7

El último grumete de la Baquedano (*The Last Cabin Boy of the Baquedano*) (Coloane) 41
United Kingdom *see* Britain
University of Dar es Salaam 94
University of Limpopo 279
Uruguay 115, 116
Ussher, Jane, photography of 171, 172–4, *174*

Vaca, Joseí María Toribio (*Antártida, mi hogar* (Antarctica, my Home)) 108
van Breda, Denver 19
Vandermerwe, Meg (*The Woman of the Stone Sea*) 145, 150–2
Varma, Sreejith 54, 56–7, 58
Vaughn-Williams, H. 260
Veit-Wild, Flora 161
Venezuela 102
Vera, Yvonne (*Butterfly Burning*) 152, 261
La vida en la Antártida (Life in Antarctica) (Soria) 108–9
Vila Labra, Óscar (*Chilenos en la Antártica* (*Chileans in the Antarctic*)) 43
Vladislavić, Ivan 119
'La Voz del Témpano' (The Iceberg's Voice) (Coloane) 46, 47

Wainschenker, Pablo 41
Washerwoman's Secret, The 195–6, *195*
Watermeisie (water spirit) 146, 150, 151

water torture 163
Webb, Eric 190, 193, 197
Wells, Julia 247
Whorf, Benjamin 14
Wicomb, Zoë 119
Wild, Frank 188, 194, 197
Williams Álzaga, Enrique 106
Williams, Billy 192
Wilson, Edward 177, 178
Winch, Tara June (*The Yield*) 18–19, 22
wireless operators 202, 206
    see also Jeffryes, Sidney
wireless technology *see* radio communications
Wiwa, Ken (*In the Shadow of a Saint*) 81, 82, 83–4, 85, 87–8
Woman of the Stone Sea, The (Vandermerwe) 145, 150–2
women
    feminine agency, water spirits in southern African literature 150–2, 153
    Hersko's collage technique 179, 182
    nature writers making slow violence visible 56
    Rorke as a marginalized colonial woman (*Melina Rorke: Her Amazing Experiences in the Stormy Nineties of South Africa's Story Told by Herself*) 259, 261, 263, 264
    violence towards (South Africa, portrayal in *Mogau Grace*) 279, 280, 281, 282
words 14, 18–19
World War I *see* First World War
Wright, Alexis 53, 54–5
Wylie, John 172, 175

Xhosa wars 239, 246

Yahgan people 43–4, 45, 47
Yang, Wayne 72
Yield, The (Winch) 18–19, 22
Yusoff, Kathryn 233

Zimbabwe
    indigenous knowledge and environmental protection 149
    literary scholarship 159, 161–2
    river god Nyamimyami 146
    see also Rhodesia (unrecognized state of); Southern Rhodesia (British colony)
Zimunya, Musaemura 159

www.ingramcontent.com/pod-product-compliance
Lightning Source LLC
Chambersburg PA
CBHW060943230426
43665CB00015B/2047